"THE VEIL OF *MĀYĀ*": SCHOPENHAUER'S SYSTEM AND EARLY INDIAN THOUGHT

"THE VEIL OF *MĀYĀ*": SCHOPENHAUER'S SYSTEM AND EARLY INDIAN THOUGHT

DOUGLAS L. BERGER

Global Academic Publishing
Binghamton, New York
2004

Library of Congress Cataloging-in-Publication Data

Berger, Douglas L., 1970–
The veil of Maya : Schopenhauer's system and early Indian thought / by Douglas L. Berger
p. cm.
Includes bibliographical references

ISBN 1-58684-243-9 (pbk. : alk. paper)

1. Schopenhauer, Arthur, 1788–1860. 2. Knowledge, Theory of
3. Maya (Hinduism) 4. Philosophy, India. I. Title.
B3149.K7B47 2003
193--dc22

2003021296

Published by Global Academic Publishing
Binghamton University, LNG 99
Binghamton, New York 13902-6000 USA
Phone: (607) 777-4495. Fax: (607) 777-6132
E-mail: gap@binghamton.edu
Website: http://academicpublishing.binghamton.edu/

Table of Contents

Preface and Acknowledgements

I belong to a surprisingly long list of Western students of philosophy who, for the past century and a half, were introduced to the philosophical traditions of Asia, and in this case specifically India, through the works of Arthur Schopenhauer. Of course, all of these forgoing students, including myself, have had much work to do in separating out Schopenhauer's peculiar representation of Indian philosophical thought from the historical and textual realities of the classical Indian *daršanas* and their long and recondite heritage of debate. The task of this separation has been abundantly rewarding, and indeed, for a real appreciation and knowledge of Indian philosophical reflection, one is best advised to turn to the source texts of that tradition itself, as well as to the much better informed modern commentators on those source texts. For the last few generations of scholars who have investigated Schopenhauer's relationship to Indian thought, his reception and interpretation of that tradition, bound by Romantic, Orientalist, and his own particular personal and cultural interests, have been largely a disappointment, and even embarrassment. Within the span of a hundred years, during which time studies of the Indian tradition in the West have vastly improved, the initial naïve trust in Schopenhauer as an interpreter of the Indian tradition among Nietzsche and Deussen in the 1870's and 1880's has deteriorated into a suspicion akin to that of Gerald James Larson, who in the mid 1980's wrote that there was something markedly psychotic about Schopenhauer's fascination with India.

Perhaps this demise of appreciation for Schopenhauer as a student of early Indian philosophical thought has paralleled a more general progressive denigration of Schopenhauer's merits as a philosopher in his own right. Even those who would acknowledge his influence on both continental philosophy through Nietzsche and on analytic philosophy through Wittgenstein, as well as on aesthetics through Richard Wagner, Thomas Hardy and Thomas Mann, loudly lament the hopeless inconsistency of his own philosophical system.

As for myself, I share in both forms of this disillusionment with Schopenhauer as systematic thinker and interpreter of Indian thought. While Schopenhauer's own creative thought gripped me as an undergraduate student, and some of his arguments still hold some intuitive or emotional appeal, I tend to agree with the outstanding Schopenhauer exegete Christopher Janaway, who has written that the centerpiece of Schopenhauer's system, his metaphysics, "seems to collapse under even the gentlest analytic prodding." Still, there are some things about Schopenhauer as a thinker that I admire. There was his oft-noticed lonely challenge to the Hegelian progressivism and exclusivism of European culture. The vitalism and irrationalism of the "metaphysics of will" which allowed him to take this "counter-cultural" stance, while they did in some respects grow out of Romantic sensibilities, were largely the result of his own unique genius. Most fascinating to me about the character of his thought was its refusal to completely give in to either the thoroughgoing rationalism of the Idealists or the iconoclastic irrationalism of the Romantics and Existentialists. This willingness to examine both the rational and irrational, giving each their respective philosophical due, perhaps still holds something of value for contemporary philosophy, with analytic, phenomenological and hermeneutic schools on one side attempting to salvage the possibility of knowledge, and post-structural, relativist and deconstructionist schools on the other, who reduce the project of knowledge to hidden desires for power and cultural ascendancy. A modern interpreter would likely see Schopenhauer as more a forbearer of the second of these movements, and this is certainly right from the perspective of the early twenty-first century. But Schopenhauer himself seems to have believed that, in order to give an acceptable explanation of the human "world," one had to resist the temptations to explain knowledge completely away in terms of human interests or to pretend that knowledge could, in most cases, do anything but be at the service of human interests. In order to explain human experience, that is, one had to acknowledge the scope and limits of both knowing and willing in all their apparent contradictions, as most of us actually live and act from within the framework of those contradictions. Such a stance that is found perpetually in between these two poles is difficult to maintain, both personally and philosophically, and so it always seemed to me that we should be less surprised that Schopenhauer had difficulties in remaining there, and should be more appreciative of those insights he derived from that stance that are perhaps still of some worth.

I was fortunate enough during my graduate studies to learn more about the Indian philosophical tradition form some of the best commentators both in print and in classes. The more I learned, of course, the more convinced I became that Schopenhauer could not be relied upon as an interpreter of Indian thought. What continued to fascinate me about Schopenhauer's reception of Indian philosophical and religious worldviews during my education was how polarized the reaction to this reception had been in the scholarly literature, as I mentioned above. In his reading of pre-systematic Indian philosophical thought, mostly from the Upaniṣads and early Buddhism, Schopenhauer was as much a hero for his early readers as a villain for his later ones. He struck his readers during these periods as first a reliable interpreter and then a willful distorter, first as someone who understood the essentials of Indian thought and then as exemplifying hermeneutical naiveté and who was most worthy of hermeneutic suspicion, first as someone who possessed the vision to see beyond the bounds of his own cultural understanding and then as an ethnocentric, even racist, Orientalist.

While somewhat more balanced readings have emerged within the past fifteen years, no thorough book-length study was available to detail the encounter between Schopenhauer and India. This book is meant to fill that lacuna. While Schopenhauer did indeed treat some aspects of Indian religious and philosophical thought superficially, subordinating his interpretation to his own ideological and cultural interests, there were more positive aspects of his readings of early European presentations of classical Indian thought. After reading Schopenhauer for some years, I became convinced that some crucial aspects of his system, specifically how he made argumentative transitions from epistemology to metaphysics to ethics, transitions about which much dispute still rages in the secondary literature, could not be well assessed without taking into consideration how Schopenhauer understood the Upaniṣadic and Vedāntic notion of *māyā*. What he in fact makes of *māyā* is a falsification thesis, or an interpretation of Kantian epistemology which renders representational knowledge a distortion, concealment or something that "veils" to our eyes the world's true nature. This fabrication has implications for each aspect of Schopenhauer's system, and so an appreciation of the influence of presystematic Indian philosophical concepts on his thought was in my estimation pivotal to interpreting how the parts of his system hung together.

In the field of cross-cultural philosophical research, Schopenhauer remains a very significant case study, both for his failures and successes, in both his misunderstandings and misrepresentations of the early Indian tradition as well as for the extent to which he allowed some concepts from that tradition to influence the formation of his own philosophy, for both his stigmatizations of Indian philosophy as irrational, fundamentally mystical and pessimistic and his assessment that the study of Indian thought would prompt a kind of Western philosophical Renaissance. Rather than being polarized, Schopenhauer's encounter with India was culturally and ideologically complex, and cross-cultural philosophy can only benefit from an accurate appreciation for this complexity. And so, it is hoped that both devoted readers of Schopenhauer as well as cross-cultural philosophy scholars will find rewards in this book.

Warm thanks go to all those who encouraged, supported and advised me during the research and writing of this work. Special thanks go to Lori Vandermark and Olga Perelmuter and

Global Publications of Binghamton University for editing and printing this book. A great debt of gratitude is owed to Irfan Omar, who helped me to advertise and prepare the manuscript.

Beyond that, it is fair to say that this project was a good fifteen years in the making. I began reading Schopenhauer as an undergraduate in the late 1980's, and was encouraged in my philosophical studies by a number of professors then at Dickinson State University and the University of North Dakota, most notably Mark Box, Debbie Heller, Dave Solheim, LeRoy Oberlander, Mike Hastings, Barb Mayer and Gerald Lawrence. This encouragement continued through my graduate studies in Tübingen, Germany and Temple University in Philadelphia. A year and a half of exchange research at Tübingen was facilitated by Thomas Kesaris, then of International Programs at Temple. The work matured under the instruction of Tübingen's Friedrich Kümmel and Temple's Thomas J. Dean, to the latter of whom I am particularly thankful for his close reading of this manuscript. This project was enriched immensely through my studies of the Indian religious and philosophical traditions. Timothy Cahill, currently of Loyola University in New Orleans, skillfully and patiently tutored me in Sanskrit and helped me gain access to source texts, and I was fortunate to benefit from the very best of careful and critical guidance through these traditions under Heinrich von Stietencron of Tübingen, J. N. Mohanty and the late Bibhuti Singh Yadav of Temple University. This project is particularly indebted to the late professor of Indian philosophy at the University of Pennsylvania, Wilhelm Halbfass, who both recommended readings and shared a great deal of enthusiasm for my project during a semester of independent study in the spring of 1996. I can only hope that this project serves as a fitting tribute to his memory, being as he was both one of the foremost scholars on the Indian philosophical tradition in the West and a lifelong lover of Schopenhauer's works.

Most grateful thanks to family, friends and colleagues who encouraged and personally supported me all throughout my research and writing. I would like especially to mention the names of Yang Haiying, Phil Bender, Gereon Kopf, Eve Mullen, Mark

Conard, Shang Geling, Zhang Zao, Li Fan, Stephanie Theodorou, Ralph Marshall, Jiang Tao, Pamela Winfield, Ho Wan-li, Chen Meei-Hwa, Tsai Yuan-lin, Helen Schroepfer, Helen Johnson, Walter and Misao Hunley, Noriko Horiguchi, Bai Park, Kaori Yamagishi, Zhang Xiao-rui, Anita Chan-Randall, Jon Dalrymple, Kay Summers, Jeff Kingston, Lee Roser, Zhang Ying and Holly Graff.

Douglas L. Berger
Evanston, Illinois
January 29, 2004

Introduction

This book will focus on what effect Arthur Schopenhauer's appropriation of pre-systematic Indian *Upaniṣadic* philosophical speculation had on the shaping of his own system. Specifically, the thesis of this work is that Schopenhauer's reading of Anquetil Duperron's early nineteenth century translations of, and most importantly commentary on the *Upaniṣads* provided him with the notion of *māyā,* which served as a foundation for his thematization of an epistemological falsification thesis. This thesis in its turn was the linking concept that bound Schopenhauer's systematic theory of knowledge, metaphysics and ethics together. A thorough understanding of how Schopenhauer appropriated the idea of *māyā* from the pre-systematic Indian philosophical tradition sheds more light than his commentators have thought on how his system is constructed.

Schopenhauer's enigmatic philosophy has always been difficult to assess. He has been dismissed as an irrationalist and pessimist by commentators from Nietzsche to Frederick Copleston to David Cartwright, and all of his readers have lamented the inconsistencies that seem to riddle his system. The inspirations of and influences on his own thought were many; Kantian idealism and the Platonic Ideas were among those he admitted, though Schellengian metaphysics as well as the theories of the French and English physiologists Flourens and Thomas Reid also played important roles. The varying degrees of these influences made many parts of the system conflate oddly with one another. A great deal of the difficulty then in assessing Schopenhauer's philosophy consists in the problem of determining which of the system's "parts," epistemology, metaphysics, aesthetics or ethics, had a thematic priority, which was foundational. The most prevalent solution of this problem, begun with Nietzsche and following through to Copleston and John Atwell, has been that Schopenhauer's metaphysics was based on his moral evaluation of the human character, which is motivated by irrational will to possess and causes unspeakable evil. That is to say, it is Schopenhauer's moral sensibilities that compel him to formulate his unique metaphysics of will, with all its "pessimistic" theoretical and axiological implications.

I propose that this assessment is inaccurate, not in its portrayal of Schopenhauer's ethical theory, but rather in the thematic priority his ethics is given with respect to the rest of the system. Schopenhauer insisted that the elements of his system hung together coherently in such a way that each one of its propositions followed from and mirrored all the others. But this is misleading, for it is hard to see how his volitionist ethics, will-body identity thesis and soteriology of resignation could necessarily lead to the idealism he held. In fact, Schopenhauer constructs his system so as to demonstrate exactly the reverse; the epistemological idealism he argues for is a falsification of the world and its nature, and the deception of human beings by this falsification helps put them into a moral situation from which they desperately need to be extricated.

Schopenhauer's epistemological idealism is not a strictly Kantian one as is often thought, rather it is a Kantianism seen through the eyes of the first translator of the *Upaniṣads* into Latin, Anquetil Duperron. It was Duperron who first suggested that the doctrines of Kant and the *Upaniṣads* were fundamentally the same. After Schopenhauer is introduced to Duperron's translations and commentary by Friedrich Majer in 1813, his epistemology undergoes a radical transformation; the "principles of sufficient reason" of his 1813 dissertation become "*māyā,* the veil of deception" in his "chief work" of 1818, *The World as Will and Representation*. Never before an ethical theorist, he propounds an ethics of identity and compassion unprecedented in the Western tradition demanded by the deceptions of epistemological falsification, as well as a metaphysics of will construed as being its impetus. Schopenhauer becomes a lifelong adherent of Duperron's translations, despite subsequent improvements, a devoted collector of scholarly works on Asian thought, and in his later works refers to himself as a "Buddhist." It is therefore my thesis that the thematic priority in Schopenhauer's system, which provides the basis of metaphysical inquiry and founds his ethics, belongs to the falsification epistemology which he, through Duperron, attributed to the "sages of India."

Schopenhauer's "global" assessments of the *Upaniṣads* have been rightly discounted, and it is not the purpose of this book to defend Schopenhauer's interpretations as accurate nor to comparatively justify his appropriations. Rather, its purpose is to understand, philosophically and hermeneutically, how Schopenhauer incorporated his understanding of Indian thought into his own system, and how the thematic priority of its epistemology of falsification, derived from the notion of *māyā,* helped give that system its peculiar character. Much attention will be paid to the development of Schopenhauer's system between the years 1814 and 1818, and how that development included his initial encounter with the *Upaniṣads* and other elements of classical Indian thought. Several chapters will then be devoted to the logical relatedness of the "parts" of that system, epistemology, metaphysics and ethics, in order to clearly demonstrate how Schopenhauer's falsification thesis was pivotal to it.

While the references to Schopenhauer's indebtedness to Indian thought are for the most part superficial and made in passing in the mainstream Western philosophical scholarship, the literature devoted specifically to Schopenhauer's relationship with Indian thought has grown through several generations. Nietzsche considered Schopenhauer a reliable authority on India, and this led to his derogation of Indian thought and particularly Buddhism, as he understood them through Schopenhauer, as a "nihilism" opposed to "Greek affirmation." Nietzsche's classmate and friend Paul Deussen devoted much of his Indological studies to demonstrating that the Schopenhaurian system was consistent with Vedāntic philosophy in his *Philosophy of the Upaniṣads* and *Sixty Upaniṣads of the Veda,* along with a number of articles he wrote in the still-published *Schopenhauer Jährlich*. As one of the leading European Indologists of the period as well as the former president of the *Schopenhauer-Gesellschaft*, Deussen's attempt at syncretism proved compelling and exciting not only to the members of the German academy, but to a number of major literary figures, most notably Thomas Mann, as well.

The reaction to Schopenhauer in India was, opposed to the original Western response, either antagonistic or silently dismissive. Rajendralal Mitra, the nineteenth century Indologist, believed the 2nd century CE author of the *Yogasūtra*, Patanjali, had superseded Schopenhauer's philosophy. Twentieth century Indian philosophers have taken opposition to Schopenhauer's characterization of India's classical thought. Sri Radhakrishnan and Vivekananda have both argued that Schopenhauer's presentation of Hinduism and Buddhism was little more than superficial, even though the latter at Deussen's suggestion defended the "ethics of compassion" Schopenhauer represented as one that was advocated by the *Upaniṣads* and *Bhagavad Gītā*. Both were at any rate interested in dispelling the Schopenhaurian myth of the "pessimism" of Indian philosophy and its exclusively otherworldly soteriology. Aside from this, modern Indian thinkers have largely ignored Schopenhauer in their attempts to highlight the logical sophistication and formulations of India's classical philosophical systems.

A few Western scholars more hermeneutically sensitive than the first generation began to critique Schopenhauer's understanding of India. Most notably, Paul Hacker devoted much criticism to Schopenhauer's interpretation of *Upaniṣadic* concepts, particularly his making the formula *tat tvam asi* (you are that) the basis of his ethical system, a suggestion that had appealed to some Neo-Vedāntins. The philological reliability of the sources and commentators Schopenhauer had relied on in his understanding of Indian thought has for the most part been undermined; better translations and histories have been written, making Schopenhauer's appropriations seem simply outdated from a scholarly point of view. The interest of scholars has thus turned to the hermeneutical issues involved with Schopenhauer, and the nineteenth century German academy in general. Helmuth von Glasenapp and J. I. Gestering have both done studies of how nineteenth century German interest in India was motivated by the pessimism of German Romantic thinkers such as Herder and the Schlegel brothers about the philosophical and cultural future of Europe, and that their images of India were consequently hermeneutical projections bearing their own historical and cultural interests. A recent work by J. W. Sedler attempted to accurately separate the typically "German" and "Indian" concepts held by both Schelling and Schopenhauer. Foremost among contemporary authors on this subject has been Wilhelm Halbfass, who in several articles and book chapters has outlined the hermeneutical complexity of Schopenhauer's outlook on India, finding in it at once attitudes of admiration and condescension, an openness and inspiration as well as a syncretistic spirit and a feeling of superiority exposing the extent to which he was, like Hegel, a "son of his times."

Two opposed tendencies have characterized the scholarship dealing with Schopenhauer and India, namely hermeneutical naiveté and hermeneutical suspicion. The first generation of Western readers of Schopenhauer believed, based on the quality of the recently translated sources they had before them along with the assumptions of "Romantic hermeneutics" explicated by Gadamer, that Schopenhauer was a reliable exegete and even representative of Indian thought. Such a naiveté, manifested particularly in Deussen, simply matched up various thematized concepts of Schopenhauer and the classical Indian texts and pronounced them equlvalent, lacking sufficient respect for the temporal, cultural and philosophical distance distinguishing Schopenhauer from the classical *Upaniṣads* and later Vedānta commentators. The following generations of scholars, including Glasenapp and Sedler have had much work to do in separating out these issues and in rightly critiquing Schopenhauer's interpretations and appropriations of the Indian materials with which he was familiar. Even so, the "pessimistic," "other-worldly" and "life-denying" stereotypes with which Schopenhauer and his later readers stigmatized Indian philosophy have to this day far from disappeared.

For this reason, a great deal of hermeneutical sensitivity is necessary to a study such as this one. Schopenhauer, as Gestering, Glasenapp, Sedler and Halbfass have ably shown, must be contextualized into his own philosophical and cultural setting, a setting in which Romantic German ideas as well as a somber outlook on Europe's own intellectual and political *Sitz im Leben* were being projected by scholars from the Schlegel brothers to Hegel, Schopenhauer and Nietzsche into Greek and Indian antiquity. On the other hand, I think this hermeneutical sensitivity must not allow Schopenhauer's fascination with India to be reduced into mere cultural sedimentation. Schopenhauer was after all one of the first, and likely the most serious of nineteenth century Western philosophers confident that the study of Asian thought could prove fruitful to Western philosophy. As this book proposes to show, his study of it, while dependent on far from perfect resources, led him to completely reshape the course of his own philosophical thinking and helped him thematize and construct his entire system. Such a figure is deserving of more serious attention than the relative ambivalence or platitudinous rejection commonly dealt him by modern philosophers.

I wish therefore to attempt to tread a different path than the aforementioned hermeneutical naiveté and suspicion. This study will be largely textual and historical, drawing on the resources Schopenhauer used as well as the philosophical environment of epistemological idealism into which he was educated. The hermeneutical and scholarly labors of the last fifty years especially will be taken into account in assessing his use and misuse of Indian philosophical concepts. But it will also critique the criteria that have heretofore been employed in determining whether or not Schopenhauer can be thought to have been genuinely influenced by some of what he learned of pre-systematic Indian thought, and will attempt to formulate more reliable criteria. These efforts at contextualization and criteria reformulation will combine to yield a clear picture of how Schopenhauer, inspired by

Duperron and others, built an "original" Western philosophical scheme to a considerable measure from the elements of his contact with classical, pre-systematic Indian thought.

For the most part, this work will contribute to the field of Schopenhauer scholarship. Specifically, it takes a position opposed to arguments formulated by Patrick Gardiner, Christopher Janaway and John Atwell, who have all argued, in various fashions but all taking cues from Frederick Copleston, that Schopenhauer's epistemology demands no inquiry such as Schopenhauer in fact made into metaphysics, that his metaphysical inquiry has nothing to do with the epistemological skepticism they see Schopenhauer espousing. This conclusion leads them to look for other inspirations for Schopenhauer's system, and thus to either ignore or dismiss the role Schopenhauer's early acquaintance with the Indian philosophical tradition may have had on his completed philosophy. Their positions are, I believe, based on a misconstrual of what in Schopenhauer's system has thematic priority. Before his major work, *The World as Will and Representation* was composed, Schopenhauer's philosophical writings concentrated on theories of perception and judgment which were influenced by Kant, Hume and Goethe. His concern with ethics had not yet been awakened and his attitude towards metaphysics was skeptical and almost non-existent. Despite his own later somewhat misleading statements to the contrary, his philosophical outlook changes dramatically after his reading of Duperron's translations and commentary on the *Upaniṣads*. He appropriates Duperron's material and therewith reassesses Kant to include within idealism a falsification theory, which in Kant's philosophy as well as in places of Schopenhauer's own writings originally was not to be found. He followed this up with an understanding of ethics and asceticism which he thought were demanded by the falsification thesis, not to mention to have precedents in Indian religion. Schopenhauer's metaphysics and ethics are made possible by the aepistemological falsification theory inspired by his understanding of the concept of *māyā*, and it is this thesis I would like to establish as opposed to the other attempts to find other foundations, scientific or moral, for Schopenhauer's metaphysical inquiry. Because it is concerned with the formation of Schopenhauer's system, this study will take as the main works of focus Schopenhauer's dissertation, his *Nachlass* from the years 1814 to 1818, and the first edition of his "main work," *The World as Will and Representation* which appeared in 1819. We will however trace in detail the theoretical transformations Schopenhauer's system underwent in the 1830's, 40's and 50's, confronting the common penchant in the secondary literature to see Schopenhauer's thought to have been uniquely stable throughout his career, and also exposing the recent tendencies in Schopenhauer scholarship, found especially in Julian Young and John Atwell, to take the later versions of his system as the normative and stable ones. It will also trace through these decades Schopenhauer's growing familiarity with and increasingly odd stigmatizations of classical Indian religious and philosophical thought.

The book also proposes to make a significant contribution to the larger field of "cross-cultural" philosophy. Much of the work that has been done in this field in the last few decades has concentrated on inquiries as to whether "comparative philosophy" is possible between cultures, or to more or less superficial comparisons between the ideas of philosophers of different times and cultural contexts. "Comparisons" of ideas obviously happen, they happen among people of different cultures when confronting "difference" as a matter of course. Cross-cultural philosophy would benefit much more from concrete studies of how ideas are hermeneutically understood and appropriated when philosophers of one culture learn about and confront thinkers and ideas of another. What is often forgotten is that cross-cultural philosophy does not, and has never consisted in a detached, "objective" and hermeneutically immune comparison of ideas merely for the purpose of apprehending their similarity or difference. Interpretation is hermeneutically motivated, and always involves conceptual appropriation, appropriation which inevitably leads to some misrepresentation, but at the same time can also be the inspiration for creative thought. As one of the only philosophers of the Western tradition for whose system ideas of the pre-systematic Indian philosophical tradition had a measurable impact, Schopenhauer represents an invaluable benchmark for the study of cross-cultural philosophy. As the most extensive investigation of Schopenhauer's relationship to classical Indian philosophical thought to date, this study hopes to affect how Schopenhauer is read not only in the West, but in India as well, and among all those interested in cross-cultural philosophy.

Schopenhauer's encounter with Indian religion and philosophy has had two major legacies for cross-cultural philosophy. The first has had to do with the stigmatization of the Indian tradition with "irrationalism," "primitivism" and "pessimism," stigmas which helped lead for many decades to the complete non-attention to or and dismissal of the Indian philosophical tradition in the West. Schopenhauer's adoption of Romantic representations of India and its religious traditions causes him, in his later thought, to treat India as the originator of a trans-historical, trans-cultural "perennial philosophy," of which Europe is now the recipient and authorized interpreter. He believes, based to a certain degree on the materials on Indian antiquity available in Europe at the time, that Indian philosophical thought is "mythological" and not "systematic," leaving him to serve as the more "logical" representative of the Indian tradition to the West. Most disturbingly, Schopenhauer formulates a completely untenable hermeneutic of "pessimism" with which to measure the religions of the world, and proposes to elevate Indian "pessimism" against Jewish "theistic optimism."

But there is another legacy that I would like to propose Schopenhauer's appropriation of the notion of *māyā* had for philosophy in Europe, though it has been much less visible than the first. Through the theory of epistemological falsification, Schopenhauer inaugurated a new epistemological and ethical orientation in the West which, rather than assuming knowledge to be reliable and even all-powerful, critiqued its. potentialities, claims and scope, not to mention the axiological and ethical values this former confidence in knowledge and metaphysics had assumed. It is through Nietzsche, a life-long Schopenhauer admirer and antipode, in somewhat altered form, that Schopenhauer's falsification thesis, and so indirectly some elements of classical Hindu and Buddhist thought, inspired an entirely different trend in Western thought which has led from Nietzsche to contemporary trends in Continental thought.

CHAPTER 1

The Question of Influence

1.1 CRITERIA AND CONDITIONS OF INFLUENCE

That Arthur Schopenhauer appropriated certain concepts and themes from pre-systematic Hindu and Buddhist philosophical and religious thought has always been clear to those interested in Schopenhauer's philosophy. One ongoing issue with regard to this appropriation has been in what manner it took place and what interests Schopenhauer entertained in incorporating concepts and themes from the Indian philosophical tradition into his own reflection. For the past fifty years, scholars interested in the problem of the relationship between Schopenhauer and classical Hindu and Buddhist thought have in the main tended to separate Schopenhauer's philosophical appropriation of Indian thought from the possibility that it influenced the formulation and thematization of his philosophical system. The consensus which seems to have been reached as a result of this scholarship has been that Schopenhauer first formulated his own philosophical system and then selectively chose, for a variety of hermeneutical reasons, whatever ideas from the Indian tradition he could as supportive illustrations of his existing beliefs. Schopenhauer has in this way become an enigmatic case study of someone who appropriated certain philosophical ideas without having been influenced by them, a situation which, despite all of the historical, textual and hermeneutic evidence solicited to demonstrate it, seems curious.

As we began to delve once again into the problem of Schopenhauer's appropriation of classical Indian religious and philosophical thought, this chapter and the next will attempt to reopen the possibility that his studies of the Indian tradition did have a measurable effect upon the formulation and thematization of Schopenhauer's philosophy. Before turning to the historical evidence for this possibility in Chapter 2, we must first re-examine what criteria have heretofore been applied to the investigation of this question of influence, and by seeing how they have been (in most cases inadvertently) misapplied, venture to formulate a more minimal though perhaps clearer set of criteria which will help us determine whether Schopenhauer's thought was indeed influenced by his studies of the Indian tradition.

The two strands of scholarship through which we shall approach the relationship between Schopenhauer and India's pre-systematic religious and philosophical thought present to us similar negative conclusions regarding the degree to which the systematic formation of Schopenhauer's philosophy was influenced by his encounter with them. But these conclusions have been reached with different conceptions of what precisely constitutes influence. Given the varying objects of research of these two strands, this is understandable. The historians of both Indian and nineteenth century German philosophy have posed questions which focus on the accuracy of Schopenhauer's understanding of Indian philosophy given the resources available to him as well as questions meant to discover his own hermeneutical situation in the environment of German Idealism and Romanticism. The Western philosophical commentary on Schopenhauer on the other hand has tended to limit itself to what it considers the marginal role played by Schopenhauer's knowledge of Indian thought and how inconsistently it fits into the large-scale systematic structure of Schopenhauer's philosophy. In order to pose once again the question of influence with clarity, we must examine and assess the conflicting criteria of influence employed by these strands of research.

1.1.1 Interpretive Accuracy

Turning to the historical examination of the impact of Hindu and Buddhist thought on Schopenhauer to start, we find that the first major criterion applied to the investigation was that of interpretive accuracy. The initial confidence in Schopenhauer's understanding of Indian thought, indeed his capacity to represent it to the Western philosophical tradition exhibited in Nietzsche and Paul Deussen, has been significantly undermined. It appears that Nietzsche, a self-proclaimed one-time disciple of Schopenhauer turned philosophical opponent, trusted him as a perfectly reliable interpreter of Vedānta and particularly Buddhism. From Nietzsche's early ruminations on Greek tragedy and how it typified an antipode of a Schopenhaurian and "Buddhist negation of the will" (*Birth* 59) to his late oft-repeated attacks on Buddhism and Schopenhauer, as "nihilistic" and "under the spell and delusion of morality" (*Beyond* 68), Nietzsche never felt the need to make any fundamental distinctions between them. They are both made to fit into his typological classification of philosophies of "life-denial" and are dichotomized against those of "life-affirmation," among the latter of which are included ancient Greek thought and surprisingly some elements of an "affirming Āryan religion" of Manu (*Sämtliche* 380).[1]

Nietzsche praised his friend and former Schulpforta classmate Paul Deussen for "keeping the faith" of Schopenhaurian pessimism in his Indological studies (qtd. in Halbfass *India* 129). Nietzsche took great pride in having converted Deussen to Schopenhauer, the crucial turning point in the latter's decision to pursue Indological research. Deussen's formidable body of historical and philological work on Indian philosophy, including his 1883 *System of Vedānta* along with his independent 1887 translation of the *Brahmasūtrabhāsya* and *Sixty Upaniṣads of the Veda*, is accompanied by a philosophical corpus just as large, most notably represented in his 1877 *Elements of Metaphysics* and six *volume General History of Philosophy*. His devotion to Schopenhauer, though it did not prevent him from engaging in his own philosophical speculation, was consistent from his self-labeled "conversion" to Schopenhauer in 1868 (Deussen *Jahrbuch* 14) to his editing of a third critical edition of Schopenhauer's works as well as the *Yearbook of the Schopenhauer Society*. He dedicated his 1887 translation of sixty *Upaniṣads* to "the manes of Arthur Schopenhauer" and expended a great deal of synthetic effort in an attempt to show how Schopenhauer's philosophy brought with Śaṅkara's a perfect revival of the "idealism" of the *Upaniṣads* from the "atheism of the Sāṃkhya system and the apsychism of the Buddhists" (*Vedanta* 17–24)[2] Nietzsche's and Deussen's penchant for constructing historiographies of philosophy which, despite their respective differences, were thematically typological allowed them to see Schopenhauer's idealism and pessimism as falling within a philosophical continuum leading back to the very premises of pre-systematic Hindu and classical Buddhist thought. They never questioned Schopenhauer's understanding of these traditions, and given Deussen's unquestionable Indological expertise and reputation, such an assessment of Schopenhauer's understanding of Indian thought carried special weight.

This confidence in Schopenhauer's understanding was however contested even by contemporaries of Deussen. Though he wrote of Schopenhauer that "if he had done nothing else but decipher the awful translations of Anquetil Duperron, this would be enough to assure him, even among philosophers, an honorable place as interpreter" (417), Max Müller personally disputed with Schopenhauer over whether the *Vedas* or *Upaniṣads* were more "worthy" of historical research. Max P. Hecker, though he persisted in finding few fundamental substantive differences between the respective sotereologies of Schopenhauer, Vedānta and Buddhism, was able to make some distinctions between what he saw as the idealistic metaphysical monism of the former two and the realistic pluralism of the latter (34).

In 1928, Franz Mockrauer had to concede that most present Indologists, in rejecting Deussen's privileging of Śaṅkara's Vedānta over all other systems of Indian philosophy and his superficial correlations between Vedānta, Buddhism and Christianity, implicitly rejected Schopenhauer's characterizations of Indian thought (17). This did little to affect Mockrauer's own praise of

Schopenhauer as "the great European who uncovered for us the soul of India, who gives us the key to understanding the greatness of one Mahātma Gandhi" (22).[3] Mockrauer listed eight supposed affinities between Schopenhauer and various Indian schools including everything from idealism to the doctrine of the imperishability of the soul, the ethical necessity of compassion and the ascetic practice of the renunciation of the will-to-live (9). He defends Schopenhauer's comprehension of Indian thought on very peculiar generalist grounds.

> If he was unable to understand the details of Indian literature, if to a certain degree his distance from Indian culture was so great, we could still ask whether he was for these very reasons in a much more fortuitous situation than the contemporary specialists of Indology. Could he not inerrantly and more clearly grasp the characteristically essential forms of the Indian world out of this distance than those who lose themselves in details and fail to gain the measure of the essential? If he acknowledged and prized as the most important movements in Indian thinking idealism, the doctrine of the unity of *Brahman* and *māyā,* and the *tat tvam asi* and *samyasin* ideals and the later pessimism, atheism and *nirvāna* of Buddhism, there is little that could contradict this. (Mockrauer 18)

This essentialist picture of the Indian religious and philosophical tradition along with the interpretive privilege it confers on cultural distance doubtless represent the hermeneutical naiveté which is at one side of the polarized interpretation of Schopenhauer's conception of Indian thought that must be rejected.

In 1955 the Indologist Helmuth von Glasenapp was able to identify serious shortcomings in Schopenhauer's assessments of Indian history, culture and thought. He points out the inaccuracy of Schopenhauer's chronological placement of the *Upaniṣads* before any of the *Vedic* texts (Glasenapp 490–91), his failure to make clear distinctions between Vedānta and Buddhism (493) or clear distinctions between the different kinds of monism found fragmentarily in the *Upaniṣads* and his own metaphysics of will (498–99). Schopenhauer is also blind to the fundamental differences between the metaphysical absolutization of will in his own system and the relegation of will to a merely phenomenal and contingent status by the Buddhists (501). Glasenapp concludes:

> Schopenhauer was interested in India solely for its religion and philosophy. Furthermore, he restricted himself to systems such as Vedānta and Buddhism, in which he believed could be found confirmations of his own philosophy. That his views do not correspond to the findings of modern research is not surprising, for in the hundred years that separate us from the works of the sage of Frankfurt, Indology has not only gained an enormous range of new material, but also numerous methods which have improved upon and enriched earlier representations of the course of Indian spiritual history. It can certainly be said that, in the last decade of Schopenhauer's life, some researches were already available which would have necessitated corrections in his views. But Schopenhauer was much too subjective a thinker to have been able to change those views he had already formed at some later time. (501)

In spite of all this however, Glasenapp believed a debt of gratitude is owed to Schopenhauer for having inspired so many European scholars, Deussen, Neumann and Grim not least among them, to pursue Asian studies. He also believed Schopenhauer had captured the quintessential foundations for the ethics of non-violence as taught by both Buddhism and Gandhi in his own thought (Glasenapp, 502).

The belief that Schopenhauer, despite any other misunderstandings of the Indian spiritual tradition he may have entertained, accurately characterized the ethical spirit of both Hindu and Buddhist thought was in fact widely held until Paul Hacker, one of the great twentieth century European scholars of traditional and modern Vedānta, subjected the contention to a rigorous textual, hermeneutical and conceptual critique. Schopenhauer had, Hacker showed, cited very few passages from the *Upaniṣads* and the *Gītā* in very incidental and superficial ways to support his belief that the *Upaniṣadic* formula *tat tvam asi* ("thou are that") serves as a basis for an ethics of compassion (qtd. in Halbfass *Philology*, 273–4). He went on to demonstrate that Schopenhauer's understanding of the passages in question was not contextually appropriate, for this formula was originally understood to be a metaphysical teaching on the true relationship between the human being and *brahman* in the *Upaniṣads* and Krishna in the *Gītā* and not an ethical maxim.[4] Though Schopenhauer's interpretation, what Hacker referred to as the "*tat tvam asi* ethic," had been espoused by Deussen and even appropriated by Neo-Vedāntic thinkers such as Vivekananda, Bāl Ganghādhar Tilak and Sarvapali Radhakrishnan, it was simply impossible to support the interpretation by reference to any source texts or commentaries of the Indian tradition (299). Furthermore, Hacker maintained, any ethic premised on a monism such as Schopenhauer's, a monism which ultimately denies the reality of the individual and consequently any real relationship between persons, can only be a "logical monstrosity" (306). Rather that having been genuinely influenced by classical Indian thought, it was Schopenhauer who was attempting to validate his own ethical doctrines with isolated and badly understood passages from the ancient texts, and the subsequent reappropriation of Schopenhauer's "*tat tvam asi* ethic" by Neo-Vedāntic thinkers was only one of many modern examples of "the deep wound which is left in the Indian mind" in the midst of the colonial period (308). Hacker looked foreword to the day when twentieth century Indian philosophers would be able to contribute to the growth of their intellectual and spiritual tradition with ideas taken from their own roots rather than with those taken from the West.

Wilhelm Halbfass has pointed out that the association of Schopenhauer's philosophy with irrationalism and pessimism led to a silent or antagonistic reaction to his thought by twentieth century Indian philosophers (*India* 120). Indeed Schopenhauer, on the rare occasions he is mentioned by twentieth century Indian thinkers, is treated tentatively and with ambivalence. Vivekananda's project of transforming the ancient monism of Advaita into engaged ethical social action, the establishment of a "practical Vedānta," while it was ostensibly based solely on traditional Hindu teachings, did incorporate Schopenhauer's "*tat tvam asi* ethic." Hacker chronicled in great detail Vivekananda's 1896 visit with Paul Deussen and convincingly demonstrated that, while before their encounter Vivekananda had preached an ethics totally consistent with the *Gītā's* doctrine of *karmayoga,* he was all-too-willing after his discussions with Deussen to advocate Schopenhauer's moral interpretation as if it had come from the Vedāntic tradition itself (Halbfass *Philology* 291–98). This interpretation, which subsequently appears in Neo-Vedāntic thinkers from the preachers of the Ramakrishna mission to Tilak and Radhakrishnan as well as in the works of the most careful commentators like M. Hiriyanna, is introduced in ways which according to Hacker either subtly attempt to represent the "*tat tvam asi* ethic" as belonging to classical Hindu teaching or by suggestively calling for its incorporation into contemporary Vedāntic thinking (*Philology* 298–305). This would seem to imply that twentieth century Neo-Vedāntic thinkers, while having been reluctant to openly discuss the issue of how well or inadequately Schopenhauer understood the *Upaniṣads* or the *Gītā,* tacitly accepted his understanding by their willingness to adopt his interpretation. For Hacker this acceptance was unfortunate and symptomatic of the colonized mentality of the Neo-Vedāntins in their representation of their tradition to the West. But if any such acceptance of Schopenhauer's ethical reading of *tat tvam asi* existed on the part of Neo-Vedāntins, their silence as to the source of this reading in a Western philosopher reveals their ambivalence about Schopenhauer's hermeneutical circumstances. Even Radhakrishnan, with whom Hacker was particularly harsh for defending the "*tat tvam asi* ethic" of Schopenhauer, made references to the inadequacy of Schopenhauer's reading of Vedānta and Buddhism. "The modern pessimistic philosophy of Germany," he wrote, "that of Schopenhauer and Hartmann, is only a revised version of ancient Buddhism. It is sometimes said to be 'little more than Buddhism vulgarized'" (Radhakrishnan *Indian Philosophy* 342). He also criticized Deussen for being overly eager to regard the fundamental doctrine of the *Upaniṣads* as the doctrine of *māyā;* "having come to that conclusion on independent grounds, he is anxious to find support for his doctrine in the philosophic systems of ancient India, the *Upaniṣads* and Śaṅkara . . . and modern Germany, Kant and Schopenhauer" (*Indian Philosophy* 189). Even those then who have been most receptive to the so-called "*tat tvam asi* ethic" have not been uncritical of the accuracy of its founder's interpretation of their tradition. In fact, there has never been any directly articulated confidence in the reliability of Schopenhauer's understanding of ancient Indian thought by Indian philosophers, particularly given the limitations of the resources on Indian philosophy available during his lifetime combined with his seemingly fanatical enthusiasm for the subject.[5]

The initial response to Schopenhauer's reception of presystematic Hindu and classical Buddhist thought which we find in Europe in the late nineteenth and early twentieth centuries exhibits a historical and hermeneutical naiveté. The thematic equivocation of various concepts such as *brahman, māyā* and the *tat tvam asi* formula with equally generalized notions such as the absolute in the Western tradition presuppose the essentialist definitions of philosophy as well as the rudimentary historiographies of philosophy which thinkers the caliber of Nietzsche and Deussen advocated without skepticism.[6] But with the compilation and translation of a steadily increasing number of texts and commentaries of the Indian religious and philosophical tradition, which revealed their complexity and sophistication, such a naiveté was naturally abandoned by Western Indologists. The discoveries of Glasenapp and Hacker of Schopenhauer's misunderstandings of many of the broad outlines and specific details of the Indian spiritual and intellectual tradition ruled out for them the possibility of genuine influence. Instead, Schopenhauer's assertions about Indian thought began to seem much more his own philosophical presuppositions, and his willingness to idealize the Indian tradition in his works seemed symptomatic of his desire to have his own doctrines confirmed by classical Hinduism and Buddhism.

1.1.2 Hermeneutic Preclusion

The few scholars who remained concerned with the question of the extent to which classical Hindu and Buddhist thought influenced Schopenhauer turned to the issue of his own hermeneutical situation. The general consensus which emerged from the researches of this new generation of scholars was that, far from being influenced by his beloved *Upaniṣads* or the early texts of Buddhism, Schopenhauer selectively appropriated whatever ideas he could from available materials which served to confirm positions he had already arrived at in the context of his own philosophical environment. The irrationalism, vitalism and pessimism of the Romantic movement were seen to be even greater influences on his philosophical development than the idealism of Kant and Fichte in which he was formally trained,[7] and these influences both directed and infected all he chose to highlight of the Indian tradition. One of the overriding concerns with Schopenhauer was no longer whether he understood anything of the Indian tradition, but rather to what extent and in what ways he could be considered to have been an Orientalist.[8]

Jean W. Sedler praises Schopenhauer for his remarkable ability to comprehend the ungrammatical Latin translations of the *Upaniṣads* by Anquetil Duperron he cherished so dearly (15–16) and admits a number of general but considerable similarities between Schopenhauer's ethical and soteriological principles of compassion and renunciation of will and various Hindu and Buddhist doctrines.[9] But even these similarities were ones which Sedler believes Schopenhauer himself overestimated, owing to his "propensity to find corroborations between his own ideas with as many thought-systems as possible" (180).[10] Schopenhauer's philosophy is much more informed by his own intellectual environment. Sedler proposes that Schopenhauer's metaphysics of will was influenced not by the *Upaniṣadic* notion of *brahman* but rather by F. W. J. Schelling's so-called "ground of God," the unconscious urge of God to manifest himself into the plurality of the world which is opposed to the purity of God's intellectual nature (71–3). She points out further that Schopenhauer's notion of denial of the will-to-live was not a product of his acquaintance with Indian asceticism, but rather "may well have been suggested by his own pronounced aesthetic sensibility" (Sedler 213).[11] More importantly however, Sedler believes that the historical development of Schopenhauer's thinking, outlined very clearly in the writings of the philosopher himself, rules out the possibility that Indian thought could be considered to have influenced the formation of his system. Even though Schopenhauer's acquaintance with Indian thought dates back to the inception of his system, she points out, the references to India in his notes from 1814 to 1818 are "few and far between . . . incidental" and "offer no evidence that he owed any of these notions to India in the first place" (Sedler 221). Considering Schopenhauer's later studies of Buddhism, she notes that the increase of his knowledge, while it lead him to more frequent mention of Buddhism and Hinduism, did not in any way change the principles upon which he first based the system (Sedler 222). The most characteristic feature of Schopenhauer's ethics, his notion of denial of the will, was worked out before he ever had any knowledge of Buddhism, and in fact could not have been influenced by what he later learned of Buddhism through the inadequate scholarly writings of Spence Hardy and Izak Schmidt combined with the murky traveler's reports he read (212–14). Sedler concludes that "Schopenhauer did not derive his philosophy from Indian prototypes, but rather employed Indian ideas as illustrations or conformations of his existing beliefs" (231).

J. I. Gestering agrees with Sedler that Schopenhauer's interest in Indian thought can be better explained through reference, not only to his own philosophical environment, but also to his cultural *Zeitgeist*. It is all too evident for Gestering that Schopenhauer's inordinately high praises for Duperron's translation of the *Upaniṣads* was due to the fact that their Latin appealed to his Romantic taste for classical literature (34). He cannot help but have been effected by the Romantic obsession with cultural and philosophical origins which inspired so much interest in India among German literati of the period, among whom in fact Schopenhauer first gained acquaintance with Indian thought in Weimar. But more problematic still for Gestering is the fact that Schopenhauer, given his anti-historical biases against Hegel's progressivist views of history, dwells in a cultural unreflectivity which leads him to engage with Indian thought as if it needed "no hermeneutic" (59). Schopenhauer has no idea that "India, objectively speaking, behaves culturally in some incompatible manner" (Gestering 58). Schopenhauer's major legacy then becomes the association of Indian thought with his own pessimistic views of the egocentric culture in which he lived and participated, for he extracts from his study of India only concepts of anthropological "negativity" such as suffering and denial of the will-to-live. This leads him to treat India "as if it were some other European philosopher" (Gestering 59), and shows how blind he is to the fact that his own involvement with the Indian tradition "reflects axiological principles inherited from his own culture" (58). Schopenhauer's appropriation of Hindu and Buddhist ideas not only cannot count as a genuine influence for him, but rather the manner in which he employs these ideas to serve his own philosophical interests is a sure sign of his ethnocentricity. Gestering's account, while in some ways insightful in its exposition of Schopenhauer's characterological judgments of culture, cannot really be said to be an altogether fair picture of the matter. While Schopenhauer does display a good deal of hermeneutical naiveté in his equations of so many thinkers from so many time periods such as Plato, Kant, Eckhart and himself as well as his imputation of a fundamental pessimism to Hinduism and Buddhism, he at times levels sharp criticisms at what he feels are hermeneutically unreflective approaches to Indian culture and thought. He belittled the Christian missionaries of England who believed they could replace the age-old religions of India with their own (Schopenhauer WWRI: 356–7), he found certain translations of the *Upaniṣads* by Colebrooke, Röer and even Rammohan Roy, even though they unlike Duperron's were made directly from Sanskrit, contemptible for the European "theism" which he believed had been injected into them (PP II: 348).[12] The notion that he treated India as if it were another European philosopher, always projecting familiar philosophical conceptions onto an alien tradition, is also mistaken. At one point in the midst of a detailed discussion on Kant's Transcendental Dialectic, Schopenhauer questions whether the three "unconditionals" to which Kant believes human reason necessarily comes, namely soul, world and God, are really universal conceptions:

> Accessible and familiar as these concepts have become . . . through the philosophers of pure reason (*Vernunft*), it is by no means certain from this that, even without revelation, they were bound to result from the development of everyone's faculty of reason, as a creation peculiar to the nature of this reason itself. To decide this it would be necessary to make use of historical research, and to find out whether the ancient and non-European nations, especially those of Hindustan, and many of the oldest Greek philosophers, actually arrived at those concepts, or whether only we, by translating the *Brahma* of the Hindus or the *Tien* of the Chinese quite falsely as "God," charitably ascribe such concepts to them, just as the Greeks encountered their gods everywhere; whether it is not rather the case that theism proper is to be found only in the Jewish religion, and the two religions that have sprung from it. (Schopenhauer WWRI, 486)

Nonetheless, Gestering's suggestion that Schopenhauer's legacy was the association of Indian thought with German pessimism certainly rings historically true, especially when one considers the extent to which this association was taken up by Eduard von Hartmann and Phillipp Mainländer, two nineteenth century pessimistic philosophers who took their departures largely from Schopenhauer (67–89).

Wilhelm Halbfass, who devoted a great deal of careful study to Schopenhauer's appropriation of Indian philosophy and religion, shows that Schopenhauer prided himself on having brought conceptual and systematic clarity not only to the religious teachings of the Buddha and the "Hindu sages" but also to those of Meister Eckhart and Christianity. Hence for Schopenhauer, "Indian philosophy appears not so much as a source of inspiration or revelation, but rather as a mirror and medium of self-representation and self-confirmation" (Halbfass *India* 114). Schopenhauer's frequent invocation of the vocabulary of Vedāntic and

Buddhist thought such as *māyā, brahman, tat tvam asi, jivātman* and *nirvāna* are meant not to give an accurate textual explication of what these concepts mean within their ancient Indian philosophical contexts, but rather to "illustrate and express his own thoughts" (Halbfass *India* 110). His faithfulness to Duperron's translations of the *Upaniṣads* was not merely a commitment to their various ideas, but also to Duperron's own parallelization of the *Upaniṣads* with Kantian philosophy (Halbfass *India* 110).[13] The encounter with Indian thought was for Schopenhauer also a very European encounter, for with the help of his appropriation of Indian thought in the clarification of his own ideas, Schopenhauer marshaled a radical critique against both Judeo-Christian theological, anthropological and historical presuppositions and more contemporary Western rationalism and progressivism, which can very easily be seen as a prolepsis to a similar critique raised by Heidegger some hundred years after him (Halbfass *India* 120). Thus, even though Halbfass makes some important distinctions between Schopenhauer's interest in Indian thought and that of his Romantic contemporaries,[14] it is perhaps in this radical critique of the present that Schopenhauer's idealization of Indian thought can be seen to be hermeneutically aligned with similar critiques by Herder and Schlegel, which Hegel so vehemently opposed in his own reception of Indian thought.

It is these criticisms of Western "rationalist and materialist philosophy" which puts Schopenhauer in tune with the Romantics, according to J. J. Clarke (68). He argues that "Schopenhauer's own understanding of Indian philosophy, however inadequate, is an outstanding representative of the Orientalist aspiration to use Eastern thought in pursuit of a fundamental rethinking of the Western intellectual tradition" (Clarke 69). Schopenhauer merits inclusion among the number of thinkers of the nineteenth and twentieth centuries whom one can justifiably label an "Orientalists," but for Clarke this designation signifies a cultural phenomena more diverse and less pernicious than what Edward Said believed to have identified in his work, *Orientalism*. Far from being merely a homogenous Occidental discourse which masked its interest for colonial domination under the rubric of cross-cultural research, the Orientalist movement in Germany in the nineteenth century, Clarke maintains, had virtually no colonial interests in either India or China; the Romantic thinkers and Indologists of the period were more interested in using Indian thought as a "corrective mirror" of the deficiencies and degeneration of their own culture (25–28). There is much in such an achievement if indeed it can be supposed that Schopenhauer used Indian thought in such a way, and indeed many of the historians cited above praise Schopenhauer for his extraordinarily unique openness to the Indian religious tradition. But such praise would have to be balanced against Schopenhauer's stigmatization of Hinduism and Indian Buddhism as fundamentally "pessimistic" and excessively "mythological," assessments that had such a great effect on Nietzsche and the many subsequent generations of historians of Western philosophy who for these very reasons refused to even confer the title "philosophy" upon the intellectual productions of the Indian tradition.

What became important for this generation of scholars interested in Schopenhauer's relationship to India was not the issue of whether there were inadequacies in his comprehension of *Upaniṣadic* and Buddhist thought, but rather how he misunderstood them. Schopenhauer's inextricable relationship with the Romantic movement, his conceptual immersion in the Idealist philosophy into which he was educated, his insistence on seeing his own ideas confirmed by the reflections of philosophers of such tremendous cultural and historical diversity defined his hermeneutical situation. They also precluded the possibility for them that Indian thought could have in any way influenced the course of Schopenhauer's philosophical thinking

1.1.3 The Problem of Consistency

The relationship between Schopenhauer and Indian thought in the secondary literature on his philosophy is often almost entirely ignored.[15] John Atwell cited Schopenhauer's acknowledgment of the influence of Plato, Kant and "ancient Indian wisdom" on the formation of his system, but then explicated only the roles played by the former two (*Character* 76–80). D. W. Hamlyn mentions the "veil of *māyā*" as it was used by Schopenhauer when he discusses Schopenhauer's metaphysics and ethics, but only in passing and with no explication (146). Bryan Magee, though he acknowledges some general affinities between Schopenhauer's theses of epistemological construction and those of Vijñānavāda, states that Schopenhauer could not have been influenced "to any decisive degree" by Buddhist thought and that, where affinities do exist, they were reached "independently" in German Idealism (340–44). Patrick Gardiner maintains that the doctrines of "metempsychosis" and "resignation of the will" had influenced Schopenhauer, but finds Schopenhauer's "mystical" tendencies problematic given his oft-repeated Kantian conviction that knowledge is restricted to the phenomenal (293–300). The great Jesuit historian of Western philosophy Frederick Copleston also believed Hinduism and Buddhism were primarily the areas where Schopenhauer found validation for his ascetic doctrine of renunciation, which for Copleston himself was inferior to the more "dynamic" and "active" ethical teachings of Christianity, which contrary to the religions of India was for Copleston "a religion of life" (178–80).

Where some space has been devoted to the instrumental role which may have been played by the *Upaniṣads* and Vedānta on Schopenhauer's systematic development, it has been suspected that the doctrine of "illusion" appropriated by Schopenhauer through his understanding of māyā runs counter to the rest of his epistemology. Early in the century, the German scholar Hans Naegelsbach concluded that Schopenhauer's conflation of Kantian and *Upaniṣadic* "idealism" was contradictory and unfaithful to the senses of both doctrines in their specific contexts. He wrote:

> Schopenhauer reinterprets Kantian idealism and Indian illusionism by setting them into a correlative relationship. Kantian idealism in connection with the doctrine of the thing-in-itself grows into an idealistic tension between world and self, with the knowing subject on one side and the thing-in-itself on the other, such that both reality and knowledge become problems for a critical

> epistemology. . . . In India the transparent consciousness of the highest knowledge becomes one with final reality. In the certain knowledge of unity, plurality becomes an illusion. Illusionism is charged with the most powerful religious sentiment carrying the metaphysical idea of the reality of all things, which of course later on strives toward a philosophical justification through a theory of knowledge. The Indian's knowledge . . . becomes for him the highest reality, while on the other side, no illusionism exists for Kant which originates in the consciousness of universal oneness. Schopenhauer attempts a synthesis between Kantianism and Indian wisdom without himself being clear about the origin of Kantian idealism within a strictly epistemological inquiry nor about the origin of illusionism in a fundamental religious and metaphysical conviction. . . . Both standpoints, originating from entirely different relationships, run next to one another in Schopenhauer and intersect in a wholly contradictory fashion. (Naegelsbach 151–2)

Naegelsbach believed that this untenable correlativity between illusionism and idealism was merely used by Schopenhauer to find an inroad to his metaphysics of will and the "pessimistic feeling of life" to which it led (152–56).[16] While Naegelsbach conceded that Schopenhauer was undoubtedly influenced by Indian thought, more so by Hinduism than Buddhism, this influence consisted ultimately in allowing him to find a voice and phraseology for his pessimistic "religiosity" (147–9).

The only contemporary Western Schopenhauer scholar to have paid serious attention to the question of influence has been Christopher Janaway. After presenting a short but accurate chronology of Schopenhauer's acquaintance with Indian thought, Janaway concludes rightly that Buddhism could not have had any initial impact on Schopenhauer's philosophy and that Schopenhauer was later gratified to have found so many correspondences with it (29). He concludes further that, if Schopenhauer can be trusted in his claim that his system was conceptually finished by 1814, his acquaintance with the *Upaniṣads* could have only "dovetailed with the rest of his thoughts towards the end of the process of completion"

(Janaway 29). Whatever impact the *Upaniṣads* may have had on Schopenhauer, Janaway feels that its consequences were unfortunate as regards the consistency of Schopenhauer's epistemology. The "leitmotif of the veil of *māyā*" creates an obsession on Schopenhauer's part that the world of representations was a mere "illusion," which is not only entirely un-Kantian, but pushes idealism towards a Berkeleyian subjective solipsism which Schopenhauer actually explicitly rejects (Janaway 168–9).

For most of the philosophical commentators on Schopenhauer, the effects of Hindu and Buddhist ideas on him are so negligible that they do not even deserve mention. For those who do attend to the matter, it is either Schopenhauer's religious and ascetic tastes that explain his enthusiasm for India, which at best is incidental to the conceptual structure of Schopenhauer's thought and at worst at positive odds with it; or it is his fancy with the "illusionism" of the *Upaniṣads* which not only fails to add anything to his system, but distorts his comprehension of idealism and corrupts the consistency of his own epistemology. Nothing instrumental or philosophically constructive results from any influence Indian philosophy may have had on Schopenhauer according to these views.

1.2 A REAPPRAISAL OF THE CRITERIA

Having considered the various criteria applied to the investigation of the influence of Indian thought on Schopenhauer's philosophy, we now turn to the question whether these criteria, either separately or taken together, constitute sufficient grounds for either accepting or rejecting the possibility of influence in this specific case. Does the fact that Schopenhauer had a merely fragmentary and superficial understanding of both the rich and diverse tradition of Indian philosophy as a whole and the context and content of those ideas with which he was familiar preclude us from saying that it was really Indian philosophical and religious speculation which affected him? Does Schopenhauer's hermeneutic immersion into the cultural and philosophical contexts of the nineteenth century, colored as these contexts were by the German

Orientalists, entail that everything from his selection of materials to his understandings of their meanings was so inescapably European as to compel the conclusion that Schopenhauer, far from being influenced by Hinduism and Buddhism, projected his own ideas into their vocabulary from the start? Does the conjecture, held by many scholars, that Indian thought contributed nothing but inconsistency to the conceptual content of Schopenhauer's systematic philosophy justify the reluctance to treat Indian thought as influential to it?

The answer to the first of the above questions must be "no." The correct interpretation of a body of philosophical texts, even if one single such interpretation were naively supposed to exist, cannot be a condition for the influence of those texts upon the course of one's own reflection, misguided or not. Schopenhauer admitted three major sources of philosophical inspiration aside from his own personal observations, the *Upaniṣads,* Plato and Kant (MR1 467). Almost all the philosophical secondary literature on Schopenhauer accuses him of misunderstanding and distorting both Plato's theory of Ideas and Kant's epistemology, putting his own questionable interpretations of these theories to the service of his own system, and yet no student of Schopenhauer's works would deny that both were of immense importance for the formation of his own philosophy. There could be no more *a priori* reason to exclude Schopenhauer's contact with Indian thought through Duperron's translations of the *Upaniṣads* and the early studies of *Asiatic Researches* from those ideas which influenced him than there could be such an exclusion of Platonic or Kantian philosophy from the sphere of influence. There can be no question that Schopenhauer's understanding of Indian philosophical and religious ideas was in many cases inadequate, as we shall have further occasion to see later. It would be much better to say that thorough knowledge of both Sanskrit and the historical richness and diversity of its philosophical tradition would have been the ideal circumstances under which to have been influenced by classical Hindu and Buddhist thought. But such circumstances are not a condition of influence, and the fact that Schopenhauer did not have such knowledge does not preclude the possibility that his early acquaintance with the materials which were available to him affected the course of his philosophical development.

It is certainly true that Schopenhauer first gained acquaintance with India through information he imbibed from nineteenth century European Orientalists, that some, though certainly not all, of his idealizations of ancient India carry Romantic sentiments. He most certainly did employ Indian religious and philosophical concepts as a "mirror" to confirm a wide variety of his own philosophical beliefs, though saying this does not necessarily imply that all of these beliefs were inherited from the European tradition. The scholarship of Sedler, Gestering and Halbfass has been invaluable in correcting the hermeneutical naiveté with which Schopenhauer's relationship to Indian thought had often been previously approached and brought the historical realities of this relationship to light. However, if it was hermeneutically naive to once suppose that Schopenhauer had an inerrant grasp of the Hindu and Buddhist traditions as Nietzsche and Deussen once did, it would also be naive to suppose that Schopenhauer should or could have had any understanding of these traditions which was not bound and conditioned by those very historical realities which led him to their study. Though Schopenhauer may indeed have often been entertaining his own philosophical preconceptions in the ways he appropriated ideas of the *Upaniṣads*, the *Gītā* and early Buddhist texts, these "prejudices" must at least in part be, as Gadamer put it, "conditions whereby . . . what we encounter says something to us" (*Hermeneutics* 9). Our historical belonging to a tradition, and for Gadamer the ontological structure of our very understanding, means that not only the way a given text "addresses" us as significant is mediated by the sedimented meanings available to us through our own tradition, but that this tradition itself ensures that "the significance exists at the beginning of any such research . . . in choosing the theme to be investigate, awakening the desire to understand" (Gadamer *Truth* 282). From the intriguing encounters between Alexander's soldiers with the Indian "*gymnosophists*" to the attempted synthesis of Roman and Indian gods in the sixth book of *Caesar's Gaelic Wars*, from the Christian missionary ventures in India to Jones' pioneering grammatical studies, from Schelling's ruminations on Hindu mythology to Hegel's dismissal of the same as an empty "religion of substance," the encounter of the West with India had been charged with many-faceted and often self-searching meanings in the history of the Western tradition. That Schopenhauer's reception of Indian thought was first prompted and later developed within this history and these acquired meanings does not constitute an apology for the pessimistic, world-denying and obfuscating stereotypes with which he stigmatized Indian religion and philosophy. Neither does it entail that Schopenhauer accepted all of the sedimented meanings which his contemporaries, the Romantics, cherished in their respective views of India.[17] In point of fact, Halbfass and Clarke show some admiration for Schopenhauer precisely because his openness to Indian thought prompted him to fundamentally rethink many of the central philosophical and religious ideas of the Western tradition.[18] The hermeneutical naiveté of Deussen and Mockrauer need not however be replaced with a hermeneutical suspicion which reduces the entirety of Schopenhauer's encounter with Indian thought into either a masked expression of his ethnocentricity or an attempt to mirror a set of independently arrived-at and fixed beliefs. Hermeneutically situated as he was and as any interpreter must be, the historical circumstances and many-layered contexts through which he came to value the new translations of Hindu and Buddhist literature as well as the growing scholarship devoted to their research need not have been what prevented their influence upon his own philosophy, but rather were inevitably the very conditions for such influence. As unfortunate as his misunderstandings of the Indian philosophical tradition may have been, the fact that Schopenhauer's own appropriations of Indian ideas were European appropriations is nothing more than a hermeneutical truism, not a fact that would rule out the possibility of influence.

Addressing briefly the final issue of how consistently Indian concepts such as *māyā, brahman, tat tvam asi* and *nirvāna* fit in with the rest of Schopenhauer's philosophical system, we must also deny that formal consistency is a condition for influence.

Consistency may indeed be an ideal for systematic philosophical thinking, and Schopenhauer himself prizes it as belonging to his own system above all others.[19] This latter claim can and has been much contested and with very good reason; the number of thinkers who figure prominently in Schopenhauer's early philosophical development is extraordinarily diverse, ranging from Plato and Kant to the skeptic G. E. Schultze, his first philosophical advisor, to Fichte, a onetime teacher, to the writings of the French physiologist Flourens and the theologian Matthias Claudias. Heterogeneous elements were being combined in his reflections from the beginning and as a result conflate oddly with one another in his system's actual thematization, as we shall see in the next chapter. They were nonetheless fundamental to his philosophic development, and remained so throughout his writings.

It must be noted that the considerations of the degree of accuracy in Schopenhauer's interpretation of the *Upaniṣadic* and Buddhist concepts which he most often referred to, such as *brahman, māyā, tat tvam asi* and *nirvāna,* and the nature of his own hermeneutical situation were not always initially held to be criteria of influence. They were sometimes used as methodological criteria aimed at answering the question of how faithful or mistaken Schopenhauer's understanding of the content and context of these various concepts happened to be. Nonetheless, the answers to these questions, with the initial investigators positive and with most recent scholars negative, over time transformed these objects of inquiry into actual criteria of whether or not Indian thought had any positive influence on Schopenhauer or not. We have found them as criteria of influence wanting.

1.3 A BRIEF SKETCH OF MINIMAL CRITERIA OF INFLUENCE

As a general consideration, some care needs to be taken with the issue of whether one text, set of ideas or tradition had an influence on a given thinker. In the case of an interpreter and a text, we may often be tempted to speak of influence in psychological parlance by saying that an interpreter was compelled by some particular idea or passage in the text. When Gadamer speaks of the interpreter and the text as partners in a hermeneutic dialogue, he wishes to stress much more the content, subject matter or issue (*Sache*) of the text and how it "addresses" the reader, or alternatively, what sort of "question" the text puts to the interpreter which forces the interpreter to requestion the text. Nevertheless, Gadamer still speaks on occasion of "our being perplexed by the traditionary word," (*Hermeneutics* 373) which becomes the impetus, as it were, for this dialogue to proceed. Hence, it would be very difficult even in this context to avoid the language of psychologism when discussing influence. For Gadamer, we may not be able to get inside the head of the author of the text to discover his or her original intention, but the various meanings the text presents prompt a reaction in the reader which furthermore must be a reaction of a certain kind in order for reader and text to become diologic partners.

Perhaps such language is to a certain degree unavoidable, for influence as it may exist between text and interpreter would seem to involve some sort of positive valuation on the part of the latter, a mental act accruing worth. However, with respect to the present case, it would be best to make the texts in question the final court of appeal as to whether Indian thought had an influence on Schopenhauer or not. The texts in question would in this instance be Schopenhauer's published philosophical writings, his notes, his correspondence and the works he read on Indian thought and how he assessed them. But what set of general criteria can be employed in order to determine from this textual evidence whether Hinduism and Buddhism had any affect on Schopenhauer's philosophy?

Two such criteria will be proposed here, and they are meant to fulfill the conditions of influence in the minimal sense. This approach should not be taken as an attempt to avoid the hermeneutical complexities of Schopenhauer's situation; on the contrary, these will be taken into consideration throughout. They are rather meant to clarify in a more reliable way than the criteria employed by previous scholarship whether we can say that the thematic formulations of Schopenhauer's philosophical system were inspired, introduced or revised through his encounter with pre-systematic Hindu and Buddhist thought. They are thus meant to meet the very simple conditions that, in order for us to tell whether a philosopher was influenced by a concept, text or tradition of thought, we should be assured that he or she both knew about these and that they had some sort of measurable effect upon the way his or her own thinking was thematized. The first criterion we will therefore call the criterion of acquaintance, and it is concerned not only with what knowledge Schopenhauer had of Indian thought and from what sources he gained his knowledge, but also when during the course of his own studies and writings he gained it. These matters will be dealt with in the next chapter when we turn to the development and revision of Schopenhauer's philosophical system in his early *Nachlass*. Many commentators have maintained that Schopenhauer's philosophy was extraordinarily thematically stable and never underwent any major changes or revisions, and furthermore, given the chronological inception of the system combined with its stability, Schopenhauer's study first of Hindu and later Buddhist texts and secondary literature came too late to have had any effect on his thinking. I shall undertake in the this work to contest both the monolithic and unrevised conceptions of Schopenhauer's system as well as the supposition that such revision did not coincide with his investigation of Indian thought.

The second criterion will occupy us for the remainder of this work, and I will call it the criterion of thematic effect. It will revolve around what measurable philosophical effects Schopenhauer's knowledge of Indian thought had on his conceptual scheme. These effects will be seen to go beyond the mere use of Sanskrit vocabulary which so many believe to be merely incidental, but will rather involve how the concepts expressed through this terminology were incorporated into his system so as to help him make the two major transitions in his philosophy he always felt to be most important, the transition from epistemology to metaphysics and the transition from metaphysics to ethics.

We shall along the way be inquiring as to the reliability of the sources of Schopenhauer's acquaintance with India and how they measure up against both the source texts and commentarial traditions of the *Upaniṣads*, the *Gītā* and early Theravāda and Māhāyana Buddhism. This will be done in order to correct certain pervasive misconceptions Schopenhauer both adopts and himself formulates with regard to these traditions, but also in order to see where and how Schopenhauer could have contributed to the continuing, living conversations of these traditions. Despite Paul Hacker's despair at the Neo-Vedāntins having employed a Schopenhaurian interpretation of one of the central formulas of the early *Upaniṣads* which did not belong to the commentarial tradition, their very use of it is not only disclosive of their own hermeneutical interests, it also seems to reveal that Schopenhauer as a creative thinker receptive to their tradition was able at least in this instance to contribute to that conversation, which for a person with no understanding of or insight into that tradition would hardly have been possible.

CHAPTER 2

Māyā in Schopenhauer's Philosophical Development

2.1 THE SIGNIFICANCE OF THE NACHLASS

As seen from the preceding chapter, one of the major reasons so many commentators have discounted the possibility that Indian thought played any significant role in the development of Schopenhauer's systematic philosophy was its apparent insignificance in the notebooks in which Schopenhauer built his system between the years 1814 and 1818. Jean Sedler has maintained that the references to Indian ideas are in these notes rare, incidental, and meant to confirm beliefs Schopenhauer had already arrived at and thus could not be counted as having influenced his system (221, 231). This is an assessment Janaway has agreed with (29). Alfred Schmidt has claimed that, while Schopenhauer was very familiar with pre-systematic Indian thought during these formative years, its influence on him was far from unmediated, and he echoes Glasenapp's judgment that "Schopenhauer is much too subjective a thinker not to extract from foreign sources that which belongs to his own thought" (*Wharheit* 125). Schopenhauer's most recent biographer, Rüdiger Safransky, has argued that, while the notes making reference to Indian thought between 1814 and 1818 are important because they are there "directly lined up with major points in Schopenhauer's nascent philosophy," they can at best be taken as "confirmations" and "illustrations" of Schopenhauer's independently reached philosophical conclusions (201–202). In the present chapter, an attempt will be made to controvert this reading and assessment through a reexamination of the formative role Indian philosophical conceptions, and specifically Schopenhauer's understanding of the idea of *māyā,* play in the forming system built in these notes. This will involve first an examination of the notes as the laboratory where Schopenhauer's system is first thematized, as well as a hermeneutic reassessment of previous readings of these notes discounting Schopenhauer's knowledge of Indian thought as playing a significant role in them. Next we shall examine the set of themes which Schopenhauer synthesizes into a philosophical system, and finally, we shall examine how his understanding of the notion of *māyā* gets incorporated into this developing set of concepts, which later serves as a fundamental key to how the different parts of the system hang together.

2.1.1 The Formation of the System

Schopenhauer's notebooks from these years do contain the formation of the philosophical system found in the first volume of his self-styled "main work," *Die Welt als Wille und Vorstellung* (*The World as Will and Representation*), which was published in 1819. Though several major themes of his metaphysics and ethics were rethought and redefined from the year 1824 to the publication of the second edition in two volumes of *The World as Will and Representation* in 1844, Schopenhauer prided himself on the consistency the system retained throughout his entire philosophical career. The beginnings of his attempt at a system are announced in a note of early 1813.

> In my hands and perhaps in my mind there is developed a work, a philosophy, which is to be ethics and metaphysics *in one,* for hitherto these were just as falsely separated as man was into body and soul. The work expands and the parts grow together slowly and by degrees like a child in the womb, I do not know which was the first and which was the last to come into existence,

> just as with the child in the womb. I who sit here and whom my friends know, do not understand the origin of this work.... That is to say, I write something down without worrying about how it will fit into the whole, for I know that everything has sprung from one foundation. (Schopenhauer MRI, 59)

Before writing his dissertation in that year, Schopenhauer had indeed been recording his philosophical reflections on various topics such as the issues of idealist epistemology, the ethical and aesthetic status of Platonic Ideas, the relationship between Kantian and Platonic thinking, but also more existential reflections on the transitoriness and futility of life and the necessity of morally and aesthetically transcending it through a phenomenon he called "the better consciousness." He was beginning to envision a system of an ethical metaphysics, but he admits here of not knowing in what order the "parts" needed to be fit together in order for the "whole" of such a system to emerge. His philosophical journey had begun a mere four years before this note, when after a short career as a merchant in Hamburg he matriculated as a medical student at Göttingen University in 1809 and in 1810 transferred to the philosophy department with the help of G. E. Schulze, the author of the famous 1792 skeptical essay *Anesidemus*, whose lectures on metaphysics, psychology and logic Schopenhauer attended between 1810 and 1811. According to an autobiographical letter Schopenhauer wrote to Johann Erdmann in 1851, Schulze had advised him to concentrate his studies on Plato and Kant, although he also encountered the thought of Fichte, Schelling, Jacobi, Wolf, Hume, Berkeley and Leibniz in his classes (GB 261).[1] Schopenhauer transferred to the University of Berlin in 1811, looking forward to studying under Fichte, whose lectures on the "Facts of Consciousness" and "Doctrine of Science" Schopenhauer transcribed and commented upon in his notes from 1811 to 1812.[2] As he tells Erdmann many decades later, his fascination for and enthusiasm with Fichte soon turned into incomprehension and disdain (GB 261). In addition to continuing science courses and a few reading classes on Plato, Schopenhauer also attended a lecture by Friedrich Schleiermacher on the "History of Philosophy

During the Period of Christianity," from which due to his unfamiliarity with the material he got very little. After his stay in Berlin, he went to the quiet village of Rudolstadt to write his dissertation from June to September of 1813, for which he received a doctoral degree in October from the University of Jena. He then set about for the next five years to compose his "main work," which would put the parts of the ethical metaphysics he had envisioned at the beginning of 1813 together.

According to Schopenhauer's later recollection, the entirety of his system was conceptually complete in 1814. Indeed, much of the thematic content of his metaphysics is introduced in this year, as is evidenced by his working through a will-body metaphysics (MR1, 115–16; 144; 156–58; 170–71; 189–97). However, there is much evidence to show that the system had not fully come into being until 1816 at the earliest, for many ideas concerning his metaphysics, epistemology and especially ethics are rethought and reformulated in the years 1814 to 1816, as we shall see below. He first makes a chart outlining the thematic structure of his metaphysics in 1816, and his decisions on how to present the argument of the coming book are also laid down in the notes from this year (MR1, 578; 446). The first announcement that he has successfully united the "parts" of his thought into a systematic "whole" ready to be presented in a book comes in mid-1816.

> It is only a single thought which I am trying to impart through this whole book, and I could not think of any way of conveying it briefly other than by the whole book. It can of course be analyzed and thus communicated after being broken down into its parts. It can also be considered from several quite different points of view and we can point out several ways, which can lead to it. However, it is not the parts but the whole out of which these exist; it is not the points of view but that which has them and the ways are only that whereby we can arrive at it. Whoever has not found it too laborious to consider in succession the parts and points of view and to follow the way, will have been able to make himself master of the thought, and then he no longer requires the means

> whereby it was awakened in him. . . . Accordingly, in the thought imparted he can possess now a system of ethics and again one of metaphysics, then one of aesthetics or again one of natural right, but always neither more nor less than a mirror, a faithful portrait, of the visible world in which and from which he exists. (Schopenhauer MR1, 426–7)

That Schopenhauer's philosophy is meant to encompass a "single thought" which is to be supported by a system composed of organically related "parts" has been highlighted in recent years by Rudolph Malter and John Atwell.[3] But this "single thought" undergoes continuous reformulation through the years Schopenhauer contemplates about the parts. In 1812, he proposes a teleological worldview in which the natural world can be observed to "will life and well-being as complete and for as long as possible" for "every different species of creature," and so human beings, since their innermost essence is at one with nature's, must strive with a "pure will" to advance this cause as a "categorical imperative" (MR1, 22). By 1814, this Romantic conception of metaphysics gives way to the idea that the world as thing in itself is an unknowing, ever-striving and insatiable will, which as phenomenon becomes a knowing and self-reflective will, and because of all the suffering it brings about, this metaphysical will must be "turned away from" (MR1, 184–5). In 1815, this picture of the world is said to be will as the Kantian thing in itself, the Platonic Ideas as its perfect knowledge communicated through art, and as phenomena the world as known through "the principle of sufficient reason" (MR1, 319). Finally in 1817, the formulation of the "single thought" which Malter and Atwell consider to be the kernel of Schopenhauer's system is given; "the whole of my philosophy can be condensed into one expression, namely: the world is the will's knowledge of itself" (MR1, 512).[4] The system as Schopenhauer has envisioned it, a system built on "a single thought," cannot be considered to be complete until that single thought or "one foundation" has been determined, and as long as that "single thought" is undergoing reformulation, the system is still being worked out. The boundaries of the working out of this system then are rather well defined in these notebooks. The first rudiments of system crystallize in the entries preceding the dissertation in 1813, and seem to reach full explication and organization in the years 1816 and 1817. Though some valuable pieces of the system, and the "pessimism" which has been perceived for so long to underlie it are evident in entries before 1813, it is from the notebooks of these years that his system arises.

2.1.2 Indian Thought in the Notes: A Reappraisal

The *Nachlass* from these years then contains a strenuous effort to think and rethink the foundations, implications, and support for the ethical metaphysics Schopenhauer first set out to establish in 1813. These notes represent the laboratory in which Schopenhauer synthesizes the elements of his system, and as many of the passages from his notes find their way almost verbatim into his published works, they reveal the thematic parameters of his thinking. Those who have attempted to gauge the degree of influence Schopenhauer's knowledge of Indian philosophy and religion had upon the shaping of his system have thus rightly appreciated the importance of the *Nachlass* and the evidentiary role it plays in establishing or denying such influence. The general consensus among commentators has, as we have seen, tended to discount the possibility that Indian thought played an instrumental role in the shaping of Schopenhauer's philosophical system because 1.) they have taken Schopenhauer at his word that his system was conceptually complete by 1814, and since he only first encountered the *Upaniṣads* in this year, his acquaintance with them came too late to have an impact on the system's conceptual structure, 2.) the notes mentioning Indian thought are relatively sparse when compared to the number of notes devoted to other philosophical topics more familiar to Schopenhauer and thus must be far less significant than the latter, or 3.) when he makes reference to Indian philosophical or religious concepts, he uses them not to explicate their meanings within their own nascent contexts, but rather invokes their antiquity and exotic vocabulary only to confirm a belief he has arrived at independently of his acquaintance with them. The presence of Indian thought in Schopenhauer's notes of these formative years could for them only be a marginal one.

We have already seen that Schopenhauer's recollection concerning when his system was conceptually complete was somewhat inaccurate, as the gestation period of the working out of his epistemology, metaphysics, aesthetics and ethics, not to mention the "single thought" of which they were supportive, lasted at least three or four years. During this time, Schopenhauer gained a great deal of familiarity with some source texts and much commentarial literature on India's pre-systematic philosophical and religious traditions His first intellectual contact with Indian antiquity occurred during his attendance at the lectures of the historian Arnold Heeren at Göttingen in 1809 and 1810.[5] The Swiss scholar Urs App, in careful reexaminations of Schopenhauer's formative *Nachlass* in the Frankfurt Schopenhauer Archive, has shown that Schopenhauer's notes for Heeren's 1811 Ethnography lecture were much more copious that had been previously thought, and both his familiarity with the journal *Asiatic Researches* and his initial knowledge of Buddhism in south Asia, Tibet and east Asia stemmed from this very early period.[6] During his stay in Weimar from November 1813 to May 1814, after having completed his doctoral degree, Schopenhauer recalls, "unsolicited, the Orientalist Friedrich Majer introduced me to Indian antiquity, which has had an essential influence on me" (GB 261). Majer, a disciple of Herder's enthusiasm for India, wrote several essays and prefaces on Indian religion and literature as well as a book entitled *Brahma: on the Brahminical Religion of India* in 1818. It was he who suggested to Schopenhauer that he read the first translations of the *Upaniṣads* made into a European language by Anquetil Duperron.[7] Just after this meeting, Schopenhauer read a translation of the *Bhagavad Gitä* by Majer and then checked these volumes out from the Weimar library on March 26th and returned them on May 18th, during which time according to Schopenhauer's early biographer Gwinner they were constantly open on the table and were the last reading Schopenhauer did before going to bed in the evenings (Merkel 164). Two years after this initial encounter, Schopenhauer wrote, "I confess that I do not believe my doctrines could have come about before the *Upanishads*, Plato and Kant could cast their rays simultaneously into the mind of one man" (MR1, 467). But this was just the beginning of Schopenhauer's studies of Indian religion and philosophy. Along with Duperron's *Oupnek'hat*, Schopenhauer checked out an essay by the Swiss East India Company employee de Polier of Lausanne, containing her reflections on "Indian mythology," which he sent back in early August after having moved from Weimar to Dresden.[8] In Dresden, his studies continued; in the early months of that year he read Schlegel's *Uber die Sprache und Weisheit der Indier*, and in March and April he borrowed a series of volumes of the *Researches Antiques* from which he later made citations and comments, mostly from volume XIII, *Colebrooke on the Vedas*, in his notes (Merkel 165–66; MR2, 459–61). He again borrowed a copy of the *Upaniṣads* at this point for a month and a half, and after returning it, made arrangements to buy the two-volume translations of Duperron himself.[9] As App shows, these translations were so heavily annotated in subsequent years and decades that the content of Schopenahuer's marginal notes sometimes exceeded the amount of printed material on the page he was reading ("Notes by Schopenhauer Relating to Volumes 1–9 of the *Asiatick* Researches" 1998, 13). From the 15th to the 26th of August he had a book called *Hindu-Gesetzgebung* written by August Hüttner and from September 24th to October 19th he was in possession of a two volume work by a colleague of Majer's, Oktober J. Kloproth, the *Asiatische Magazin*, which together with passages from the *Oupnek'hat* are referred to in the first volume of his "main work" (Merkel 166; WWRI, 388). In addition to the books he borrowed from the Dresden library however, he also had access to various works on India from a neighbor in Dresden named Karl Christian Friedrich Krausse, who knew Sanskrit and whose writings on Indian metaphysical doctrines and compassion would find their way to Spain and become incorporated into a solidarity ethics proposing itself as a foundation for socio-liberal progressivism known as "Crausismo" (Safransky 201).[10] Finally, Schopenhauer later claimed in an 1856 letter to Adam von Doss that agreements between his philosophical doctrines and those of Buddhism were "wondrous" precisely because while he wrote the first volume of his *Welt als Wille und Vorstellung* between the years 1814 and 1818, he "didn't know, could not have known" anything about Buddhism because of the lack of work that had been published on it during that time (GB 384). Certainly the specific doctrines he mentions in this letter do not appear to be known to him during these formative years. But Schopenhauer's notes of 1816 and 1817 demonstrate his awareness of central concepts from Buddhist teaching such as "*nibbana*," some specific Theravāda teachings concerning vegetarianism and ethical conduct, as well as some rudimentary familiarity with Buddhism as it appeared in East Asia (MR1, 456; 488; 515; MR2, 459).[11] Schopenhauer's studies of Indian philosophy and religion did not begin when his systematic thinking was complete, nor do they "dovetail" the completion of his independently formulated mature philosophy. Rather these studies coincide with the formulation of the system, with the written reflections on Indian thought increasing in number as he goes about thematizing it.

As to the rarity of the mention of concepts and doctrines of the Indian philosophical tradition in the early *Nachlass*, there can be no question that these are not invoked frequently.[12] But mere frequency of mention is not necessarily a measure of philosophical significance in these notes, for they do not present a systematic, arranged argument, but are merely recorded, entry by entry, as ideas occur to Schopenhauer. Taking for example the *Erstlingsmanuscripte* of 1816 as a representative case, we find in that year a total of one hundred twenty three entries whose lengths vary from one sentence to several pages. Of these one hundred twenty three entries, only thirteen make reference to concepts or themes from the Indian philosophical and religious traditions, and this is the year when references to Indian thought are more frequent in his notebooks than from any other year from 1814 to 1818. As can be expected, his entries concerning his metaphysics of will are much more abundant, well over two dozen dealing directly with various aspects of will, and over twenty more about issues of knowledge and ethics that are implied by this metaphysics. On the other hand, issues that no commentator would deny are as crucial as any to Schopenhauer's completed system as is found in the first volume of *Welt als Wille und Vorstellung* enjoy rather conspicuously rare treatment in the notes from this year. The Platonic Ideas are mentioned in only five notes, and the various aspects of Schopenhauer's philosophy of art which they give rise to appear in only six other entries, and yet these two subjects make up the third part of *World as Will and Representation,* its second longest section. Kant, who is the subject of the longest section in the book, is only directly dealt with in four entries and mentioned in conjunction with Plato and Indian thought in three others.[13] Schopenhauer's ethical doctrine which is concerned with various forms of will-renunciation, is only treated in six entries, and its discussion occupies a significant portion of part four of his main work. The entries in the manuscripts of these years are quite varied and deal with a range of interrelated topics which Schopenhauer organizes into a sustained argument in his published works. When dealing with these notes, the mere frequency of mention cannot be taken to be indicative of what importance a particular idea plays in Schopenhauer's philosophical development, for in almost all his entries in the notebooks of these years, ideas are being combined and increasingly complex formulations of his arguments congeal as he goes along. It is *how* his ideas are synthesized with others and what affects these syntheses have on the developing system that is significant. As we shall see below, the synthesis of his understanding of certain ideas he appropriates from the Indian philosophical tradition with his developing epistemology, metaphysics and ethics plays an important role in how the system is constructed.

Perhaps the most prevalent criticism of Schopenhauer's treatment of ideas from the Indian philosophical and religious traditions of which he is aware is that he merely uses them as confirmations or illustrations of his existing beliefs (Glasenapp 501; Sedler 231; Gestering 58; Halbfass *India* 114; Schmidt *Wahrheit* 125; Safransky 203). There can be no question that Schopenhauer does match up ideas and even deities from the Indian tradition with his own ideas often in his notes, as when he explains the symbolism of Shiva's *lingam* with his own doctrine of the will-to-live, of the fire sacrifice as having to do with his ideas on will-renunciation, his identifying the notion of *māyā* with Plato's idea of the "eternally becoming" and Kant's phenomena, the "myth of metapsychosis" with his conception of the mere phenomenality of the individual (MR1, 181; 449; 286; 247; 332; 419; 389). However, what is happening in many of these cases is not merely an exercise in conceptual subordination or a domestication of an alien vocabulary into Schopenhauer's own philosophical melieu, but more broadly a process of appropriation.

In his examination of the hermeneutics of appropriation, Paul Ricoeur has written:

> 'Appropriation' is my translation of the German term *Aneignung*. *Aneignen* means 'to make one's own' what was initially alien. According to the intention of the word, the aim of all hermeneutics is to struggle against cultural distance and historical alienation. Interpretation brings together, equalizes, makes contemporary and similar. This goal is attained only insofar as interpretation actualizes the meaning of the text for the present reader. Appropriation is the concept which is suitable for the actualization of meaning as addressed to someone. It takes the place of the answer in the dialogical situation, in the same way that 'revelation' or 'disclosure' takes the place of ostensive reference in the dialogical situation. (185)

Ricoeur wished hermeneutics to avoid the errors of historicism and subjectivism in its theory of interpretation. For historicism, the only possible meaning a text can have was the one understood by the original audience, making the historically distanced interpretation which inevitably occurs under very different circumstances untenable; and for subjectivism, either the reader imposes her own interpretation on the text or is the only measure of meaning the text can have in the present (Ricoeur 192). Neither of these models of interpretation and appropriation of meaning are satisfactory for Ricoeur, for both in their varying fashions focus too exclusively on the subjective constitution of meaning resulting from the irretrevability of some inaccessible original meaning of a text and thus fail to take into account what must be a necessary element in any theory of interpretation, namely the text's presentation of its subject-matter to a receptive reader. Ricoeur's theory of appropriation, like the others, requires that meanings be actualized for readers through a rendering present of the text's subject matter, but also requires that the reader be "addressed" by the world of meanings "disclosed" by the text. Ricoeur continues:

> What is made our own ... is the projection of a world, the proposal of a mode of being-in-the-world, which the text discloses in front of itself by means of its non-ostensive references. Far from saying that a subject, who already masters his own being-in-the-world, projects the *a priori* of his own understanding and interpolates this *a priori* in the text, I shall say that appropriation is the process by which the revelation of new modes of being—or if you prefer Wittgenstein to Heidegger, new 'forms of life'—*gives* the subject new capacities for knowing himself. If the reference of a text is the projection of a world, then it is not in the first instance the reader who projects himself. The reader is rather broadened in his capacities to project himself by receiving a new mode of being from the text itself. (192)

One need not accept, as Ricoeur seems himself to indicate here, the Heideggerian ontology of having "modes of being-in-the-world" projected by the text to the reader to appreciate the fact that the relationship between reader and text in general is a dynamic or dialectical one in which the reader must be addressed and "broadened" by the meanings disclosed in a text so that she can, and inevitably does, project her own understandings onto those disclosed meanings.

The common penchant to see Schopenhauer's appropriations of concepts, not only from the Indian philosophical tradition but also from the European, as mere exercises in assimilation to his own philosophical doctrines betrays a persistent historicism masquerading as hermeneutical explication. Schopenhauer is taken to task for having not understood the "original meanings" of the religious and philosophical ideas of the Indian tradition to which he makes reference (as if those ideas were in their respective "original" contexts synonymous), and then identifying his misunderstandings of these concepts with the utterly alien conceptions of his own tradition and his own specific philosophical teachings. It is then claimed that these hermeneutical circumstances preclude the possibility that Indian thought influenced Schopenhauer's philosophical thinking, but they somehow did allow him to use his understanding of Indian thought to "rethink" and "critique" his own tradition (Halbfass *India* 120; Clarke 69). Hence the curious but persistent view that Schopenhauer appropriated ideas by which he was not actually influenced. Little consideration is entertained that Schopenhauer's own philosophy becomes thought and rethought through his studies of the Indian tradition because the interpretive premises of this kind of critique have lost sight of the most basic facets of a hermeneutical approach and have fallen back into the assumptions of historicism. That notions such as *brahman, māyā, karma* and so on are not understood by Schopenhauer as they were within the Indian philosophical tradition, but rather from the works of Romantic Orientalists, is taken to be conclusive evidence that Schopenhauer's own philosophical reference to these notions can only amount to the results of his own historical projections. This is precisely, according to Ricoeur, the error of historicism; "to conceive of appropriation in terms of the primacy of the original audience with which one seeks to coincide, to discover to whom a text was addressed and to identify oneself with that original audience" (190). The idea that Schopenhauer or anyone else could appropriate philosophical ideas without having been directly or indirectly influenced by them can only be considered a hermeneutical impossibility. Rather, the two are merely two moments in the dialectical process of interpretation as hermeneutics understands it.

The above is not meant to invalidate the difficulties and complexities which have been found by generations of scholars to problematize Schopenhauer's encounter with Indian thought. For it is undeniable that Schopenhauer did not in many cases have an understanding of philosophical and religious notions that would resemble the corresponding thematizations of those notions from within the Indian tradition. Neither is it meant to excuse him for the stigmatizations he burdened the perception of Indian thought in the West with by linking it to his own existential "pessimism."[14] Complicating matters are the hermeneutical circumstances of the early German Romantic Orientalists themselves from whom Schopenhauer learned so much about Indian thought, as well as his own apparent acceptance of the Romantic ideas about interpretation as a direct understanding of the intentions of the author, a transition of meaning from "genius to genius" as it were. What it is rather meant to illustrate is that a true hermeneutic assessment of Schopenhauer's appropriation of ideas from the Indian philosophical tradition does not merely stop with these issues, does not merely rest with the fact that Schopenhauer uses Indian ideas to "illustrate" or "mirror" or "confirm" his own, but goes on to discover why he believed such confirmations were possible. As we shall see in the course of this work, Schopenhauer does not only in his appropriations redefine Indian ideas in terms of his own thought, but just as often redefines his own thought in terms of his understandings of Indian ideas. Insofar as a thorough investigation of this dynamic appropriation process has not been presented, there has yet not been a fully hermeneutic investigation of Schopenhauer's encounter with Indian thought. This work proposes to contribute to a more comprehensively hermeneutic reading of this encounter.

2.2 DEVELOPMENT OF THE SYSTEM'S MAJOR THEMES

As mentioned above, in order to gain an appreciation of what sort of impact Schopenhauer's appropriation of ideas from the Indian philosophical tradition had on the formulation of his own system, it is necessary to examine how the major ideas of that system are thematized and determine whether and how they were reformulated in the process of this appropriation. In this section, some of these major themes will be looked at as they develop in Schopenhauer's thinking through the building of his system in the notebooks. This will serve the double purpose of making ourselves familiar with the most important ideas in Schopenhauer's philosophy and allowing us to see how these ideas develop and are conceptually redefined and refined in the formative years of the mature system.

2.2.1 Platonic Ideas

Schopenhauer began his philosophical studies with Plato, and of all the themes that he touched upon during his fifty-year philosophical career, the Platonic Ideas were the most permanent element of his thinking. They are from the beginning of his philosophical contemplation associated with aesthetic representation; in art they are presented as the "eternal verities" of ontology and morality. In 1810 he writes, "as all poetry is the image of the eternal in time, *the (Platonic) Idea of the real, inexplicable and unconditioned evil* is awakened by images of earthly misfortune, and an awareness of eternity is thus brought home to us. This is tragedy" (MR1, 9). In 1813, he notes that the Platonic Ideas are what are revealed in still-life paintings of nature, for in these "we are snatched out the eternal flux of all things" by an artistic abolition of the ordinary knowledge of a thing "determined by time and the conditions of the understanding," at which point "only the *Platonic Idea* is left" (MR1, 42.). It is the transcending of time-bound existence, which Schopenhauer conceives to be so essential to the resolving of the human existential dilemma, that is effected by the Platonic Ideas, as he writes in 1814;

> He has taken a big step towards wisdom to whom it is clear and certain that *the difference between past, present, and future is only apparent* and quite unreal. He will now see that, instead of pining for the future, wishing ourselves back in the past, and striving with all our senses for the insubstantial and illusory present, we really have nothing to do but grasp the timeless Platonic Idea of the *whole* of life and then decide whether or not we *desire* this

> whole. . . . And that choice is the only thing that actually leads the way. (MR1, 108)

The Platonic Idea is later called that "adequate representation of the concept" which brings about "a knowledge of the true nature of the world" (MR1, 139–140). This knowledge of the Platonic Ideas was for Schopenhauer distinguished from empirical knowledge in that the eyes of the "artist" or "contemplative genius" considered objects not as they are determined by the logical, linguistic, conceptual knowledge of reason (*Vernunft*), not through the causal connections that obtain between them and other things as apprehended by "understanding" (*Verstand*), not as the objects of willing and motivation, nor as they are located within a temporal sequence of events; rather, for the contemplative, "the object must, so to speak, be torn out and isolated entirely from the stream of world events" (MR1, 139).

Schopenhauer begins to struggle with how to explain the Platonic Ideas when in 1814 he develops his metaphysics of will, for up to that point, knowledge of the Platonic Ideas was tantamount to knowledge of things as they are in themselves, whether those things be object-universals as represented through architecture and painting or value-universals as represented by arts such as poetry, tragedy and music (MR1, 193–4).[15] When these are supplanted by his initial conception of will as thing-in-itself as we shall see below, he must work out how the Ideas stand in relation to will. He first calls the "Platonic Idea, the *thing in itself*, the *will*, for they are all the same," and explains that the thing-in-itself manifests itself in all phenomena without being affected by time, which brings the individual phenomena to an end (MR1, 205).[16] A few entries later Schopenhauer claims that "the Ideas are not the wills, but the way in which the wills become knowable, become knowledge," and here, because there is more than one Platonic Idea, there must be more than one will; a notion Schopenhauer dispenses with quickly since he claims that the knowledge of will as thing-in-itself transcends all categories of plurality (MR1, 219). We find him continuing to struggle with the theory of Ideas in 1815, when he says that a "significant and suggestive (Platonic)

Idea" is presented when a thing's parts are contemplated as having "a very definite, thoroughly significant and manifold relation to one another," whereas before Ideas were said to be known outside the conceptual categories which were the conditions of spatio-temporal relation (MR1, 275).[17] However, what emerges in the entries of 1815 and 1816 approaches his systematic conception of the Ideas as what is perceived in things when the epistemological subject is freed of her normal interested, willful mode of perceiving and "brackets" the forms of sensibility through which particulars are apprehended. In 1815, he writes:

> Aesthetic contemplation is, on the one hand, the consciousness of myself as the pure subject of knowing and, on the other, knowledge of the thing in itself or of the Platonic Idea and these two are inseparable, are one, which the first objection states subjectively and the second objectively. With the advent of aesthetic contemplation I am no longer a person, but the pure, will-free subject of knowledge and the beautiful object is no longer a single thing in space and time, but the (Platonic) Idea. (MR1, 275)

In the following year, we find the note:

> The *Platonic Idea* of an object and the *pure subject of knowing* are complete correlatives; they enter consciousness always simultaneously and with such entrance all difference of time vanishes at once, for the two lie outside time.... Only the phenomenon and the individual lie in time. For example, if I perceive a tree with artistic eyes, so my entire consciousness is engrossed in this representation and I contemplate, not the tree's relation to anything outside it, but only its form, expression of its inner nature (which is the visibility of the will at this stage), then I have the Platonic Idea of this tree and am the pure subject of knowing. It is now a matter of complete indifference whether it is precisely this tree or its ancestor of a thousand years ago and likewise whether I am this or any other individual. The two differences have disap-

> peared entirely; the tree and I have stepped out of time and out of the entire principle of sufficient reason. All that remains are the pure subject and the Platonic Idea, which together constitute the pure objectivity of the will at this definite stage of it. (MR1, 442–3)

The Platonic Ideas in these passages are what is apprehended in a particular mode of perceiving, aesthetic contemplation, where both the subject and object of a cognition are temporarily free of the epistemological *a priori* filters of time and causality. As James Chansky has pointed out in his assessment of the Platonic Ideas in Schopenhauer's published works, this does not mean that the apprehension of the Ideas eliminates the categories of perception and thinking, nor does it involve the permanent elimination of willing. He clarifies the doctrine in the following way:

> Now, this possibility of the sort of perception and knowledge peculiar to the Platonic Ideas begins, as we saw, "when we relinquish the ordinary way of considering things" (WWR, v. 1, 34, p. 178). Of course this does not at all imply that our consciousness is suddenly unburdened by the principle of sufficient reason, for consciousness of any sort is no more possible without this essential form than can any object be an object of knowledge without appearing in accordance with these forms. Rather what is relinquished is the *way* of considering things under the guidance of this principle, the subjective seeking out of reasons, grounds, and causes, the specification of an object's location in a specific space and time as if all these relations and qualifications were attributes of an essential nature. Instead of demanding answers of an object to questions posed by the principle of sufficient reason, questions, that is, posed by the interested will of the perceiver, we *let the thing itself speak to us*, let *it* address *us*, not as individual knowers seeking to relate the object to our wills ... but simply as pure knowers in relation to the object as pure object, pure representation. (Chansky 75–76) [18]

Since the Platonic Ideas will not be considered in the coming chapters when we turn to Schopenhauer's systematic philosophy as laid out in his published works, a few considerations about their role in his thinking are given here. While the Platonic Ideas were indeed the most permanent element in Schopenhauer's philosophical thinking and while they did provide him with an explanation of aesthetics (which greatly influenced nineteenth and twentieth century artists such as Richard Wagner and Thomas Mann), and the gradations of beings in nature, their explication and role in Schopenhauer's epistemology and metaphysics has been widely criticized. Patrick Gardiner has cast serious doubts on whether a comprehensive interpretation of art can be given in terms of the revelation of Platonic Ideas (207–234). D. W. Hamlyn has suggested that Schopenhauer introduces with the Platonic Ideas elements of an "alien ontology" which are meant to relate Schopenhauer's thing-in-itself, an undifferentiated will to the plurality of phenomena in the world, an attempt which is bound to fail since, merely because they are "intermediary" elements between will and phenomena does not necessarily prove that the Ideas mediate between them (107; 122). Bryan Magee has referred to the Ideas as "*ad hoc*" explanations of genera and species and believes they are expendable both to Schopenhauer's metaphysics and theory of the arts (239–40). In opposition to Hamlyn and Magee, Atwell has offered a more sympathetic reading of the Ideas as being, in addition to the basis for Schopenhauer's theory of the arts, the presuppositions of a "classificatory theory of natural types and natural forces," and so is an extraordinary attempt to explain the metaphysical underpinnings of both science and art in one swoop (*Character* 130). It must also be noticed that the appropriation of the Platonic Ideas into Schopenhauer's system is not at all dissimilar to that of Indian thought from a historical perspective, for while Plato certainly did believe knowledge of the Ideas transcended phenomenal, empirical experience and was the special province of the philosopher, he never used them as Schopenhauer did as explications of either aesthetics or as a metaphysical account of natural forces or physics. Plato understood the Ideas first, with Socrates, as the essence of value-universals and later as the essential, eternal, intelligible forms of phenomena. They are a very curious class of representations as Schopenhauer presents them; objects of a kind of intuition that is supposed to be non-spatial and non-temporal, explanations of natural forces which can have no basis in intelligible explanation, an intermediary ontological class of objects whose mediation between representations and will is unaccountable. Magee is certainly mistaken in supposing that the Ideas are *ad hoc* and disposable from Schopenhauer's system; their appropriation into that system is invoked on very specific logical and metaphysical grounds, but they in the end may be, among the other ideas of the system, out of place.

2.2.2 Epistemological Issues

One of the first important epistemological themes set down by Schopenhauer already in the notes of 1812, a kind of idealist precursor to the later intentionality thesis of Brentano's and Husserl's phenomenology, is his "subject-object correlativity thesis." While still a student at the University of Berlin enmeshed in the reading of contemporary Idealist philosophers, Schopenhauer writes that "I cannot conceive the intelligence, the subject, except as having representations or mental pictures," that "the two are one" (MR1, 26–7). This correlativity of subject and object is further spelled out in an 1813 note on concepts and judgments, where Schopenhauer conceives the thesis to be the solution to the argument between realism and idealism; for while external objects must exist because representations depend upon them for their "material," our representations are the "sole condition" by which we can determine that an object "affected" our sensibility (MR1, 61). The relationship between subject and object cannot be construed as a causal one, for if we accept that the object causes the subject to perceive, we have realism, whereas if we assert that the subject causes the existence of objects, we end up with a Berkeleyan or Fichtean idealism. For Schopenhauer, subject and object "mutually condition each other" (MR1, 228). Schopenhauer clearly employs the subject-object correlativity thesis in an attempt to give a subjectivist theory of cognition that does not absolutize the subject, an error he believes Fichte to have been guilty of. He notes at one point in 1814 that the rules of the principle of sufficient reason supply the "conditions of objects, and these exist only *for* the subject . . . not *in* the subject" (MR1, 237). The problem that Schopenhauer is attempting to solve with the subject-object correlativity thesis is a problem at the heart of Kantian transcendental idealism, a problem initially identified by Schopenhauer's first instructor of philosophy, G. E. Schulze, in his 1792 essay *Anesidemus*. Kant had established, according to Schulze, that the notion of cause could not be applied outside of the categorical framework with which the understanding (*Verstand*) synthesized intuitions (*Anschaungen*) *a priori*. This did have one effect Kant intended, namely of undermining realism, but on the other it obviated Kant's presupposition that "things-in-themselves" could somehow "affect" sensibility and provide it with a "manifold" (*Mannigfaltigkeit*) of sense-data to be synthesized by the cognitive apparatus. All of the Idealists who followed, K. L. Reinhold, Jacobi, Fichte and Schelling, had accepted this incoherence in Kant's notion of things-in-themselves and attempted to provide an epistemological theory in which the basis of objectivity and knowledge was provided by what Dieter Henrich has called a "basic power" of consciousness, whether it was construed as Reinhold's "principle of consciousness," Fichte's "activity of consciousness" or Schelling's "intellectual intuition."[19] Schopenhauer wishes to steer clear of the metaphysical problems which he believes burden idealism by merely saying, in effect, that every conscious state is conscious of an object, and that no object is conceivable without being an object for consciousness. Their correlativity is not locative in nature; in which case one would conceive of objects being produced or lying somehow "within" consciousness, this would give us one or another form of idealism. Rather their relation is adverbial; all conscious states have objective content and all objects have as a condition of their objectivity consciousness as such. The comprehensive replacement of "representations in us" with "representations for us" is meant to give us a more metaphysically neutral subjectivist epistemology.

Nonetheless, from the very beginning of his philosophical thinking, Schopenhauer prizes highly a certain kind of subjectivism for which the subject may perceive and know in a "disinterested" way. As he writes in 1813, "What is to be desired?—An eye that sees the sun set from a prison as well as a palace" (MR1, 76). At several points in his notes from 1814, he speaks of subjectivity in salvific terms.

> By reflecting and becoming aware of myself as *the eternal subject of knowing,* I express with pride and confidence the undeniable truth that those worlds are my representation or mental picture and that therefore I, the eternal subject, am the bearer of this universe, whose entire existence is nothing but a relation to me. Where now is the shudder, where the alarm? I am, nothing else exists; supported on me the world rests in the peace that emanates from me. How could it terrify me, how could I be frightened by its size which is always only the measure of my own greatness that always surpasses it? This knowledge is the feeling of the *sublime.* (MR1, 229)

Schopenhauer in his systematic philosophy turns "pure, will-less subjectivity" into a soteriological goal which can emancipate human existence from the insatiable will which underlies all desire and suffering. This notion of "pure subjectivity" which serves as the support for all objective existence was, as we shall see below and in the following chapter, to be profoundly affected by Schopenhauer's reading of Duperron and his translations of the *Upaniṣads.*[20]

With the exception of a short period at the beginning of his philosophical career when he preferred Plato to Kant, Schopenhauer was a Kantian. He takes a great deal from Kant's epistemology, including the latter's doctrine of the *a priori* forms of sensibility and a slightly revised and simplified version of Kant's faculty psychology of the epistemological subject. His Kantianism does not prevent Schopenhauer from constructing his own epistemology, which ended up being on the one hand a carefully balanced medium between idealism and empiricism, and on the other, a doctrine of falsification.

Schopenhauer's two published works which appeared before *The World as Will and Representation* were both on epistemology; the first being his 1813 doctoral dissertation entitled *Über die vierfache Wurzel des Satzes vom zurreichenden Grunde* (*On the Fourfold Root of the Principle of Sufficient Reason*) and the second the 1816 essay that was directed against a theory of colors presented by Goethe six years earlier, *Über das Sehn und die Farben* (*On Vision and Colors*). The theoretical construction of neither of these works receives any extensive treatment in Schopenhauer's notebooks. However, the notion of the "principle of sufficient reason" enjoys great significance throughout Schopenhauer's philosophy, for he always considered his dissertation on this subject an "introduction and propaedeutic" to his "main work" which had to be read in order to understand his philosophy (WWRI, xiv). According to that work, the principle of sufficient reason stipulates, as was succinctly formulated by Wolf, that "nothing is without a ground or reason why it is" (FR 6). The principle of sufficient reason had traditionally received either ontological formulations in terms of discovering the cause for every event, or logical formulations in terms of discovering what rational justifications were given for a claim (FR 9–32). Schopenhauer wishes to redefine the principle within a more Kantian vein; objects are only objects for a subject, representations, and these representations stand to one another in a regular *a priori* connection which is determined by the principle of reason (FR 42).

This principle is separated into four classes. The first class is the one Schopenhauer devotes the most time explicating, and this he calls the principle of sufficient reason of becoming, or the law of causality (FR 52–3). The objects of this principle are objects of intuitive perception (*Anschaung*), representations which have been synthesized out of raw sensation according to the forms of sensibility, time and space. This principle is applied by the understanding, or intellect (*Verstand*) when it connects states of affairs according to a regular succession (FR 55). This conception of causality is interesting in that Schopenhauer believes it to be a mistake to suppose that mere objects, or representations cause one another; rather the existence of an entire "state of affairs" (*Zustand*) consists of a number of factors which bring about a change, it causes another state of affairs to obtain. The objective external world we are empirically familiar with is brought about because perception is "intellectual"; the understanding does not merely sense, does not merely represent objects in isolation by means of time and space, rather by employing the principle of causality, it makes experience coherent through a regular successive connection of states of affairs (FR 75). The second class of this principle is called the principle of sufficient reason of knowing (FR 156). Its objects are abstract concepts (*Begriffe*) of reason (*Vernunft*) (FR 145). Concepts are thought by the "isolation" or "abstraction" of the qualities of an object familiar through intuition, and while concepts can for this reason be called "representations of representations," they enable thought to group together however many representations can be thought through them depending on their degree of generality (FR 146–7).[21] The application of the principle of knowing takes place in judgment, which combines or separates two or more concepts based on their logical, empirical, transcendental or "metalogical" relationship (FR 156–63). That is to say, concepts are combined in judgment if they are logically or empirically compatible, if taken together they make experience or thought possible, and distinguished from one another if they together accomplish none of these. Concepts and judgments on the one hand are specifically human; they make possible all thought, deliberation and reflectively intentional action, but on the other hand also are the supports of the emptiest and most misleading doctrines of philosophy and religion.[22] The third form of the principle is labeled the principle of sufficient reason of being, and it consists of the "pure intuitions" of time and space which make all empirical perceptibility possible (FR 194–5). The final form is the principle of sufficient reason of acting, which has as its object "the immediate object of the inner sense, the subject of willing, which is object for the knowing subject" (FR 207). When we act, we always introspect as to why we so acted, and such an inquiry is an inquiry into motivation. Motivation is here a special kind of causality, a "causality seen from within" (FR 214).[23] This principle allows us to determine how motivations necessitate actions in human conduct. According to the dissertation then, the fourfold principle of sufficient reason allows us to determine the ground or basis upon which anything has come to be. Each principle exercises its influence over a specific science; the principle of being is applied in all mathematics, the principle of becoming in physics, chemistry and geology, the principle of knowing in all classificatory sciences such as zoology, botany and mineralogy, and the principle of acting in the study of history, politics and psychology (FR 230–1). What Schopenhauer believed to have accomplished with the dissertation was on the one hand a determination of the subjective conditions of all knowledge through a proof that the principle of sufficient reason was an epistemological and not an ontological or logical phenomenon; and secondly the establishment of a strict philosophical method by which every "why" could be traced back to its reason in accordance with strict epistemological rules (FR 232–3).

If Schopenhauer set out to define the positive functions of the principle of sufficient reason in his dissertation, the working out of his metaphysics in his notes serve to set the limits and limitations of the principle. He begins to reflect in the notes of 1815 that every metaphysical inquiry, every question which pursues an explanation to its end, must halt at the principle of sufficient reason, for it contains within itself all the conditions which make objectivity possible (MR1, 257–8). Schopenhauer finds such a subjectivist end to all metaphysical inquiry progressively less satisfying as time goes on. He soon calls all philosophizing according to the principle of sufficient reason "false philosophizing," for if the principle of sufficient reason is thought to pertain to real things in the world, then useless theological questions concerning the nature of God and the origin of the world are indulged in, while if the principle is restricted to subjective reflection, it can only "derive mere concepts from one another" (MR1, 270). He goes on to say that the principle of sufficient reason is that in which all suffering consists, as the principle is the ground of all necessity, and necessity either inhibits and subdues our will or makes it very difficult to fix representations as objects of sustained contemplation (MR1, 272). By the end of 1815, in the light of his developing metaphysics of will and epistemological falsification thesis, knowledge according to the principle of sufficient reason has almost completely lost its value, for all objects are according to it temporal, and as temporal, transient, and as transient, non-existent, non self-subsistent.

> Whoever perceives and knows ... the individual thing ... is still involved in knowledge according to the principle of sufficient reason, and this is never an adequate knowledge of the will. For such a person knows the given actual thing only in so far as it exists *here, now and under these circumstances*. From these he derives it completely, and for him the thing is also disposed of with the place, the time and the circumstances. He has therefore made no further progress in the knowledge of the will which lies outside time and is therefore adequately known only in the (Platonic) Idea, which is extratemporal. Such a person knows something that exists and yet at the same time does not exist, for time is precisely that by virtue of which opposite determinations are attributed to a thing. Therefore every phenomenon in time is again always *non*-existent. The existence of all individual things, even of ourselves as individuals, also of our joys and sorrows, is likewise also a non-existence. (MR1, 382)

The same fate befalls another epistemological principle which will be very important in our examination, namely the so-called *principium individuationis*, or "principle of individuation." Schopenhauer gets the terminology from the Scholastics, but identifies this principle with the subjective forms of sensibility, time and space, which he classified as the third form of the principle of sufficient reason (MR1, 309). The *principium* is an epistemological necessity for obvious Kantian reasons; for it is space and time that delineate things in succession and spatial relation, and therefore make all representations determinate. But in the developing scheme of Schopenhauer's metaphysics, for which the world consists of undifferentiated will, Platonic Ideas and phenomenal things, space and time can be applied only to knowledge of the third class and thus cannot supply us with knowledge of things as they are in themselves. But reflective knowledge about the nature of the *principium individuationis* is central to Schopenhauer's philosophy, for it opens the door for him from epistemology to metaphysics on the one hand and from metaphysics to ethics on the other. In 1815, he makes the following entry in his notes.

> Only because we perceive and know things not *in themselves* but through the medium of our cognitive forms *space* and *time*, do the phenomena of life present themselves to us as separate, detached and quite different, and not as the objectivity of the one and only *will-to-live*. And so great pleasure appears as one thing and great pain as another, whereas the two are only one and the same, a phenomenon of life, objectivity of the will. Moreover, one man appears as a torturer and murderer and another man as a sufferer. The man who with violent and intense desire grasps, seizes and clings to great pleasures and delights, does not know that at the same time and by the same act, that is to say through an expression of will, he seizes and presses to himself with just such violence all the pains and frightful afflictions of life. Through space and time, which are the *principium individuationis*, what is one appears as separate and different. This knowledge is the *genuine theodicy* and furnishes us with an explanation why in this world one man lives in great pleasure and happiness and another dies at his door painfully of cold and destitution. (MR1, 373)

In terms of epistemology, space and time are the transcendental conditions of all objectivity. In terms of metaphysics, they present (*vorstellen*) a falsely diversified picture of a pluralistic world which is really at bottom an undifferentiated will. In terms of axiology, they are the grounds upon which human beings make all distinctions of value, allowing them to differentiate between self and other, pleasure and pain and so on. In terms of ethics, it helps us to explain evil as being the result of too rigid distinctions between self and other and a consequent egoism fueled by will which causes human beings to preserve and value the self at the expense of the other. From these bases, Schopenhauer quickly develops an ethics of compassion which requires an epistemological transformation, namely, the recognition of all phenomena as spatio-temporal manifestations of one will, which allows human beings to identify the sufferings of another as if they were one's own. "The ultimate ground of all virtue, or rather its real and essential nature, is a knowledge of the identity of one will in all its phenomena, and of the illusion of the *principium individuationis*, whereby the individualities of others appear to be different from one's own, and likewise their sufferings" (MR1, 323). In many senses then, the idea of the *principium individuationis* as being the transcendental subjective condition of all objectivity, a condition which falsifies and renders "illusory" our ordinary empirical knowledge of the world, serves as the transitional doctrine which makes possible Schopenhauer's metaphysics and ethics. The central role played by the "principle of individuation" in Schopenhauer's system is all the more significant since, as we shall see below, it is not only identified with, but is effected in its very philosophical thematization by an idea Schopenhauer encountered first through his studies of classical Indian philosophy, the notion of *māyā*.

2.2.3 Metaphysics of Will

Schopenhauer began his philosophical career thinking about the notion of will in a traditional moral sense. He first considered willing to be something related to and sometimes encumbered by external circumstances (MR1, 16). He struggles briefly in 1812 with the alternative of whether human beings can morally emulate the "pure will" of nature in providing the greatest well-being to the greatest number of creatures or whether the human will in opposition to nature is bound to go wrong (MR1, 22; 28). He writes in early 1814 about the ultimate existential choice as being identification with a "better will" over against the insatiably desiring "will-to-live" (MR1, 98).

This conceptualization of a duplicity of wills or motivations corresponding to different species of moral choice is abandoned in 1814, when suddenly Schopenhauer declares that "the body (corporeal man) is *nothing but the will that has become visible*" (MR1, 115). As all passions and emotions are embodied experiences, and the movements and actions they prompt human beings to are also embodied, the body shows itself to be the objectivity of an underlying metaphysical will. All existence we are familiar with is embodied existence, and therefore the will reveals itself in every bodily movement in nature, whether it be an expression of human moral character, animal motivation, plant growth, vegetation and reproduction or the interplay of inorganic chemical process like crystallization or natural forces such as gravity (MR1, 156-8). The will thus becomes for Schopenhauer the metaphysical foundation of the world, and all phenomena are merely objectifications or manifestations of this will at different "grades" as represented by space, time, causality and the principle of sufficient reason.

We can arrive at the knowledge of the will through the fact that the body is not only known to us a representation, that is as a spatio-temporal object which conforms to the principle of sufficient reason just as every other object does. We also know the body "immediately," that is through movements of will which compel and are objectified in bodily acts (MR1, 170-71; 196-7).[24] The relationship between will and body cannot be accounted for in causal terms; will does not cause bodily actions since causality applies only with respect to objective representations. The will itself is not an object, nonetheless it becomes objectified in bodily acts. There is no way for us to make any intelligible distinction between a movement of will and a bodily activity, for even were we not to do something with regard to a willing event, any willing has physiological consequences which are known to us, as in cases such as hunger or passion. It is precisely because every bodily act is an act of will that we can infer that the will is the metaphysical basis of all natural activity; first because every natural activity is physical and embodied in some way, and second because will is outside the categories of differentiation, it must be one, unitary will that underlies all natural activities.

The consequence of all phenomena in the world being manifestations of will does not in any way make existence a pleasant affair for these phenomena. Each manifestation of will, being a phenomenal individual, has individuated interests and therefore, moved by will, fights against every other phenomenon for the preservation and prolongation of its own existence. This situation makes life a constant striving and suffering, for either what is willed in specific situations is unattainable or hindered from grasp, or is attained and soon laid aside as "boring" at which point the willing individual pursues something else. This perpetual willing Schopenhauer calls the "will-to-live." But for the human being who realizes what a horrific and violent world is supported by its own metaphysical foundation, what would seem far more preferable to a continued affirmation of the will is a "denial of the will-to-live." This is not accomplished through some change in moral character, which Schopenhauer considers impossible, but through a "turning" of the will.

> Man as such is a phenomenon of the will-to-live. The wicked man is the concentrated phenomenon of this will-to-live, and as with the will-to-live, its phenomenon, life, and consequently all the horrors and agonies of life are assumed (since all these are only one), so to others and to himself, virtually to the subject of knowing in general, is the wicked man a frightful phenomenon just because the will-to-life, revealing itself in him to such a high degree, is essentially bad and infamous. . . . His opposite is the saint who is the phenomenon of *not* willing to live, of a will that is *not* concerned with life. It is true that his body as such is a phenomenon of life-willing. . . . His character is, however, that is to say the common element in the whole series of his actions, is a phenomenon of the will which is not concerned with life, in other words has turned, so that it is not the will whose phenomenon is the body as such. . . . Here of course, we can *express ourselves only negatively*, just because the material

> in which philosophy works, namely concepts, are representations and are therefore conditioned by life and belong to this. And so for our point of view the turning of the will, holiness, salvation, bliss are certainly a transition into *nothing*. (MR1, 269)

Schopenhauer identifies several ways in which the will can be denied; one is through knowledge, as when he writes in 1815, "abolition of the will-to-live is . . . knowledge of the (Platonic) Ideas" (MR1, 250). Another, as we have seen above, is compassion, which is elicited upon the realization that the world is indeed one will, an insight which brings an end to the rigid distinctions that are normally made between another individual's sufferings and one's own.[25] The complete and permanent abolition of the will takes place in asceticism, in which all worldly desires are renounced, and in such a state, as shown above, the world can only be described from the perspective of a concept-bound and distinction-dependent philosophy, as "nothing." It is this metaphysics of will and the doctrines of virtue and saintliness that follow from it that have made Schopenhauer's philosophy seem to so many commentators "pessimistic." Nietzsche in the end believed Schopenhauer's philosophy to be the ultimate expression of Western nihilism, as for it the affirmation of life Nietzsche sought so diligently was not only impossible, but also morally reprehensible. However, as we shall see in the coming chapters, Schopenhauer did not intend his picture of asceticism and renunciation to be categorical imperatives, moral "oughts," but more explications of how these phenomena looked in the light of his metaphysics of will.

2.3 THE NOTION OF MĀYĀ *IN THE EARLY* NACHLASS

Now that we have gained a basic familiarity with the themes around which Schopenhauer built his system, we will be in a better position to appreciate his encounter with pre-systematic Indian philosophical thought. Schopenhauer appears often to feel almost compulsively driven to relate what he learns about classical Indian thought, in particular from "the *Vedas* and *Upaniṣads*" as he understood them, to his own developing philosophical ideas, though these various attempts and parallelization were not all equally convincing to Schopenhauer himself. Some of them he dropped from consideration quickly, others he struggled with for decades, and still others remained permanently crucial to him. One of the notions from *Upaniṣadic* and Vedāntic speculation he became familiar with, the notion of *māyā*, was to become a key linking concept of the system as he first envisioned it.

From the time he first gained familiarity with classical Indian religions, the Hindu, Buddhist and Jaina traditions, Schopenhauer frequently muses about some of their doctrines and symbolism which struck him as having a resonance with his own philosophy. He sometimes comments on the worship of Shiva, and specifically on the symbolism of the *lingam* as paralleling his doctrines about the "will-to-live" (MR1, 181; 371; 440). He mentions the *Vedic* fire sacrifice after his reading of Colebrooke's essay on it in volume eight of the *Asiatic Researches* in 1815 in connection with his developing ideas on the "resignation" of the will (MR1, 286). He is especially impressed with the doctrine of "metapsychosis" or "transmigration," in fact believes it to be superior as a religious idea to those of the Western tradition concerning the afterlife, for the former shows that the individual is only a passing, transient "phenomenon" which will not survive death in contrast to the "will-to-live" which survives death and passes from one individual to the next in the succession of generations (MR1, 389; 487–88). He finds in the "sacrifices, pilgrimages, the worship of gods and ceremonies of all kinds" among "the Hindus" an "indication and expression of the awareness of life's inadequacy and of its inability to satisfy the spirit and the mind" (MR1, 381). It is for the most part due to these very superficial reflections and identifications that so many have found it difficult to see in Schopenhauer anything more than a kind of conceptual subordination of non-Western and even Western religious thought to his own doctrine, owing to his "propensity to find corroborations between his own ideas with as many thought systems as possible" (Sedler 180). There can be no question that Schopenhauer did have this propensity and that it appears not only with respect to Indian thought, but also in his discussions of Western "mystics" like Eckhart, Boehme and Giodarno Bruno on occasion. However, this propensity does not account for all of Schopenhauer's reflections on concepts he discovers from the pre-systematic philosophical period in India, some of which he rejects and some which he accepts and himself appropriates, and there is much there that becomes the subject of sustained philosophical reflection.

For instance, we find in his early thinking in the notebooks of these years a struggle with the ideas he encounters from the Indian tradition, struggles that would end up lasting for decades. In 1816, for instance, he writes that the denial of the will-to-live by the ascetic is tantamount to "nothingness," as "for those whose will has turned, this very real world of ours with all its suns and galaxies is—nothing," and that this characterization of resignation of the will is preferable to "meaningless words such as *Brahma*, reabsorption in the primordial spirit, or the *Nibbana* of the Buddhists (see *Asiatic Researches* and *Upnek'hat*)" (MR1, 455–6). He claims also that the "denial-of-life, of not willing" is only "something additional, as ethics and asceticism" in the "*Vedas* and *Puranas*" which in the form presented in those texts as he knows them, he believes to be only "half true" (MR1, 453). Later, of course, Schopenhauer would take the concept of *brahman* very seriously, seriously enough to try to understand it in accordance with his notion of will in light of Müller's translation of the term as "force, will, wish" (Halbfass, *India* 111).[26] After a very short interval following the above rejections, Schopenhauer can be found calling those who renounce the will-to-live "*Sanyassi*" and identifying as the "morality of the Hindus" the "giving-up of the will-to-live" by making reference to "the *Vedas, Puranas . . . Oupnek'hat, Life of Foe* in the *Asiatic Researches, Bhagavadgita, Laws of Manu,* Madame de Polier's *Mythologie des Hindous*" in 1817 (MR1, 461; 514–15). Schopenhauer's dependence on the early essays of the German Orientalists of the time helps to account for the great generalizations he makes concerning the "morality of the Hindus" and other such references. Nevertheless his oscillations on these issues, which begin in the notebooks of these years and continue through his entire philosophical career, testify to the effort of Schopenhauer to understand ideas from pre-systematic Indian thought not only through his own philosophy, but to redefine and rethink his own ideas through his encounter with Indian religion and philosophy.

It seems clear however that the greatest impact of this encounter was worked upon his epistemological thinking. We have seen above how important Schopenhauer's reading of the *Upaniṣads,* and especially the specific presentation of them given by Duperron, was for him. It will be helpful in what follows to keep these observations of Halbfass in mind:

> Even though the essential points of his own thinking had probably been taking shape even before he had heard of the work, the *Oupnek'hat* nevertheless had an enduring and far-reaching effect upon Schopenhauer's life and thought. Yet all too frequently, the fact is overlooked that his encounter with the *Oupnek'hat* was by no means a purely "Indian" encounter. It was also an encounter with Anquetil Duperron's own ways of thinking and interpreting, with his methods of comparing and parallelizing, and with the manner in which he incorporated the *Upaniṣads* into the context of contemporary European philosophy. Anquetil himself had repeatedly asserted and attempted to demonstrate that the sages of all countries and all times have basically "all said the same" or at least meant the same, and that the *Upaniṣads* in particular have parallels in European doctrines. It is especially remarkable that Kant was very explicitly cited in these comparisons, indeed an entire "Paragon" in the first volume was devoted to the relationship between Kantianism and the *Upaniṣads*. There, Anquetil claimed that the two do not greatly differ with respect to their emphasis upon man's self-discovery and return to his inner reality.... Schopenhauer's stubborn adherence to the *Oupnek'hat* in the face of all the European translations of the *Upaniṣads* which he subsequently became aware of is certainly also an expression of approval for the very personal and explicitly philosophical approach of Anquetil. (Halbfass *India* 115–16)

There can be no question that Schopenhauer was made very much amenable initially and throughout his life to Duperron's renderings and commentaries on the *Upaniṣads* and what he believed to be their affinity with the Kantian philosophy precisely because of his own strong Kantian leanings. Some of what Duperron wrote in one of his appendices to the first of his two volumes of translations, called "*De Kantismo*," can be found echoed in Schopenhauer's notes. Duperron had claimed that both Kant and classical "Brahminical doctrine" had taken account of "transcendental" considerations of knowledge, also that the *Upaniṣadic* notion of *ātman* was, like the Kantian consciousness, "absolutely unitary . . . undifferentiated, a singular entity," and that *jñāna*, like Kantian knowledge, was "conjoined in the intellect by the intellect" and that "everything traditionally labeled real was actually cognitive" (711; 712). The idealism of the *Upaniṣads*, according to Duperron, stipulated that "everything outside of me is only a phenomenal appearance" and that the "positivity and negativity in known objects does not exist in them but in me as the essence of cognition" (712). Duperron's insistence that Kantian idealism was compatible with the teachings of the *Upaniṣads* appealed to Schopenhauer's subjective idealism. He writes in early 1814, shortly after first checking out the *Oupnek'hat* from the Weimar library:

> The theoretical childish and foolish dogmatics has tried to explain everything through the relations of *objects*, especially through the *principle of sufficient reason or ground*; it represented a God as constructing the world, deciding the fate of men, and so forth. The wiser Indians started from the *subject*, from *Atma*, *Jivatma*. The essential point is that the subject has representations or mental pictures; it is not the connexion of the representations with one another. If, after the manner of the Indians, we start from the subject, the world together with the principle of sufficient reason ruling in it suddenly stands before us, no matter from which side we begin to consider it. If we start with the object and build, as we must do, one stone on another with the mortar of the principle of sufficient reason, then we are never able to find the foun-

> dation on which the building is to rest or the top which is to carry the building's wreath. (MR1, 116)

Duperron's conviction that *Upaniṣadic* and *Vedic* thought can be looked at through a Kantian lens continued to be a guiding principle in Schopenhauer's reading.[27] In the following year, upon reading selections from the eighth volume of the *Asiatic Magazine*, containing the essay "Colebrooke on the *Vedas*," he annotates several passages illustrating the emanation of the world from the primordial "person" (*puruṣa*) as evidence of the "dependence of the object on the subject" and that "only for the subject of knowing does the world exist" (MR2, 459-60).[28] Schopenhauer's persistent predilection to interpret Indian thought by the standard of Kantian subjectivism was certainly, as Halbfass has concluded, a reflex of his introduction to Indian thought by the Kantian Duperron.

But more than this was to come out of Schopenhauer's reading of the *Upaniṣads*, for as Alfred Schmidt, in rather problematic terms, has written, in Schopenhauer's works we find not only a "Kantianization of the Orient" but also an "Orientalization of Kant" (*Wahrheit* 125). Long before Schmidt, Naegelsbach put the matter a bit more accurately by saying, as we saw in the last chapter, that Schopenhauer "synthesized" in a wholly unjustifiable manner the subjectivism of Kant with the "illusionism" of the "Indian" doctrine of *māyā* (151-2).[29] In the strict sense, Schopenhauer's developing understanding of *māyā* comes neither from the *Vedas* or the *Upaniṣads*, as he claims is does, but rather more from the Advaita Vedāntic interpretation of this concept, for *māyā*, from the root *mā* "to measure," is most often identified in the *Vedic-Upaniṣadic* texts to be the magical power of God employed to create the world and then to hide behind the matter out of which it was made.[30] It was only the Advaitins, specifically Śaṅnkara, Sureśvara and Sarvajñātman, who many centuries later redefined *māyā* as the epistemological "ignorance" (*avidyā*) which caused human beings to mistake their changeless, eternal, undifferentiated innermost self (*ātman*) for the empirical, transitory individual person (*jiva*).[31] Still later Advaitins like Vidyāraṅya explicated *māyā* in an even more elaborate fashion, as the "constructive power" (*nirmānaśakti*) of the mind to "project" (*vikṣepa*) its objects that works in conjunction with the "veiling power" (*āvaraṅaśakti*) of *avidyā* to make a unitary metaphysical reality appear as the plurality of things in empirical experience.[32] Schopenhauer develops an understanding of *māyā* over time which makes it at once an epistemological category of falsification and an existential fetter that causes human beings to comport themselves towards others and toward the world as a whole in an ethically pernicious way.

More specifically, Schopenhauer believes *māyā* to be a way the world appears to us as something it is not. This takes place in several ways. Epistemologically, māyā entails an erroneous perception of things and a fallacious assessment of their nature; axiologically, it is the inauthentic valuation of world and other; metaphysically, it is the mere phenomenal appearance of a noumenal reality; and ethically, it leads to an unjustifiable alienation of other from self. These various connotations of *māyā* are never distinctly separate either in the notes or in the published works. However, they do amount to a falsification thesis, which is certainly not the only nor necessarily the overriding thematic in Schopenhauer's philosophy; logically speaking it conflates oddly at times with Schopenhauer's other doctrines, which we will see later. It does nonetheless play a key role in how the "parts" of Schopenhauer's system are conceived to run together.

The epistemological and axiological implications of Schopenhauer's understanding of *māyā* converge from his very first entries on the subject. He writes in 1814:

> In so far as he is alive . . . a human being . . . is doomed not merely to *sin* and *death*, but also to *illusion*, and this *illusion* is as real as life, as real as the world of the senses itself, indeed it is identical with these (*Māyā* of the Indians). On it are based all our desires and cravings, which again are only the expression of life, just as life is only the expression of illusion. To the extent that we live, will to live, and are human beings, the illusion is truth; and only in reference to the better consciousness is it illusion. If peace, quiet and bliss are to be found, then the illusion

> must be abandoned, and if this is to be abandoned, then life must be given up. (MR1, 113–14)

"Life," with all its passing "desires and cravings," is said to be opposed to the contemplation of the "better consciousness" of the Platonic Ideas, and while our desires seem to us elements of the "real" and "actual" world, their transience and the suffering they cause proves them to be "illusory." The "real" world is not what we believe it to be; instead of being a "field" for the fulfillment of our desires, it is merely an "expression" of the will-to-live as it appears in time. A few entries later, we find the following.

> We constantly imagine that the desired object can put an end to our willing.... (The) release from willing occurs through better knowledge, and so *Oupnek'hat*, Vol. II page 216 says "the moment knowledge appeared on the scene, thence abated desire," here by "desire" is meant *maya* which is just this willing, that love (for the object), whose objectification or appearance is the world. As the fundamental error it is at the same time, so to speak, the origin of evil and of the world. (MR1, 130)

Schopenhauer here takes *māyā* to be a "willing," "desire" or "*amor*" for an object that will not satisfy the desire; but beyond that, it is also an "error" which is at once the origin of evil and the world. It is here that the axiological conception of *māyā* becomes worked into Schopenhauer's epistemological framework. In 1815, an entry specifically marks this change of conception.

> The world is the objectivity of the will (to live). This will's most vehement phenomenon is the sexual impulse, which is the *eros* of the ancients . . . the principle of the world, that which creates; the *Maya* of the Indians means the same thing.
>
> N. B. not quite the same; *Maya* is rather the objectivity of the will, Kant's *phenomenon*, knowledge according to the principle of sufficient reason. (MR1, 332)

What was formally considered the "will" or the creative "*eros*" which served as the metaphysical basis of the world as well as the axiological basis of all desires, is now "knowledge according to the principle of sufficient reason," that is, the way the world appears through the forms of sensibility, the category of causality and concepts. In Schopenhauer's subjectivist epistemology, the principle of sufficient reason is the condition of all objectivity in a Kantian sense. In this vein, *māyā* has become for Schopenhauer precisely that kind of knowledge which brings about desire and perpetuates the will-to-live, for desires are only made determinate by the objectifications effected by the principle of sufficient reason. But these desires are, as we have seen, illusory; and so are the objects of those desires *if they are taken to be real* (*wahrgenommen*) and satisfying by the subject.

Simultaneously, *māyā* is incorporated into Schopenhauer's evolving metaphysical scheme. In 1814, he makes reference to it as "the endlessness of the material world," its "inner driving force" (MR1, 148). This more concrete, naturalistic sense of *māyā* quickly fades away and taking its place is the frequent invocation of *māyā* as the "immaterial and insubstantial" world presented by the principle of reason, the "actual world, Kant's phenomena" (MR1, 247). In 1816, Schopenhauer arrives at a thematization of *māyā* that will last throughout his philosophical career; "the *māyā* of the *Vedas,* Plato's 'what eternally becomes but never is' and Kant's 'phenomenon' are one and the same thing, are this world in which we live, are we ourselves in so far as we belong to it" (MR1, 419, 444). This identification of Plato's "becoming" and Kant's "phenomenal" is, from a historical perspective, one of the most puzzling and unjustifiable identifications Schopenhauer makes, for the Platonic forms, the Kantian thing-in-itself, the *Upaniṣadic brahman* and Schopenhauer's own notion of will are vastly different in their respective thematizations. How these respectively manifest themselves in the empirical world are also different in these various traditions. Schopenhauer's insistence that they are synonymous and refer to the same thing can from this perspective certainly be taken as evidence of Schopenhauer's own extreme a-historicism and hermeneutical naiveté in his interpretive approach. And yet, there is something of philosophical and hermeneutical importance even in this apparently absurd formula. As we have seen above, the conception of *māyā* most familiar to the authors of the *Upaniṣads* is the medium or "power" through which Indra or Iśvara created a world of multiplicity, a world of "names and forms." The two fundamental metaphysical realities in Schopenhauer's thinking are "will" as initially "thing-in-itself" and "representation" whose explication gives an account of how the empirical world appears before consciousness. What his "main work" is meant to provide is a satisfactory explanation of how the will becomes representation, how the will "objectifies" itself and in the process is spun into the phenomenal world of our experience. Instead of presenting this explanation in the "mythological" terms of the *Upaniṣads,* which he found suspect, and worse in the traditional "theistic" terms of the Western religious and philosophical tradition which he found objectionable, Schopenhauer wants to find adequate philosophical vocabulary to describe the mediation through which will becomes represented. The vocabulary he chose was the vocabulary most familiar to him, one which was ingrained in him from his earliest days of philosophical studies with Schulze, who advised him to focus his studies on Plato and Kant. It does not appear to be the case that Schopenhauer merely believes that these three terms, Plato's "becoming," Kant's "phenomena" and the *māyā* of the *Upaniṣads* have the exact same sense. Rather, all their senses must be called to mind when we consider how a unitary, eternal thing-in-itself can become the differentiated, changing representations of human experience. In order for the will to become objectified, it must first descend from its atemporality into the field of time, which is the sense of Plato's "becoming" but never "being"; it must become accessible to human knowledge in a determinate way, which is meant to be explained through Kantian subjective idealism; and it must appear as something it is not, for since it cannot be known apart from representations and the body, it cannot appear as it is in itself but must appear falsely, and this is the work of *māyā.* Rather than understanding this identification of Plato, Kant and the *Upaniṣads* only as a glaring instance of Schopenhauer's hermeneutical naiveté, we may also understand it as an expression of the necessary conditions that must obtain in order for the thing-in-itself to appear as the world of our experience, and *māyā* as falsification must be, for Schopenhauer, one of these conditions. This interpretation of *māyā* is not evidence, as J. I. Gestering has taken it to be, of the absence of a hermeneutic in Schopenhauer's methodological approach, but rather the result of a properly hermeneutical appropriation as Ricoeur has formulated it.

The idea of *māyā* as the principle of sufficient reason began to have implications for the ethical sphere as well in the notes of 1816. Legal and moral punishment, as Schopenhauer saw them, were attempts to realize a kind of "eternal justice" in which "the one who caused pain in another again experiences exactly the same amount of pain" (MR1, 429). These attempts, no matter how justifiable we believe them to be, are for Schopenhauer the result of a kind of transcendental confusion. A man demands justice because

> he is involved in the *principium individuationis* and demands of the phenomenon that which belongs only to the thing in itself. In themselves, not in the phenomenon, the tormentor and the tormented are, as I have often shown, the same, however differently *Maya* shows them. (MR1, 429)

He continues this thought in a further entry.

> Only for the representation, not in himself, only by means of the form of the representation, namely the *principium individuationis* which is *Maya*, is he the author of another's suffering, different from the sufferer. On the other hand, in themselves, in what the world still is other than representation, both are the one will-to-live, and so the sufferer and the one inflicting the suffering are only one. Thus dazzled and deluded by *Maya*, the will-to-live falls into conflict with itself, since, by seeking enhanced well-being in one of its phenomena, it causes in precisely this way great suffering in the other, and only the will itself must endure this suffering, whereby it atones for the violation of *eternal justice*. . . . For *temporal justice starts*

> simply from the *principium individuationis* and hence from egoism. The individual, endowed with the faculty of reason, is interested in looking after himself in that he enters into an agreement that no one shall inflict injury on another, and such *temporal justice* is the source of *natural right*. But *eternal justice* sees through the *principium individuationis,* and in this way one perceives that the tormentor and the tormented are *in themselves* not different. (MR1, 446–7)

If judging by the *principium individuationis,* the "forms of sensibility" of time and space, we take the world to be composed of multifarious things of heterogeneous natures, then this judgment when carried over to ethics creates the distinction between the agent and the patient in an action. The self or ego is the most immediate representation of the subject, and so her will takes priority over the other's will, at which point reason calculates an action based on the difference between self and other and how good can accrue to the self. Thus, acting under the guidance of the *principium,* people are egoists; they seek their own well-being either with indifference to or positive contempt for the well-being of others. "Natural right" or systematic ethics, social law and state policy are based on a system of blame and punishment which strives to atone for the sins or crimes of an evildoer by inflicting on him the suffering he caused to others. This is all well and good, according to Schopenhauer; he is not attempting to mount an argument against ethics or law, but merely wishes to point out that it is based on the same transcendental mistake made by the evildoer. This transcendental mistake is brought about under the influence of *māyā,* which deludes the individual into thinking his difference from the other is absolute and not merely phenomenal. The will is only differentiated in terms of phenomena, but in itself is undifferentiated. In words which sound as if they were taken from similar formulations in the *Bhagavad Gītā,* "the tormentor and the tormented are the same" insofar as they are both manifestations of will.[33] In the realization of the metaphysical oneness of all phenomena as manifestations of will, the individual no longer acts under the guidance of the *principium,* at which point the "veil of *māyā*" will be removed and the human being will be able to perform acts of compassion, "suffering with" the other in the knowledge of metaphysical identity (MR1, 322–4; 342–3; 469). This will become known in Schopenhauer's published works as what Hacker has labeled the "*tat tvam asi* ethic," the formula of metaphysical identity Schopenhauer takes from the *Upaniṣads*.

We shall discuss the philosophical tenability and problematic implications of these ideas in the coming chapters. What is required for the present is for us to see what an important role the notion of *māyā* as Schopenhauer understood and appropriated it was to the formulation of his philosophical thinking. At the beginning of his philosophical reflections in 1813, Schopenhauer envisioned a system which was a "metaphysics and ethics at the same time," a system whose "parts" would be organically related and offer at once an epistemology, a metaphysics, an aesthetics and an ethics. Schopenhauer has made the "single thought" of his system the tenet that "the world is the self-knowledge of the will." During the formative years of the system, between 1814 and 1818, the concept of *māyā* becomes thematized in epistemological, axiological, metaphysical and ethical terms, and as a necessary condition of the will appearing as representation through a falsification of the world's true nature, serves as a crucial linking concept connecting different "parts" of that system into a "whole." *Māyā* is for Schopenhauer's systematic philosophy not merely a "leitmotif," not merely an instance of his "confirming his own thoughts in the light of other thought-systems," but an irreplaceable premise which helps support Schopenhauer's "single thought."

CHAPTER 3

Representationalism and Falsification

3.1 MĀYĀ *IN SCHOPENHAUER'S REPRESENTATION THEORY*

The two criteria of influence set forth in this work for determining whether Schopenhauer's knowledge of pre-systematic Hindu and Buddhist philosophical thought was incorporated into his system are the criterion of acquaintance and the criterion of thematic effect. They are meant respectively to establish whether Schopenhauer possessed knowledge of source texts from and commentarial literature on these traditions at a time which would allow for their themes to find their way into his system, and whether his appropriations of concepts of these traditions significantly impacted his own theoretical reflections on epistemology, metaphysics and ethics. In the preceding chapter, it was found that Schopenhauer's *Nachlass* of the years 1814 to 1818, the laboratory in which his system was initially built, was compiled precisely during the period in which Schopenhauer was first familiarizing himself with pre-systematic Hindu and Buddhist thought, and that his own philosophical reflections were measurably effected through his encounter with these traditions. In the present chapter, these criteria will be applied to question of whether the epistemological theory of Schopenhauer's *opus*, *The World as Will and Representation*, can be said to have been influenced by ideas from the early Indian philosophical tradition, and in particular by the *Upaniṣadic* and Vedṟntic notion of *māyā*.

For the most part, this chapter will focus on the epistemological argumentation of the first edition of *The World as Will and Representation*, completed in 1818 and published in 1819. What will be confirmed here is that the concept of *māyā* plays a significant role in Schopenhauer's representation theory, providing him with one of the major justifications he gives for the necessity of the transition from epistemology to metaphysics in this first edition. The supplementary essays to this first volume which were published together twenty-five years later in the second edition of the *opus* in 1844, and which were further amended fifteen years after that, witness some fundamental changes in the way Schopenhauer conceptualizes idealism and justifies metaphysics. The falsification thesis of the first edition, so critical to Schopenhauer's linkage of epistemology to metaphysics, becomes naturalized and psychologized in these later works, revisions which on the one hand broaden the purview of epistemological falsification and on the other diminish its theoretical importance to Schopenhauer's later metaphysics and epistemology. The thesis of epistemological falsification, the result of the philosophical appropriation of the concept of *māyā*, is pivotal to Schopenhauer's epistemology and metaphysics in the first edition, and its importance has either been overlooked or badly assessed by most of Schopenhauer's serious commentators. It plays a diminished and problematic role in the second volume of the much later second and third editions of *The World as Will and Representation*, and we will also account for this in the next chapter.

Our procedure then will be first to review Schopenhauer's admitted theoretical indebtedness to the "*Vedas, Purānas* and *Upaniṣads*," as well as identify his couching of some major principles from his representation theory in *Upaniṣadic* and Vedāntic terminology. It will then be shown how Schopenhauer develops his understanding of the notion of *māyā* into a falsification thesis, a thesis which draws theoretical consequences from his characterizations of representational knowledge as a limited, incomplete, "unsatisfying" and fundamentally flawed view of the world.

3.1.1 The Upaniṣads *as Groundwork for the System*

In the previous chapter, we investigated the influences on the formulation of Schopenhauer's philosophical system. G. E. Schulze recommended to Schopenhauer during his attendance at Göttingen University that he study Plato and Kant, and indeed, Schopenhauer's reformulation of the Platonic Ideas as the eternal forms of aesthetic perception and the universal principles of gradations of physical force were the most permanent elements of his thinking, just as Kant's philosophy bore the heaviest weight on his system. Schopenhauer's encounter with Anquetil Duperron's translations of fifty *Upaniṣads* also counted as a major influence on his work. The *Upaniṣads* are mentioned frequently in the *Nachlass* of 1814 to 1818 in conjunction with Plato and Kant as pivotal to Schopenhauer's philosophical development (MR1, 247; 419; 444; 467; 578).

These influences are acknowledged quite readily in the Preface to the first edition of *The World as Will and Representation*. Schopenhauer uses this preface to recommend to the reader what sort of preparation she needs in order to be most open to the content of the work. His first admonition is that his own dissertation, *On the Fourfold Root of the Principle of Sufficient Reason* be read, for as a treatise on Schopenhauer's epistemology, it serves as an "introduction and propaedeutic" to it and "is always presupposed" in it (WWRI, xiv). After paying intellectual gratitude to Kant as well as warning that there are severe critiques of Kant coming, Schopenhauer writes:

> Kant's philosophy is therefore the only one with which a thorough acquaintance is positively assumed in what is to be here discussed. But if in addition to this the reader has dwelt for a while in the school of the divine Plato, he will be the better prepared to hear me, and the more susceptible to what I say. But if he has shared in the benefits of the *Vedas,* access to which, opened to us by the *Upanishads,* is in my view the greatest advantage which this still young century has to show over previous centuries, since I surmise that the influence of Sanskrit literature

> will penetrate no less deeply than did the revival of Greek literature in the fifteenth century; if, I say, the reader has also already received and assimilated the divine inspiration of ancient Indian wisdom, then he is best of all prepared to hear what I have to say to him. It will not speak to him, as to many others, in a strange and even hostile tongue; for, did it not sound too conceited, I might assert that each of the individual and disconnected utterances that make up the *Upanishads* could be deduced as a consequence from the thought I am to impart, although conversely my thought is by no means to be found in the *Upanishads*. (WWRI, xv–xvi)

The relationship Schopenhauer articulates here between his own thought and the "*Vedas, Upanishads*" and "ancient Indian wisdom" is much more complex than most have taken it to be. Those familiar with classical Indian philosophical thought are held to be "best of all prepared" to enter into Schopenhauer's system. He shares the high estimation of the Romantics that the texts of the classical Indian tradition will create a new intellectual Renaissance in Europe. He decries those who find the works of that tradition to be written "in a strange and even hostile tongue," and by these he may have Herder, Schlegel and even the early Hegel in mind, who all took notable account of Indian religion and philosophy while at the same time holding in deep suspicion many of the doctrines of classical Hinduism and Buddhism, such as reincarnation, a doctrine Schopenhauer particularly admired. He then asserts that, while each of the "individual and disconnected utterances" which mediate the teachings of the *Upaniṣads* could be "deduced" from his own philosophical conclusions, the converse, finding Schopenhauer's thought in the *Upaniṣads*, could not be done. Several important points arise from these assertions. First, Schopenhauer takes what is philosophically significant in the *Upaniṣads* from "individual and disconnected utterances," a claim that is in line with traditional Vedāntic exegesis, which builds its systematic philosophy from the so-called "great sayings" or *māhāvakyas* of the Upaniṣads, not from any system found within those texts. Secondly, Schopenhauer is not here advocating the kind of perennialism one finds in some of his other claims, to the effect that he, Plato, Kant, Eckhart and the *Upaniṣads* "say the same"; he does not treat the *Upaniṣads*, as if they need "no hermeneutic," as some other "European philosopher," as Gestering held (59). Schopenhauer is aware in this passage of the nature of his appropriation insofar as he realizes that the *Upaniṣads* espouse a philosophy distinct from his own. Nonetheless, he downplays here as well as in other places the extent of the influence of the *Upaniṣads* on his own systematic philosophy when he writes that his thought is "by no means" to be found in them, for as we shall attempt to demonstrate in the rest of this work, some major elements of his systematic thought were significantly impacted by his reading of Duperron's translations. How else could it be said after all that one who has read the philosophical texts of classical India would be "best of all prepared" for Schopenhauer's thought, and how could each of the "great utterances" of the *Upaniṣads* be "deduced" from Schopenhauer's principles if he believed they held nothing in common philosophically? The notion then that a certain interpretation of *Upaniṣadic* thought Schopenhauer was aware of cannot be found in his own writings is highly misleading.

Schopenhauer entertains two constant attitudes with respect to those thinkers he believed were his "predecessors." He is generally very forthcoming about acknowledging his intellectual debts by naming the philosophers and books he admires. He calls Kant "marvelous" and Plato "divine," he often also labels "ancient Indian wisdom" "divine" or believes it to be "inspired." He heaps high praise on others who effected his thinking greatly, poets such as Goethe, physiologists such as Reid and philosophers such as Lammarck. In the same vein, he shows no trepidation about leveling critiques at philosophers by name: often they are the same philosophers he admires. The longest section of the first volume of *The World as Will and Representation* is devoted to a thoroughgoing criticism of Kant, and a very extensive criticism of Kant also makes up most of his 1841 essay *On the Basis of Morality*. He singles out Fichte, Schelling and Hegel for retribution by name, and in this his written criticisms are starkly contrasted from theirs.[1] In like manner, he often chastises Indian thought as being "too mythological," and believes his own work brings systematic clarity to concepts which, despite their truth, are clouded in mystery by the religious context those concepts arose out of in the Indian tradition. These comments should not be taken as utter denigrations of the Indian philosophical tradition. Schopenhauer was after all very little aware of the systems or *darśanas* of the Indian tradition, and where certain affinities were suggested by some of his contemporaries between Greek and Indian logic and intimations were made that the former derived from the latter, he rejected those suggestions (WWR1, 48). Schopenhauer believed his system was the culmination of philosophy itself, and in fact he thought all philosophers proposing new systems believed this. His particular elitism is more of a personal than a cultural one, and in fact in his notes for an 1820 University of Berlin lecture on the theory of representation, Schopenhauer wrote: "What I have to present agrees very precisely with the ancient Indian principles. Yet it is also connected with the entire development of philosophy in the Occident; it is historically contiguous with it and follows from it" (qtd. in Halbfass *India* 116). His admitted indebtedness to Indian thought as well as his various criticisms of it, while obviously both open to historical assessment and question, are measures of how central and not peripheral it was to his own reflection.[2]

3.1.2 Māyā *and the Questions of Metaphysics*

Schopenhauer's frequent association of the *Upaniṣads* with Kant and Plato, as suggested in the last chapter, is much more revealing of Schopenhauer's appropriation of ideas of classical Indian thought than the outlandish oversimplification which it has seemed to be to many commentators. The *Upaniṣadic* notion of *māyā* was in a very pointed sense for Schopenhauer the Vedāntic version of the basic metaphysical question he saw in Plato and Kant, the question of appearance and reality. Schopenhauer uses quotations and concepts from the *Upaniṣads* liberally to thematize some of the main conceptions of his representation theory which, in his mind, necessitate an inquiry into metaphysics.

Schopenhauer opens *The World as Will and Representation* with the assertion that "the world is my representation" (WWR1, 3). This proposition is one which he thinks Kant made obvious, by proving all objects are the results of the perceiving and thinking subject's cognitive processes, what Schopenhauer himself in his dissertation identified as the "principle of sufficient reason." But to say that the world is specifically "my representation" is also to posit that representations exist only by virtue of the correlativity of object and subject. All representations are divided into the known and the knower, the object and subject, and this division is the most fundamental form of representation as such (Ibid.). In the second paragraph of the work, he writes:

> This truth is by no means new. It was to be found already in the skeptical reflections from which Descartes started. But Berkeley was the first to enunciate it positively, and he has thus rendered an immortal service to philosophy, although the remainder of his doctrines cannot endure. Kant's first mistake was the neglect of this principle.... On the other hand, how early this basic truth was recognized by the sages of India, since it appears as the fundamental tenet of the Vedānta philosophy ascribed to Vyasa, is proved by Sir William Jones in the last of his essays, "On the Philosophy of the Asiatics" (*Asiatic Researches*, vol. IV, p. 164): "The fundamental tenet of the Vedānta school consisted not in denying the existence of matter, that is, of solidity, impenetrability, and extended figure (to deny which would be lunacy), but in correcting the popular notion of it, and in contending that it has no essence independent of mental perception, that existence and perceptibility are convertible terms." These words adequately express the compatibility of empirical reality with transcendental ideality. (WWR1, 3–4.)

At the opening of the second section of the book, Schopenhauer continues:

> That which knows all things and is known by none is the *subject*. It is accordingly the supporter of the world, the universal condition of all that appears, of all objects, and it is always presupposed; for whatever exists exists only for the subject. Everyone finds himself as this subject, yet only in so far as he knows, not in so far as he is the object of knowledge. But his body is already object, and therefore from this point of view we call it representation. . . . Like all objects of perception, it lies within the forms of all knowledge, in time and space, through which there is plurality. But the subject, the knower, never the known, does not lie within these forms; on the contrary, it is always presupposed by these forms themselves, and hence neither plurality nor its opposite, namely unity, belongs to it. We never know it, but it is precisely that which knows wherever there is knowledge. (WWR1, 5)

In these opening passages, Schopenhauer familiarizes his readers with a central notion of his representation theory, the subject-object correlativity thesis, by making allusions to Vedānta and the *Upaniṣads*. The fundamental doctrine of Vedānta, Schopenhauer learns from William Jones, is that all experienced objects depend essentially upon the constructive cognitive apparatus of a knowing subject.[3] This is not a doctrine meant to deny matter, but rather establishes the "transcendental ideality" of all objects, as objects can be objects only as known.[4] One of the fundamental keys to this tenet of subject-object correlativity is that, while the object is known to the subject, even when that object is the body of the knower, the knowing subject can never itself become an object of knowledge. Time, space and causality, the *a priori* forms of the understanding, apply only to objects and the relationships between objects, the subject, though "one half" of any representation, is not conditioned by any of these forms and thus cannot be objectified. Schopenhauer introduces the idea of the subject-dependence of all objects, an idea he first imbibed from Fichte's lectures of 1811 and 1812 in Berlin but reformulated, with the proposition that the subject is "that which knows all things and is known by none." In the opening passage of the book, Schopenhauer describes the mind-dependence of all representations with the words "he does not know a sun and an earth, but only an eye that sees a sun, a hand that feels an earth" (WWR1, 3). Maurice Mandelbaum has taken this diction to indicate the "physiological orientation" Schopenhauer's epistemology had from the start, given that it makes reference to eyes seeing and hands touching (52). Christopher Janaway takes the phrase as an illustration of Schopenhauer's "inadequate" espousal of Kantian idealism against subsequent idealists like Fichte and Schelling who both held that the "Absolute" was the full knowledge of both object and subject (119). These formulations however appear to be paraphrases of passages read from the *Bṛhadāraṅyaka Upaniṣad*, which speak of the self as "the unseen seer, the unheard hearer, the uncognized cognizer, the unthought thinker."[5] The knowledge of the self cannot be accomplished if one seeks to "get behind," as it were, the perceptual and cognitive process, since the putative "agent" of this process itself cannot be objectified. We cannot then know ourselves as knowers, but, Schopenhauer will uncover, we can know ourselves immediately as willers. The subject-object correlativity thesis, often thematized with passages taken from the *Upaniṣads* and Vedāntic exegesis, sets up one of the major problems which for Schopenhauer necessitates an inquiry that goes beyond epistemology and into metaphysics.

It is Schopenhauer's appropriation of *māyā* that provides other crucial keys for understanding his undertaking of a metaphysical inquiry. The fact that all things appear in time, for example, ensures that all things will be "fleeting and empty," "relative." This leads to a metaphysical view that "in essence is old":

> In it Heraclitus lamented the eternal flux of things; Plato spoke with contempt of its object as that which for ever becomes, but never is; Spinoza called it mere accident of the sole substance that alone is and endures; Kant opposed to the thing-in-itself that which is known as mere phenomenon; finally the ancient wisdom of the Indians declares that "it is *māyā*, the veil of deception, which covers the eyes of mortals, and causes them to see a world of which one cannot say either that it is or that it is

> not; for it is like a dream, like the sunshine on the sand which the traveler from a distance takes to be water, or like the piece of rope on the ground which he regards as a snake." (These similes are repeatedly found in innumerable passages of the *Vedas* and *Puranas*.) But what all these meant, and that of which they speak, is nothing else but what we are now considering, namely the world as representation subordinated to the principle of sufficient reason. (WWR1, 7–8)

The problem presented to us by the nature of representations is that they are impermanent, insubstantial, imperfectly known, as Heraclitus, Plato, Spinoza and Kant have taught us. But they are also "deceptive," "like a dream," characteristics "ancient Indian wisdom" calls *māyā*. The mode of givenness in representations leaves us with experience in which objects present themselves to us as ungrounded, incorrigibly relative, as it were, and hence as not quite real. Schopenhauer takes up this motif again in the following section, in which he considers whether there is any way to distinguish epistemologically the dream from waking life, which in turn leads to the question of whether life as a whole may nor be a dream, a question he finds in Pindar, Shakespeare, and in India. "The *Vedas* and *Puranas* know no better simile for the whole knowledge of the actual world, called by them the web of *māyā*, than the dream, and they use none more frequently" (WWR1, 17).

The problem of *māyā* is taken by Schopenhauer to be the age-old problem of metaphysics, the relationship between what appears and what is real. But it gives this fundamental problem of metaphysics as traditionally conceived in the West a new twist. In the opening pages of his appendix to the first volume of *The World as Will and Representation*, his "Criticism of the Kantian Philosophy," he writes:

> Kant's separation of the phenomenon from the thing-in-itself propounded, quite originally and in an entirely new way the same truth found from a new aspect and on a new path, which Plato untiringly repeats and generally expresses in his language as follows: "This world that

> appears to the senses has no true being, but only a ceaseless becoming; it is, and it also is not; and its comprehension is not so much a knowledge as an illusion.... The same truth, although presented quite differently, is also a principle teaching of the *Vedas* and *Puranas,* namely the doctrine of *Maya,* by which is understood nothing but what Kant calls the phenomenon as opposed to the thing-in-itself. For the work of *Maya* is stated to be precisely this visible world in which we are, a magic effect called into being, an unstable and inconstant illusion without substance, comparable to the optical illusion and the dream, a veil enveloping human consciousness, a something of which it is equally false and equally true to say that it is and that it is not. Now Kant not only expressed the same doctrine in an entirely new and original way, but made it a proved and incontestable truth through the most calm and dispassionate presentation. Plato and the Indians, on the other hand, had based their contentions merely on a universal perception of the world; they produced them as a direct utterance of their consciousness, and presented them mythically and poetically rather than philosophically and distinctly." (WWR1, 419)

Obviously unaware of the centuries of systematic commentaries of Advaita Vedāntins on the relationship between knowledge, perception and ignorance, the last of which was construed as *māyā,* Schopenhauer takes *māyā* in its "mythical presentation" by the "*Vedas* and *Purānas,*" the latter of which he actually knew very little and spoke of them elliptically under the exegetical authority of the *Upaniṣads*. Nonetheless, the basic effectiveness of *māyā* is to be distinguished from the "metaphysical riddle" explicated by Plato and Kant. Metaphysics does not merely consist in the Platonic distinction between the flux and instability of the everyday world and the eternal Ideas, nor only in the Kantian gulf that separates empirical perceptions conditioned by the subject from things as they are in themselves.[6] In addition to these, *māyā,* "illusion" (*Wahn, Schein*) is that power of cognition and reason whereby we take this phenomenal and insubstantial world of our experience to be real and independent of our own being.

> All previous Western philosophers had imagined that these laws according to which all phenomena are connected to one another, and all of which-time and space as well as causality and inference—I comprehend under the expression the principle of sufficient reason, were absolute laws conditioned by nothing at all, *aeternae veritates*, that the world itself existed only in consequence of and in conformity with them, and that under their guidance the whole riddle of the world must therefore be capable of solution. The assumptions made for this purpose, which Kant criticizes under the name of the Ideas of reason (*Vernunft*), really served only to raise the mere phenomenon, the work of *Maya*, the shadow-world of Plato, to the one highest reality, to put it in the place of the innermost and true essence of things, and thus to render the real knowledge thereof impossible, in a word, to send the dreamers still more soundly to sleep. (WWR1, 420)

Strictly speaking, it is not possible to attribute a falsification thesis of any kind to Plato or Kant, despite the fact that Schopenhauer, who at times uses the *Upaniṣads* as a hermeneutic device through which to read them, does. Phenomena are for Plato imperfect "copies" of the eternal Ideas, their imperfection lying in their temporality and the incomplete way in which they manifest their requisite Idea.[7] This incompleteness and imperfection does not itself amount to a falsification theory. To extend the principles of phenomena to things in themselves was for Kant certainly fallacious, but this is far from saying that phenomena falsify the thing in itself. This would by Kant's own assessment be impossible to assert, since to prove such falsification, the thing in itself must be knowable, which for him it is not.[8] For Schopenhauer, the extension of the principles of reason to the objects of experience serves not only as the ground for their objectivity, but is also the reason that we take these objects to be real and independent of the knowing subject. This is the basic paradox of Schopenhauer's epistemology, which necessitates the particular inquiry into metaphysics he undertakes. For reasons we shall clarify in more detail in the present chapter, representations provide the objectivity of everything given in experience, they provide all the conditions whereby objects are known, they attribute reality to those objects of experience. At the same time, those very representations leave the subject of knowledge, the knower, forever hidden and unknown. The conditions representations supply which give experienced content objectivity ensure that the object in question will be experienced as fleeting, insubstantial, almost phantom-like, giving us the impression that the reality attributed by the representation to itself is empty and fabricated. Representational knowledge, Schopenhauer will surmise, is unsatisfactory, for it offers us knowledge of the world on the one hand and deprives us of it on the other, it simultaneously posits that the world of our experience is self-subsistently real, and makes it impossible for us to have confidence in such an attribution. This fundamentally paradoxical nature of representation forces us to ask what Schopenhauer conceives to be the proper question of metaphysics, namely "is the world anything besides representation?" Upon the discovery that the answer to the above question is affirmative, and what the world is besides representation turns out to be a timeless and unified will, it is explicated how representations are not only paradoxical, but out and out falsifications of what the world is in essence. The notion of *māyā,* appropriated by Schopenhauer from the Indian philosophical tradition, is explicated in his representation theory as a falsification thesis, which provides one of the fundamental justifications Schopenhauer gives for an entry into metaphysics, and the metaphysics in turn shows how epistemological falsification objectifies the unitary and timeless essence of the world as a differentiated, temporal world of heterogeneous things and persons.[9]

We have in these two sections shown that pre-systematic Indian philosophical thought, particularly some motifs and concepts from the *Upaniṣads*, did have a positive influence on Schopenhauer's systematic philosophy. He admits his indebtedness to the Indian tradition, and actively imports its terminology into his representation theory, which leads him to find one of the most important keys to justifying an inquiry into metaphysics. The result of Schopenhauer's appropriation of the notion of *māyā* into his epistemology is a theory of falsification, which plays a central role in Schopenhauer's system. We now turn to the detailed examination of this theory of falsification in the context of Schopenhauer's epistemology.

3.2 FALSIFICATION AND THE NATURE OF REPRESENTATION

In the first volume of *The World as Will and Representation*, Schopenhauer devotes the entirety of the first book and the first third of the second book to the demonstration of how representations are not only inadequate means through which to know the world, but also that representations falsify the world's true being. The project that this self-styled "main work" of Schopenhauer undertakes is an interpretation of the world. "The present philosophy," Schopenhauer says of his system, "by no means attempts to say *whence* or *for what purpose* the world exists, but merely *what* the world is" (WWR1, 82). "The world" is what philosophy accounts for through the systematic relation of concepts (WWR1, 82–3). Representational knowledge, for other philosophers, gives as complete and exhaustive an account of what the world is as can be hoped for. Schopenhauer fundamentally disagrees with this, and comes to the conclusion that what the world is cannot be given a thoroughgoing interpretation through representational knowledge alone, but also must be explicated in terms of what he shall call will. There are basically three reasons why critical philosophy comes to the conclusion that representations, and an explanation of what constitutes them, cannot bear full witness to what the world is. Representational knowledge is after all limited; while it is the condition whereby in the strict sense anything can become as object for us, it also by its very nature conditions that knowledge in such a way that certain things about what is known, and about the knower who apprehends the known, are either thoroughly relative and groundless, or totally hidden. Representational knowledge, being incomplete, cannot occupy a standpoint outside of its limited modes of knowing, and thus cannot complete an explication of the world, cannot in fact even assure us that it is not all merely dreamt. Furthermore, by attributing a self-subsistent reality to objects it constructs, representational knowledge deceives us about the nature of those objects, for upon critical reflection it can be found that the objects of representational knowledge cannot have any such self-subsistent reality independent of the machinery of knowledge. We shall now enter in detail into Schopenhauer's arguments for the conclusion that representational knowledge is an insufficient and deceptive medium in giving an interpretation of the world, necessitating for him a metaphysical inquiry that purports to give such an interpretation.

3.2.1 Objects, Subjects and the Limits of Knowledge

As mentioned in the previous chapter, one of the first and most permanent elements in Schopenhauer's epistemology, the subject-object correlativity thesis, was initially conceived during his attendance at the lectures of Fichte in Berlin.[10] Schopenhauer believed that one of the major distinctions between his own philosophy and those of his contemporaries was that, instead of taking as its starting point an inquiry into whether representations were produced by objects, as in realism, or by subjects, as in idealism, his thought began from the representation itself (WWR1, 25; 34). The most basic form of any given representation is the presence of a known content and a knower who apprehends that content. This is announced as early as the 1813 dissertation, *On the Fourfold Root of the Principle of Sufficient Reason*.

> Our knowing consciousness, appearing as outer and inner sensibility (receptivity), as understanding and as faculty of reason (*Vernunft*), is divisible into subject and object, and contains nothing else. To be object for the subject and to be our representation or mental picture are the same thing. All our representations are objects of the subject, and all objects of the subject are our representations. Now it is found that all our representations

> stand to one another in a natural and regular connexion (*sic*) that in form is determinable *A PRIORI*. By virtue of this connexion, nothing existing by itself and independent, and also nothing single and detached, can become an object for us. (FR 41–2)

The first distinctive feature to note about this definition of representations is that it is, at least in part, asserted as an alternative to Kant's notion of the "transcendental unity of apperception." In his *Critique of Pure Reason*, Kant had attempted to account for the possession of knowledge by a subject with the maxim: "It must be possible for the 'I think' to accompany all my representations, for otherwise something would be represented in me which . . . at least would be nothing to me" (152–3). Schopenhauer recognizes in this maxim a kind of correlativity thesis, for Kant introduces it to account for the experiential fact that "the abiding and unchanging 'I' (pure apperception) forms the correlate of all my representations in so far as it is to be at all possible that we should become conscious of them" (146). But Schopenhauer believed there were many serious problems in the way Kant formulated his apperception maxim. In the first place, Schopenhauer thought that there could be no separation between two cognitions such that the first was perceptive and the second apperceptive. It is not possible, he thought, to separate the objective content of representations from the fact that this content is known to someone even in reflection, and so the separation of the cognition "this is known" from the cognition "this is known to me" can only be the result of the most meaningless abstraction (FR 208–9). This is relevant in that he thought that the formulation as Kant gave it was logically odd, for to say that "it must be possible for the 'I think' to accompany all my representations" offered "a problematical-apodictic enunciation . . . a proposition taking away with one hand what it gives with the other" (WWR1, 451). That something must be possible could not amount, for Schopenhauer, to asserting that it was true all the time, and therefore could not serve as a basis upon which a unitary subject's apprehension of all its cognitions could be established.[11] In addition, the maxim seemed to imply to Schopenhauer that Kant equated perceiving with thinking, an implication Schopenhauer believed to be philosophically disastrous, for it obscured the separations between the epistemological faculties Schopenhauer thought it so important to maintain (WWR1, 451).[12] Through his thesis of the subject-object correlativity in representations, Schopenhauer believed he had resolved these issues. His thesis offered a clear definition of consciousness as representational knowledge, as necessarily involving apprehension, and as proving that the subject-object complex of every state of consciousness was an analytic truth *a priori*.[13]

But besides fixing the grounds for knowledge, the subject-object correlativity thesis also more firmly established what precisely subjects and objects were, in Schopenhauer's mind, than Kant had. As the definition above stipulates, "objects" can be referred to as nothing but "representations" for a knowing consciousness. Kant had obfuscated this problem by making distinctions between "objects of representations" (*Gegenstände der Vorstellungen*) which affect sensation, the "transcendental object" which is an object of categorial thought, the representation or appearance, and the thing in itself (WWR1, 442–5). This confusion is "the source of all Kant's errors," for it ensured that Kant would require for his epistemology things outside the mind which produce sensations, appearances which are causally unrelated to those things but are constructed by the cognitive apparatus, and empty objects of thought which are required in order to make experience conceivable to us. Schopenhauer decides that this problem can be solved by making "object" and "representation" interchangeable terms (FR 59; WWR1, 3; 444). Objects as representations then are not distinguishable in kind, but rather in terms of form. For Schopenhauer, as we saw in the last chapter, there are four forms of representations which are correlates of the four different "roots of the principle of sufficient reason," which serve as subjective grounds for knowledge. The are objects of intuition, constructed through the application of time, space and causality to the "sense data" which affect the body, that is to say, intuitive objects are creations of the intellect (*Verstand*) (FR 45–8).[14] There are abstract objects, concepts, which are created by the isolation of certain empirical qualities of intuitive objects effected for the purposes of thinking by reason (FR 145-7; WWR1, 40–1).[15] The third class of objects consists of the "pure, *a priori* intuitions of time and apace" according to which all other representations are supposed to be organized (FR 194-5; WWR1, 6–7). The final class of object is "the immediate object of the inner sense, the subject of willing, which is object for the knowing subject" (FR 207). To know oneself as a willing being is the objective correlate of self-consciousness, for it is not the "I think," for Schopenhauer, that unites all representations in one consciousness, but rather the subject of willing, and so the unity of the subject of knowing with the subject of willing is for once "immediately," though inexplicably "given" (FR 211). In *The World as Will and Representation*, this final notion will be fundamentally revised, in that will in this "main work" of Schopenhauer is no longer, and can no longer be an object, for it falls outside the province of the principle of sufficient reason and is given in an "entirely different way" from representations (WWR1, 102). Our objective experience is exhausted by representations that bear a rule-governed, and hence relative relation to other representations. The "being" or "existence" of these "objects" of our knowledge extends no further than the spatial, temporal and causal relation they exhibit toward one another, and those relations themselves are supposedly all subjectively constituted. The objects of our knowledge do not appear to us by virtue of some power they themselves exert over us; that is to say, their appearance is not caused by anything or anyone, but rather is merely an appearance "for" beings in whom the conditions of appearance reside. This means that objective experience is completely relative, completely subjective, and as such is utterly "groundless."

> I maintain that the principle of sufficient reason is the common expression of all these forms of the object of which we are a priori conscious. . . . I have shown in detail how every possible object is subordinate to it, that is to say, stands in a necessary relation to other objects. . . . This extends so far that the entire existence of all objects, in so far as they are objects, representations, and nothing else, is traced back completely to this necessary relation

> of theirs to one another, consists only in that relation, and hence is entirely relative. (WWR1, 6)

Another important point in equating the terms "object" and "representation" is that it confines knowledge to the subjective determination of appearances through rules of combination and connection that are strictly epistemological. Objective knowledge is here limited to representations and the merely epistemological principles which govern their combination.

> Object and representation are the same thing. . . . The demand for the existence of the object outside the representation of the subject, and also for the real being of the actual thing . . . has no meaning at all. . . . All causality is only in the understanding and for the understanding. The entire actual, i.e., active, world is therefore always conditioned as such by the understanding, and without this it is nothing. We must absolutely deny to the dogmatist the reality of the external world when he declares this to be its independence from the subject. The whole world of objects is and remains representation, and is for this reason wholly and for ever conditioned by the subject; in other words, it has transcendental ideality. (WWR1, 14–15)

And:

> The whole of empirical perception remains throughout on a *subjective* foundation, as a mere occurrence in us, and nothing entirely different from and independent of it can be brought in as a *thing in itself*, or shown to be a necessary assumption. Empirical perception actually is and remains our mere representation; it is the world as representation. (WWR1, 436)

Commentators in recent decades have shown some dissatisfaction with Schopenhauer's limitation of knowledge to subjective representation. Patrick Gardiner has written that the subject-object correlativity thesis "provides no insight into the logical character of the concept of knowledge itself," for it "seems merely to reflect in a dramatized 'material' mode the grammatical structure of sentences in which claims to knowledge are normally made" (82). Using a propositional distinction first introduced by Rudolf Carnap, Gardiner is saying that Schopenhauer is reifying the "subject" and "object" of knowledge in a "material" sense by merely observing that sentences which express knowledge have a grammatical "subject-object" structure, as in "I know this."[16] This however provides no insight into what knowledge actually may be.[17] Christopher Janaway has objected that, while the correlativity thesis was meant to straighten out inconsistencies in Kant, and also to defeat skepticism in an idealist fashion by removing any conceivable barrier between objects and subjects, it in no way argumentationally established that objects are only representations of consciousness and nothing else (79, 154). Whatever the force of these objections, and they do indeed seem to carry some considerable weight, Schopenhauer's correlativity thesis is an attempt to say something meaningful about the character of knowledge, albeit only by way of definition and not explication. First, knowledge is according to this account always intentional, always of some objective content. Second, the objective content of cognitions is transcendentally ideal, it is appearance that is ordered and constructed according to epistemological and not ontological principles. Third, there can be nothing that warrants the supposition that in knowing "objects," representations, we know anything about the things "outside of the mind" as they may be in themselves, for all of the qualities which make them familiar to us are supplied by the structure of our own cognitive apparatus. Fourth, no objects of our consciousness are known according to any determination intrinsic to those objects themselves, but rather all representations are spatially, temporally and causally relative to one another. The import of this final point that has implications for the falsification thesis is that no object as representation is knowable as a "thing in itself," for as a representation each object can only come to be a thing in a dependent and relative relation to all other representations and to the representing subject.

That these objects or representations are subject-dependent or "mind dependent" is, according to John Atwell, "the fundamental tenet of Schopenhauer's epistemological or transcendental idealism" (34).[18] Indeed, Schopenhauer repeats innumerable times that all objects are only such insofar as they are representations for a knowing subject. But, as we have seen above, the subject is the "unknown" side of the subject-object complex, for none of the principles which determine objects can apply to the subject of knowledge, cannot objectify it.

> The world as representation . . . has two essential, necessary and inseparable halves. The one half is the object, whose forms are space and time, and through these plurality. But the other half, the subject, does not lie in space and time, for it is whole and undivided in every representing being. Hence a single one of these beings with the object completes the world as representation, just as fully as the millions that exist. And if that single one were to disappear, then the world as representation would no longer exist. Therefore these halves are inseparable even in thought, for each of the two has meaning and existence only through and for the other; each exists with the other and vanishes with it. They limit each other immediately; where the object begins, the subject ceases. The common or reciprocal nature of this limitation is seen in the very fact that the essential, and hence universal forms of every object, namely space, time and causality, can be found and fully known, starting from the subject, even without the knowledge of the object itself, that is to say, in Kant's language, they reside *a priori* in our consciousness. To have discovered this is one of Kant's chief merits, and it is a very great one. (WWR1, 5-6)

There is much that is highly ambiguous in this passage. It is not clear for instance what Schopenhauer means by saying that the subject and object "limit each other" in such a way that "when the object begins, the subject ends." In his dissertation, Schopenhauer had claimed that one of the advantages of the subject-object correlativity thesis was that it made the metaphysical debate between realists and idealists somewhat superfluous, since according to the thesis, "it is immaterial whether I say that objects have such and such special and inherent determinations, or that the subject knows in such and such ways. It is immaterial whether I say objects are divisible into such and such classes, or that such and such different powers of knowledge are peculiar to the subject" (FR 209–10). So why suddenly change tracks now and say knowledge of the subject is somehow primary? How can it be said that the critical philosopher could discover the *a priori* forms of knowledge "starting from the subject, even without the knowledge of the object itself," since transcendental philosophy purports to be a method for discovering what makes the kinds of experience we have possible? But even if Schopenhauer had stuck to the line he took in his dissertation, *The Foufold* Root, and maintained that the subject and object "have meaning and existence" only through one another lends some credence to Gardiner's objection, cited above, that the subject and object in Schopenhauer are reifications of a "material mode" of propositions about knowledge claims. As we have seen, Schopenhauer's commentators are mostly justified in wondering how well his formulation of subject-object correlativity clarifies the logical character of knowledge.

As Schopenhauer conceives it, however, the fundamental problem posed to knowledge by the subject is that it is itself unknowable, for it does not lie inside the bounds of space and time and hence cannot become an object for any cognition. As we have seen above, Schopenhauer frequently uses allusions to the *Bṛhadāraṅyaka Upaniṣad* to illustrate this point, saying that the individual "does not know a sun and an earth but only an eye that sees a sun, a hand that feels an earth," and further, the subject is "that which knows all things and is known by none . . . the supporter of the world, the universal condition of all that appears" (WWR1, 3; 5). Christopher Janaway again has serious doubts about this. Though we may be able to concede to Schopenhauer that, logically, all experiences need an experiencer, this in no way implies that this experiencer, the transcendental subject, is completely unknowable (Janaway 119). While the subject may not be an object of "acquaintance," that is, I may not know (*erkenne*) the subject, I can know of (*weiss*) the subject as an object of thought, as a fact of experience, and so it makes no sense for Schopenhauer to claim that one cannot know that one knows (Janaway 121–2).[19] It is certainly the case that, if we accept Schopenhauer's own account, we know lots of things about the subject; we know that it is unitary, unbound by space, time and causality, though it applies these to all intuitive perceptions and as such is the condition of all objective experience.

But these objections do not exactly capture Schopenhauer's point about what sorts of limits subject-object correlativity imposes upon representational knowledge. These limits are limits on our ability to "ground" representational knowledge, to find an ultimate "basis" for our knowledge claims. The subject of knowledge is, as we have seen above, also "groundless," for it, like the thing in itself, lies outside the province of the principle of sufficient reason.[20] But say we were, on Schopenahuer's behalf, to ontologically reduce the subject to nothing more than the workings of the principles of sufficient reason. According to Schopenhauer, every objective representation, be it an intuition, a concept, even a motivation, has a ground in one of the principles of sufficient reason, it falls into one of the four "roots" of sufficient reason depending upon what form the representation takes. But when we attempt to justify our knowledge of the principle of sufficient reason itself, we again reach a dead end, we cannot bear witness to what the principles of reason, the *a priori* rules that govern experience, are themselves based upon.

> Two things are absolutely inexplicable, in other words do not lead back to the relation expressed by the principle of sufficient reason. The first of these is the principle of sufficient reason itself in all its four forms, because it is the principle of explanation, which has meaning only in reference to it; the second is that which is not reached by this principle, but from which arises that original thing in all phenomena; it is the thing-in-itself; knowledge of which is in no wise subject to the principle of sufficient reason. (WWR1, 81)

It is this very groundlessness of the subject-object complex which constitutes representations that first initiates, according to Schopenhauer, a pondering about metaphysics, a pondering that is undertaken in a quest for the "inner nature of the world."

> We start neither from the object nor from the subject, but from the *representation*, as the first fact of consciousness. The first, essential, fundamental form of this is the division into object and subject; again the form of the object is the principle of sufficient reason in its different aspects. Each of these rules has its own class of representations.... The complete and universal relativity of the world as representation according to its most general form (subject and object) as well as to the form that is subordinate thereto (principle of sufficient reason) suggests to us, as we have said, that we look for the inner nature of the world in quite another aspect of it which is *entirely different from the representation*. (WWR1, 34)

Any knowledge which is ungrounded is for Schopenhauer by definition insufficient. What we have discovered in finding out that the world of objective knowledge is based upon the groundless principle of sufficient reason and the groundless subject is that knowledge according to representation is incorrigibly limited. To know the world only as representation is in effect not to know the world at all, or at best to know it incompletely from only one aspect, for representational knowledge is ultimately baseless. It then prompts the first instance of the fundamental metaphysical question as Schopenhauer conceives it, namely "what is this world of perception besides being my representation" (WWR1, 18)? As John Atwell has pointed out, this question becomes the most poignant when it is turned back upon the self:

> Notice how one would be wondering: Is the world exhausted by the subject-object knowing relationship? Is the world nothing more than a world of knowledge, consisting of two interdependent halves? Is representation or knowledge all there is? More poignantly, am *I* nothing more than a knowing subject, on the one hand, and

> merely a representation or perceived object on the other? Schopenhauer's answer is no. I suggest therefore that with the correlative conception of the representation there is a natural tendency to wonder about the "something else," the "other than representation," particularly with regard to oneself. And if to wonder about this is to initiate a metaphysical inquiry, then the very notion of the world as representation tends to prompt that inquiry. In short, if the world as representation is merely the world as knower and known, and if the human being feels a natural reluctance to restrict the world to mere knowledge—which Schopenhauer no doubt believes—and if to wonder what "more" the world is to raise a metaphysical inquiry, then the very idea of the world as representation does naturally lead into metaphysics. (*Character* 51–2)

There is no question then that for Schopenhauer, the very limitations in which representational knowledge finds itself may first prompt a metaphysical question; "is the world nothing besides representation, am I nothing besides representation?" But prompting a metaphysical inquiry and justifying it are two different things. One could simply remain skeptical about the matter in an early Humean or Kantian fashion and hold that we do not know the world or the self as they may be in themselves, but only as they appear. In fact, in his dissertation, Schopenhauer explicitly critiqued the notion of the "thing in itself" precisely because it could not be accounted for by the principle of sufficient reason, could not be "grounded," and therefore fell outside the bounds of legitimate philosophical inquiry (FR 233–4). He had espoused the thesis of subject-object correlativity ever since his days as Fichte's student in Berlin from 1811 to 1812, and in fact had rejected Fichte's and Schelling's metaphysics of the "absolute ego" for the very reason that he thought the ego could never be its own object. By the time he writes his self-styled "main work," *The World as Will and Representation* in 1818, Schopenhauer adds other considerations of representationalism to its limitations which justify for him a metaphysical inquiry, and to these we now turn.

3.2.2 Representation and the Standpoint of Knowledge

In presenting the epistemological falsification thesis of Schopenhauer's philosophy, it is important to understand those passages in which he speaks about illusion. In the strict sense, there is an important distinction to be made between illusion and falsification. To fall prey to an illusion is to perceive, think or have some sort of awareness of a thing which is not there, or at least not there at the time or place in which one believes oneself to be aware of it.[21] That is to say, illusion is a mistake concerning the existence of a thing, or a particular instance of its existence. Falsification, on the other hand, is an error not about the particular existence of something at a certain place or time, not a false assessment of a certain characteristic that a thing may or may not possess, but rather is an error concerning the nature of a thing. Put more simply, an illusion is an error *that* something is, or *that* something is or is not the present case, while falsification is an error about *what* something is, about its nature. An illusion is an incidental perceptual error, while falsification is a conceptual, reflective metaphysical error. So, for instance, to argue that the world as we know it may be illusory is to argue that it may not, in fact, exist, while to argue that the world is falsified by us is to assert that, the world as we normally take it is not what we take it to be. In Schopenhauer's representation theory, we find arguments which are meant to lead one to conclude that, while the world as representation is no illusion, though in some ways comparable thereto, the manner in which it is given in representation deprives us of the possibility of knowing its "inner nature," in fact falsifies what the nature of the world is. We turn to these arguments in this and the next section.

In one of the opening sections of *The World as Will and Representation*, Schopenhauer claims that "the controversy about the reality of the external world," a controversy in which realistic or idealistic dogmatism is opposed to skepticism, is "foolish" (WWR1, 13). Realists, he maintains, try to establish the external world's existence by showing how the external object causally affects the subject's knowledge of it. Idealists, in the manner of

Berkeley and Fichte, attempt to establish that the subject causally produces the object. Both of these views are rebuked by skepticism, which drives a wedge between subject and object such that no real knowledge of the object can be possessed by the subject. While this account of these strands of philosophy must be conceded to be superficial, Schopenhauer constructs it in order to represent his own philosophical system as providing a solution to the age-old dilemma of the eternal world posed by these schools. There is, Schopenhauer posits, no causal relationship between subjects and objects, there is only a causal relationship between objects; but these objects are themselves representations, and as such, are known to a subject, and hence there is no gap for skepticism to exploit between subjects and objects. The implications of this solution is that, while representations are themselves the unity of the subject-object complex, objects, or the contents of knowledge are nothing but representations. Lest this implication would bother one with the worry that there is something illusory about the contents of representations, Schopenhauer is quick to point out:

> The whole world of objects is and remains representation, and is for that reason wholly and for ever conditioned by the subject; in other words, it has transcendental ideality. But it is not on that account falsehood (*Lüge*) or illusion (*Schein*); it presents itself as what it is, as representation, and indeed as a series of representations whose common bond is the principle of sufficient reason. As such it is intelligible to the healthy understanding, even according to its innermost meaning, and to the understanding it speaks a perfectly clear language. To dispute about its reality (*Wirklichkeit*) can occur only to a mind perverted by over-subtle sophistry; such disputing always occurs through an incorrect application of the principle of sufficient reason. (WWR1, 15)

What Schopenhauer is defending here is the phenomenological givenness of the world as representation to any subject of knowledge. Now this may at first seem problematic, for when an object or cognitive content is "given" to us, it seems at first to be "given" as what it is, that is, as the content, a table, chair, stone or whatever. But Schopenhauer asserts that things are given as representations, that is, their representationhood must be given along with their content. This is not at all clear, for if it were true, critical philosophy itself would seem superfluous, for we ought then to know immediately in any case that objects are representations, vitiating the need for any epistemological controversy. One can nevertheless maintain, and Schopenhauer seems to take the view, that representationhood is given along with every cognitive content, but in our normal attention to the content, the mode of givenness as representation is obfuscated, only to be recovered by reflective, transcendental philosophy. The representationhood of objects is perhaps particularly easy for Schopenhauer to deduce. He consistently associates the "being" of objects with their "acting" (*wirken*), their "effectiveness" upon one another in the causal nexus, and consequently, "reality" is to be understood more as "actuality" (*Wirklichkeit*), and cause and effect lies only within the province of representation, is in fact the correlate of the understanding (WWR1, 8–9).

But, Schopenhauer stresses, the fact that representations, mental contents, are "only representations" should not be construed as leading to the inference that they are "falsehood" (*Lüge*) or "illusion" (*Schein*). Now it is certainly the case, as we shall see below, that Schopenhauer believes representations are ultimately falsehoods, but they are not falsehoods "on this account" (*nicht dieserwegen*), that is, not because they are transcendentally ideal. Transcendental idealism shows that representations are constituted by the understanding according to space, time and causality *a priori* for the knowing consciousness of every subject. That means that intersubjectivity is provided for by the theory of transcendental idealism, and what is consistently and reliably intersubjective cannot be a mere illusion. This point is very important, for it has been the habit among commentators throughout the century to suppose that, by his constant insistence that "Kant's phenomena and the *Maya* of the Indians" were the same, Schopenhauer confuses idealism with illusionism. Janaway accuses

Schopenhauer of conflating transcendental ideality with illusion, and struggles to separate this conflation into the two assertions that, while the world of representation is real, it is ephemeral and therefore not the "highest" reality (167–70). Atwell similarly accuses Schopenhauer of running together the idea that causal explanations of the world are unsatisfactory with that of each object of representation being finite, ever passing away, and as a result Schopenhauer demands a perspective of the world from which its essential nature can be seen as eternal (*Character* 75–6). Fredrick Copleston concluded that, since for Schopenhauer all knowledge is phenomenal and illusory, then my knowledge of subject-object correlativity is illusory; so is my knowledge of the will, for in order to know it, one has to objectify it; and so, all knowledge being illusory, the entire Schopenhauerian system negates itself (69).[22] The supposed conflation of idealism with illusionism was perhaps best articulated by Hans Naegelsbach in 1927, in a passage that was cited in the first chapter and is worth quoting here again in full.

> Schopenhauer reinterprets Kantian idealism and Indian illusionism by setting them into a correlative relationship. Kantian idealism in connection with the doctrine of the thing-in-itself grows into an idealistic tension between world and self, with the knowing subject on one side and the thing-in-itself on the other, such that both reality and knowledge become problems for a critical epistemology.... In India the transparent consciousness of the highest knowledge becomes one with final reality. In the certain knowledge of unity, plurality becomes an illusion. Illusionism is charged with the most powerful religious sentiment carrying the metaphysical idea of the reality of all things, which of course later on strives toward a philosophical justification through a theory of knowledge. The Indian's knowledge . . . becomes for him the highest reality, while on the other side, no illusionism exists for Kant which originates in the consciousness of universal oneness. Schopenhauer attempts a synthesis between Kantianism and Indian wisdom without himself being clear about the origin of Kantian idealism within a

> strictly epistemological inquiry nor about the origin of illusionism in a fundamental religious and metaphysical conviction.... Both standpoints, originating from entirely different relationships, run next to one another in Schopenhauer and intersect in a wholly contradictory fashion. (Naegelsbach 151–2)

There can be no question that Schopenhauer attempted a synthesis between Kantian and classical Indian thought in a relatively problematic fashion, but as we see here, this synthesis does not involve a conflation of illusionism and transcendental idealism. The forgoing commentators fail to make a distinction between illusionism and falsification, a distinction which needs to be understood not merely for a proper interpretation of Schopenhauer, but for comprehending some Vedānta thought as well.[23] To argue that representations are illusions would be tantamount, for Schopenhauer to arguing that representations are not there, that the do not really present what they present, and for him such a confusion would be absurd.

But if representations and illusions are not akin phenomenologically due to the transcendental ideality of the former, then on what account are they akin? The answer comes when one considers what Schopenhauer believed to be the ultimate challenge of skepticism.

> The question of the reality of the external world ... has yet another origin, quite different from the purely speculative one so far mentioned, a really empirical origin, although the question is always raised from a speculative point of view, and in this form has a much more comprehensible meaning than it had in the former. We have dreams; may not the whole of life be a dream? Or more exactly; is there a sure criterion for distinguishing between dream and reality, between phantasms and real objects? The plea that what is dreamt has less vividness and distinctness than real perception has, is not worth considering at all, for no one has held the two up to comparison; only the *recollection* of the dream could be compared with the present reality. Kant answers the ques-

> tion as follows: "The connection of the representations among themselves according to the law of causality distinguishes life from the dream." But even in the dream every single thing is connected according to the principle of sufficient reason in all its forms.... To institute an inquiry in accordance with this criterion as to whether something was dreamt or really took place would, however, be very difficult, and often impossible. For we are by no means in a position to follow link by link between any experienced event and the present moment; yet we do not on that account declare that it is dreamt. (WWR1, 16)

It has been suggested on many occasions, Schopenhauer notes, that the whole of life is a long dream; this suggestion has been offered by "the *Vedas* and *Puranas*" with their doctrine of *māyā*, by Shakespeare, Plato, Pindar and Calderón (WWR1, 17). No solution to the question about whether all life is not a dream is completely satisfactory, not even, according to Schopenhauer, his own, "the wholly empirical criterion of waking up" (WWR1, 17). The formal similarity between waking experience and dream cannot be denied philosophically, he says, for both are experiences of objects, both connect representations through causal relation, and neither can give a comprehensive causal account of their respective states of awareness (Ibid.).[24] While we can and most of the time do in fact make distinctions within our representational experience between dreams and waking life based upon the empirical fact of waking up, this criterion does not suffice to distinguish the contents of these states as representations, and so does not really distinguish sharply between waking life and dream in any critically meaningful way, for both kinds of experience are representational. In fact, phenomenologically, dream and waking life are similar in more respects than the ones outlined above. In both, objects are ephemeral, fleeting, do not reveal their nature to the subject, even if in the course of those experiences one is fully convinced of the veracity and reality of everything in them.

> Thus, although individual dreams are marked off from real life by the fact that they do not fit into the continuity of experience that runs constantly through life, and waking up indicates this difference, yet that very continuity of experience belongs to real life as its form, and the dream can likewise point to a continuity in itself. Now if we assume a standpoint of judgment external to both, we find no distinct difference in their nature, and are forced to concede to the poets that life is a long dream. (WWR1, 18)

Now the most important point is introduced in the final sentence of the above reflection, namely, the possibility of assuming a "standpoint" external to representational knowledge, that is, external to both waking and dream. There must be a standpoint, according to Schopenhauer, from which we can make certain judgments about representational knowledge as a whole, just as we can determine what a dream is once we have stepped outside of the standpoint occupied in that dream. What we realize, however, when we have transcended the standpoint of representational knowledge is just that there can be little or no critical distinction made between dreaming and waking life, and in this respect "life is a long dream."

It is with this latter point that we return to the discussion initiated at the beginning of this section on the distinction between falsification and illusion. Schopenhauer could not maintain that dream and waking life are the same based on the idea that both are illusory, for that would amount to arguing that the objects of representation were in some sense not there, that is, not presented as such. But Schopenhauer does not hold this view: he maintains that the world "presents itself as what it is, as representation" and presents itself as such "to the healthy understanding," for which representations "speak a perfectly clear language." The objects of experience are there, they are there because of rule-governed causal laws that are grounded in transcendental subjectivity, and in that sense, they are perfectly real (*wirklich*). As representations, objects are not falsified. To attempt to prove that representations are illusions is, in a sense, for Schopenhauer to attempt to argue that the world is not presented to the knowing consciousness as representation; but since we all as knowing consciousnesses inhabit a represented workd, those attempts Schopenhauer has judged to be "foolish." On the other hand, representations do falsify the world's nature, that is, while the world as we know it is there, representations present it to us in an incomplete, insufficient, indirect, misleading and ultimately "unsatisfying" way on their own. What is required to determine this is another "standpoint" from which the world's true nature is available to us. In fact, this other standpoint is one Schopenhauer thinks is available to us all the time, and it is from this standpoint that we find the world as representation is revealed as in itself unsatisfactory. Before turning to this other standpoint in the next chapter, we must consider the first respect in which Schopenhauer believes representations falsify the true nature of the world to the knowing consciousness.

3.2.3 Realism and the Fabrication of Knowledge

As mentioned above, Schopenhauer places his own philosophy into a historiographic typology of philosophies which he calls "Dogmatism" and "Skepticism." Skepticism cannot hold good since no gap can be exploited between the subject and object such that the former cannot know the latter, for Schopenhauer's correlativity of subject and object is the fundamental form of any representation. "Dogmatism" can be divided into two camps, idealism and "materialism." Schopenhauer devotes some time opposing the idealism of Fichte, Schelling and Hegel, accusing them of elevating to an ultimate philosophical status the really empty notion of the "Absolute" by proving that the subject produces all objects out of itself (WWR1, 25–6; 33–4). He spends more time however, addressing the position of "materialism," the epistemological basis of which is realism. There are several kinds of materialist philosophy, according to Schopenhauer. The first kind deals with the "real world," represented by "Thales and the Ionians, Democritus, Epicurius, Giordano Bruno and the French materialists." There is a materialism based on the doctrine of substance, as was presented by "Spinoza and the Eleatics." There is a materialism which holds that matter behaves according to mathematical laws, such as is found in "the Pythagoreans and the Chinese philosophy of the *I Ching*." Finally there was the theological materialism of the "Scholastics" which posited that the material world was the creation of God *ex nihilo* (WWR1, 26–7). It is the first form of materialism that is most worthy of consideration, for Schopenhauer believes that it is the "most consistent" doctrine in this family of thought (WWR1, 27). It seems also that he addresses it in the most detail because it is closest to the "natural attitude" of accepting the world of objects as self-subsistently real and independent of the knowing subject. According to the methodical extension of this realistic natural attitude, namely natural science, it was the world of independently existing objects which first brought the subject, the human being and her mind, into being. Schopenhauer's criticisms of the realistic position, which is the basis of scientific materialism, reveal much about his own epistemology, and particularly that facet of it with which we are here primarily concerned, the thesis of falsification.

Schopenhauer has three major objections to realistic materialism. The first is that it passes over the fact that all things in the world are not mind independent, as the realist normally holds them to be, but on the contrary, it is only on the basis of being known that anything can be said about objects or the world at all. " 'No object without subject,' " he writes, "is the principle that renders all materialism for ever impossible" (Schopenhauer, WWR1, 29–30).

> The objective method can be developed most consistently and carried furthest when it appears as materialism proper. It regards matter, and with it time and space, as existing absolutely, and passes over the relation to the subject in which alone all this exists. Further, it lays hold of the law of causality as the guiding line on which it tries to progress, taking it to be a self-existent order or arrangement of things, *veritas aeterna,* and consequently passing over the understanding, in which and for which alone causality is. It tries to find the first and simplest

> state of matter, and then to develop all the others from it, ascending from mere mechanism to chemistry, to polarity, to the vegetable and animal kingdoms. Supposing this were successful, the last link of the chain would be animal sensibility, that is to say, knowledge, which, in consequence, would then appear as a mere modification of matter, a state of matter produced by causality. Now if we had followed materialism thus far with clear notions, then, having reached its highest point, we should experience a sudden fit of the inextinguishable laughter of the Olympians. As though waking from a dream, we should all at once become aware that its final result, produced so laboriously, namely knowledge, was already presupposed. (WWR1, 27)

Schopenhauer does not infrequently speak of the result of the enlightenment of knowledge brought on by transcendental philosophy in its critique of realism to be like "waking from a dream." A citation from the beginning of this chapter found Schopenhauer suggesting that the assumptions of realism "really served only to raise the mere phenomenon, the work of *Maya*, the shadow-world of Plato, to the one highest reality, to put it in the place of the innermost and true essence of things, and thus to render the real knowledge thereof impossible, in a word, to send the dreamers still more soundly to sleep" (WWR1, 420). In realism, it is thought the existence of independent things in the world causally brings about a knowledge event, and is the ultimate court of appeal for validating true knowledge. Critical philosophy, the basis of Schopenhauer's version of which is the subject-object correlativity thesis, reveals to us that the conditions for perception in the proper sense and for all objective knowledge lie within the subject.

The second major objection Schopenhauer has to realism is that it leads to a scientific account of the world that is fundamentally insufficient. The goals of science are twofold; first science attempts to explain comprehensively the workings of nature through an explication of natural forces and the objective laws which govern those forces and different kinds of matter in their interactions. Secondly, science in the end would justify the realism and materialism which it first set out with as premises, it would prove through its comprehensive explication of nature that the world is objectively real and, in the end, composed only of matter and force. Neither of these overarching goals can be attained, according to Schopenhauer. Science does not in the first place explain the relationships of mind-independent entities to one another, but merely uncovers the relationships of representations to one another according to the principle of sufficient reason, and this does not reveal to us the "inner nature" of the world at all, an "inner nature" science would have us believe is matter. Science, and the materialism and realism which serve as theoretical supports of it, is involved in a manifest self-conceit, in illegitimately extending the principles of sufficient reason beyond their province of governing representations, and into the world "outside the mind."[25] The fact that scientific explanations only amount to discovering how mere representations relate to one another lands it into a relativism and against an epistemological barrier to the world as it may be in itself which frustrates the scientific goals outlined above.

> At bottom, the aim and ideal of all natural science is a materialism wholly carried into effect. That we here recognize this as obviously impossible confirms another truth . . . that all science in the real sense, by which I understand systematic knowledge under the guidance of the principle of sufficient reason, can never reach a final goal or give an entirely satisfactory explanation. It never aims at the inner nature of the world; it can never get beyond the representation; on the contrary, it really tells us nothing more than the relation of one representation to another. (WWR1, 28)

At the beginning of the second book of *The World as Will and Representation,* Schopenhauer offers an ironic characterization of this predicament of science in the way of justifying a metaphysical inquiry. What science promises us is what Schopenhauer calls an "etiological" explanation of the world, insisting that the relations of things to one another are based on "natural forces," but it leaves unexplained what precisely those natural forces are. The natural forces of science are therefore what Schopenhauer dubs "*qualitas occulta*" or "occult qualities." This leaves us not knowing in the end what things themselves really may be, like a man at a party who is introduced to strangers only by what relation they have to one another.

> The philosophical investigator must always feel in regard to the complete etiology of the whole of nature like a man who, without knowing how, is brought into a company quite unknown to him, each member of which in turn presents to him another as his friend and cousin, and thus makes them sufficiently acquainted. The man himself, however, while assuring eachperson introduced of his pleasure at meeting him, always has on his lips the question: "But how the deuce do I stand to the whole company?" (WWR1, 98)

Some commentators have argued that Schopenhauer's characterization of science is flawed. Patrick Gardiner has contended that Schopenhauer's view of science is simplistic and truncated, for the natural and human sciences do not merely attempt to describe the world or prove that the interpretive premises of those sciences were accurate. Rather, science attempts to render the relationships of natural phenomena predictable, and its high level theories and their periodic revision also constitute arguments not merely about the relationships between things, but about what kinds of things there are and what sorts of interpretive models are best employed in their investigation (Gardiner 131–2).[26] Paradigm shifts in science are not merely about revising theories of natural law, but about determining what kinds of entities there are between which natural laws obtain; some even question whether putative natural laws are laws at all. And so, to use Schopenhauer's own metaphor against him, the sciences do not merely introduce the philosophical investigator to strangers at a party, but take the investigator to altogether different parties at which altogether different kinds of company are celebrating altogether different kinds of relationships. Nonetheless, it is possible to concede Gardiner's qualification in this regard without the force of Schopenhauer's argument being lost. For instance, one could argue on the transcendental idealist's behalf that, while paradigms of science do indeed change concerning what kinds of phenomena are held to be there and what kinds of relationships obtain between them, the basic structural aims of scientific theorizing remain the same, aims directed toward descriptions of what there is, how what is behaves with respect to everything else, and how we can know the rules of that behavior and make use of them. The fact that there are many different kinds of science is one Schopenhauer well recognized, after all, for he held each science to be beholden to a different form of the principle of sufficient reason (FR 230–1). That there are occasional paradigm shifts in the sciences only shows that sciences is open to corrections of the methods it happens to be using in the investigation of the world, not that the basic structural aims themselves undergo any fundamental revisions. Insofar as science purports or aims to be such a description of the "real world," it will always be deficient, for it is confined, according to Schopenhauer, to merely telling us what relationships representations bear to one another. "We can never get at the inner nature of things *from without*. However much we investigate, we obtain nothing but images and names" (WWR1, 99). The second predicament of trying to know the world exhaustively through representations, "from without," Schopenhauer illustrates by employing another phrase from the *Upaniṣadic* and Vedāntic traditions, that we can only know the "images and names" (*nāma-rupa*) of things, never their "inner nature."

Finally, the pretensions of realism are not only inadequate means to know the world because they ignore that all knowledge is subjectively constituted. They are not merely incomplete in the sense that they only reveal to us how representations relate to one another and nothing beyond that. Realism is an epistemological pretense that actively falsifies the true nature of things.

> In truth, everything objective is already conditioned as such in manifold ways by the knowing subject with the

> forms of its knowledge, and pre-supposes these forms; consequently it wholly disappears when the subject is thought away. Materialism is therefore the attempt to explain what is directly given to us from what is indirectly given. Everything objective, extended, active and hence everything material is regarded by materialism as so solid a basis for its explanations that a reduction to this (especially if it should ultimately result in thrust and counter-thrust) can leave nothing to be desired. All this is something that is given only very indirectly, and is therefore only relatively present, for it has passed through the machinery and fabrication of the brain, and hence has entered the forms of time, space and causality, by virtue of which it is first of all presented as extended in space and operating in time. (WWR1, 28)

That is to say, the objective content of representations is not only one "pole" of the representation, nor is it only an incomplete and "indirect" mediation of objective content, but is the result of the "fabrication of the brain." The problematic relationship "the brain" bears to the intellect, the understanding and reason of a subject's cognitive apparatus, will be dealt with more when we come to consider the second edition of the *World as Will and Representation*, for there a comprehensive theory of what I shall call "brain idealism" exists which is on the whole very different from the epistemological theory of the first volume we are now considering. Schopenhauer had made some extended reference to the role of the brain and the eyes in the perceptual process in his first two published works, *On the Fourfold Root of the Principle of Sufficient Reason* and *On Vision and Colors*. But the idea that the brain's interpretive powers, in these works identified with the understanding, were fabrications is nowhere to be found in their respective original editions. According to these early works, the brain's activity in interpreting the data mediated to it by sensation consisted in things such as inverting the visual image so it could be seen right-side-up, making a single object out of an optically doubly sensed content, estimating the extension of external bodies, determining their distance, all conclusions Schopenhauer drew from his early studies of physiology at Göttingen (FR 86–97, 237–55). These descriptions become systematized and amended in the second volume of *The World as Will and Representation*, as we shall have further occasion to see in the following chapter. The major point in the present context of the first volume is that the realistic materialist does not merely make some elementary or facile theoretical mistake in considering the objective content of representations to be external to her. The most that the realistic materialist can be accused of is not sufficiently reflecting theoretically on the indirect and subjectively constituted manner in which representations appear as external objects. Not only the realist, but all people normally take the objective content of representations to be mind-independent because the cognitive forms of space, time and causality present things as if they are extended in space and operating in time in the first place. Schopenhauer is unique among the Idealists for labeling the *a priori* forms of sensibility and intellect not merely "conditions of knowledge," but also "fabrications." It is in the very nature of representations themselves to falsify, for they present the world to the knowing subject according to principles which in no way can be said to belong to anything but the cognitive apparatus of the subject itself. Representations, that is, present to the knowing consciousness objects which appear as extended, temporal and heterogeneous, but only because the forms of knowledge which exist within the knowing subject are precisely space, time and causality.

Now such an argument does not at first appear to be extraordinarily divergent from "orthodox" Kantianism, for Kant too held that the forms of intuition were subjective and could not be predicated of things in themselves. In fact, one might even suspect the Kantian position of being deficient, for while it may establish that certain forms of perceptibility lie within the subject, things as they are in themselves might still possess the properties of spatiality, temporality and behave according to causes. This is the so-called argument for the "neglected alternative." As Christopher Janaway has pointed out partly in defense of Schopenhauer, it is hard to see how Kant could have conceived of anything such as "objects of sensation" that affect the subject, or given his "Refutation of Idealism" against Berkeley had he not at least to a certain degree conceded this possibility, or in the alternative was flatly inconsistent (63, 68)? John Atwell was skeptical that Schopenhauer ever subscribed to a Kantian epistemology in the first volume of *World as Will as Representation,* and if he did, such a position could not justify a metaphysical inquiry at all (*Character* 41–4). Given Schopenhauer's own admitted preoccupation with Kant in his early works, along with the clear idealism he espouses there, Atwell's speculations on this matter are problematic. Schopenhauer, Janaway maintains, was "scrupulous" about avoiding these problems because he had the kind of metaphysical doctrine he had, a doctrine which stipulated that plurality did not obtain for the inner nature of the world, the unitary will, whereas Kant's trenchant skepticism precluded the possibility that his epistemology could have any such falsification theory built into it (68). Indeed, as has been mentioned several times in the previous chapter and this one, Schopenhauer is able to subscribe to a falsification thesis because he believes that knowledge of the world's inner nature is possible. The theory of falsification, how the mind "fabricates" the true nature of the world through its representational activities, will be further fleshed out in the next chapter when we turn to the metaphysics of will.

What has concerned us in the present chapter has been Schopenhauer's appropriation of the notion of *māyā* as well as other terminology from the classical *Upaniṣads* and their early eighteenth and nineteenth century Western readers into his representation theory, an appropriation which played a key role in justifying a metaphysical inquiry. Schopenhauer's representation theory led to a metaphysical inquiry for three basic reasons. First, representations, though they are constituted the correlativity of subject and object sought after by the post Kantian Idealists, leaves the objective content of the representation a mere epistemological product, and the subject of knowledge itself hidden and unknown, "the eye that sees but is seen by none." Second, representations account for all experience of an objective kind, and the implication of this is that waking life is not distinguishable from dream, leaving us to wonder if the world was anything besides representation. Finally, representations can be found to falsify the world, presenting objective content as external, temporal and mind-independent which is actually given all of these determinations by the subject. All of these reasons bear the stamp, as we have seen, not of Kant, the Idealists or Plato only, but also of *Upaniṣadic* and Vedāntic thought. These reasons cumulatively compel one, for Schopenhauer, into seeking the nature of the world upon a path "entirely different" from the representation.

> What now prompts us to make enquires is that we are not satisfied with knowing that we have representations, that they are such and such, and that they are connected according to this or that law, whose general expression is always the principle of sufficient reason. We want to know the significance of those representations; we ask whether this world is nothing more than representation. In that case, it would inevitably pass by us like an empty dream, or a ghostly vision not worth out consideration. Or we ask whether it is something else, something in addition, and if so what that something is. This much is certain, namely that this something about which we are inquiring must be by its whole nature completely and fundamentally different from the representation, and so the forms and laws of the representation must be wholly foreign to it. (WWR1, 98–9)

There have been several attempts in recent years to understand Schopenhauer's metaphysics, most of them assuming that Schopenhauer's system was basically consistent from the first to the second editions of *The World as Will and Representation* that were separated by twenty-five years. Julian Young has maintained that what Schopenhauer was attempting with his metaphysics was an explication of the natural, and not the transcendent world, and as this could not be completed with the "third person" account natural science is partial to, it would have to be finished through the kind of "first person" account Schopenhauer envisions his philosophy of will provides, a philosophy which makes the world "significant" for us (50–4). John Atwell relied a great deal on Young's thesis, and added that Schopenhauer believes accounts of natural forces which the sciences pursue must be supplemented by an account of the most immediate force, the will, and its manifestation in the individual, the intelligible character (*Character* 60–4). There is much Schopenhauer says to suggests that these analyses are valid, though while reserving a more detailed discussion of this problem for the next chapter, it does not seem that this perspective applies well to the first formulation of Schopenhauer's system in 1818. It is very doubtful whether Schopenhauer wished his philosophy initially to be a supplement to natural science, although this ambition did grow from the early 1830's on and flowered in the two late editions of Schopenhauer's main work, published in 1844 and 1859 respectively. In the passage above, Schopenhauer concludes that what gives representations "significance" is not accounted for by representations themselves, for if we consider the world as representation in isolation, it would seem to us like an "empty dream, a ghostly vision not worth our consideration." Scientific knowledge is representational knowledge systematically governed by the principle of sufficient reason, and in searching for the "inner nature" of the world, what the world is "in itself," Schopenhauer says that representational knowledge is not adequate to the search. To discover the "inner nature" of the world, we must follow a path "entirely different" from the one laid out by representation. The principles of sufficient reason are "totally foreign" to this path. It is highly dubious then whether it can be said that Schopenhauer's metaphysics as conceived in the first edition of *The World as Will and Representation* is meant to "ground" the natural forces of science, for these natural forces are according to the early Schopenhauer not explanations of the world of representation at all, they are rather "occult qualities." Representations give an incomplete, ungrounded, ephemeral, and falsified picture of the true inner nature of the world, and hence are to us totally unsatisfactory. The only way we can make the judgment that they are unsatisfactory however is that we can know the "inner nature" of the world, we can occupy a standpoint outside of representational knowledge and its limitations in order to make such judgments. The falsification thesis has thus played a vital role in justifying the inquiry into metaphysics, and its full explication through that metaphysics will be the subject of the next chapter.

CHAPTER 4

Māyā, Plurality and the Metaphysics of Will

4.1 MĀYĀ, *WILL AND FALSIFICATION*

In the previous chapter, we saw how Schopenhauer incorporated various ideas and vocabulary from the pre-systematic Indian philosophical tradition, in particular the notion of *māyā,* into his representation theory as a thesis of falsification. This thesis was one of the keys to Schopenhauer's justification of a metaphysical inquiry in the first edition of *The World as Will and Representation*. But as has been mentioned several times in Chapter 2, Schopenhauer wished his philosophy to be at once metaphysics and ethics, and his understanding of *māyā* during the compilation of his *Nachlass* from 1814 to 1818 gave it epistemological, metaphysical, axiological and ethical significance.[1] As the metaphysics of will is certainly the centerpiece of the Schopenhauerian system, the "single thought," as Schopenhauer called it, that tied the whole system together, the theory of falsification receives its fullest explication through that metaphysics, an explication which will later give it ethical and axiological weight in the system.

In the present chapter, we will examine this centerpiece of Schopenhauer's philosophy, the metaphysics of will, and specifically how the falsification thesis relates to it. Schopenhauer based the need for a metaphysical inquiry on where we had been left by representation knowledge, a mode of knowing judged to be an incomplete, ungrounded and even fabricated picture of "the world" of our experience, a picture that in the end could not even be critically distinguished from the kind of experience we have when we dream. It is an immediate experience of our own will, Schopenhauer believes, which grounds us in the world, makes the world of representation significant to us, and upon reflection, reveals the will as the undifferentiated, timeless "thing in itself" of all beings. In this light, the representational faculty, in revealing the world to us through what Schopenhauer calls the "*principium individuationis*" or the "principle of individuation," falsifies the world's true nature, and so becomes synonymous with "the veil of *māyā*, the veil of deception." We shall take a look not only at how Schopenhauer justifies these conclusions, but also at the problems of his argumentation for the metaphysics of will.

One of the most important reasons Schopenhauer's falsification thesis and the role it plays in his metaphysics has been overlooked by commentators of recent decades has been that, believing Schopenhauer's system to have been more or less stable throughout the fifty years of his productive career, they have interpreted that system in the light of the second and third editions of *The World as Will and Representation*, published in 1844 and 1859. Beginning in the early 1830's and especially in his 1836 book *On the Will in Nature*, Schopenhauer began attempts to make his metaphysics of will consistent with the most recent findings in natural science, particularly biology, physiology and astronomy. While his interest in the natural sciences was constant from his first days as a university student in Göttingen in 1809, there had not been so much an attempt to make the metaphysics of will consistent with science in the 1819 edition of *The World as Will and Representation* as an effort to ground the natural sciences, all products of representational knowledge, in that metaphysics. By the time Schopenhauer had completed the supplementary essays that comprised the second volume of the second edition in the mid-1840's, his epistemology had taken on a much more physiological character, and was transformed into what I shall call "brain idealism." The metaphysics of will was greatly impacted by this, and in fact, the will was pulled from the status of "complete otherness" from the knowledge of representation in the second and third editions into representational knowledge, for the will must be, according to Schopenhauer at least, apparent insofar as it becomes known in and through the sensible form of time. That is to say, Schopenhauer's epistemology becomes much more naturalized and his ontology markedly more realist. With these transformations, Schopenhauer's falsification thesis is broadened in its purview to include the knowledge of will, and yet at the same time it becomes diminished in theoretical importance to Schopenhauer, receiving itself a naturalized and psychologized interpretation. In the second part of the present chapter, we will undertake a detailed examination of these transformations of Schopenhauer's epistemology, ontology and falsification thesis, and also assess the somewhat unstable ontology to which they gave rise.

4.1.1 Satisfaction, Significance and Groundedness

Schopenhauer's project in his *opus* was to give a philosophical account of what he called "the world." It is at first sight very curious to attempt to give an account of the "world," for the question immediately comes to mind, "about which world are we speaking, what precisely is the world of which we are supposed to give an account?" Schopenhauer's use of "world" in this context seems to be relatively equivalent to that which presents itself to "human experience." Schopenhauer, in his first edition of *The World as Will and Representation*, believes that metaphysics is possible because he holds a conception of metaphysics that diverges from Kant's. Kant had believed that metaphysics offered itself as "the science of that which lies beyond the possibility of all experience," and since the *a priori* forms of our understanding and reason do not allow us to investigate this realm of the "beyond" legitimately, metaphysics was for Kant impossible (Schopenhauer, WWR1, 426). For Schopenhauer, this conception of metaphysics was only one of Kant's unchecked assumptions, for while "the world and our own existence present themselves to us necessarily as a riddle . . . the solution must be sought only in what we can arrive at . . . by means of inferences from universal principles *a priori*" (WWR1, 427). That is to say, "the task of metaphysics is not to pass over experience in which the world exists, but to understand it thoroughly, since inner and outer experience are certainly the principle source of all knowledge" (WWR1, 428). To understand the world is to understand experience, and to understand experience is to understand those principles which make experience possible. It is of course still open to question, even given this revised definition of metaphysics, as to whether or not those principles which make experience possible are indeed universal, and if they are not, how many worlds are indeed open to "metaphysical" inquiry. With respect to this problem, as John Atwell has pointed out, Schopenhauer is certainly an "essentialist," for his project involves an interpretation of experience according to which experience can be explicated through representation and will, with will being the primary element (*Character* 119). Atwell emphasizes the point that the "knowledge" to be gained about "the world," since it cannot be accounted for through representation, is "interpretive . . . more of a matter of decipherment than a manner of acquaintance" (*Character* 119). This echoes a claim found in Schopenhauer's most recent biographer, Rüdiger Safransky, that Schopenhauer's philosophy of will is not so much an "explanation" of the world as it is a "hermeneutics of existence" (213–4).

However, as we saw in the last chapter, Schopenhauer does not believe an adequate account of "the world" of human experience can be given through representational knowledge alone. Representations leave us with an incomplete picture of the world, for while each objective content of our experience can be grounded in the principle of sufficient reason, that principle itself has no ground of its own, since it is not viable to extend the grounding principles of reason in anything outside itself. Though it is perfectly clear, to Schopenhauer, that all objective content is known to a subject, that subject of knowledge itself is forever hidden and unknown, "the eye that sees but is not seen." All objective content is relative, and at least critically indistinguishable from the kind of experience we have in dreams, for both waking life and dream are intentional and representational in more or less the same senses. Furthermore, representational knowledge, by presenting objective content as external, temporal and causally independent of the knowing subject, must falsify that content, for it receives its form from the subject, and not from itself as the representation testifies. This leaves us, according to Schopenhauer, "unsatisfied," at least unsatisfied enough to ask the fundamental question of metaphysics, namely, what the world is besides representation.

> What now prompts us to make enquiries is that we are not satisfied with knowing that we have representations, that they are such and such, and that they are connected according to this or that law, whose general expression is always the principle of sufficient reason. We want to know the significance of those representations; we ask whether this world is nothing more than representation. In that case, it would inevitably pass by us like an empty dream, or a ghostly vision not worth out consideration. Or we ask whether it is something else, something in addition, and if so what that something is. This much is certain, namely that this something about which we are inquiring must be by its whole nature completely and fundamentally different from the representation, and so the forms and laws of the representation must be wholly foreign to it. (WWR1, 98–9)

We are not satisfied, or it is not enough for us ("*es uns nicht genügt*") to know the world as representation, for if that is all it is, it would "pass us by like an empty dream . . . not worthy of our consideration." It is an obvious fact of experience, however, that the world has significance or meaning (*Bedeutung*) for us, it catches our interest and engrosses our attention (Schopenhauer, WWR1, 95). What can account for the fact then that the world is not "meaningless" or as Atwell better translates it, "uninformative" (*nichtsagend*) (55)? A contemporary response would perhaps be that the meaning of experience, what allows us to interpret it in the first place, is language. If Schopenhauer's philosophy is indeed a "hermeneutics of existence," as Safransky calls it, shouldn't it have language at its center? Schopenhauer, while he did have a high regard for language, considered it to be intimately related to conceptual knowledge, and so at best was not that which originally enables us to be interested in the world, but was rather the mere medium through which that interest was expressed.[2] Schopenhauer insists that what makes the world as representation "meaningful" does not derive from the representation itself.

> If the objects appearing in these forms are not to be empty phantoms, but are to have a meaning, they must point to something, must be the expression of something, which is not, like themselves, object, representation, something existing merely relatively, merely for a subject. On the contrary, they must point to something that exists without such dependence on something that stands over against it as its essential condition, and on its forms, in other words, must point to something that is *not a representation*, but a *thing in itself*. (WWR1, 119–20)

Now an important question must be asked. It was mentioned in the preceding chapter that the prompting of a metaphysical inquiry and the justification of it are two different things, and even if we are compelled by Schopenhauer's account of representations, as well as his belief that the paradoxicality, insubstantiality and incompleteness of representational knowledge may naturally lead us to ask if the world is nothing more than representation, it may still not be clear that a metaphysical inquiry is warranted. This suspicion, that a metaphysical inquiry is not warranted, may be strengthened when one takes into consideration Schopenhauer's criterion for such an inquiry, namely the "dissatisfaction" Schopenhauer assumes we feel at the "meaninglessness" of representational knowledge. What kind of criterion is this? Why should it be compulsory upon us to undertake a metaphysical investigation because Schopenhauer finds the limitations and conditions by which human knowledge is bounded "unsatisfying" and "unmeaningful?" One may in fact object that "satisfaction" is often found in our experience precisely in discovering the right connections between representations, for learning about the relationships that obtain between things adds to the meaningfulness of our experience. Schopenhauer would perhaps respond that this dissatisfaction with representational knowledge is not merely a subjective impression of his own, but something that follows from two things. First, as we have seen, Schopenhauer considers reasons which justify certain phenomena sufficient when those phenomena can be exhaustively explained by those reasons. The explanation to which we have recourse for any matter of representational knowledge is the principle of sufficient reason, but this principle, as we have seen, along with the subject of knowledge are themselves both groundless. Science may, Schopenhauer says, provide explanations of the relationships of all given representations to one another, but it can do so only in terms of unexplained and inexplicable "natural forces." Epistemology may offer us a model of how knowledge is constituted, but must leave the constituting principles of knowledge themselves unfounded. "What," Schopenhauer rhetorically asks of this predicament, "is the use of explanations that ultimately lead back to something just as unknown as the first problem was" (WWR1, 125)? The first kind of "grounding" Schopenhauer is seeking then is a theoretical one, and he assumes, in the manner of Descartes, that any explanation which is not exhaustively intelligible cannot be satisfactory. Atwell has pointed out, if Schopenhauer's argument for metaphysics is merely that, since appearances are dependent on one another and the whole series of representations depends on the subject, the world of appearances and the subject must depend on a thing in itself, that argument is invalid (74–6). This, however, is not exactly the argument Schopenhauer is offering; it is rather that any claim to knowledge must be grounded in something in order to be intelligible, and that since the claim representational knowledge makes to know the world can itself be found to be ultimately ungrounded, our knowledge of the world, if we possess it, must be grounded in something else. It is certainly possible to question the premises of such an argument, that we can know the "inner nature" of the world and that every knowledge must be "ultimately" grounded in order to be intelligible, but the argument itself is not invalid.

The second kind of grounding to which Schopenhauer makes reference is more of an ontological than an epistemological one. He believes that representational knowledge is not satisfying to us, because we can know the world is not merely representation, because we ourselves are not merely representation, but are the thing in itself. We have, according to Schopenhauer, a "double knowledge" of ourselves, from one aspect, we know ourselves as representation like other representations, and from another aspect we know ourselves "immediately" and in a way "entirely different" from the representation, as will. Will is what makes the world of representation "interesting," "meaningful" and "significant" to us, it is what roots us in the world of our representational experience and ties us to it. Without will, Schopenhauer believes, representations would be utterly unimportant to us, and so what we are in essence, will, makes the idea that the world is only representation one we cannot accept. We shall go into Schopenhauer's proposed evidence for these views in the next section. It could be asked at any rate what sort of an "argument" this is, for it assumes what Schopenhauer needs to prove in order to justify the inquiry, and at the same time is what that inquiry is supposed to establish. There can be little doubt that a circularity exists here. Whether that circularity is vicious may depend on how successfully the metaphysical arguments are carried out. We now move to the heart of Schopenhauer's metaphysics.

4.1.2 The Knowledge of Will and Representation

Now that the bases have been given for a metaphysical inquiry, it falls to Schopenhauer to determine whether or not we know what he alternatively calls the "inner nature" and the "thing in itself" of the world. We have established thus far that, if such a knowledge is possible, it must be knowledge of an "entirely different" kind than representational knowledge, it must be non-objective, immediate and in need of no further grounding. These are criteria that most commentators have recognized must obtain if Schopenhauer is to prove his metaphysical contentions, and with respect to the first volume of *The World as Will and Repre-*

sentation, they have been singularly unimpressed with Schopenhauer's ability to meet those criteria. One further criterion that will be added here is that the knowledge of the thing in itself must not only be non-objective, immediate and in need of no further grounding, but as meeting all these criteria, it is a kind of knowledge that cannot be falsified, cannot be a kind of knowledge which of its nature brings suspicion on itself. The thing in itself must, in Schopenhauer's estimation, be known incorrigibly. We shall see in this section how Schopenhauer's epistemological falsification thesis played into his arguments about the knowledge of the thing in itself. Most commentators have to a certain degree missed this element of falsification in Schopenhauer's arguments about the knowledge of the thing in itself, and as a result have not assessed those arguments altogether accurately. Schopenhauer's metaphysical arguments about the nature of will and how it is known are notwithstanding not without grave problems, but a consideration of Schopenhauer's falsification thesis does bring a measure of greater clarity to them.

Schopenhauer asserts at the opening of the second book of the first edition of *The World as Will and Representation* that the key to metaphysical knowledge is provided by our own bodies.

> The meaning that I am looking for of the world that stands before me simply as my representation, or the transition from it as mere representation of the knowing subject to whatever it may be besides this, could never be found if the investigator himself were nothing more than the purely knowing subject (a winged cherub without a body). But he himself is rooted in this world; and thus he finds himself in it as an *individual,* in other words, his knowledge, which is the conditional supporter of the whole world as representation, is nevertheless given entirely through the medium of a body. . . . For the purely knowing subject as such, the body is a representation like any other, an object among objects. Its movements and actions are so far known to him in just the same way as the changes of all other objects of perception, and they would be equally strange and incompre-

> hensible to him, if their meaning were not unraveled for him in an entirely different way. (WWR1, 99)

We know all things in the world as representations, and can understand the relationships of those things to one another according to the principle of sufficient reason, though we do not know them as they may be in themselves. But this proposition meets an important qualification when it comes to our knowledge of ourselves. Our knowledge about ourselves is partly accounted for through representation, for the body and its parts are given to us as representations like other objects. But there is a very "immediate" sense in which we experience our own bodies not only as representations, as "moved" or "effected" not merely through objective causes, but through what Schopenhauer decides to uniquely characterize as "will."

> This body is given in two entirely different ways. It is given in intelligent perception as representation, as an object among objects, liable to the laws of these objects. But it is also given in quite a different way, namely as what is known immediately to everyone, and is denoted by the word *will*. Every true act of his will is also at once and inevitably a movement of his body; he cannot actually will the act without at the same time being aware that it appears as a movement of the body. The act of will and the action of the body are not two different states objectively known, connected by the bond of causality; they do not stand in the relation of cause and effect, but are one and the same thing, though given in two entirely different ways, first quite directly, and then in perception for the understanding. The action of the body is nothing but the act of will objectified, i.e., translated into perception. . . . The whole body is nothing but the objectified will, i.e., will that has become representation. (WWR1, 100)

There is nothing that we know more immediately than our own will. Schopenhauer cites a number of reasons for this conclusion. Among these are the facts that we cannot and do not understand the movements of our bodies in a causal fashion only, but in conjunction with what we will. He also makes reference to the "impressions" on the will such as pleasure or pain, which cannot be attributed to the object or the objective body, and are therefore "affections of the will," an argument Berkeley also used.[3] He says that violent movements of passion or emotion are also not objective states, but states of will known immediately. Now what is it that exempts these states of awareness of will from being representational? It would seem from the examples Schopenhauer uses that states of will are only known in conjunction with states of the represented body, and were it not for this conjunction, we could not be aware of will at all.[4] Schopenhauer may have to admit that will is discovered through finding it to be ever-present in conjunction with bodily states objectively known, but he would hasten to add that the immediacy of the knowledge of the will consists in what kind of conjunction obtains in all these bodily states. Objects in representation are related through space, time and causality, and because they are related through these epistemological forms, representations are mediated by them. The knowledge of will is not spatial; for even though it accompanies movements of the body that are spatial, the will occupies no space. The knowledge of will is not temporal; for even though it accompanies bodily movements that take time, willing is common to them all, it is itself never temporally absent from our experiences of ourselves under normal, that is, non-aesthetic, non-ascetic conditions. The knowledge of will is not causal; for although it accompanies bodily states, it cannot be distinguished from them in the objective fashion necessary to identify it as a cause. Now in the way of assessing this argument, while it does have a kind of intuitive appeal, it is probably flatly false when one takes into consideration all of the examples Schopenhauer uses to demonstrate it. While it may be the case that a bodily movement always occurs simultaneously with some sort of internal "volition," this does not render it philosophically nonsensical to speak of such movements of will as causes, and as has been mentioned, in his 1813 dissertation, Schopenhauer had himself called will or motivation at once "immediately an object for the knowing subject" and a kind of "causality seen from within." He also speaks of pain and pleasure as being "immediate affections" of will, and yet it is almost inconceivable to imagine a spaceless pain or an uncaused pleasure. And what of these "violent movements of passion" that Schopenhauer equates with will? Are these violent movements somehow outside of time, for even through they may occur simultaneously with a bodily event, do they still not take time, or have a duration? The merit of Schopenhauer's argument seems to be that we do not in fact know our bodies only as "objects" or "objective content" or as "a thing extended" that behaves according to impetuses we must discover and are not "immediately familiar" with. We do possess, at least in most cases, a familiarity with our bodies and their own states of volition that we do not possess with respect to other "objects." It may be phenomenologically possible to explain certain senses in which my knowledge of my own body and will is distinctly more intimate than knowledge of other bodies and wills. That does not necessarily lead to the conclusion, however, that we know about this will in an "entirely different" way than representationally, for given all the examples Schopenhauer has provided, we can only know about the will through some empirical state that is subject to the *a priori* forms of sensibility in some way or other. This problem leads Schopenhauer to revise his ideas about the knowledge of the will in his later work, and we shall examine this below. Schopenhauer concludes without any basis that, because acts of the will are known "simultaneously" with bodily acts, will is "unmediated" (*unvermittlet*). Perhaps had Schopenhauer maintained that we merely know the will "simultaneously" (*gleichzeitig*) with bodily acts, the claim would have been less problematic, but in that case it would not have achieved what Schopenhauer had wanted of a metaphysics. What he argues instead is that the will is known "unmediated" (*unmittelbar*), that is, apart from the forms of sensibility, space, time and causality, which does allow for a metaphysics of will, but leaves that metaphysics open to almost paralyzing objections.[5]

For his own part, Schopenhauer makes much out of the conclusion that the knowledge of will is unmediated, for it allows him to draw the inference that such unmediated knowledge is precisely what gives us access to the thing in itself. "All representation," he tells us, "be it of whatever kind it may, all object is *phenomenon*. But only the *will* is *thing-in-itself*, as such it is not representation at all, but *toto genera* different therefrom. It is that of which all representation, all object is the phenomenon, the visibility, the *objectivity*. It is the innermost essence, the kernel of every particular thing, and also of the whole" (WWR1, 110). In an explanation of why he has chosen the word "will" to identify the Kantian "thing in itself," Schopenhauer writes:

> Now if this *thing-in-itself* (we will retain the Kantian expression as a standing formula) – which as such is never object; since object is its mere appearance or phenomenon, and not it itself – is to be thought of objectively, then we must borrow its name and concept from an object, from something in some way objectively given, and therefore from one of its phenomena. But in order to serve as a point of explanation, this can be none other than the most complete of all its phenomena, i.e., the most distinct, the most developed, the most directly enlightened by knowledge; but this is precisely man's will. We have to observe, however, that here of course we use only a *denominatio a potiori*, by which the concept of will therefore receives a greater extension than it has hitherto had. . . . The word will, which, like a magic word, is to reveal to us the innermost essence of everything in nature, by no means expresses an unknown quantity, something reached by inferences and syllogisms, but something known absolutely and immediately, and that so well that we know and understand what will is better than anything else, be it what it may. (WWR1, 110–11)

Schopenhaur theoretically prioritizes knowledge that is more immediate, roughly, knowledge which is clearest and in the least need of explication, and this is very much in line with the philosophical debates of the preceding centuries. Empiricists such as Locke and Hume maintained that the most clear and distinct knowledge was afforded by perception as opposed to concepts, while rationalists such as Leibniz had contested that conceptual knowledge was more clear than perception. But one of the basic distinctions between these schools was exactly about what kind of knowledge they considered the clearest. Schopenhauer takes a new departure from this debate, and declares that the clearest and most immediate knowledge we have is not of some objective content, but rather of will. At one point, Schopenhauer even connects this notion of the knowledge of the will, which is supposedly nonrepresentational knowledge on its own, with the theme of what sort of knowledge is most "meaningful" and "significant," and thus metaphysical, to us, when he remarks, "the clearer and more satisfying it is, the less is its purely objective content, or the less reality (*Wirklichkeit*), properly so called, is given to it" (WWR1, 122). And so, as will shows itself to be the most immediate, clearest knowledge we have of ourselves, it provides the key to the "inner nature," the "thing in itself" of "the world as representation." That being understood, it must be admitted that the position is striking for its plain oddity, for it is counterintuitive at best to say that the less intentional any given knowledge happens to be, that is, the less objective content is related to or within it, the more meaningful it is. What exactly could be meaningful about a knowledge that was in no sense relational? From the passage above, however, Schopenhauer believes that will gives us the key to our inner nature and hence is more informative about what we are in essence than any other representation could be. The knowledge of will informs and makes meaningful representational knowledge, in which relations obtain. But even on this point, there is a great deal of dissembling, for will is first equated with the thing in itself, then it is claimed that our label of the thing in itself, which is never an object, has to be borrowed from an extension of the word "will," a concept that is objectively meaningful. But the word will nonetheless does reveal the inner nature of the world to us by naming not an unknown quantity, but by being so immediately and absolutely known. The whole justification of using the word "will" to identify the thing in itself leaves us totally unsure as to whether the will is the closest known relative to the thing in itself, which is never an object, a position Schopenhauer expressly adopts in the second edition of *World as Will and Representation*, or whether the will is the thing in itself become object, the position he advocates in the first edition.

The commentators on Schopenhauer, though at odds on many other fundamentals of the Schopenhauerian system, seem unanimous in the view that the position of the first edition, that the world is the objectification of the will as thing in itself, is untenable. They believe the position of the second volume, which we shall examine in detail below, makes more sense and in one way or another represent it as Schopenhauer's actual metaphysics of will. The idea that the will is the thing in itself as Schopenhauer has formulated it above, is not established by the arguments provided in its support. Frederick Copleston, the Jesuit historian of Western philosophy in his initial research on the Schopenhauerian system, concluded that, in effect, since for Schopenhauer all knowledge properly so called was phenomenal, then the knowledge of will would have to be phenomenal too, would have to make will an object, and thus could not be knowledge of a thing in itself, nullifying the possibility for any metaphysics (64–6). After Copleston, Patrick Gardiner has similarly objected that, if it is the case, as Schopenhauer claims, that we gain knowledge of our will only by observing it in bodily movements or acts, then we learn about it as "spectators," that is, empirically and not immediately, and this undermines the whole thrust of the metaphysics (168). The commentators that followed attempted to show that Schopenhauer's argument that the will was the thing in itself was in one or another of its constructions invalid. D. W. Hamlyn proposed that, even were we to grant Schopenhauer the premises he expressly states, that 1.) all representational knowledge is conditioned, 2.) that we know all bodily actions in an unconditional way, at least in part, then we can conclude that there is an element of action that is non-representationally known (93). But nothing else follows from this argument, neither that the will is the non-representational part of action nor that the will is the thing in itself, and in fact, Schopenhauer merely assumes that everything not a representation is a thing in itself without proving it (Hamlyn 93). Christopher Janaway reasoned that, if the thing in itself were itself never known as such, there would be no way of relating anything to it in a more or less immediate fashion, and while Schopenhauer may be taken to have proven that will is "incorrigibly known, non-inferential, without observation," any other conclusions he draws about it are unwarranted (197). Julian Young, in his advocacy of the idea that Schopenhauer believed that metaphysical knowledge could never be knowledge of the thing in itself, but only of will as its nearest relative, also believed Schopenhauer's characterization of knowledge made the knowledge of a thing in itself impossible (27). Finally, John Atwell, who to a large degree followed the interpretation of Julian Young, held that the most we could get from Schopenhauer's arguments was an immediate knowledge of the will as the "inner nature" of all representations, but not an explication of any "thing in itself" (*Character* 107–9).

The attention that is paid by these commentators to how Schopenhauer could have arrived at his metaphysics through epistemological considerations is certainly correct. But the conclusions of Gardiner, Young and Atwell are more relevant to Schopenhauer's reconceptualization of metaphysics in the second edition of *The World as Will and Representation*, as they consider the later edition to contain a more tenable argument. The early Schopenhauer almost unreservedly considered the knowledge of will to be the knowledge of the thing in itself, and this view was held from the first formulations if this idea in his *Nachlass* of 1814 all the way through his "main work" and to the notebooks of at least 1824.[6] The position of the later metaphysics, that the will itself is actually the most direct appearance of the thing in itself crystallized slowly over the next twenty years. For the present, we address the argument about the possibility of knowing the will as the thing in itself. Hamlyn and Janaway, as noted, believe that Schopenhauer's arguments concerning representation and will can lead us only to the conclusion that we can know will, to use Janaway's words, in an "incorrigible" way, or in Hamlyn's words, in a non-representational fashion. Both of them believe that Schopenhauer's unexamined premises must have been something along the lines that anything known non-representationally must be a thing in itself, and that the will was the thing in itself, though he did nothing to establish these assumptions. What both seem to miss is that Schopenhauer's argument, though it does accept the Kantian distinction between the phenomenon and the thing in itself, assumes in its premises something not about the thing in itself, but about representational knowledge. What it assumes specifically is the idea, explicated in the preceding chapter, that representational knowledge falsifies the world's true nature when left to its own devices. It is very important for Schopenhauer's argument that he establishes that there is one thing, namely our own bodily, "lived" existence of which we have a "double knowledge" (*ein verdoppelte Erkentniss*). We know ourselves, presumably, as we know other representations, in a mediate way.[7] We know our bodies as will "immediately" also. Copleston and Gardiner both claimed that Schopenhauer's argument that the will was the thing in itself was invalid because for Schopenhauer, all knowledge was of the "phenomenon" of "representation," and hence to know will must be to make it phenomenal. Both overlook the so-called "double knowledge" Schopenhauer claims we have of our bodily existence, as representation and as will, and thus overgeneralize Schopenhauer's epistemology. But, if Schopenhauer believes that mediated or representational knowledge is a falsification of the world's true nature by the mere virtue that such knowledge is mediate, and as seen in the last chapter, he certainly believes this, then any knowledge that is "immediate" does not falsify, but reveals the world's true nature. The one thing Schopenhauer does indeed assume upon his redefinition of the Kantian conception of metaphysics, is that the "thing in itself" is really the "inner nature of the world." But Schopenhauer's contention that representational knowledge leaves us with an incomplete, insubstantial and fabricated knowledge of the world because it is a mediation of the world through the forms of sensibility is central to the metaphysical argument he makes here. The argument Schopenhauer has built to establish his metaphysics of will is not the incomplete one Hamlyn construes, but is rather more like the following: 1.) To know the world as representation, and even to know the body as representation, is to know these in a mediated, hence incomplete, indirect and deceptive fashion. 2.) I know my body not merely as representation, but in an immediate way as animated, moved, engrossed in the world, by will. 3.) To know immediately is to know in an entirely different way than to know through representation, because the whole nature of representational knowledge is mediation, and immediate knowledge must be the opposite of this. 4.) Therefore, my immediate knowledge of my will is a complete, direct and unfabricated knowledge. All one needs to do then is accept Schopenhauer's redefinition of metaphysics, the knowledge of the thing in itself is the knowledge of the inner nature of the world, and the argument establishes what Schopenhauer wants it to, namely, that the knowledge of will is a complete and "incorrigible" knowledge of the world's inner nature, the thing in itself.

Now as we have addressed above, this argument is at great pains to convince us of its conclusions about the knowledge of will as being non-representational and immediate in nature. In fact, the argument seems to collapse under the least scrutiny. The purpose of this section has not been to defend the argument as much as to demonstrate how crucial Schopenhauer's falsification thesis is to it. Without the falsification thesis, the argument Schopenhauer offers in the second book of *The World as Will and Representation* fails to establish what he wanted it to. It is not the case, as Hamlyn has suggested, that the unexamined premise Schopenhauer needs to prove in order to complete the argument that the will is the thing in itself goes something like, "everything not a representation is a thing in itself." This would in fact be a nonsensical premise in the context of what Schopenhauer says about representations and "things," as technically according to him every "thing" can only be a representation. The premise Schopenhauer has carried over into the metaphysical argument from his representation theory is that representational knowledge, being incomplete and fabricated, fails to reveal to us the world's true nature. If it is possible for any knowledge to reveal something immediately, that is, complete, clear and unfabricated, then we can trust that such a knowledge is the key to that true nature of things. Immediate knowledge is possible, it is possible of will. Neither Hamlyn nor Janaway contest that Schopenhauer has successfully demonstrated that the knowledge of will is immediate, and if they submit to this, and accept Schopenhauer's reformulation of the thing in itself, Schopenhauer's argument needs nothing more than to show how the world, being one unified and timeless will, appears as representation in the first place, and how we can be sure the will is the thing in itself not merely of my own body, but of all phenomena. We now proceed to these explanations.

4.1.3 Will, Falsification and Plurality

What Schopenhauer now must shed light on is, if the will is the inner nature of the world, if our knowledge of it reveals it as the unitary ground upon which all phenomenal existence is based, then how do we account for representational knowledge in the first place? If the world is, as Schopenhauer suggests, from one aspect will and from another representation, and if will is the true reality of the world that everyone finds as the inner essence of their own being, then how is it that we become so taken up in the world as representation so as to forget, as it were, all about will? Again, the falsification thesis serves as the explanation of how the world as will is experienced as the world as representation.

> The will as thing in itself is quite different from its phenomenon, and is utterly free from all the forms of the phenomenon into which it first passes when it appears, and which therefore concerns only its objectivity, and are foreign to the will itself. Even the most universal form of all representation, that of object for subject, does not concern it, still less the forms that are subordinate to this and collectively have their common expression in the principle of sufficient reason. As we know, time and space belong to this principle, and consequently plurality as well, which exists and has become possible only through them. In this respect, I shall call time and space the *principium individuationis*. . . . For it is only by means of time and space that something which is one and the

> same according to its nature and the concept appears as different, as a plurality of coexistent and successive things. Consequently, time and space are the *principium individuationis*, the subject of so many subtleties and disputes among the Scholastics which are found collected in Suarez. . . . The will as thing-in-itself . . . is free from all *plurality*, although its phenomena in time and space are innumerable. It is itself one, yet not as an object is one, for the unity of an object is known only in contrast to possible plurality . . . but it is one as that which lies outside time and space, outside the *principium individuationis*, that is to say, outside the possibility of plurality. (WWR1, 112–13)

Now on the one hand, the assertion that there can be no multitude of things outside of the *a priori* forms of knowledge looks straightforwardly Kantian. But Schopenhauer believed Kant had fundamentally violated his own principle in this regard by speaking of things which affected sensibility and served as the "grounds" for our intuitions of things (WWR1, 436). What lies outside of space and time, in Schopenhauer's case will, cannot be subject to those principles which govern representations. The principles he has specifically in mind in the present argument are time and space. It will be remembered that Schopenhauer's dissertation had defined these as the third class of objects of the principle of sufficient reason, the objects of "pure intuition" in a Kantian vein. They are, along with the subject-object correlativity of all knowledge, the basis upon which anything can become an "object" for us. "Objects" are in his view only identifiable insofar as the are delineated by spatial boundaries and relations, and are temporal, becoming "present" in a succession of cognitive states. Anything that can become known outside of this epistemological mediation provided by space and time can therefore not be anything but undifferentiated, because it could never become bounded or spatially delineated nor could it ever become "present" in a temporal manner, it could not become an "object." This is one of the reasons Schopenhauer concludes that the will is unitary and exists whole and complete not merely in the knowledge of one's own body, but in all phenomena.

> The plurality of things in space and time that together are the objectivity of the will, does not concern the will, which, in spite of such plurality, remains indivisible. It is not a case of there being a smaller part of will in the stone and a larger part in man, for the relation of part and whole belongs exclusively to space, and has no longer any meaning the moment we have departed from this form of intuition or perception. More or less concern only the phenomenon, that is to say, the visibility, the objectification. (WWR1, 128)

What is particularly relevant for our purposes is that this notion of the *principium individuationis* is responsible for representational experience. The form of space is responsible for making things appear as extended, the form of time makes everything appear as though in succession, and both in concert facilitate the appearance of a world that is independent of the knowing subject and containing different things and persons whose natures seem to be heterogeneous. Considering the discovery that the true, inner nature of the world is an undifferentiated will, it becomes evident that the *principium* presents the world to the knowing consciousness falsely. This is especially clear when we examine the *Nachlass* of 1816, which contain notes dealing with the construction and thematization of Schopenhauer's system. Schopenhauer did indeed take the notion of the *principium individuationis* from the Scholastics, but in the debates of the Scholastics, this principle was bound up with the creation or emanation of the world from God's power or nature. Schopenhauer turns the principle into an epistemological process, and it appears in his notes on ethics in 1816 as synonymous with the notion of *māyā* (MR1, 429, 446–7). The "principle of individuation," is the epistemological mechanism of falsification, and as such, it does the work of *māyā*, it covers over or "veils" the true nature of the world as will.

As in all systems of metaphysics, Schopenhauer makes a fundamental distinction between appearance and reality, and once such a distinction is made, some account is needed as to how the two are related, and how to transcend the appearance in order to gain insight into reality. The notion of *māyā,* appropriated from the Vedāntic philosophical tradition, is the cognitive apparatus through which the world not only appears to the knowing consciousness as representation, but also by virtue of which the "inner nature" of the world is falsified by representation. Only by piercing the veil of *māyā* through an unmediated knowledge of the will can we ascertain the world's, and the self's true essence. Without the "principle of individuation," the world as representation would have no way to appear to consciousness as it does. It is in this light that the theory of falsification is revealed as central to Schopenhauer's system.

4.1.4 Attributing Reality: The Possibility of Metaphysics

What Schopenhauer has so far maintained with respect to the will is that it is known directly and immediately as the true nature of the body and its actions, while apart from this the will is known mediately as representation. We have also seen that Schopenhauer holds that the mechanics of representational knowledge, the forms of intuition of time and space, make the unitary and eternal essence of the world, will, appear as a plurality of heterogeneous objects and individuals. But this may tempt us to infer that the will of the self, or the individual investigator following a Schopenhauerian metaphysical inquiry, is the only essential reality, and that the other representations, objects or individuals the investigator encounters do not share this essential nature, since, as Schopenhauer himself has claimed, one knows only one's own body directly as will and representation, while one knows other things only as representation. Schopenhauer characterizes that kind of inference as leading to "theoretical egoism," and he rejects it.

> Whether the objects known to the individual only as representations are yet, like his own body, phenomena of a will is, as stated in the previous book, the proper mean-

> ing of the question as to the reality of the external world. To deny this is the meaning of *theoretical egoism,* which in this way regards as phantoms all phenomena outside his own will, just as practical egoism does in a practical respect; thus in it a man regards and treats only his own person as a real person, and all others as mere phantoms. Theoretical egoism, of course, can never be refuted by proofs, yet in philosophy it has never been positively used otherwise than as a skeptical sophism, i.e., for the sake of appearance. As a serious conviction, on the other hand, it could be found only in a madhouse; as such it would then need not so much a refutation as a cure. Therefore, we do not go into it any further, but regard it as the last stronghold of skepticism . . . a small frontier fortress. Admittedly, the fortress is impregnable, but the garrison can never sally forth from it, and therefore we can pass it by and leave it in our rear without danger. (WWR1, 104)

The parallelism Schopenhauer suggests here between "theoretical" and "practical" egoism will come back to us in the next chapter, for it is his belief that "theoretical" egoism leads to "practical" egoism, the latter of which is morally reprehensible and is, it will turn out, another of the effects of *māyā*. For the present, Schopenhauer dismisses the position of "theoretical egoism" as more of a disease than an argument, even though, curiously, he concedes that the argument that the self may be the only truly existing being, while all other objects and persons may be mere "phantoms," is logically unassailable. Why such ambivalence about the position, such simultaneous respect for the logic of the argument and derogatory dismissal of its conclusion? Because, according to Schopenhauer's own formulation, the individual's "double knowledge" of herself and "singular" representational knowledge of everything else, makes the question genuinely philosophical. Schopenhauer writes: "Our knowledge, bound always to individuality and having its limitations in this very fact, necessarily means that everyone can *be* only one thing, whereas he can *know* everything else, and it is this very limitation that really creates the need for philosophy" (WWR1, 104).

Contrary to the position of "theoretical egoism," Schopenhauer certainly believes that all phenomena share the same being, namely will. That is, all representations, not merely the representation of the individual's body alone, are will. How does he justify this belief? He proposes to do so by "attributing" or "transferring" the essential reality of the will to all other representations.

> We shall judge all objects, which are not our own body, and therefore are given to our consciousness not in the double way but only as representations, according to the analogy of this body. We shall therefore assume that as, on the one hand, they are representation, just like our body, and are in this respect homogeneous with it, so on the other hand, if we set aside their existence as the subject's representation, what still remains over must be, according to its inner nature, the same as what in ourselves we call will. For what other kind of existence or reality could we attribute to the rest of the material world? From what source could we take the elements out of which we construct such a world? Besides the will and the representation, there is absolutely nothing known or conceivable for us. If we wish to attribute (*beilegen*) the greatest known reality to the material world, which immediately exists only in our representation, then we give it that reality which our own body has for each of us, for in each of us this is the most real of things. . . . We can nowhere find another kind of reality (*Realität*) to attribute to the material world. If therefore, the material world is to be something more than our mere representation, we must say that, besides being the representation, and hence in itself and of its inmost nature, it is what we find immediately in ourselves as will. (WWR1, 105)

A few pages later, Schopenhauer continues his argument about the will as the essential nature of "the world" with the following:

> The reader who with me has gained this conviction, will find that of itself it will become the key to the knowledge of the innermost being of the whole of nature, since he now transfers (*überträgt*) it to all those phenomena that

> are given to him, not like his own phenomenon, both in direct and indirect knowledge, but in the latter solely, and hence merely in a one-sided way, as *representation* alone. He will recognize that same will not only in those phenomena that are quite similar to his own, in men and animals, as their innermost nature, but continued reflection will lead him to recognize the force that shoots and vegetates in the plant, indeed the force by which the crystal is formed, the force that turns that magnet to the North Pole, the force whose shock he encounters from the contact of different metals of different kinds, the force that appears in the elective affinities of matter as repulsion and attraction, separation and union, and finally even gravitation, which acts so powerfully in all matter, pulling the stone to the earth and the earth to the sun, all these he will recognize as different only in the phenomenon, but the same according to their inner nature. (WWR1, 110–11)

There has been some significant disagreement among scholars as to what exactly Schopenhauer's argument here is. He seems to be suggesting that there is some kind of "analogy" between the self and the world such that we can conclude that both are will. But in what does this "analogy" consist, such that we can "attribute" or "transfer" the essential reality of ourselves to the world of phenomena as a whole? D. W. Hamlyn has suggested that the key to this is the insight into "agency" offered by introspection; that is, as we find in the immediate knowledge of will the key to human motive, and because motive is a species of cause, we can infer that the phenomena of representation act causally upon one another due to will (96–8). Hamlyn's suggestion doesn't seem right given the fact that his argument leads him to conclude that causes such as those which condition phenomena are not really believed by Schopenhauer to be different from acts conditioned by will, whereas Schopenhauer says time and time again that will is not a cause (Hamlyn 98). Janaway basically goes along with Hamlyn though, saying that Schopenhauer believes motives are a kind of cause known immediately, and so we can infer that all things have their immediate cause in motives, which are grounded in will (215–16). Both these arguments are very misleading, for the most part because they use Schopenhauer's 1813 dissertation, *On the Fourfold Root of the Principle of Sufficient Reason*, where Schopenhauer calls will an "object for the knowing subject" and a "kind of causality seen from within," as a hermeneutic device through which to interpret the metaphysics of will in *The World as Will and Representation*. But in the latter work, Schopenhauer in no way holds will to be an object: in fact it is because it is not an object of any kind that it does not fall within the principle of sufficient reason in his "main work" and thus cannot be called or considered a cause of any kind. Now it might seem from the second passage cited above that the analogy between bodily actions and other phenomenal actions which allows us to conclude both are essentially grounded in will is this observation of "force" in both. Schopenhauer frequently attempts to illustrate some kinds of empirical confirmation of the will as the essential nature of all phenomena by pointing to the forces behind natural actions, as when he speaks of the "irresistible impulse" with which water flows downward, the "persistence and determination" of magnets, the "vehemence" of electric currents, the "striving" in the formation of crystals, the "pressure" exerted by gravity (WWR1, 118). Were we to count these illustrations as argumentative proofs, we might have to agree with Georg Lukács that Schopenhauer's philosophy amounts to nothing more than an amateurish anthropomorphization of nature, which for Lukács was an element of a "bourgeois irrationalist mysticism" (89).

John Atwell has captured much more precisely Schopenhauer's argument. Atwell has noted that, if he is offering as an argument some kind of analogy between the knowledge of the self and the knowledge of the world, Schopenhauer is treading on thin ice, since "arguments from analogy are notoriously weak, they yield at most a probable conclusion, and perhaps not even that. But if they are to be at least minimally convincing . . . the two things figuring in the analogy must be exactly alike in one regard and the more regards the like, the better" (Atwell *Character* 89). As we have seen, if this is Schopenhauer's contention, Atwell believes the argument fails, since Schopenhauer maintains from the beginning that the experience of the body is fundamentally different from that of other objects because the body is known in two ways while other things are known only in one way (Atwell *Character* 90). Atwell concludes:

> The transference of self-knowledge to world-understanding does not take place by means of an argument from analogy contrary to . . . what Schopenhauer sometimes suggests himself. He does not really intend to argue that we find ourselves to be representation and will, we find other things to be representation, therefore we may infer that other things are, or probably are, will also. Granted there is a hint of such an argument, but, I think, Schopenhauer takes a rather different course: The human being cannot know or even conceive of anything except—using the most general terms—representation and will, hence if he or she is to denominate the natural world as something other than mere representation, then he or she must call it will. There simply is no alternative except of course to leave it absolutely unknown or, backtracking now, to relegate it to mere representation. (*Character* 102)

Atwell has made an admirable exegetical attempt to defend Schopenhauer's metaphysical arguments, or at least his own versions of them, but all the exegesis in the world will not redeem the weakness of the arguments under examination here. As seen from the first, and central passage of Schopenhauer's metaphysics cited above, he certainly does believe, as Atwell portrays him to believe, that only two things are known to us, will and representation, and that if the "material world" is to be as real as ourselves, then it must be essentially will just as we are. There seem to be three major problems with this argument however. The first is that, contrary to Atwell's defense of him, Schopenhauer explicitly posits an analogy between the body of the individual and other objects of representation, for he insists that the body is known, in part, just as other objects are, as a representation like other representations. Atwell's has rightly objected to this argument because there can be no proper analogy between the body of the individidual, which is experienced as Atwell puts it, "as the locus of sensations," whereas other objects are not known to us as loci of sensations in the same "immediate" way (*Character* 90). Atwell tries to circumvent this valid problem by saying that Schopenhauer never offered this analogy, which in the crucial passage quoted above, Schopenhauer clearly did offer. The second problem is the status of this "material world" which suddenly stands in need of having its existence proven. Before this point, Schopenhauer thematized the problem of metaphysics as one of establishing the reality of "the world" or the "external world," but never the "material world." On the one hand, the "material world" is for Schopenhauer the "correlate of the understanding," that is, the realm of causes and effects in which representations interact according to the subjective principles of sufficient reason (WWR1, 10–11). He says in the passage quoted above that matter exists only "in the subject." But in other places in the same work, and in the midst of passages stipulating the subjectivity of matter, the same is called "the foundation of all things . . . not subject to any becoming or passing away; consequently it always has been and always continues to be" (WWR1, 472). Matter is according to these passages outside the forms of sensibility, specifically time, and so, matter can from this point of view replace the superfluous category of substance (WWR1, 490). If there is some sort of "material" world independent of representation but still in need of being established as will, then will and representation are not all there is to "the world" of human experience. What matter is for the Schopenhauer of the first edition of *The World as Will and Representation* is not entirely clear, but if matter is a construction of subjective representation, then "attributing" the reality of the will to it would amount to saying that representation is itself essentially will, whereas one of the central tenets of Schopenhauer's philosophy is that these two as aspects of the world are totally different. If, however, the material world is something independent of representation, a something of which there are modifications in form but in itself stays the same, then Schopenhauer must account for its relationship to will independently of his account of how representations are related to it. The invoking of the "material world" in the midst of Schopenhauer's discussion of how we can know representations are will complicates his ontology, especially when he is himself not always clear on what its ontological status is.

But these are problems that may be addressed in some fashion or other. The most glaring difficulty of Schopenhauer's argument showing that will is the nature of all phenomena is that it may not be an argument at all. Having set up the problem of relating representation and will, and having ruled out the possibility that the world might only be representation despite that position's logical consistency, Schopenhauer pleads, "if we wish to attribute the greatest known reality to the material world," we shall call it will, since will is the most immediate reality of our own embodied existence. Again, if we have come to the realization that will is known immediately and as the true, unfalsified nature of our own existence, we will "transfer" that essential nature to all other phenomena upon the conclusion of "continued reflection" that failing to do so will leave us with "theoretical egoism." That means that, to a very considerable degree, we are supposed to be compelled to accept Schopenhauer's contention that all phenomena of our experience are essentially will because of the conditional, "if we wish to attribute the greatest known reality" to them, we will do so. It is almost nakedly obvious here that Schopenhauer is ruling out alternatives he doesn't like by fiat, and attempting to make his reader acquiesce to this ruling in the face of a position that is "unsatisfying" to Schopenhauer. It would perhaps be plausible to say that, on the whole, human beings have felt a need to engage in metaphysics, have felt a need to discover the true nature of the world. Schopenhauer would in fact devote a lengthy and eloquent essay in the second volume of *The World as Will and Representation* in 1844 to this very thought, showing how this "metaphysical need" of human beings has been incarnated throughout their cultural history in religion, science and philosophy (WWR2, 160–91). But describing that need empirically and prescribing it as the basis of metaphysics are far from the same thing. Perhaps the best Schopenhauer could get out of this approach would be to say that, if metaphysics were possible, it would be his. But proving that we wish to find "the greatest known reality" in things, showing that metaphysics is indeed possible, and proving that his version of metaphysics is the correct one require different, and not the same, arguments. Nevertheless, perhaps Schopenhauer's "argument" here, though falling far short of establishing what he wanted it to, was more instructive in a negative sense than that of any philosopher who came before him in the Western tradition. After all, it is at the most crucial juncture of Schopenhauer's metaphysics that we find to what extent his attempt to establish a metaphysics of "the world" is the project of wishful thinking. At the bottom of the metaphysical project, that is, dwells the "wish to attribute the greatest known reality to the world," or to find something to which we can "transfer" the greatest "reality" of our own experience. Metaphysics, that is, does not derive from the "things" which we find ourselves confronted with in our experience, but from our will to represent those things as real. It is perhaps for this reason that Schopenhauer found admiration with Nietzsche even after Nietzsche had ostensibly abandoned the metaphysical project, for in his wishful thinking, Schopenhauer exposed himself as the most "honest" practitioner of the ancient, all-too-human wayward art of world making.

4.2 NATURALIZING FALSIFICATION: THE LATER SCHOPENHAUER

Beginning with his notes in the year 1824, five years after the publication of his so-called "main work," Schopenhauer began to revisit the idea of the will as the thing in itself in his reflections. He found himself troubled by the problem of how we can know will if, as he maintained in his early metaphysics, it can only be found on a path "entirely different" from that of representational knowledge. He was also troubled by the problem of the thing in itself, and whether the will, if the will was in fact knowable, could be identified with it. After he fled Berlin in 1831 at the outbreak of the cholera epidemic, an epidemic that took his former colleague Hegel's life, he arrived in Frankfurt, where he began immersing himself in the studies of the natural sciences at the Sneckenberg Natural Research Society (Safransky 282). He composed his next work, *On the Will in Nature,* in 1836 as the fruit of these studies, as he believed to have found in the recent investigations of biology, physiology, chemistry and astronomy confirmations of he metaphysics of will.[8] This belief, and the attempt to make his will thesis consistent with the recent findings and discoveries of natural science, ended up fundamentally changing his epistemology and metaphysics however, as the former took on a markedly more physiological interpretation and the latter became more realistic in nature. These changes come to full fruition in the second edition, published in 1844, of *The World as Will and Representation,* which came in two volumes, the second of which was a collection of essays elaborating on each of the sections of the first volume. It is the doctrines of this second volume which commentators have come more and more to believe represent Schopenhauer's authentic system, and in fact they now assess the first volume of Schopenhauer's "main work" by its standards. In the present section, we shall examine some of these fundamental changes to Schopenhauer's epistemology and ontology, and see what implications they hold for the falsification thesis of his epistemology and metaphysics found in the first edition of *World as Will and Representation*. We shall see how this fundamental change resulted in a broadening of the purview of "the veil of *māyā*," while at the same time diminishing its theoretical importance to Schopenhauer's later metaphysics.

4.2.1 The Unstable Ontology of Brain Idealism

As will be remembered from the previous chapter, Schopenhauer's early definition of representation was the correlativity of object and subject, that is, the presence to consciousness of some sort of object content (FR 41–2; WWR1, 5). The early definition was a statement of subjective idealism in which consciousness was actively intentional, that is, it carried within itself the conditions of the objectivity of the objects that were its contents. In the second edition of *The World as Will and Representation,*

Schopenhauer significantly altered this definition. "What is knowledge? It is above all else and essentially *representation*. What is *representation*? A very complicated *physiological* occurrence in an animal's brain, whose result is the consciousness of a *picture or image* at that very spot" (WWR2, 191). Schopenhauer consistently refers to representations as "brain phenomena" in this work, representations are productions of the brain and exist in the brain. Schopenhauer writes on the one hand of the brain that it is the condition of all representations in the same vein as the subject was their condition in the first edition of his *opus*. On the other the brain becomes physiologically distinguished from sensation because sensations take place at the body's "nerve extremities" while perception takes place within the nervous center of the brain (WWR2, 19). Schopenhauer believes that English physiologists such as Thomas Reid proved that perception takes place through the brain's processing of sense-data, and that this proof is a confirmation of Kant's *a priori* ideas (WWR2, 19–20; 285–6). He in fact devotes an entire essay in the second volume of *The World as Will and Representation* to two views of the intellect he believes need to be brought into agreement, the "subjective view" of Kant and the "objective view" of the physiologist (WWR2, 273; 290). On this synthesized view of the mind, the brain is the "organic pulpy mass . . . nature's final product, which presupposes all the rest" and at the same time, the entire objective, "external world" is nothing but the epistemological construct of the "pulpy mass in the skull" (WWR2, 22; 273). This attempt to synthesize the Kantian and physiological accounts of knowledge is what I will call Schopenhauer's brain idealism.

Now this brain idealism as Schopenhauer formulates it is impossibly and at times outrageously incoherent. One gets the clear impression from Schopenhauer's discourses on the brain that it is an organ of the body, of all animal bodies, in the straightforwardly realistic sense. The organism first develops knowledge because it must relate itself to individuals in the world and survive among them (WWR2, 201; 273; 277). The brain is able to perceive objects intuitively because "space first arises from the knowing subject seeing outwards" (WWR2, 274). All of nature exhibits an "intellectual aristocracy" in that, the more complicated an animal's brain structure, the more sophisticated its intellect and hence its ability to survive (WWR2, 144–6; 278-9; 282-4). This "intellectual aristocracy" of Schopenhauer is mentioned a few times as extended over the geographical and hierarchical dimensions of cultures, as when he maintains that "northern peoples," faced with more demanding environments, are intellectually superior to "southern peoples," and when he speaks of social and occupational classes in society as differentiated along the lines of intellectual sophistication (WWR2, 282–4). He even goes so far as to say that "knowledge presupposes the existence of the world," and because "knowledge is limited to the relations between existing things," we can see how "the intellect is conditioned by nature, resides therein, belongs thereto, and therefore cannot be set up in opposition to nature" (WWR2, 287–8). But, simultaneously with all of this, Schopenhauer retains the idealist vocabulary which characterizes the forms of sensibility, space and time, as *a priori* knowledge of the subject which helps construct the "objective" world of our experience. Immediately before declaring that knowledge presupposes the world's existence and that the intellect is conditioned by nature, Schopenhauer asserts that time, space and causality are forms of the intellect (WWR2, 287). He argues at the beginning of the second volume of the second edition, in view of establishing idealism, that there can be no intelligible or imaginable objective world that existed apart from the knowing subject (WWR2, 5–10). He says that causality is rooted in a form of knowledge in the brain (WWR2, 11). He continues to speak of spatial determinations in a thoroughly idealistic fashion.

> *Outside us* is an exclusively spatial determination, but space itself is a form of our faculty of perception, in other words, a function of our brain. Therefore, the "*outside us*" to which we refer objects on the occasion of the sensation of sight, itself resides inside our head, for there is its whole scene of action; much the same as in the theater we see mountains, forest, and sea, and yet everything remains within the house. . . . For things are *in space*

> and consequently *outside us* only in so far as we *represent* them. (WWR2, 22)

He continues to maintain that time, along with space, is a form of knowledge of the subject, and only appears as if it were outside that subject (WWR2, 35). He claims that, since the form of causality is known *a priori* to the understanding, "it is immaterial whether the *sensation* . . . occurs through . . . the impression of light on the retina or of sound on the auditory nerve," for those impressions are only perceived as external because the understanding has applied causal rules to those impressions (WWR2, 37). Examples could be multiplied to show how these accounts of the intellect, one idealistic and the other physiological, are intentionally run parallel to one another in the 1844 edition. The instant examples will suffice to show how oddly these two views of the mind conflate with one another. One would assume safely enough that if the brain is an organ of the body in the real sense, if its importance in terms of knowledge can be accounted for through physiological factors, if the brain's functioning helps the individual navigate her way through the world of other individuals, then the brain is something "inside" the body, whose structure has its own "inside" and "outside," and that it resides in an individual for whom in turn there is an "inside" and "outside" in a straightforwardly realistic vein. To naturalize knowledge by calling it a "phenomenon" or "function of the brain" is to stipulate a realistic ontology. But upon being told these things, we are told at the same time that space, in this instance, is actually inside the brain, that all conceptions of "outside" are produced by the brain's "innate" forms of representing, indeed that "this intellect itself *appears* objectively as brain" (WWR2, 286). These two accounts, which Schopenhauer glibly fancied himself to have joined, leave us with an ontology that is markedly more realistic and naturalistic than the one found in the first edition of *The World as Will and Representation*, but in the same breath leaves us utterly confounded as to whether the brain as an objective representation is the product of the intellect, or whether the intellect is the production of the physiological functions of the organism that resides in its brain. Schopenhauer himself is not by any means unaware of this instability, but stubbornly refuses to balance it in favor of one account or the other in the name of reconciling two mutually exclusive doctrines which both found favor with him.

Schopenhauer's commentators of the last two decades seem agreed that one of Schopenhauer's most outstanding accomplishments as a philosopher was his insistence that the human person is rooted in the world by embodiment, and that self-knowledge can only be intelligible through this embodiment. The laudability of the metaphysics of will for them lay in its intimacy with Schopenhauer's persuasive arguments that the body and the will are one and the same. They were thus drawn more to the physiological account of knowledge and the revised metaphysics that Schopenhauer espoused in the second edition of *The World as Will and Representation* of 1844. Nonetheless, they also all lamented the inconsistency of the physiological account of knowledge with the idealistic one. D. W. Hamlyn suspects the convergence of these two accounts for two reasons. First, as Hamlyn puts it, "the argument is supposed to use the empirical reality of certain representations to prove the transcendental ideality of all representations," that is, it purports to use the empirical fact that the brain produces all knowledge to show that all knowledge, even that about the brain, is representational (Hamlyn 70). He also held that Schopenhauer took no proper steps to show that the brain was the subject, and if he leaves any doubt about this by making it possible that they are not the same, the account will fail (Hamlyn 71). Maurice Mandelbaum was the most ardent defender of Schopenhauer's physiological doctrines of epistemology, and he maintained that this physiological orientation of Schopenhauer's was always an element of his philosophy, from his days at Göttingen through his dissertation, to his studies of the French and English physiologists in the '30's and '40's, and this shows us just how un-Kantian Schopenhauer always was (257).[9] Mandelbaum is somewhat unique in his contention that Schopenhauer's talk of the brain and other bodily organs in such a realistic vocabulary should not bother us in terms of their status as representations, for Mandelbaum reminds us, nothing for Schopenhauer is merely representation but also will, and so all organs of the body are both representation and will (56–7). The most compelling analysis of this problem was given by Christopher Janaway. Janaway recognized that Schopenhauer's evolving realistic stance was strengthened by a changing assessment of matter, and that this stance resulted in a conflation by Schopenhauer of idealism and materialism. Indeed, in the second volume of the second edition of *The World as Will and Representation*, while matter remains for Schopenhauer the correlate of the understanding as it was in the first edition, it also becomes the substratum of natural forces and the condition for all experience.

> Now if we deprive the *subject* of all the particular determinations and forms of its knowing, all the properties in the *object* also disappear, and nothing but *matter without form and quality* is left. This matter can occur in experience as little as can the subject without the forms of its knowledge, yet it remains opposed to the bare subject as such.... The world as representation, the objective world, has thus, so to speak, two poles, namely the knowing subject plain and simple without the forms of its knowing, and crude matter without form and quality. Both are absolutely unknowable, the subject because it is that which knows, matter because without form and quality it cannot be perceived. Yet both are the fundamental conditions of all empirical perception.... This matter is not given in any experience, but is pre-supposed in every experience. (WWR2, 15)

It will be remembered from the preceding chapter that one of the crucial and basic elements of Schopenhauer's early epistemology was the subject-object correlativity thesis, which posited that the difference between Schopenhauer's system and all other systems of philosophy was Schopenhauer's doctrine that all consciousness consisted of an intentional objective content and an unknowable subject (FR 41–2; WWR1, 5)[10] Now he says that with his philosophy, "matter and intellect are inseparable correlatives . . . both together constitute the *world as representation*" (WWR2, 16). In the new, revised version of the correlativity thesis which serves as the condition for all representational knowledge, the objective content of every representation in the first edition has been replaced by matter. The "eternal" substrate of matter has become one of the conditions of all knowing, with the perceiving subject as the other condition, ordering matter through the familiar forms of time, space and causality. This movement, Janaway insightfully notices, results in a crucial confusion between idealism and materialism, two very different doctrines whose combination is according to Janaway grossly absurd (137; 181).[11] The results of this confusion at any rate allow Schopenhauer to locate the subject within the material world, and thus to explain experience as possible only through the contact between a knowing being and a material world. This explanation in its turn gave Schopenhauer room to speak more and more of knowledge as a physiological process, which was, at the same time, transcendentally ideal in terms of how the knowing subject ordered its experience in the brain.

Janaway's account is certainly a plausible exegesis of the strange courtship between idealism and materialism in the later Schopenhauer's philosophy. But as he rightly notes, this strange courtship does not result in the successful union of these two doctrines that Schopenhauer had intended. One can perfectly well maintain an indirect or representational realism in which the brain orders its experience according to its own physiological rules. But in order to do this, one requires a realist ontology in which space, time and causality are real characteristics of the world. Idealism requires a complete skepticism about whatever characteristics the world may possess in itself, and must claim in one way or another that all objective experience is produced through space and time, which are not characteristics of the world but of the knowing subject itself. Any attempt to combine these two positions such as is found in Schopenhauer can only result in an ontology which is completely unstable, or just nonsensical. However, this naturalization of epistemology by Schopenhauer had two other major effects on his early system which concern us here. The first is the phenomenalization of will, which before had been hidden and placed beyond all representational knowledge.

The second is the psychologization of Schopenhauer's falsification thesis.

4.2.2 The Appearing Will and the Veil of Time

As will be remembered from the first edition of *The World as Will and Representation*, Schopenhauer first considered that "the veil of *māyā*" was what kept the thing in itself, the will, hidden from representational knowledge. The fact that representational knowledge is incomplete, insufficient, insignificant and deceptive necessitated a path to the thing in itself that was "entirely different" from the representation, another "immediate" and "unfabricated" knowledge. Schopenhauer did believe that we possess such a kind of knowledge, a knowledge of will, a non-objective familiarity with ourselves in terms of what engrosses us in the world and what impels bodily actions. As we have seen above, this argument was problematic because Schopenhauer suggested that will is known through bodily actions, but bodily actions or movements are known partly through representation, and so it is difficult at best to do anything but concede that will must be known at least partly through representation. And if will is known at least partly through representation, then it is not known in a manner "entirely different" from representation, bringing the whole bifurcation between the two by the metaphysics of will into doubt. Schopenhauer became aware of this problem a few short years after the publication of the first edition of his "main work," and by the time he composed his expository essays which expanded the second edition into two volumes, Schopenhauer had fundamentally revised his position on the matter.

Schopenhauer hints at this change early in the second volume of the second edition in a discussion of time. After explaining once again that time is a subjective determination of the principle of sufficient reason and not an objective "thing," Schopenhauer writes: "*Time* is primarily the form of the *inner sense*. Anticipating the following book, I remark that the sole object of the inner sense is the knower's own *will*. Time is therefore the form by means of which self-knowledge becomes possible to the individual will, which originally and in itself is without knowledge" (WWR2, 35). Later on, in a discussion of metaphysics which characterizes it as an interpretation of "the world" which connects "inner and outer experience," Schopenhauer makes the first explication of his revised theory of the will.

> Although no one can recognize the thing-in-itself through the veil of the forms of perception, on the other hand everyone carries this within himself, in fact he himself is it; hence in self-consciousness it must be in some way accessible to him, although still only conditionally. Thus the bridge on which metaphysics passes beyond experience is nothing but just that analysis of experience into phenomenon and thing-in-itself in which I have placed Kant's greatest merit. For it contains the proof of a kernel of the phenomenon different from the phenomenon itself. It is true that this kernel can never be entirely separated from the phenomenon, and be regarded by itself as an *ens extramundanum;* but it is known always only in its relations and references to the phenomenon itself. The interpretation and explication of the phenomenon, however, in relation to its inner kernel can give us information about it which does not otherwise come into consciousness. . . . Therefore this thing-in-itself must express its inner nature and character in the world of experience; consequently it must be possible to interpret these from it, and indeed from the material, not from the mere form of experience. (WWR2, 182–3)

The first important admission here is that, although he still maintains that we can tell what the thing in itself is because we are in essence the thing in itself, we cannot know that thing in itself completely apart from the phenomenon. Only because it was encountered within experience could the "kernel" of the thing in itself help us interpret our experience. Schopenhauer then draws out the full implications of this.

> Even the inward observation we have of our own will still does not furnish an exhaustive and adequate knowl-

> edge of the thing-in-itself. It would do so if it were a wholly immediate observation. But such an observation is brought about by the will, with and by means of corporization, providing itself also with an intellect (for the purpose of his relations with the external world), and then through this intellect knowing itself in self-consciousness (the necessary reverse of the external world); but this knowledge of the thing-in-itself is not wholly adequate.... Inner knowledge is free from two forms belonging to outer knowledge, the form of *space* and the form of *causality* which brings about all sense-perception. On the other hand, there still remains the form of *time*, as well as that of being-known and knowing in general. Accordingly, in this inner knowledge the thing-in-itself has indeed to a great extent cast off its veils, but still does not appear quite naked. In consequence of the form of time which still adheres to it, everyone knows his *will* only in its successive individual *acts*, not as a whole in and by itself.... The act of will is indeed only the nearest and clearest *phenomenon* of the thing-in-itself.... Accordingly, we have to refer the whole world of phenomena to that one in which the thing-in- itself is manifested under the lightest of all veils. (WWR2, 196–7)

In this passage, there is not a complete identification between the thing in itself and the will, rather, the act of will is only the "nearest and clearest phenomenon" of that inner nature of the world, will.[12] One of the forms of the principle of sufficient reason, time, mediates the knowledge of the will to us. It is significant that Schopenhauer writes of the will as having cast off most of its "veils," of the thing in itself as manifesting itself under the lightest of veils. This means that the "veil of *māyā*," the falsification of the inner nature of the world by representational knowledge, has now enveloped the will also, and this envelopment has made a knowledge of the will an "inadequate" knowledge of the will.

Now commentators have taken this revised metaphysical doctrine as Schopenhauer's authentic position. Julian Young has used the passages cited above to support his interpretation that Schopenhauer's metaphysics was not an attempt to know the thing in itself, but a project of interpreting the world through self-knowledge (27–35). John Atwell has paid much attention to these passages as well to buttress his view that Schopenhauer thought the will was "the thing-in-itself in appearance" (*Character* 48; 107–14; 126). What strikes one as of particular interest though is how this new thesis of will, that it is only the "nearest and clearest phenomena" of the thing in itself, is maintained alongside the old one, that the will is the thing in itself, in the very same volume. He supports continuously the view that plurality is the reflex of the forms of knowledge of the knowing subject, which is "foreign to the thing-in-itself, to the inner, primary force manifesting itself in things" (WWR2, 322). He continues to hold that "the illusion of plurality (*Maya*), resulting from the forms of external objective apprehension, could not penetrate right into the inner, simple consciousness, hence this always meets with only one being" (WWR2, 321). He persists resolutely to justify the earlier thesis of the unitary will as the thing in itself, and even to turn back to support from the pre-systematic Hindu philosophical tradition to prop up that thesis.

> Why is our consciousness brighter and more distinct the farther it reaches outwards, so that its greatest clearness lies in sense perception, which already half belongs to things outside us; and on the other hand, becomes more obscure as we go inwards, and leads, when followed to its innermost recesses, into a darkness in which all knowledge ceases? Because, I say, consciousness presupposes *individuality*; but this belongs to the mere phenomenon, since as the plurality of the homogeneous, it is conditioned by the forms of the phenomenon, time and space. On the other hand, our inner nature has its root in what it no longer phenomenon, but thing-in-itself, to which therefore the forms of the phenomenon do not reach; and in this way the chief conditions of individuality are wanting, and distinct consciousness ceases therewith. In this root-point of existence the difference of beings ceases. . . . The will as thing-in-itself is entire and undivided in every being. . . . Therefore it is said also in the *Bhagavad-Gita*: Undivided it dwells in beings, and yet

> as it were divided, it is to be known as the sustainer, and producer of beings (xiii, 16, trans. Schlegel). Here of course we fall into mystical and metaphorical language, but it is the only language in which anything can be said about this wholly transcendent theme. (WWR2, 325–6)

All of the tensions between the two different versions of the metaphysics of will, and all of the inconsistencies of the naturalized epistemology of the second edition converge unhappily in this passage. Sense perception is said to "half belong to things outside us," and yet space and time are said to be only forms of our knowledge. At the ultimate point of introspection, all individuality is obliterated, and consciousness ceases, and yet this introspection leads us to somehow know that the will is the thing in itself. The *Gītā* is solicited to support the doctrine of the eternal and undifferentiated will with its "mystical and metaphorical language," a doctrine Schopenhauer could not make such clear sense of himself in his supposedly more systematic mode of expression. Schopenhauer performs this veritable metaphysical high wire act with a not too subtly articulated awareness that the two positions he has advocated in these essays that make up the second volume of his *opus* are inconsistent, and with a frank admission that he is not sure how to reconcile them systematically.

> The *unity of the that will* here alluded to, which lies beyond the phenomenon, and in which we have recognized the inner being of the phenomenal world, is a metaphysical unity. Consequently, knowledge of it is transcendent; that is to say it does not rest on the functions of our intellect, and is therefore not really to be grasped with them. The result is that this unity opens itself to the consideration an abyss whose depth no longer grants an entirely clear and systematically connected insight, but only isolated glances that enable us to recognize this unity in this or that relation of things; now in the subjective, now in the objective. In this way new problems are again raised, and I do not undertake to solve all these, but rather appeal here to the words *est quadam prodire tenus* ("advance up to a certain limit"),

> more concerned not to set up anything false or arbitrarily invented than to give a thorough account of everything; at the risk of furnishing here only a fragmentary statement. (WWR2, 323)

The "new problems" that have been created as a result of Schopenhauer's revised epistemology, his brain idealism, and his wavering between an early and late metaphysics of will, are ones he cannot satisfactorily solve even for himself. The intractability of the metaphysical problems Schopenhauer has created is matched only by the integrity of his frankness about being bested by them.

In the second volume of the second edition of *The World as Will and Representation,* Schopenhauer revised his metaphysics of will to show that will is not the unknowable, unobjectifiable thing in itself, but only its most immediate relative in the world of appearance, representation. This means that the falsification thesis of representation has now encompassed even will, making will an inadequate knowledge of the thing in itself. One would expect for this reason that the motif of "the veil of *māyā*" would increase in theoretical importance to the system as a result of such a broadening of its purview, but in fact, in the later Schopenhauer, we find the notion of *māyā* more and more psychologized.

4.2.3 The Psychologization of Māyā

Again, as it will be remembered from the previous chapter, the falsification thesis of Schopenhauer's epistemology in the first edition of his "main work" was the result of his appropriation of the notion of *māyā* from the pre-systematic Vedāntic tradition. That falsification thesis went to the nature of representational knowledge as Schopenhauer conceived it. Representations, according to the early Schopenhauer, were flawed because they pictured the world to the knowing consciousness in an incomplete, insubstantial, ungrounded, unsatisfying and fabricated way. The grovel of the thesis was thoroughly epistemological: it purported to establish something about the representational mode of knowing as such. The notion of falsification in the second edition of *The World as Will and Representation* deals not so much with how representations falsify the world, as in the early works, but with the "essential imperfections of the intellect," the incompleteness of the intellect's knowledge of the world, and the subservience of the intellect to the will, the motivating force of the individual.

With his revised and naturalized epistemology of brain idealism, some of Schopenhauer's later discourse on falsification revolves around the brain's determination of knowledge. In the first edition of *The World as Will and Representation* for instance, Schopenhauer had argued that representations and dreams were not subject to any critical epistemological distinctions, for both kinds of experience were subjectively intentional and related their contents through the causal form of understanding (WWR1, 16). At the opening of the second volume of the second edition, Schopenhauer still finds dreams and representations comparable, but now because both are productions of the brain (WWR2, 4). He devotes an entire essay in the second volume to "the essential imperfections of the intellect," and makes an attempt to enumerate these. He argues that, because of the form of time, what he later calls the last "veil" covering the thing in itself, thought is fragmentary, we can only entertain one thought at a time, and our thoughts and focus are therefore fleeting and scattered (WWR2, 137–8). Along familiar lines, he contends that the intellect cannot show us the "kernel of things" but only their "outer shell" (WWR2, 176). This is the case because, as is repeated *ad infinitum*, it is bound by the *a priori* forms of understanding, which cannot apply to things as they are in themselves.

These points can be considered structurally epistemological, but they are mentioned in passing and not emphasized to any marked degree. The most important imperfection of representational knowledge according to the later Schopenhauer is that it is a slave of the will, and thus not meant for the purpose of knowing things completely, but for satisfying the will's ends.

> These inner and essential imperfections of the intellect are further increased by a disturbance to some extent ex-

> ternal to it but yet inevitable, namely, the influence that the will exerts on all its operations, as soon as that will is in any way concerned in their result. Every passion, in fact every inclination or disinclination tinges the objects of knowledge with its color. Most common of occurrence is the falsification of knowledge brought about by desire and hope, since they show us the scarcely possible in dazzling colors as probable and well-nigh certain, and render us almost incapable of comprehending what is opposed to it. The defective nature of the intellect here described will not surprise us, however, if we look back at its origin and its destiny. . . . Nature has produced it for the service of an individual will; therefore it is destined to know things only in so far as they serve as the motives of such a will, not to fathom them or to comprehend their true inner essence. (WWR2, 141–2)

The will is the essential element of all being, and thus of human being, while the intellect remains its mere physiological product, and with every excitation of will, the intellect is compelled to will's aims (WWR2, 215). If the desired thing which the individual wills cannot be grasped or is not present, the will upsets the intellect with its imagination, does not let the mind rest in pursuit of what is desired (WWR2, 216). Schopenhauer enters into many engaged discussions of the psychological ramifications of the desires of the will upon the intellect, which establish for him that the intellect is nothing more than the practical tool of the will. While it is for Schopenhauer certain that the intellect is the servant of the will, their relationship and interaction is a dynamic one, with each feeding off of the other's activity. The will itself, though incarnated in an individual human being, wills "blindly," it is merely a striving that always strives to continue striving. Armed with an intellect in a human or animal, the will becomes individuated, seeks its own interests, is drawn to some objects and repelled by others. The intellect, with the forms of understanding, time, space and causality, aided and abetted in the human being by the concepts of reason, organizes experience and presents the self with a world in which she is engrossed. Once the will has "selected" an object of desire, it compels the individual to seek it, colors the thoughts concerning that desired object, obsesses the person with its possession. The will's employment of the intellect allows it to live and thrive off individuality, the individuality of the self, whose limitation is the identity of the body and will, and the individuality of the things and persons which are distinguished and prioritized according to importance in experience. The will, with the help of the fabrications of the intellect, are what in unison effectively make the individual want to live in the world, this is the "will-to-live."

The consequences of this kind of existence are nonetheless grim, for while the will makes the world "significant" for the individual, it also ensures that the very same world will inevitably be experienced as a world of suffering. For as will is the "inner nature" of every individual, each individual is bound in harsher or gentler ways to combat against every other for the preservation and prolongation of existence, for the possession of mutually desired objects, for supremacy, love, honor, and the whole gamut of willed "goods." The psychologized notion of falsification allows Schopenhauer to construct a compelling account of contest, struggle and suffering among animals, human beings, even for him organic and inorganic phenomena in their unconscious action and interaction. It also creates what for Schopenhauer was the basic ethical problem of all philosophy, the problem of suffering and how to transcend it. Only by transcending the standpoint of knowledge which is bound to individuality can human beings see into the true nature of things, and in compassion renounce the will that chains them to an otherwise frightful world. The theory of falsification which has been carried over into the metaphysics of will allows Schopenhauer to realize the vision of a philosophy he first nurtured in 1813, "a philosophy that is to be ethics and metaphysics at once." "The veil of *māyā*" reaches into every avenue of Schopenhauer's thought, and has profound implications for how he links his epistemology, metaphysics and axiology. It will also provide him a solution to that one outstanding phenomena which first excited in him a philosopher's wonder, though it was a dreadful wonder, the phenomenon of suffering.

CHAPTER 5

Falsification and the Ethics of Identification

5.1 MĀYĀ, *IDENTIFICATION AND A METAPHYSICAL ETHICS*

At the opening of the final chapter of the first edition of *The World as Will and Representation*, the chapter dealing with the ethical part of Schopenhauer's system, it is asserted that ethics can fairly be said to be the "most serious" aspect of philosophy since the practical matters of everyday conduct are of interest to all (WWR1, 271). Nitezsche saw Schopenhauer's entire philosophy, in its attempt to represent the world as nothing but suffering, as a prolepsis to an imperative ethics of world-renunciation, an ethics Nietzsche took to be nothing more than an "instinct of decadence" (*Beyond* 490).[1] Leaving aside for the moment Nietzsche's contentions that the Schopenhauerian ethics is an imperative one and that it signaled the depths of Western nihilism, we can certainly understand how Nietzsche came to the conclusion that ethics constituted to a certain degree the crux of Schopenhauer's view of the world. As D. W. Hamlyn has pointed out, this much could be gleaned merely from noticing that the length of the essays on ethics in the three editions of *The World as Will and Representation*, accompanied by his two major essays on ethical themes, *On the Freedom of the Human Will* and *On the Basis of Morality* outstripped by far the number of pages Schopenhauer wrote on epistemology, metaphysics or aesthetics (123).

Not unlike these other "parts" of his system however, Schopenhauer's ethics has been found by generations of scholars to be riddled with unsettling inconsistencies. To some degree, this is perhaps to be expected given the various theoretically synthetic ends that ethics is meant to achieve. Patrick Gardiner sees Schopenhauer's reflections on ethics as attempting to make consistent the doctrines of moral freedom and necessity of actions, while at the same time working out a sensible position for which, while human actions are subject to necessity, the agents of these acts are morally responsible for them (248). Using slightly more technical terminology, John Atwell reached similar conclusions about Schopenhauer's ethics and some moral theories it tried to join that we are accustomed to perceiving as inconsistent. Schopenhauer's ethics is on the one hand trying to merge practical reductionism, for which doers cannot be considered to be anything but their deeds, and practical causalism, for which doers stand apart from and are responsible for their deeds (Atwell *Human* 32). That is, according to Schopenhauer's idea of every bodily act being an act of will, doers are completely and solely their actions, their being is their acting, and so no intelligible notion of responsibility can attach to any putative agent, since the agent and act are one (WWR1, 8, 9). At the same time however, according to Atwell, every individual on Schopenhauer's account possesses an inborn character, a Kantian "intelligible character" to which the morality or immorality of any given act is attributable according to the Scholastic formula *"operari sequiter esse"* or "actions follow from essence" (*Human* 36). While we normally would take these two versions of reductionism and causalism to be mutually exclusive positions, Schopenhauer believes that synthesizing them will at once demonstrate to us that agents are non-contingently related to their deeds and provide us with a formula of human moral responsibility (*Human* 37).[2] In addition to these significant attempts to create a theory of ethics that would combine insights from normally opposed positions, Schopenhauer's moral philosophy also delved into other complex issues, such as the disparities and relationship between Kant's notions of the "empirical character" and the "intelligible character." It dealt with finding a more accurate definition of moral freedom and strove to reconcile that notion of moral freedom with the larger whole of Schopenhauer's metaphysics of will. It proposed to give an account of asceticism and sainthood, as well as psychologically and morally evaluate suicide. This great diversity of themes which Schopenhauer takes upon himself to fit into a comprehensive ethical theory has the effect it normally does on systematic thinking, namely, provides it with both unique insights and philosophical instabilities and incoherences.

Schopenhauer insists nonetheless, consonant with his vision of 1813 to create a philosophy that was "at once ethics and metaphysics," that his moral system hangs together intimately with his epistemology and doctrine of the will. Thirty-one years after he had committed himself to the project of a metaphysical ethics, Schopenhauer proclaimed proudly in the second edition of *The World as Will and Representation* in 1844 that he had successfully saw that project to fulfillment. "My philosophy . . . is the only one that grants to morality its complete and entire rights; for only if the true nature of man is his own *will*, consequently only if he is in the strictest sense his own work, are his deeds actually entirely his and attributable to him" (Schopenhauer, WWR2, 589). That is to say, Schopenhauer believed that the centerpiece of his system, the metaphysics of will, gives each deed of human beings moral significance, for according to that metaphysics, the actions of human beings are occasioned, in part at least, directly by their innermost nature. The deeds of every individual flow from the will, the ground of all reality, and the moral significance of those actions varies from person to person with respect to their individual characters and the motives they happen to be entertaining.[3]

As we have seen from the preceding chapters, the falsification thesis of Schopenhauer, the idea that our perception of a heterogeneous plurality of things and individuals in the world is a reflex of an epistemological fabrication of the world's true nature of a singular, unitary will, was pivotal to his metaphysics. This falsification thesis was also, as we have seen, the result of Schopenhauer's hermeneutic appropriation of the *Upaniṣadic* notion of *māyā*. We should then expect the falsification thesis, and the *Upaniṣadic* inspiration of it, to play a significant role in Schopenhauer's ethics. And play a significant role it does. Even the contemporary commentators on Schopenhauer, who otherwise normally reject the formative role Indian thought played in Schopenhauer's system, have to acknowledge its presence in the ethics, given the frequency and seriousness of its mention by Schopenhauer. The thematization of *māyā* gives Schopenhauer, according to Frederick Copleston, the basis upon which he can make distinctions between bad, just and moral people (173). Gardiner confirms this assessment when he writes: "both just and altruistic forms of conduct are possible, and the source of such conduct intelligible, only on the assumption that the world as it presents itself as 'idea' is throughout deceptive and illusory" (273). D. W. Hamlyn recognized that Schopenhauer equates loving acts, compassionate acts and the piercing through the veil of *māyā* to see into the metaphysical identity of all individuals (146). John Atwell points out that the compassionate man or the ascetic are for Schopenhauer superior to the artist in metaphysical knowledge, for it is really the former two who have broken through the *principium individuationis*, or *māyā* (*Character* 156). The importance of the falsification thesis to Schopenhauer's ethics then cannot be disputed, for Schopenhauer argues that the unraveling of the epistemological falsification of the world's true nature is supposed to be the basis, the condition upon which all truly non-egoistic, properly moral actions are grounded. The putting to an end of falsification is also, as it turns out, posited by Schopenhauer to be the hallmark of all genuine asceticism.

It is how Schopenhauer attempts to work out this formula that has been derided by his commentators. As we have seen in the opening chapter, one of the first scholars to critique Schopenhauer's hermeneutic and logical employment of *māyā* and the "tat tvam asi ethic," or the ethics of identification which followed from it, was the twentieth century German scholar of Vedānta, Paul Hacker. He contended that Schopenhauer entertained fundamental misunderstandings of the metaphysical doctrines of the classical *Upaniṣads* and the *Bhagavad Gītā*, and in addition made a "logical monstrosity" out of ethics by claiming that it was based on the illusory nature of individuality (Halbfass, *Philology* 273–4; 306). D. W. Hamlyn has pointed out that, even if we would be inclined to agree with Schopenhauer that in some way compassion, which is brought about by the cessation of falsification, was the basis for all philanthropic acts, this goes nowhere in helping us assess which acts have moral worth and which don't; that is, it fails to provide us with a theory of morality (135). Christopher Janaway finds Schopenhauer's ethics of identification, based on *māyā* and compassion, to be conceptually incoherent, for while the falsification thesis requires that all individuals in the world be in essence identical, compassion necessitates that a plurality of individuals in fact exist (271–3). John Atwell, among other objections to Schopenhauer's ethics of compassion, holds that will-less, compassionate acts of complete identification are impossible given Schopenhauer's own metaphysics, grounded as that metaphysics is in a "will-body identity thesis." All acts, including compassionate ones, are bodily acts and thus require the maintenance of individuality which the falsification thesis decries (*Human* 142). Hence, rather than following from his metaphysics, the ethics of compassion stands in direct conflict with it. The philosophical secondary literature on Schopenhauer then finds his formulation of an ethics based on the thesis of falsification to be too self-contradictory and lacking in evaluations of the moral worth of actions to be of much value.

The present chapter will attempt to address these criticisms and uncover the role played by the falsification thesis in the ethics Schopenhauer tried to articulate. In a number of instances, commentators have come to their negative assessments of Schopenhauer's ethics of identification based on an inaccurate understanding of the use to which Schopenhauer puts the falsification thesis in the context of his ethical theory. As he himself indicated on numerous occasions, Schopenhauer conceives of ethics to be not a prescriptive discipline, in which rules are laid down by which an individual should conduct herself; but rather an inquiry into what motives individuals entertain in their conduct and what sorts of characters they possess which make them amenable to certain particular motives and not others. Owing to the empirical necessities of living in the world as representation, a heterogeneous world ruled by space, time and causality, Schopenhauer thought that people normally make strong distinctions between themselves and other individuals. These distinctions in their turn leave individuals prone to more or less egoistic motivations, that is, motivations aimed at preserving the existence of the self at the expense of consideration for, or indifference to, the welfare of others. To put this matter in slightly more modern terminology, Schopenhauer believed that distinctions made between various phenomena in the world could not for human beings be merely apprehensions of difference, because human beings are impelled by will, and not merely will in general as the ground of all appearance, but their individual wills, or what he called in Kantian parlance, their "intelligible characters." Distinctions informed by will cannot merely be innocent, value-free distinctions, but rather must carry evaluations of an axiological sort, that is, distinctions which judge which phenomena and other individuals are more or less important with respect to the will-governed interests of the self. Difference, for Schopenhauer, was at great pains to be anything but axiological inequality in the normal, everyday conduct of individuals, and all axiological inequality, being inevitably in the service of egoism, was for him morally suspect. The ethical question Schopenhauer thought most central in this context was thus: "is it possible for human beings to treat other individuals as axiologically on a par with themselves, such that their conduct toward others has no egoistic motivation?" The falsification thesis and compassion provide the answer to this question, for in Schopenhauer's view, realizing that the nature of every individual is at bottom the same can engender in people the motivation to treat them as axiologically valuable as themselves, and this treatment finds its expression in compassion. To be sure, this formula is not without its difficulties, some of which we shall examine, but it has been mostly misunderstood and badly assessed by Schopenhauer's commentators, and a re-examination of it and the importance of the thesis of falsification to it will reveal that Schopenhauer's ethical thinking is at least not plagued by the kinds of problems that scholars have tended to perceive.

This chapter will therefore first put the notion of *māyā* into the larger context of Schopenhauer's theory of motivation and character, and then examine the falsification thesis itself in order to assess the intelligibility of its formulation *vis-à-vis* ethics. We will first discuss the principles by which Schopenhauer believes human beings morally conduct themselves as they find expression in their respective characters and what motives by which those characters are impelled to act. We will then go into the problem of egoism and individuality as Schopenhauer conceives them in order to discover his notion of the nature of the most important problems of ethics. Special attention will be paid to the critics' charge that Schopenhauer's ethics makes no room for the individual and consequently any real relationship between persons, and that any ethics which derogates the centrality of these concepts can be nothing more than a "logical monstrosity." The relevance of the falsification thesis to Schopenhauer's proposed "basis of morality," compassion, will then be explicated, in an attempt to show in what manner Schopenhauer can make the controversial claim that his ethics is a uniquely "metaphysical" one. The closing part of the chapter will deal with Schopenhauer's account of asceticism and the standpoint of the so-called "renunciation of will" he believes is found in the ascetic. As the major commentators have acknowledged, Schopenhauer's description of the standpoint of an ascetic, how an ascetic views the world as opposed to everyone else, owes much to his acquaintance with classical Hindu, and in this case even Theravādā and Māhāyana Buddhist thought. The full drawing out of the consequences of the falsification thesis and its unraveling occur in this last phase of Schopenhauer's account of ethics, and we shall there bring our exposition of his systematic thought to a close.

5.1.1 Character, Motives and Moral Agency

Despite his leveling of severe critiques against Kant's epistemology and ethics, Schopenhauer always paid the highest respect to Kant for his innovations in moral philosophy.[4] "Kant's greatest merit," he wrote, "is the distinction of the phenomenon from the thing in itself" (Schopenhauer, WWR1, 417). We have seen the implications Schopenhauer himself draws from this all-important distinction in the areas of theory of knowledge and metaphysics in the preceding chapters, namely that the empirical world of our representational experience is mere phenomenal appearance, while the true and undifferentiated essence of the world is will. This distinction and the metaphysical doctrine to which Schopenhauer believed it leads also have incredible moral significance, to be found in Kant's parallel distinction of the empirical and the intelligible characters. In this distinction, Schopenhauer thought, Kant showed how the empirical character is subject to determined necessity and the intelligible character is free and as such is the real moral agent.[5] In doing this, Kant demonstrates how the moral importance of our deeds derives from our inmost nature and not from the cause and effect relationships that govern the phenomenal world (WWR1, 422; BM 112). Schopenhauer's thoughts on moral conduct are so dominated by his idea of how human actions issue from the interaction of empirical character, intelligible character and motive, that no explication of Schopenhauer's ethics would be accurate without reviewing them.

Schopenhauer begins his discussion on the different aspects of character by showing how the freedom and necessity to which these aspects are subject parallel the necessity that bounds the empirical world and the freedom of the thing in itself.

> Here we have before us most clearly the point of unity of that great contrast, namely the union of freedom and necessity. . . . Everything as phenomenon, as object, is absolutely necessary; *in itself* it is will, and this is perfectly free to all eternity. The phenomenon, the object, is necessarily and unalterably determined in the concatenation of grounds and consequents, which cannot have any discontinuity. But the existence of this object in general and the manner of its existing, that is to say, the Idea which reveals itself in it, or in other words its character, is di-

> rectly phenomenon of the will. . . . Like every other part of nature, man is objectivity of the will; therefore all we have said holds good of him also. Just as everything in nature has its forces and qualities that definitely react to a definite impression, and constitute its character, so man also has his *character*, from which the motives call forth his actions with necessity. In this way of acting, his empirical character reveals itself, but in this again is revealed his intelligible character, i.e., the will in itself, of which he is the determined phenomenon. (WWR1, 287)

The notions of intelligible and empirical character correspond on the human level to Schopenhauer's "two aspect" theory of the world. Just as on the one hand the world is the phenomenal, empirical appearance that is governed through and through by the principle of sufficient reason and on the other is the will as thing in itself, so the individual human being is from one aspect the empirical self whose behavior is in every case determined, and from the other she is the unchanging "intelligible character," the manifestation of will in a particular human being.[6]

Mere parallelisms, however, are not arguments, and do not perform the functions of argument. What evidence do we have for supposing that there is any such thing as an unchanging "intelligible character" that is the moral basis of our empirical deeds? Schopenhauer gives several answers, none of which, as it turns out, are very compelling. First, despite the fact that, upon reflection we find that every deed of our empirical self was determined with strict necessity (and we will return to Schopenhauer's special notion of necessity below), we nonetheless always feel responsible for our actions; we know we are the doers of our deeds, whereas if our deeds were only the result of strict necessity, that is, if there was no "free" element in our agency, this feeling would not arise (WWR1, 289; FW 133–4). But, as Christopher Janaway has pointed out, this feeling of responsibility for our deeds cannot even be explained from Schopenhauer's own account, for if the intelligible character, which Schopenhauer further maintains is unalterable, lies behind our acts, we must accept that we were bound to act in only a certain way and thus would be irrational in feeling moral responsibility (242–3). In any event, some persistent "feeling" of responsibility cannot be solicited on its own as evidence that we are responsible agents, for that feeling itself needs to be justified. The next basis Schopenhauer gives for positing the intelligible character as the real moral agent of actions is that, when someone engages in immoral conduct, we do not tend to blame him for the motives he entertained in his misbehavior, but rather blame him for what kind of a person he is, what kind of character he has, and this kind of moral assessment is grounded in our knowledge that deeds issue from a fixed character (FW 134). Again, this proves nothing more than that we may be accustomed to make moral judgments in certain ways and not others: it in no way justifies the claims of those judgments.

The most serious argument Schopenhauer offers in support of the intelligible character really comes out of the larger context of the importance he attached to the need for some philosophical explication of responsibility or moral agency. The basis for moral philosophy has in the West been traditionally associated with theology, and even though Kant effectively put an end to speculative theology through his critical philosophy, theological morals enjoyed an unhappy and mischievous resurrection in Kant's *Critique of Practical Reason* (Schopenhauer BM 53–8). Any moral system based on theological premises must in any event be bankrupt. In the first place, since in a theological worldview, the nature of each individual is a unique creation of God, God must assume ultimate responsibility for their moral character as well, and by extension, their deeds, in which case human beings really bear no substantive responsibility for their deeds (WWR1, 374–5). Secondly, the moral incentives which a theological system inculcates in people are always informed by egoism, for that system offers in exchange for the practice of virtue, seen as duty to God, rewards in the afterlife (WWR1, 524). The rejection of theological morals has led philosophers to two others alternatives. First was the idea that the human being's moral agency lies in his or her ability to chose among several alternatives of action in any given case; that is to say, responsibility lies in our freedom of will. Schopenhauer believed however that this version of a doctrine of freedom and moral responsibility could not hold good. Moral responsibility cannot follow simply from the state of two or more possible alternatives of action existing, for to merely contemplate "I can do this" or "I can do that," has only a subjective significance; it has no more moral worth than saying, for instance, "this pole . . . can topple over to the right or to the left" (WWR1, 290–1). That an alternative action was possible in any given case is irrelevant to the moral worth of an act; what is relevant is rather that the particular agent in the given instance performed the deed he in fact did. Moral responsibility then accrues to the agent not with respect to the choices available to him, but to his "character" which led him to make the choice he did.[7] The other alternative was to assent to strict determinism, for which people inevitably perform the actions they did, not because they possess any sort of unalterable character, but because they are completely physical beings, and as such completely determined according to the laws of nature.[8] The moral consequences of this position however entail that no one can be held accountable for anything. Schopenhauer found such thinking not only flawed but perverse. The world is not merely a series of physical events that passes in front of our consciousness and incites our scientific curiosity, but rather, as we have seen, we are grounded in the world by will, which makes the world as representation significant to us. The will is also what impels us to action, for as Schopenhauer constantly insists, every bodily act is an act of will. Thus, the world has not only a physical significance, but a moral one as well. But in order to meaningfully claim that the world indeed has moral significance, we must also have an account of moral responsibility. Schopenhauer, having found the previous accounts of moral responsibility inadequate, is obliged to provide an alternative. He finds an explanation of the basis for moral responsibility in Kant's notion of the "intelligible character." In order for us to viably say that someone is responsible for their deeds, according to Schopenhauer, there must be some way that we can show that an agent is non-contingently related to the acts he performs, so that his deeds "belong" uniquely to him. The intelligible character, as Schopenhauer conceives it, is the fixed, abiding, inborn nature of an individual, and so for him fulfills the requirements of a moral agent.

> Only if the true nature of man is his own *will*, consequently if he is, in the strictest sense, his own work, are his deeds actually entirely his and attributable to him. On the other hand, as soon as he has another origin, or is the work of a being different from himself, all his guilt falls back onto the origin or originator. For *operari sequitur esse.* (WWRII, 589)

This Scholastic formula, "*operari sequitur esse,*" or "deeds follow from essence," lies at the heart of Schopenhauer's ideas on character, for only if each human being has some fixed essence can we say that his actions truly come from who or what he is. The "intelligible character" is for Schopenhauer the manifestation of will as it appears in each individual person, and so on this theory the deeds of all persons are in the end grounded in their inmost natures.[9] Commentators have lamented various aspects of Schopenhauer's view of the intelligible character. Patrick Gardiner finds Schopenhauer's doctrine of actions inevitably ensuing from character to be too determinist, almost Calvinist, to provide us with a tenable theory of moral responsibility, which for Gardiner must include some element of choice (261–3). For Janaway, as noted above, no sense of responsibility can follow from a story that tells us the only way an act was avoidable was for the agent to have had a completely different character; this position rather represents an a-moral determinism (243–4). Atwell was the lone defender of Schopenhauer's formulations of moral responsibility through an appeal to character. "It is precisely," he wrote, "when the explanation of an action ends with reference to the particular agent's character or will that the agent is most aptly said to be responsible for the action" (*Human* 42). That agent's particular contribution to the act, that is, is what gives the act moral worth, and the agent as such can reasonably be praised or blamed for it.

The great flaw that plagues Schopenhauer's notion of intelligible character is how he describes it *vis-à-vis* the "empirical character." After all, an act requires not merely a moral agent to whom blame or praise are attributed, but a person, a physical being who performs the act in question bodily. The "empirical character" is thus the physical body, the material basis of a deed, whom over time we come to know as a person. But, being part of the phenomenal world of space, time and causality, the behavior of the empirical character is bound and determined to those principles as well as to the dictates of will given it by the intelligible character. However, the intelligible character, itself outside the principle of sufficient reason and thus not subject to space, time or causality, bears an obscure and indeed dubious relation with the empirical self.

> The intelligible character of every man is to be regarded as an act of will outside time, and thus indivisible and unalterable. The phenomenon of this act of will, developed and drawn out in time, space, and all the forms of the principle of sufficient reason, is the empirical character as it exhibits itself for experience in the man's whole action and course of life. The whole tree is only the constantly repeated phenomenon of one and the same impulse that manifests itself most simply in the fiber, and is repeatedly recognizable in the construction of leaf, stem, branch, and trunk. In the same way, all man's deeds are only the constantly repeated manifestation, varying somewhat in form, of his intelligible character, and the induction resulting from the sum of these gives us his empirical character. (WWR1, 289–90)

Through the series and pattern of a person's actions, we come to know who that person is, or in other words, what sort of a character that person possesses. This is also the case with respect to our knowledge of ourselves. Schopenhauer maintains that we come to know who we are over time; as we grow in experience, we can take a fuller and fuller view of our deeds. The intellect does not have an "immediate" knowledge of the character in the same way we are said to have an "immediate" knowledge of the will in general, for the character is, in effect, the moral disposition of an individual, it has a moral content which can only be discovered through deeds in time (Schopenhauer WWR1, 290–1). Our "empirical character" is the "unfolding" or "manifestation" of our intelligible character, which is to say that we come to know who we are through what we do. Moral responsibility is traced to the intelligible character through the deeds of the empirical. The problem with this formulation, recognized readily and derided by many of Schopenhauer's commentators, is that Schopenhauer has left us no coherent way to trace moral responsibility from the empirical character to the intelligible, for he has left us no way to relate the two at all. Schopenhauer calls the intelligible character in the passage above "an act of will outside time." This definition is absurd on its face, for how are we to conceive of any act outside of time (see Hamlyn 129; Magee 207–8; Janaway 244)? If we were to attempt to reformulate the definition on Schopenhauer's behalf and say that it is really the empirical character that acts under the influence of the intelligible, we would still be pained to articulate the nature of this "influence." The intelligible character cannot cause an action any more than it can itself act, for the intelligible character is said to lie outside of time. Furthermore, how, if the intelligible character is associated in every case with a particular individual, can that character be unrelated to time in the ways Schopenhauer imagines? Schopenhauer's rigid insistence that moral agency be grounded in the "essence" of the individual, so that the significance of her actions derive directly from who she is, forces him to reject the empirical person as the moral agent, and saddles his moral theory with obscurity.

While Schopenhauer does think the intelligible character is non-spatial, non-temporal and uncaused, he cannot think this about actions or deeds themselves. As empirical phenomena, by his own definition of what constitutes empiricality, actions must be temporal, spatial, caused and necessary. The empirical character does not produce actions merely at the behest of an autonomous intelligible character, for the intelligible character, as we have seen, cannot cause actions in any event. In Schopenhauer's view, the causes of actions are motives. As early as his dissertation of 1813, Schopenhauer thematized the fourth "root" of the principle of sufficient reason, that transcendental governor of all empirical phenomena, to be the "law of motivation," or "causality seen from within" (FR 214). When we perform an act, according to the dissertation, we always ask why this act was performed and not another, we want to discover the cause of an act. In every case, for Schopenhauer, we find that a resolve to act is caused by a particular motive (FR 212). This notion is carried further in light of Schopenhauer's formulations of character in the systematic philosophy. "Every individual action follows with strict necessity from the effect of the motive on the character" (WWR1, 113). In the late 1830's, this conception of motive was defined still more succinctly. "Every action of a man is the necessary product of his character and of the operating motive. Given both of them, it follows inevitably. For a different one to originate, either a different motive or a different character would have to be posited" (FW 58). The motives are representations of desired ends, and are therefore known to the intellect, and the intellect can contemplate the motives and present them to the character "from every point of view," but the intellect does not choose to follow one motive or the other; rather "it awaits the real decision just as passively and with the same excited curiosity as it would that of a foreign will" (WWR1, 291). Schopenhauer's version of determinism in human conduct then has to do with the necessity with which the motives effect the character, and the reaction of the unalterable intelligible character that manifests itself in the empirical deed.

> If, as Kant's teaching as well as the whole of my system makes necessary, the will as thing in itself is outside time and outside every form of the principle of sufficient reason, then not only must the individual act in the same way in the same situation, and not only must every bad deed be the sure guarantee of innumerable others that the individual *must* do and *cannot* leave undone, but as Kant says, if only the empirical character and the motives were completely given, a man's future actions could be calculated like an eclipse of the sun or moon. Just as nature is consistent, so also is the character; every individual action must come about in accordance with the character. (WWR1, 292)

And again:

> The motives determining the phenomenon or appearance of the character, or determining conduct, influence the character through the medium of knowledge. Knowledge however is changeable, and often vacillates between error and truth; yet as a rule in the course of life it is rectified more and more, naturally in very different degrees. Thus a man's manner of acting can be noticeably changed without our being justified in inferring from this a change in his character. What the man really and generally wills, the tendency of his innermost nature, and the goal he pursues in accordance therewith—these can never change by influencing him from without, by instructing him, otherwise we should be able to create him anew. Seneca says admirably: *velle non discitur* (willing cannot be taught). . . . From without, the will can be effected only by motives; but these can never change the will itself, for they have power over it only on the presupposition that it is precisely such as it is. (WWR1, 294)

In other words, Schopenhauer believes that, while motives can change in accordance with an improved knowledge of how a person can attain the ends to which they are inclined, no motives can change those inclinations themselves. The example Schopenhauer seems to get the most traction out of in this regard is that of an egoist who once stored up all of his wealth, only to give it all away on being told that he would receive it back a thousand-fold in heaven. We cannot say his character has been changed under the influence of a religious doctrine; we can only say that he has found a better means, a more effective motive (albeit for Schopenhauer a fictitious one) to meet the demands of his selfish character. As Schopenhauer is fond of saying, we cannot create morally virtuous or saintly people from classes on ethics any more than we can produce great artists from classes on aesthetics. The motives cannot change the character, and in fact can only have an "effect" on the person if that person has a character of a certain kind in the first place. Thus, the motives and character produce only certain actions in any given circumstances with necessity.

Again, Atwell cane to a spirited defense of Schopenhauer's conception of motives and how they effect the character.

> The sole cause of an action is the motive, which, given a certain character, "occasions" the action, which in turn "manifests" the character or individual will of the person. The character or will is simply the "ground" on which the operating motive causes the resultant action—this "ground" being necessary for any motive to operate, since motives alone and by themselves have no power. Designating the character as the will, indeed as the "I will" that accompanies all of my actions, and conceiving of it as a susceptibility to and not a product of motives, Schopenhauer can conclude with some plausibility that I will everything that I do, that I and I alone am the doer of my deeds, and that I am fully responsible for every one of them. (Atwell *Human* 35)

The point that Atwell is pushing here is that a motive has no power in and of itself; rather, a motive is such only for someone, a motive is a motive only insofar as it impels a particular individual to act. A motive requires that someone be susceptible to it, and this susceptibility to motives that is unique to each individual is for Schopenhauer the character. Atwell uses this point to buttress the characterological theory of responsibility in Schopenhauer he finds so appealing. Indeed, this point about motives, susceptibility and character may be accepted as it stands. On the other hand, it does not prove anything regarding the supposed "inalterability," "uniqueness" or transcendental status Schopenhauer wishes to impute to the intelligible character. In fact, as we saw above, the intelligible character lies outside space, time and causality, and this makes it nonsensical not only to say that the intelligible character can "cause" an act, but also to claim that it can be "effected" by a motive. What sorts of effects can be worked upon something that in no way enters into the causal chain of events as the intelligible character does not?[10] On what basis, furthermore, can we say that "the motives effect the character with necessity" when we have no way to account for the effect, much less its necessity, to begin with, since nothing can be intelligibly said to be "necessary" about the character? While appealing in its efforts to work out a coherent formula of moral responsibility and compelling in some of the claims it posits regarding the need for a "ground" upon which motives work, Schopenhauer's theory of agency buckles under the weight of his strained and indeed Platonic definition of the intelligible character.

Schopenhauer's philosophical ruminations on motive and character are at any rate of great significance for the ethical and even acetic theories to which he adheres. There are in Schopenhauer's thought three basic "moral" and "anti-moral" incentives or motives by which human beings are moved most readily, namely egoism, malice, and compassion. Each of these motivations brings to the character its own maxims for conduct. Corresponding roughly to these three motives are three fundamental types of character, that of the "bad man," the "just man" and the "good man" who are in varying degrees susceptible to these motives. The overriding and indeed dominant motivation for human conduct Schopenhauer holds to be egoism, and thus the fundamental moral dilemma revolves around how virtue can be produced by rendering it impossible for egoistic motivations to effect the character. Egoism, it will turn out, has its basis in *māyā*, the falsification of the world brought about by the *principium individuationis*, and so seeing through "the veil of *māyā*" is central, for Schopenhauer, to any conduct properly considered virtuous. Real asceticism, on the other hand, can be brought about not merely through a reevaluation of the motives, but rather through what Schopenhauer thinks must entail a radical "destruction of the character." With Schopenhauer's doctrines of character and motive now in mind, we can proceed to a detailed consideration of these main topics of this chapter.

5.1.2 Egoism and the Basis of Moral Conduct

Schopenhauer, rejects a prescriptive ethics, that is, an ethics which lays out moral principles by which people should conduct themselves. This rejection was perhaps an outgrowth of

Schopenhauer's beliefs surrounding the freedom of the intelligible character. Schopenhauer considered freedom a "paradox," since, although every act of the empirical character is necessary with respect to the effect of the present motives on the character, the constitution of that character itself, its moral content, was the result of a free "act of will outside time." As we have seen above, this formulation is hardly satisfactory. But for Schopenhauer it meant that the moral content of the character could not be molded or altered through prescriptive or directive moral teaching. On the contrary, the individual will, the character, adopts its own maxims of conduct as its knowledge of itself grows through experience (Schopenhauer WWR1, 308).

Schopenhauer does not discuss in any detail the specifics of these "maxims of conduct" each individual will adheres to in the first volume of *The World as Will and Representation*.[11] In an 1840 essay submitted to the Royal Danish Society in response to a prize question on the basis of moral conduct, which, even though it was the only submission in response to the question, was not awarded the prize, Schopenhauer takes up this issue explicitly. The three fundamental incentives of acts of will, upon whose prompting all motives effect the character, Schopenhauer in this work identifies as egoism, a "boundless" inclination to procure one's one weal, malice, a desire for another's woe that is limited to "acts of extreme cruelty," and compassion, which desires another's weal and is the mark of all noble and magnanimous deeds (BM 145).[12] Each of these incentives, in its turn, has its own "axiom" of action. For egoism, the regulative principle of conduct is: "help no one; on the contrary, injure all if it brings you any advantage" (BM 92; 136). For malice, the corresponding principle is: "injure all people as much as you can" (BM 136). Compassion, in contradistinction to these incentives, lays down the rule: "injure no one; on the contrary, help everyone as much as you can" (BM 69). People of different "types" then are moved by these motives in varying degrees depending on what "mixtures" of moral traits constitute their characters. The "bad man" is always inclined to seek his own advantage, even if that entails that his behavior will compromise the wills or well-being of others (Schopenhauer

WWR1, 362). This inclination is a reflex of the egoism by which his character is constantly motivated and prompted to act (Ibid.). The wicked person, on the other hand, has become so spiteful in the privation of his own will's desires coupled with the beholding of the pleasures of others, that he acts no longer out of simple egoism, but with cruelty, malice and revenge to actively cause the suffering of others (WWR1, 362–3). There is then the "just man," who is motivated by a weak egoism, that is, the incentives to procure a good life for himself and his loved ones within the boundaries of the law, but not at the intended expense of others (WWR1, 370–1). Finally, we have the "good man," who performs acts of compassion because he has realized that the inmost nature of every individual is the same, and thus there is no basis for a hard distinction to be made between his own well-being and that of another (WWR1, 371–3).

Schopenhauer often complained about the simplistic nature of Kant's thought, the artificial derivation of a "symmetrical" table of categories, the formation of a disguised theological morals, and so on. But the above formulations do not exactly impress one with confidence that Schopenhauer's ethical thought was conceived with the sophistication that Kant's or anyone else's somehow lacked. On the other hand, Schopenhauer does not intend to give a comprehensive outline of the virtues nor a systematic presentation of moral principles. Indeed, Schopenhauer believed that the whole business of thematizing such systems was an exercise in talking around the central problem of ethics, namely, the discovery of a "basis" or "foundation" of moral conduct.

> The *principle* or the main *fundamental proposition* of an ethical system is the shortest and concisest expression for the line of conduct prescribed by it, or if it should have no imperative form, the line of conduct to which it attributes real moral worth. Consequently, this is its guide to virtue in general, an instruction expressed in one proposition, and thus "the what" of virtue. The *foundation* of an ethical system, on the other hand, is the "why or wherefore" of virtue, the *ground* or *reason* for that obligation, recommendation, or praise, whether

> such ground be now sought in the nature of man, in the external circumstance of the world, or in anything else. . . . The *principle*, the *fundamental proposition*, concerning whose purport all teachers of ethics are really in agreement, however much they may clothe it in different forms, will here be reduced to *that* expression which I regard as the simplest and purest of all, thus: "injure no one; on the contrary, help everyone as much as you can." This is really the proposition whose *establishment* is the constant endeavor of all teachers of morals. . . . It is the "why or wherefore" for which the "what" is still always sought. . . . The solution to this problem will furnish the real *foundation* of ethics. (BM 68–9)

It is not that moral principles and maxims are unimportant to ethical theories, and in fact for Schopenhauer, all ethical theories basically agree on the most laudable propositions of conduct. The real problem for ethics however is to justify why the moral principle of "injure no one; on the contrary, help everyone as much as you can" has more moral worth than any other alternative principle. This justification of the "highest" moral principle Schopenhauer calls the positing of the "why" of ethics, the "reason" for its particular support of moral principles, which themselves are the "what" or the moral content of ethics.[13]

All ethical thinkers of the past have tried to unite metaphysics and ethics, according to Schopenhauer, but they have done so by dissolving the difference between the "what" of ethics and the "why" (BM 68–9). This has had sometimes inspiring and sometimes disastrous consequences. Socrates tried to show that the Idea of the Good was both the paramount metaphysical and ethical reality; theological morals tried to do the same by rendering "God" and "good" synonymous; Spinoza's "pantheism" "bypassed the world's ethical significance" by calling everything "divine" and thus making nothing censurable; Hegel erred by equating morality with the State, which in truth is only an "abstraction" of the individuals that compose it (WWR2, 590–1).[14] Given these results, Schopenhauer felt it very important to hold to a clear distinction between the "why" of ethics, its foundation, and the "what" of morals, its principles. The ethical significance of actions derived for him not from any *a priori* nature of some moral maxim, nor from what a particular state or society deemed moral, nor from the effects of a specific deed, but from the intention with which the act was performed.

> The *intention* alone decides the moral worth or worthlessness of a deed, so that according to its intention, the same deed can be reprehensible or praiseworthy. Thus, whenever an action of some moral importance is discussed, everyone inquires into the intention, and by this alone is the action judged; as also on the other hand, everyone clears his character in his *intention* alone when he sees his act misinterpreted, or excuses himself if it has turned out unfavorably. (BM 66–7)

Indeed, ever since Aristotle, the moral culpability a person is thought to have with respect to her actions has much to do with the intention harbored when the act was performed, and through Roman law, much Western jurisprudence recognizes the importance of intent in adjudicating criminal acts. Schopenhauer, however, makes intention the sole measure through which we should regard particular acts as morally praiseworthy or contemptible. This notion, it would seem, had much to do with the pains Schopenhauer took to delineate the "three fundamental inclinations" by which people of different characters are moved to act, the three incentives which most color human motivation; egoism, malice and compassion. It is these motivations which for Schopenhauer make it possible for us to morally assess any given act.[15]

The motives that lie at opposed ends of the moral spectrum for Schopenhauer are egoism and compassion.

> It is therefore any action of the kind just described (acts of compassion) to which we attribute real *moral worth*. We find that their characteristic feature is the exclusion of that class of motives whereby all human actions are otherwise prompted, namely, those of self-interest in the widest sense of the term. If a self-interested motive is the

> only one, its discovery entirely destroys the moral worth of an action; and if such a motive acts as an accessory, the moral worth of the action is reduced by its discovery. The absence of all egoistic motivation is, therefore, *the criterion of an action of moral worth.* (BM 139–40)

The definition of a morally praiseworthy action given here, as characterized by "the absence of all egoistic motivation," is inadequate for Schopenhauer's own purposes, for a number of acts could be found to be free of self-interested motivation, leaving the refrigerator door open due to drowsiness or inattention, for instance, and still not be immoral on this standard. Schopenhauer thus quickly changes the definition of a morally praiseworthy act, while at the same time making more extreme the moral assessment of actions provoked by any other motive; "It is simply and solely . . . compassion that is the real basis of all *voluntary* justice and *genuine* loving-kindness. Only insofar as an action has sprung from compassion does it have moral value; and every action resulting from any other motives has none" (BM 144). Compassion is an active motive and a positive virtue for Schopenhauer, not merely "the absence of egoism from the motives." The measure of moral reproach we make of any given act though, for Schopenhauer, depends upon how egoistic we can find to have called it forth.

This is one aspect of Schopenhauer's moral philosophy with which John Atwell has taken serious issue. It is possible to perform a morally praiseworthy act on principle, even with a positive antipathy for the patient, as when a poor man returns a rich man's wallet merely because it belonged to him (Atwell *Human* 109–10). It is also possible to perform an act of beneficence for someone without compassion, that is, without perceiving them to be in any distress or suffering, as when, for instance, a professor gives a student a book for their mere intellectual betterment (*Human* 111). It is just as possible to do something highly self-sacrificial for someone without the act having any identifiable moral worth, as when one intelligent sister declines to go to college so her "duller" younger sister can go, or when parents indulge a child's selfish wish for a Porsche (*Human* 111; 113). In his doctrines of egoism and compassion, Atwell thinks, Schopenhauer has made a very unhappy moral oversight.

> Regarding this general matter, Schopenhauer has made the serious error of divorcing moral worth from what has worth. He fails to see that the moral worth of an action depends in part on the value of what it is meant to bring about. And whether another person's well-being is worthy of promoting depends largely on what his well-being amounts to and what its worth is. (Other things matter too.) If it amounts to nothing worthwhile, despite his desire for it, then actions devoted to furthering it have no moral worth. (Atwell *Human* 112–13)

This criticism echoed the complaints D. W. Hamlyn had with Schopenhauer's criteria for judging actions as moral or immoral. Hamlyn wrote that, while it is one thing to show that all truly just or philanthropic acts ensue from compassion, this does not tell us which acts are good and which not, much less does it show us the acts to which we can reasonably attach moral worth (135). These critiques are certainly sound, and make Schopenhauer's claim that the presence and degree of egoistic and compassionate motivations are the sole criteria for adjudicating moral worth hardly credible.

It is obvious, in any event, that Schopenhauer was deeply impressed by the phenomenon of egoism. He believed not only that egoism was pervasive in the widest range of human actions, but that it was an inevitable appearance of the will as it incarnated itself in a multiplicity and variety of individual creatures. The manifestation of individuality in the world from the original, homogeneous impetus of the metaphysical will gave rise to conflict, evil, and suffering. Most readers of Schopenhauer tend to agree that he is at his literary best when describing the range and consequences of egoism in the world.

> In general . . . the conduct of men towards one another is characterized as a rule by injustice, extreme unfairness,

> hardness, and even cruelty; an opposite course of conduct appears only by way of exception. The necessity for the State and for legislation rests on this fact, and not on your shifts and evasions. But in all cases not lying within the reach of the law, we see at once a lack of consideration for his like which is peculiar to man and springs from his boundless egoism, and sometimes even from wickedness. How man deals with man is seen, for example, in Negro slavery, the ultimate object of which is sugar and coffee. However, we need not go so far; to enter at the age of five a cotton-spinning or other factory, and from then on to sit there every day first ten, then twelve, and finally fourteen hours, and perform the same mechanical work, is to purchase dearly the pleasure of drawing breath. But this is the fate of millions, and many more millions have an analogous fate. (WWR2, 578)

Schopenhauer prided his ethical thinking on being centered on what actually motivates human beings rather than on categorical imperatives and universal values that would, if practiced, purportedly improve human society. He believed that it was more important to examine the principles by which people conducted themselves in their everyday lives and start one's moral philosophizing from there. But when we look at the everyday conduct of most human beings, Schopenhauer thinks, we will be overcome by the extent to which egoism informs and dominates human behavior. He at times calls egoism "colossal" and "cosmic" in its range and vehemence. Everything from the small business deals of the tradesman, the intrigues of family and interpersonal relationships to socioeconomic and legalized institutions like slavery, child labor and domestic and international politics are pervaded by egoistic motivations. The conflict and consequent suffering that are caused in the individual, social and political realms are incalculable, and have their basis in the fundamentally egoistic motivations that prompt people to seek the well-being of their own person, their own socioeconomic interests, their own nation, with either indifference to or positive contempt for the well-being of others. This "colossal" egoism was at the root then of all human misery and most of its misfortune, and so struck Schopenhauer as the most pressing problem for anyone concerned with ethics. To address the fundamental moral dilemma of human conduct is to ask how egoism becomes the operative motive of human behavior, and then to inquire into whether it is at all possible for people to be moved to act not by the interests of their own well-being, but by the well-being of others.

> How is it possible for *another's* weal and woe to move my will immediately, that is to say, in exactly the same way in which it is usually moved only by my own weal and woe? Thus, how is it possible for *another's* weal and woe to become directly my motive, and this sometimes to such a degree that I more or less subordinate to them my own weal and woe, normally the sole source of my motives? (BM 143)

Egoism Schopenhauer sees as at once an epistemological and axiological evaluation of the self as of primary importance, and so the conduct that it makes possible is ruled by maxims which affirm this priority over the beings and concerns of others. And so, the abolition of egoistic motivations involves a two-step process; first, it must be asked whether the epistemological priority egoism places on the self is in accord with the actual order of things in the world. If it is found that this epistemological centrality of the self does not square with the metaphysical nature of things, then egoistic conduct is not justifiable on moral grounds, and we must discover whether it is possible to prevent egoistic motives from effecting the character. Is it possible, that is, to effect an axiological transformation of motives, such that the well-being of others moves me with the same compelling force by which egoism once drove me? This is really the hub of Schopenhauer's system as he envisioned it, where metaphysics and ethics meet, and it is here that we discover that egoism is bound up with *māyā,* with the falsification of the world's and the self's true nature, and virtue necessitates an unraveling of this falsification through the knowledge brought by seeing through *māyā*'s "veil" and the "practical mysticism" of compassionate acts (BM, 212).

5.1.3 Falsification and Compassionate Identification

Schopenhauer begins his discussion of how the self gets its epistemological and axiological priority in egoism with the following explanation in the first edition of *The World as Will and Representation*.

> We have called time and space the *principium individuationis,* because only through them and in them is plurality of the homogeneous possible. They are the essential forms of natural knowledge, in other words, knowledge that has sprung from the will. Therefore the will will everywhere manifest itself in the plurality of individuals. This plurality, however, does not concern the will as thing-in-itself, only its phenomenon. The will is present, whole and undivided in each of these, and perceives around it the innumerably repeated image of its own inner being. . . . Therefore, everyone wants everything for himself, wants to possess or at least control everything, and would like to destroy whatever opposes him. In addition, there is in the case of knowing beings the fact that the individual is the bearer of the knowing subject, and this knowing subject is the bearer of the world. This is equivalent to saying that the whole of nature outside the knowing subject, and so all remaining individuals, exist only in the representation, and so merely indirectly, and as something dependent on his own inner being and existence. (WWR1, 331–2)[16]

Egoism has its foundation in the epistemological and metaphysical order of things, as Schopenhauer conceives it. Egoism is the axiological prioritization of the self over all other things and persons, but selfhood and individuality have their origins in the *principium individuationis,* that is to say, space, time and causality, which are the conditions that must obtain if something is to appear as a discrete phenomenon. The self is able to distinguish itself from other beings owing to these basic forms of perception.[17] But beyond this, the self, along with the world, is given in two aspects, as will and as representation. Since the will is homogeneous and indivisible, unaffected by space and time, we must say that it appears "whole and entire" in each individual, and since it is the ground of all existence, the individual, given to herself as will, takes herself to be the primary being and hence wills to possess or control everything for herself. Given to herself as representation, on the other hand, the individual recognizes that her subjectivity is the condition according to which any objects may be apprehended and thus perceived, in accordance with Schopenhauer's thesis of "subject-object correlativity."[18] This makes the individual's subjectivity "direct" and the objectivity of all that is apprehended "indirect," and this also confers upon the self priority. The self, that is, is known "immediately" as will and "directly" as representation, while others are unknown to the self as will, at least in any "direct" way, and are known according to representation as mere "indirect objects," so to speak. The primary epistemological and metaphysical position of the self then is built upon these facts of consciousness. Schopenhauer repeats the epistemological explanation of the basis of egoism in the 1840 essay *On the Basis of Morality*, though he leaves the metaphysical dimension of the above passage out of consideration.

> By its nature, *egoism* is boundless; man has the unqualified desire to preserve his existence, to keep it absolutely free from pain and suffering, which includes all want and privation. He desires to have the greatest possible amount of well-being and every pleasure of which he is capable; in fact, where possible, he attempts to develop within himself fresh capacities for enjoyment.... "Everything for me and nothing for the others" is his motto.... Accordingly, everyone makes himself the center of the world, and refers everything to himself.... This is due ultimately to the fact that everyone is given to himself *directly*, but the rest are only given to him *indirectly* through the representation in his head, and the directness asserts its right. Thus in consequence of the subjectivity essential to every consciousness, everyone is himself the whole world, for everything objective exists only indirectly, as mere representation of the subject, so that everything is always closely asso-

> ciated with self-consciousness. . . . Accordingly, everyone is all in all to himself; he finds himself to be the holder and possessor of all reality, and nothing can be more important to him than his own self. (BM 131–2)

Schopenhauer adds one more psychological aspect to the prioritization of the self above all others in *The Basis of Morality* as well as the second edition of *The World as Will and Representation* in 1848. While thinking itself most important on the "subjective view," that is, with a knowledge of the centrality of her own subjecthood to representation, the individual sees at the same time a huge multiplicity of other individuals in the world, and this incites her spiteful wrath, wanting to be regarded as the most important among them (BM 133; WWR2, 600). But the two most important bases for egoism remain the self's belief that it is the ground of all reality as will, and the ground of all representation as the subject.

The next step in the formation of the egoist's "worldview" is that, given the perceived centrality of the self in the metaphysical and epistemological scheme, the individual comes to make rigid distinctions between herself and others, distinctions which have axiological and ethical implications. If my will is experienced directly, and my subjectivity as the only subjectivity, than my personhood is experienced with a vividness and immediacy that never is presented to me in my experience of others. I come to regard myself as of a distinctly different nature from, and hence as uniquely more important than others. And so, I seek my own well-being more than I seek the well-being of others, and if it goes too far, I seek my own advantage at the expense of others. These distinctions to which egoism comes to hold fast constitute metaphysical errors, according to Schopenhauer, for metaphysically, every individual, and not just oneself, is grounded in the same homogeneous and unitary will, just as the subjectivity of every individual is not unique to them, but is at least formally transcendental. These metaphysical errors, however, are not merely conceptual confusions, but result from the epistemological falsification of the thing in itself, the will, that is effected by the *principium individuationis*, or *māyā*.

> The eyes of the uncultured (*ungebildet*) individual are clouded, as the Indians say, by the veil of *Maya*. To him is revealed not the thing-in-itself, but only the phenomenon in time and space, the *principium individuationis*, and in the remaining forms of the principle of sufficient reason. In this form of his limited knowledge, he sees not the inner nature of things, which is one, but its phenomena, as separated, detached, innumerable, very different, and indeed opposed. (WWR1, 352)

Schopenhauer repeatedly refers to the unenlightened egoist as enveloped in *māyā*, ignorant of the unity which underlies all plurality and individuality, and basing his behavior on this falsified apprehension of things. He even asserts that the "bad person," one possessed with a selfish or malicious character, occasionally has glimpses of this fundamental error.

> However densely the veil of *Maya* envelopes the mind of the bad person, in other words how firmly involved he is in the *principium individuationis*, according to which he regards his person as absolutely different from every other and separated from it by a wide gulf, a knowledge to which he adheres with all his might, since it alone suits and supports his egoism . . . there is nevertheless roused in the innermost depths of his consciousness the secret presentiment that such an order of things is only phenomenon, but that in themselves, things are quite different. He has a pre-sentiment that, however much time and space separate him from other individuals and the innumerable miseries they suffer, indeed suffer through him; however much time and space present these as quite foreign to him, yet in themselves and apart from representation and its forms, it is the one will-to-live appearing in them all which, failing to recognize itself here, turns its weapons against itself, and by seeking increased well-being in one of its phenomena, imposes the greatest suffering on another. He dimly sees that he, the bad person, is precisely this whole will; that in consequence he is not only the tormentor but also the tormented, from whose suffering he is separated and kept

> free only by a delusive dream, whose form is space and time. (WWR1, 365)

This view of egoism having its axiological and epistemic roots in *māyā* remains constant through his later works, as we find in the 1840 *Basis of Morality*. As we saw above, Schopenhauer identifies all truly morally praiseworthy actions to be those actions in which egoistic motivations have been rendered refuted and abolished, so that the person can become amenable to the motive of compassion. Hence, the prerequisite for any moral action, the basis of morality, calls for the piercing through of the "veil of *māyā*."

> If plurality and separateness belong only to the *phenomenon*, and if it is one and the same essence that manifests itself in all living things, then that conception that abolishes the difference between ego and non-ego is not erroneous, but on the contrary, the opposite conception must be. We find also that this latter conception is described by the Hindus as *Māyā*, i.e., illusion, deception, phantasm, mirage. It is the former view which we found to the basis of the phenomenon of compassion; in fact compassion is the proper expression of that view. Accordingly, it would be the metaphysical basis of ethics and consist in *one* individual's again recognizing in another his own self, his own true inner nature. (BM 209)

Especial care needs to be taken in understanding Schopenhauer's descriptions of compassion, and the "identification" with another individual that he believes compassion requires, since this has been misunderstood and badly assessed by his commentators. To see past the *principium individuationis*, the forms of time and space, means for Schopenhauer to remove the boundaries between self and other, to "identify" with the other. But this "identification" is not, as some critics believe, thoroughgoing, it does not dissolve the identity, personhood or individuality of the other, or of the self, for that matter. It does not obliterate otherness by claiming that this obliteration is the only way compassion is possible; to appropriate the other's identity into one's own, and making this the basis upon which one is motivated to relieve the other's suffering. There is nothing particularly "mystical" about Schopenhauer's notion of compassion, in that his ethics of identification requires some sort of abrogation of the world of difference and action and thereby makes a "logical monstrosity" out of the ethical purview it claims. It is merely meant to follow from his doctrine of will as unitary thing in itself, and the epistemological falsification that compels us to take the inner natures of persons to be absolutely different. Contrary to the complaints of Schopenhauer scholars, it is with his notions of *māyā* and compassion that Schopenhauer's ethical thinking probably enjoys the greatest, and not the least amount of consistency, with his metaphysics.

Schopenhauer first asserts that seeing through "the veil of *māyā*," compassion and truly morally praiseworthy acts, "acts of love," are more or less the same.

> (The noble man) *makes less distinction than is normally made between himself and others*. This distinction is in the eyes of many so great, that the suffering of another is a direct pleasure for the wicked, and a welcome means to their own well-being for the unjust. . . . Generally most people know and are acquainted with innumerable sufferings of others in their vicinity, but do not decide to alleviate them, because to do so they would have to undergo some privation. Thus a strong distinction seems to prevail in each of all these between his own ego and another's. On the other hand, in the noble person, whom we have in mind, this distinction is not so significant. The *principium individuationis,* the form of the phenomenon, no longer holds him so firmly in its grasp; but the suffering he sees in others touches him almost as closely as does his own. He therefore tries to strike a balance between the two, denies himself pleasures, undergoes privations, in order to alleviate another's suffering. He perceives that the distinction between himself and others, which to the wicked man is so great a gulf, belongs only to a fleeting, deceptive phenomenon. He recognizes immediately, and without reasons or arguments, that the in-itself of his own phenomenon is also that of others,

> namely the will-to-live, which constitutes the inner nature of everything.... The veil of *Maya* has become transparent for the person who performs works of love, and the deception of the *principium individuationis* has left him. Himself, his will, he recognizes in every creature, and hence in the sufferer also.... To be cured of this delusion and deception of *Maya* and to do works of love are one and the same thing. (WWRI, 372–3)

Several salient points emerge from this long quotation. First, the "noble man" makes *less* of a distinction between himself and others following the principles of individuality, time and space; it is not the case that he makes no distinction between ego and non-ego. The commonality that the "noble man" shares with another comes from the realization that their respective individualities are manifestations of one and the same thing in itself, the "will-to-live." Consequently, the sufferings of the other are not so foreign to the self who has seen through these principles of individuality by which most human beings normally orient themselves toward the world, for they trick the latter into believing that there exist absolute differences between self and other. But that other and his sufferings are not obliterated by the dissolution of *māyā;* rather, they are responded to compassionately by someone who sees the self and the other in their true light, who actively tries to alleviate those sufferings.

Schopenhauer further elaborates on the mechanics of breaking through *māyā* and compassion in *On the Basis of Morality*.

> How is it possible for another's weal and woe to move my will immediately, that is to say, in exactly the same way in which it is usually moved only by my own weal and woe? Thus how is it possible for *another's* weal and woe to become directly my motive? . . . Obviously only through that other man's becoming the *ultimate object* of my will in the same way as I myself otherwise am, and hence through my desiring *his* weal and not *his* woe. . . . But this necessarily presupposes that, in the case of his *woe* as such, I suffer directly with him, I feel *his* woe just

> as I ordinarily feel only my own; and likewise, I directly desire *his* weal in the same way I otherwise desire only my own. But this requires that I am in some way *identified with him,* in other words, that this entire *difference* between me and everyone else, which is the very basis of my egoism, is eliminated, to a certain extent, at least. Now since I do not exist *inside the other man's skin,* then only by means of the *knowledge* I have of him, that is, of the representation of him in my head, can I identify myself with him to such an extent that my deed declares that difference abolished. However, the process here analyzed is not one that is imagined or invented; on the contrary, it is perfectly real and indeed by no means infrequent. It is the everyday phenomenon of *compassion* ... that is the real basis of all *voluntary* justice and *genuine* loving-kindness. Only insofar as an action has sprung from compassion does it have moral value; and every action resulting from any other motive has none.... Here the difference between him and me is now no longer absolute.... In that event, we see abolished the partition which, by the light of nature (as the old theologians call the faculty of reason), absolutely separates one being from another, the non-ego has to a certain extent become the ego. (BM 143–4)

Ethical "identification" in Schopenhauer's sense means that the difference between self and not-self is "no longer absolute," that the "partition by which the light of reason absolutely separates one being from another is abolished, *to a certain extent.*" The other must exist for compassion, for it is "his weal and woe" that become "the ultimate object of my own will," his suffering that becomes my motive. I can "identify" with him only through a transformed knowledge which renders the egoistic motivation uncompelling and the compassionate motive the operative one. An operative compassionate motive in its turn leads to an act. When speaking of rending or seeing through the veil of *māyā* then, Schopenhauer does not mean that the identity of the other or the self is dissolved; rather, the person no longer acts with the strict distinctions the principle of sufficient reason lays down as his guide to conduct. The self is not more real than the other, but both are phenomena of the will; the self is not more axiologically valuable than the other, because no definitive distinction between their inmost natures is tenable. While Schopenhauer does think that compassion is "astonishing" and even occasionally refers to it as the "great mystery of ethics," and even though he believes it is awakened by some sort of flash of intuitive insight, he doesn't seem to believe it is any way a kind of esoteric phenomena. Compassion is a completely normal and everyday occurrence in the great and small deeds of countless people.

Schopenhauer does his meticulous best to ensure that his doctrine of compassion as the partial abolition of the *principium individuationis* is not misunderstood by addressing a problem he detects in the theorizing of compassion by the German philosopher Cassina.

> In consequence of the above discussion on compassion as a state of being immediately motivated by the sufferings of another, I must censure the error of Cassina, which has since been so often repeated (*Analytical Essay on Compassion* [*Saggio analytico sulla compassione*], 1788; German translation by Pockels, 1790). His view is that compassion arises from an instantaneous deception of the imagination, since we put ourselves in the position of the sufferer, and have the idea that we are suffering his pains in our person. This is by no means the case; on the contrary, at every moment we remain clearly conscious that *he* is the sufferer, not *we*; and it is precisely in *his* person, not in ours, that we feel the suffering, to our grief and sorrow. We suffer *with* him, and hence *in* him; we feel his pain as *his*, and do not imagine that it is ours. (BM 147)

From these reasonably lucid passages, it should be clear that Schopenhauer's ethics of identification does not require that the identity of the self or the other be eliminated in order for compassion to take place. Indeed, compassion and the deeds which it prompts would be completely unintelligible were we to think this.

Compassion requires, in Schopenhauer's estimation, that self and other be neither absolutely different nor absolutely identical. What seeing through the "veil of *māyā*" does is relegate the difference between individuals to a merely phenomenal status, and by doing so connects them through the grounding of both self and other in the same metaphysical unity of will. This causes the "absolute distinctions" that are believed by the egoist to obtain between himself and the person to whom he is causing suffering to be null and void, and makes the egoist vulnerable to the very suffering he believes himself only to be causing. The character, with such a transformed knowledge of the relationship of itself to others and the world, can then supposedly be effected not merely by egoistic motives, but by compassionate ones. But this connection of the motivation of compassion to the character of the agents vulnerable to it is one Schopenhauer makes problematically, and to this we will return below.

Schopenhauer sums up his ethics of identification, the beholding of the true metaphysical relationship of individuals as opposed to the fabrications of *māyā*, by borrowing yet another *Upaniṣadic* formula to label that ethics. The formula is one of the so-called *māhāvākhyas* or "great pronouncements" of the early *Upaniṣads* employed to thematize the true relationship of identity between *ātman*, the transcendental "self" of every individual, and *brahman*, the "sacred power" which underlies and supports the phenomenal world.[19] "*Tat tvam asi*" or "that you are" for Schopenhauer is not merely a metaphysical truth that points to the ultimate unity of all things and beings in the world, but also the "maxim" by which compassion operates. This follows indeed from Schopenhauer's own deep-seated and persistent conviction that metaphysical knowledge is also ethical knowledge. They meet in the formula "*tat tvam asi*."

> In Sanskrit, *tat tvam asi* (this art thou) is the formula, the standing expression for this knowledge. It is this that bursts forth as *compassion* on which all genuine, i.e., disinterested virtue therefore depends, and whose real expression is every good deed. . . . For such an appeal is a

> reminder of that respect in which we are all one and the same entity. (BM 210)

Schopenhauer refers to this "standing expression," "*tat tvam asi,*" as the very pinnacle of all moral conduct from his early to his late works (see WWR1, 220; 355–6; 374; BM 210; WWR2, 600).

Despite the lucidity and relative straightforwardness of Schopenhauer's ethics of falsification, identification and compassion, misinterpretations and inaccurate assessments of it abound in the secondary literature. There are basically four characterizations and critiques of this part of Schopenhauer's ethics by his commentators. The first is the view, held by Patrick Gardiner, that Schopenhauer's ethics of identification is basically a revised Kantian ethics of "disinterest," that is to say, to be unmoved by egoistic motives means to be open to treat others in accord with their own interests and ends and not manipulate them according to one's own interests. Compassionate action is on this view disinterested action. We then find the contention of Christopher Janaway that Schopenhauer's notion of identification with the other vitiates the identity of the ego, which he explicitly needs in order to preserve such an ethic. That is, if Schopenhauer's notion of the cessation of falsification entails the dissolution of the ego, then the intersubjectivity required in compassion is rendered impossible. Gardiner articulated the opposite horn of this dilemma, namely, if the ego is maintained in a compassionate attitude, then identification means making another's sufferings one's own, and this makes the motive to alleviate them egoistic, contrary to Schopenhauer's intentions. Next is the objection of John Atwell that Schopenhauer's thoughts about compassion, rather than supported by his metaphysics, run directly counter to what Schopenhauer actually believes about "will-body identity" and the character of willing. Finally, in the most rigorous attack on Schopenhauer's position, Paul Hacker and Konstantin Kolenda charge that Schopenhauer's ideas about the dissolution of individuality through the collapse of the *principium individuationis* make any kind of intelligible discourse on ethics impossible. While there are certainly a number of serious problems with Schopenhauer's conception of identification within and without the larger context of his system, and I shall return to these below, every one of the objections brought forward by the above critics is misguided and in fact a misrepresentation of Schopenhauer's position.

Gardiner characterizes the central point of Schopenhauer's tirades against egoism, and the central ethical question that follows from these to be: "How can a man act in a disinterested way, so that what he does is done out of respect for the interests of others, even with a desire to promote those interests, to help those around him alleviate their sufferings" (167)? Gardiner spends some time connecting Schopenhauer's thoughts on compassionate identification with his other assertions that a "just" act is one that does not impose itself on another's will and a morally praiseworthy act is one which serves the interests of the other's will (272–3). Though Gardiner does show some comprehension of Schopenhauer's statements regarding the fabricated relationship between persons the *principium* presents to us, and the need to transcend them, the association of compassion with disinterest is not consonant with Schopenhauer's definition of compassion. Unfortunately, Schopenhauer carries most of the blame for this misunderstanding, by referring to compassionate acts as works of "disinterest," especially in his "metaphysical" explication of ethics in an appendix to his essay *On the Basis of Morality*. This carelessness does not help Gardiner or us remain altogether clear about Schopenhauer's otherwise consistent thematization of the issue. Compassion, for Schopenhauer, is not merely the absence of egoistic motivations, but is itself an active motive. Schopenhauer holds throughout his writings that it is not possible for any kind of deed to take place unless the character reacts to the effect of a motive. Indeed, he defines his ethics of identification as the attempt to discover "a motive that could induce man to take a line of conduct opposed to all those deeply ingrained tendencies of his nature" (BM 137). Compassion, for from being disinterested in a Kantian sense due to its surrender of the dictates of individual separation normally demanded by the intellect, takes on the interests of others with the axiological force with which one's own interests are normally pursued. Nor is compassion a "renunciation of will," which as we shall examine shortly, is the hallmark of Schopenhauer's account of asceticism; rather compassion is the adoption of pains and conflicts of the other's will in his or her suffering rather than one's own. Compassion is an active, motivated, interested and willful identification with the other, insofar as this is possible for knowledge and action, a process by which, as Schopenhauer says, "the very heart is enlarged."

Making reference to a passage by Schopenhauer on identification that runs "others are I once more," Christopher Janaway wrote: "Schopenhauer seems to be suggesting that it is in penetrating beyond the mere world of appearance that I am able to recognize others as 'I' " (282). What this amounts to, for Janaway, is that the morally good person has a realization, not merely as Schopenhauer says that we are all grounded in will, but also that others are centers of self-consciousness just as I am (282). That is to say, "a recognition of genuine *intersubjectivity* underlies the morally good, non-egoistic view of life" (Janaway 282). Janaway believes however that this line of argument is inconsistent with Schopenhauer's claims regarding the mere phenomenality of individuality. Janaway thinks that Schopenhauer is trying to say that the morally "noble" person has to have two conflicting realizations at once; namely that others are distinct centers of consciousness, but at the same time, on the level of will, the same as myself.

> While in practical terms egoism can be overcome by seeing others as distinct from oneself but as equal centers of consciousness, the dominant metaphysical reading of "others are I once more" precludes that possibility entirely. Schopenhauer cannot make morality depend on the recognition of inter-subjectivity, and at the same time explain its possibility in terms of the absorption of all individuals into a single will. (Janaway 283)

This statement by Schopenhauer that "others are 'I' once more" for the person who has seen through the *principium individuationis* is meant to serve as a kind of heuristic maxim for the compassionate person, a reminder that all individuals share phenomenality according to time and space, and one essential nature, the "will-to-live." But it has served as a stumbling block to Janaway, in the above characterization, as well as other commentators. Patrick Gardiner thought that Schopenhauer's precondition of moral behavior, the realization that all other selves are at bottom identical to my own, unintentionally implied that egoism was the only real motive behind compassionate acts.

> Is it in any case really necessary to suppose that the notion we ordinarily have of ourselves as separate individuals should inescapably and inevitably issue in actions of an unrestrictedly egotistical kind; and that it is impossible, for instance, for a man disinterestedly to go to the assistance of another if he does not regard himself as being, in some not very clear sense, 'identical' with him? Indeed it might be argued that such an assumption tacitly presuppose the belief that egoism does in the last analysis represent the only effective spring of human behavior whatever, moral as well as immoral, inasmuch as it still treats love of self as the ultimate determinant, even in altruistic or detrimental action, explaining such action by the metaphysical device of extending the concept of self to embrace the whole of mankind. (Gardiner 276–7)

In fact, Schopenhauer's theory of compassion does not incur difficulties of the kinds suggested by Janaway and Gardiner. In the first place, Schopenhauer's doctrine of compassion is not so much an experience of "intersubjectivity" as Janaway conceives it. Compassion is not based on the realization that "others are distinct centers of self consciousness," rather it is elicited by the beholding of another's suffering coupled with the realization that the other and myself are the *same kind* of beings. The other's suffering, that is, does not become an object of sympathy for me because I feel his pain as mine, or because I realize that he is a center of self-consciousness like I am and feels pain as I do. Schopenhauer's essentialism, his conviction that all human beings are on the one hand phenomenal representation and on the other noumenal will, is what makes possible the awareness of a moral agent that others and the self are axiological equals, and this knowledge in its turn can radically change human motives. As far as Gardiner's objection is concerned; again, Schopenhauer does not maintain that others must be regarded as the self in order for compassion to be possible, for this would indeed make the motivation to remedy their sufferings a kind of twisted desire to help oneself, in the end, egoism. As we have seen from the passages cited from Schopenhauer above, our motive in compassion is precisely to the help the *other*, the other's sufferings become my motive, and "we are at every moment fully conscious that *he* is the sufferer, not *we*; and it is precisely in *his* person, not in *our's* that we feel that suffering, to our grief and sorrow" (BM 147). Schopenhauer's clumsily worded, indeed misleading, heuristic maxim, "others are 'I' once more" does not mean that "all selves are myself, and thus I should help them," but rather it is meant to communicate the idea that "as an individual, I am in essence the will-to-live, and though the other is a different individual, she is also at bottom the will-to-live. We are not the same, *but then we are not essentially different*, and so I have no reason to believe my wants more important than her privation."

This misunderstanding of Schopenhauer's tenets about the basis of compassion, and their supposed abrogation of individuality as such, also gives rise to one of the two problems Atwell raised against this part of Schopenhauer's ethics.

> To affirm the will, Schopenhauer holds, is equivalent with affirming the body. Indeed, "the fundamental theme of all the many acts of will is the satisfaction of the needs inseparable from the body's existence in health." ... Being natural and being egoistic are, in effect, synonymous. Consequently, if a human being is ever to perform a compassionate act, he must transcend his natural being, or, to say the same, his egoistic being. Schopenhauer declares as much when he states that "morality has a source that really lies beyond nature" and "morality is directly opposed to the natural will, which in itself is absolutely egoistic." It thus becomes clear, contrary to what one might have expected, that an act of virtue for

> Schopenhauer (an act of compassion) . . . has to be an act, indeed an act of will, that is not egoistic, hence one that is not concerned with preserving or maintaining the agent's body or species, and that means it has to be an act that does not have corresponding to it a bodily action, every one of which is egoistic. In short an act of compassion has to be an act of will, parallel to which no bodily action occurs . . . and if a bodily action corresponds to every act of will (as Schopenhauer insists at the beginning of WWR I, Book One), then there can be no acts of compassion. And that fact demolishes Schopenhauer's ethics (according to his own criteria of the possibility of ethics). (Atwell *Human* 141–2)

Atwell relies for this objection on Schopenhauer's "will-body identity thesis," or the notion that "every bodily act is an act of will made manifest, or objectified." Thus, Atwell reasons, if all bodily acts are willed acts, and all willed acts are egoistic, then any act that is not egoistic is not a willed act, and therefore not a bodily act, and as such, really no act at all. Schopenhauer has in this way unwittingly precluded the entire possibility that compassionate acts are possible within his own metaphysical scheme, after having made compassion the foundation of ethical conduct. Indeed, Schopenhauer in the second volume of the second edition of *The World as Will and Representation* does make assertions to the effect that bodily acts are one and all devoted to preserving the individual, and so again Schopenhauer must bear the responsibility for the unfortunate inference that Atwell draws here. But in point of fact, nowhere in his original formulations on compassion in the first edition of *The World as Will and Representation* or in *On the Basis of Morality* does Schopenhauer posit any such thing. Compassionate acts must certainly be bodily acts, and as such they must be willed acts. A compassionate act, as we have said, results from a compassionate motive effecting the character, and as Schopenhauer unremittingly insists, the intelligible character is nothing other than the individual will; therefore, a compassionate act is a willed act. Rather than this act being the affirmation of the self's own body, however, it is instead an affirmation of the other's body, the other's interests, the other's being, the other's will. But even were he to have accepted that compassionate acts are affirmative acts of will, this would not satisfy Atwell, who had an additional, more psychologically oriented objection to this alternative at the ready.

> Let us return to the alms-giver. When he looks into the deep recesses of the beggar's heart, Schopenhauer claims, he finds himself, as stated in the formula this art thou. Now if he really believed this, he would be called not compassionate but insane. What does he believe then? Or better, what is it that he finds in the "inner nature" of both the beggar and himself? Does he find anything that would help make disinterested alms-giving meaningful? What he finds is simply the will-to-live. For this and nothing else (as far as one can know) is the thing-in-itself. This means that what he actually finds is sheer egoism-a drive to perpetuate itself, an impulse to continue existing (no matter what the cost for others), an insatiable, hungry, self-devouring force! This is what the alms-giver and the beggar have in common, that is their "inner nature."... If I really "see" the thing-in-itself "in" another person, what I "see" is the will-to-live, which is neither *my* will-to-live nor the *other's* will-to-live (hence both egoism and compassion drop out of consideration)—and I am facing something I am more likely to shrink from in horror than I am to sympathize with.... I am aware of nothing that might move me to compassion. (How could one have compassion for the will-to-live?). (Atwell *Human* 122–3)

Atwell's point is a simple and at first glance compelling one. If the person who sees past the "veil of *māyā*" indeed realizes that both the sufferer and self are the same "will-to-live" in essence, and if that "will-to-live" is nothing but a blindly and insatiably egoistic impulse to perpetuate one's own existence, why should the agent feel compassion instead of disgust and horror? Again, Atwell can be found to closely align "will" and "individual egoism" in this argument, in fact to align them more closely than Schopenhauer himself does. The will often extends beyond the individual, even in ways that are, as Atwell himself admits "species-egoistic" (Atwell *Human* 141). In the sexual impulse and subsequent parenthood for instance, the will according to Schopenhauer extends itself beyond the interests of the individual and his own body, and puts itself in the service of the species (see WWR1, 328–9; WWR2, 531–60). The will often benefits others, even when it is acting on egoistic motives, as when for instance a self-interested alms-giver surrenders all his belongings to the poor for the purpose of receiving a thousand-fold reward in heaven for his charity (WWR1, 524). But more relevant to the present argument by Atwell is Schopenhauer's other principle with regard to will, namely that will as it appears in the world, incarnated in individuals, guarantees that human life will be characterized by suffering. As an individuated will, each person normally tries to assert their own needs and desires over the needs and desires of others, and this leads to the temporary well-being of the stronger, as it were, and the suffering of the weaker. This ensures that all conscious life, human as well as animal, will be suffering (WWRI, 309–10). And so, to address Atwell's question of what it is about the will I should feel compassion for in the beggar, it is precisely the individual of the beggar, in whom the suffering of the will is so immediately apparent, that brings me the recognition that to will is not only to strive and desire, but also to suffer the consequences of the will's privation. To see into the true nature of will elicits not only the horror of its consequences for human life, but compassion for the suffering to which the will condemns itself. The sufferer makes the moral agent no longer only susceptible to the vicissitudes of his own desires, but vulnerable to the suffering she sees as the will in the person of another.

As we saw in the first chapter, Paul Hacker, one of the eminent twentieth century German scholars of traditional and modern Vedānta, established that Schopenhauer's understanding of the notion of *māyā* was based on a superficial reading of a very few texts from the classical *Upaniṣads* in poor translation. No ethical interpretation of *māyā* existed within the Vedāntic tradition before Schopenhauer, and after him, for Hacker, the attempt to make Vedāntic monism into an ethical doctrine resulted in little more than a "logical monstrosity" (qtd. in Halbfass *Philology* 306). Hacker characterizes Schopenhauer's metaphysics as a "monism of will," a system which posits that everything is will. Ultimately, a Schopenhauerian "monism of will," and even a Vedāntic "monism of consciousness," both of which base their respective claims on the formula "*tat tvam asi,*" cannot be ethical in any proper sense of the term, for any philosophy that dissolves personal identity into a metaphysical all-unity negates the significance of interpersonal relationship, and with that, morality. Hacker writes:

> From the philosophical point of view, to base the *tat tvam asi* ethic on the Vedāntic monism of consciousness is a logical impossibility. But even on the basis of a monism of will, if this is to be understood in a strictly ontological sense, it does not survive close examination. Ethical behavior presupposes an interpersonal relationship, which loses its metaphysical justification if individual personhood has no ultimate reality.... Relations between persons cannot be reduced to an egoism of the universal One, as the ethics of the monism of will ultimately does.... The idea that ultimate reality is a universal One is always supra-ethical in the end. In the case of the monism of will, this feature is only superficially disguised by placing ethical behavior in the realm of true Being. For the monist of will means to *break through* the *principium individuationis,* as through a "veil of *Māyā,*" as Schopenhauer puts it. This aim he shares with the monist of cognition or consciousness. Besides, whether the principle of individuality starts from space, time and causality, as in Schopenhauer, or from metaphysical "unknowing" as in Vedāntic monism, in either case individuality must be annulled, either forever or temporarily. But personality presupposes individuality, and the possibility of ethical behavior presupposes the existence of persons. (qtd. in Halbfass *Philology* 305–6)

On Hacker's interpretation, all individuality is extinguished, and rendered philosophically irrelevant, on Schopenhauer's view that everything is grounded in one universal essence. When individuality is rendered insignificant, ethics becomes meaningless. And so, despite Schopenhauer's insistence that his was a philosophy that was at once metaphysics and ethics, Hacker claims that it is precisely the monism of Schopenhauer's metaphysics of will that makes it impossible for Schopenhauer to engage in any coherent ethical discourse.

This critique was echoed two and a half decades after Hacker by Konstantin Kolenda, from a slightly different perspective. Kolenda held that Schopenhauer claims in his philosophy a privileged position, as one speaking from the point of view of someone who saw into the nature of the one true reality, will. But that point of view actually ends up being, as Kolenda puts it, "a view from nowhere." "Speaking for the one will, he does not express a *particular* point of view which could be compared or contrasted to some *other* points of view. Instead, he proclaims the truth about the will from beyond any such views . . . he occupies a position outside all positions, and thus his view is a view from nowhere" (Kolenda 254). Kolenda concludes that this "position outside all positions," this standpoint of will Schopenhauer believes he occupies, cannot speak from within the space where ethical claims are meaningful, for that space is a community of speakers who each occupy their own position.

> To propose a course of action as morally desirable is not to appeal to some transcendent fact to which one claims privileged access, but to speak out of respect for values which those addressed can be expected to share. . . . In order for ethical language to happen, it must be addressed by someone to someone. Moral judgments can be made in good faith only by a moral subject. Such a subject, however, does not stand in an empty moral field, but must start with some commitments which relate him or her morally to other subjects. In other words, moral discourse presupposes a moral community and cannot have the form of decisions pronounced from a purely subjective, morally neutral position. (Kolenda 255)[20]

Both these criticisms, with their slightly different approaches, reach the same conclusion; that Schopenhauer's metaphysics of will, what is really a monism of will, derogates individuality as ultimately unreal, and in doing so removes itself from the arena of ethical theorizing. Whether Schopenhauer's metaphysics is a monism of will is a debatable point. True enough, Schopenhauer asserts that "no will, no representation, no world," and so the world as representation is dependent on will, emerges out of it and is supported by it. But this is not exactly the point, for merely citing that Schopenhauer believes that one and the same essence underlies all things does not make a mockery out of ethical discourse. Schopenhauer, in his philosophy, attempts to give an account of "the world," that is to say, an account of human experience, and no account of "the world" would be adequate for him that did not deal with both will and representation. Now the individual for Schopenhauer is assuredly a representation, an appearance, a phenomenon, a reflex of the conditions of perception even. This does not entail however that the individual is in any sense "unreal," for as long as there is a "world," there will be individuals in relationship, and as long as these individuals are grounded in will, their existences in the world will be ones of volition, intention and axiological evaluation, and therefore the relationships in which these individuals stand will be ones of moral significance. As we have seen from Schopenhauer's own passages dealing with compassion and have repeated against his critics above, nothing about Schopenhauer's ethical maxims abrogates individuality. A malicious, morally deplorable, just, or compassionate relationship is for Schopenhauer always a relationship between two individuals. It is merely the case, Schopenhauer contends, that in compassion, the difference between those two individuals is for at least one of the partners in the relationship no longer absolute and final, and different individuals is not all individuals are. Neither is it the case, as Kolenda contends, that anyone in a moral relationship ever occupies, as he puts it, a "privileged position," or entertains "a view from nowhere." A compassionate view is a morally engaged one, inasmuch as it beholds the hardships of another, feels them with great force, invests in them great importance and compels the agent to actively take upon herself those hardships.

It seems then that Schopenhauer's foundation of ethics, compassion which sees through the principles of individuation, "the veil of *māyā*," and thus affords the recognition that others are of equal axiological value to myself since we are both manifestations of the striving and suffering "will-to-live," is at least defensible on the grounds upon which he has based it. But then again, this may be the greatest limitation of his ethics, that is, that it is defensible *only* on the grounds upon which he has based it. The metaphysics of will and the ethics of compassionate identification are bound so tightly together in Schopenhauer that the rejection of one necessitates a rejection of the other. Schopenhauer may have pointed out something important about the "view" of the compassionate person, to the effect that the compassionate agent believes we ought to help one another because we are not, even in terms of our respective unique individualities, essentially different. But this is not all Schopenhauer thinks the compassionate person believes, for his motive to alleviate the sufferings of others is also based on the conviction that we are *essentially the same*. This is not so objectionable in the sense that it abrogates individuality, as the above commentators have in various fashions mistakenly charged. But it does hinge the motivation for compassion upon an essentialism of will that we have seen in the last chapter is itself highly questionable, and apart from this essentialism, Schopenhauer leaves any other possibility for ethical motivation closed. It is perhaps in this consequence that Schopenhauer's "good faith" as an ethical theorist is brought most seriously into doubt, for we are left to wonder whether he has committed himself to explaining to us how people can and do behave morally or immorally, or whether he is merely courteously informing us that all good people are good because they are either consciously or unconsciously Schopenhauerians, while all bad people are bad because they do not buy Schopenhauer's metaphysical picture of the world. There is of course nothing wrong with formulating an ethical theory in conjunction with some system of metaphysics, as Schopenhauer and so many other philosophers attempt to do. But a good test of the veracity of an ethical principle is to see whether such a principle retains its ethical character regardless of whether the system within which it was born itself stands or falls. While compassionate actions may indeed retain their ethically praiseworthy status irrespective of whether or not Schopenhauer's system withstands scrutiny, the particular grounds Schopenhauer thinks compassion has as a motive are not ones he considered to be metaphysically flexible.

One other major problem with Schopenhauer's ethics of compassionate identification is that he does not square it altogether clearly with the other part of his ethics, which deals with motives and character. As we have seen, compassion is what Schopenhauer has called a "moral incentive," or a "motive." It has the virtue of bringing with it a knowledge or vision of the world which renders the morally deplorable motive of "egoism" untenable and unable to effect the character in its resolve to act. This is all well and good on its own. But the significance of this possibility that the motives can be radically changed from egoistic to compassionate ones is obscured greatly when one remembers Schopenhauer's other contention about the "intelligible character," that it is unalterable. There are in Schopenhauer's scheme, as seen above, three or four basic moral "types" of character; the "wicked," the "bad," the "just" and the "good." These characters are such because we can tell, through our familiarity with a person's "empirical character," that people are susceptible only to motives of certain kinds, either malicious, egoistic or compassionate. Of course Schopenhauer thinks the situation is complicated, and that different characters have different proportions of these basic moral and anti-moral traits. He even concedes, as we cited above, that the "bad person" sometimes gets a glimpse at the true nature of suffering and the phenomenality of individuality, which is basically the content of a compassionate motive (WWRI, 365). But, he insists, the character is unchangeable, and as a result, "bad" people only respond in deed to motives which are "egoistic," while "good" people respond faithfully to motives which are compassionate.

> Everyone will be powerfully stirred by *those* motives to which he is predominantly susceptible, just as one body reacts only to acids and another only to alkalies; the one like the other cannot be changed. The motives of loving-kindness, which are for the good character such powerful incentives, can as such have no influence on a man who is susceptible only to egotistical motives. If, however, we wish to induce the egoist to perform actions of loving kindness, we can do it only by deluding him with such ideas that the alleviation of another's suffering contributes indirectly in some way *to his own advantage* (indeed most doctrines of morals are really attempts of different kinds in this sense). In this way, however, his will is merely misled and not improved. For a real improvement, it would be necessary to transform the entire nature of his susceptibility to motives. (BM 193)

Moral improvement, for Schopenhauer, is impossible, for to accomplish this it would be necessary to be able to actually change the character, which we cannot under any circumstances do. This means, in effect, that a "bad" person will never see through "the veil of *māyā*," and thus can never have any capacity to have his motives transformed so that he could act in a truly morally laudable fashion. No one, in fact, is ethically transformed by piercing through *māyā*, for the good, compassionate agent sees through it by virtue of his goodness, while the egoist is an egoist because he cannot. This makes it strange that Schopenhauer ever felt it necessary in the first place to draw out for us how and why "good" and "bad" persons view the world in the ways they do, when all he seems to have required for his characterological theory of moral agency and responsibility is that "good" people do compassionate things and "bad" people do egoistic things. What difference should their respective "views" of the world make to such a theory of ethics if changing these "views" could in no way change their characters or patterns of action?

Schopenhauer does in the end leave open one opportunity for the knowledge brought by the dissolution of falsification to definitively alter the course of human conduct. But this opportunity is one in which penetrating the "veil of *māyā*" and seeing into the true nature of the world does not change or improve the human character, but paradoxically, dramatically "destroys" it. This is the subject with which Schopenhauer closes his systematic philosophy, and even more positively links his metaphysics and ethics to his thesis of falsification. We shall thus conclude this chapter with a brief examination of the relationship the falsification thesis bears to Schopenhauer's thoughts on the "renunciation of will."

5.2 FALSIFICATION, RENUNCIATION AND "NOTHINGNESS"

Schopenhauer committed himself in his ethical theory to explain a wide range of human behavioral tendencies, and in doing so, includes in this part of his system many different psychological observations of everyone from the genius and artist to the schizophrenic and suicidal personalities. This desire to describe comprehensively the whole range of human conduct compelled Schopenhauer to also give an explanation of asceticism. Moral and spiritual asceticism Schopenhauer characterizes as a "renunciation of will." "By the expression of asceticism. . . . I understand in the narrower sense this *deliberate* breaking of the will by refusing the agreeable and looking for the disagreeable, the voluntarily chosen way of life of penance and self-chastisement, for the constant mortification of the will" (Schopenhauer WWR1, 392). In ascetic self-discipline, people renounce sexual gratification, fast, deny themselves worldly ambitions and give up their egoistic motivations. But contrary to what various religious traditions may say about the purpose of asceticism, that its ultimate goal is closeness to or unity with God or some notion of universal "Being," Schopenhauer contends that what happens in the disciplines of the ascetic is a "renunciation" or "denial" (*Verneinung*) of the unitary ground of existence, the thing in itself. An ascetic, for Schopenhauer, is an incarnate "contradiction," for while his or her body is a manifestation of the will, in all of its organs and functions, he or she renounces willing. While the sexual organs are an "objectification" of the "will-to-live" striving to transcend the individual, the ascetic renounces sex. While the stomach and gullet are manifestations of the impulse to preserve the existence of the individual in a different organ, the ascetic fasts. While the brain, hands and feet are manifestations of will put to the service of procuring and preserving the interests of the individual, the ascetic renounces worldly knowledge and ambitions (WWR1, 334; 380).[21] Schopenhauer further says of asceticism that it is the genuine realization of "salvation" (*Erlösung*), for through it, one is freed from the world of struggling and suffering, the great endless contest and conflict of the will with itself.

The aspect of Schopenhauer's doctrines of asceticism that will be emphasized in this short section will be their relationship to his thesis of falsification. Asceticism has an epistemological prerequisite, Schopenhauer believes, which demands that one see through the "veil of *māyā*" to such a degree that the will as thing in itself is completely revealed to a person. In that event, an individual recognizes the horrible fate to which the will, forever at odds with itself in the agonistic relationships of conscious beings, condemns the world, and this recognition impels one to "renounce" the will, to put an end to its tireless insatiability at least in his own body and person. When this renunciation has been thoroughly perfected by the disciplined ascetic, an extraordinary epistemological and moral transformation takes place, in which the world of will and representation becomes for the purified individual a kind of "nothing," and the character with all its moral and anti-moral inclinations is dissolved. This recognition and transformations represent the final grafting of the falsification thesis to Schopenhauer's metaphysics and ethics, and so we shall give a brief exposition of them as Schopenhauer brings his system to a close.

5.2.1 Māyā and "Eternal Justice"

In order for the individual to be motivated to renounce the "will-to-live," which animates their own existence as well as the existence of all other things, Schopenhauer believed that the suffering of the world must somehow be "seen," or "intuitively beheld."

> If that veil of *Maya*, the *principium individuationis*, is lifted from the eyes of a man to such an extent that he no longer makes the egotistical distinction between himself and the person of others, but takes as much interest in the suffering of other individuals as in his own, and thus is not only benevolent and charitable in the highest degree, but even ready to sacrifice his own individuality whenever several others can be saved thereby, then it follows automatically that such a man, recognizing in all beings his own true and innermost self, must also regard the endless sufferings of all that lives as his own, and thus take upon himself the pain of the whole world.... As he sees through the *principium individuationis*, everything lies equally near to him. He knows the whole, comprehends its inner nature, and finds it involved in a constant passing away, a vain striving, an inward conflict, and a continual suffering. Wherever he looks he sees suffering humanity and the suffering animal world, and a world that passes away.... Now how could he, with such knowledge of the world, affirm this very life through constant acts of will, and precisely in this way bind himself more and more firmly to it, press himself to it more and more closely?... That knowledge of the whole, of the inner nature of the thing-in-itself, which has been described, becomes a *quieter* of all and every willing. The will now turns away from life, it shudders at the pleasures in which it recognizes the affirmation of life. Man attains to the state of voluntary renunciation, resignation, true composure, and complete will-lessness. (WWR1, 378–9)

Schopenhauer's statements regarding this "renunciation of will" are not altogether clear and at times even conflicting. Even though he claims in the passage above that the person who has seen through *māyā* "must" deny the will because it "inevitably follows" from his transformed knowledge, he acknowledges just a few sentences later that it is possible for many of us to have small epiphanies of this "knowledge of the whole" and continue to affirm life, to "backslide" into willing (WWR1, 379–80). Again, above, Schopenhauer posits that renunciation is a "voluntary" act, and in other places says that renunciation is the result of a constant effort and struggle against one's own will, but elsewhere he attempts to persuade us that denial of will is the result of a "free" act of the will, and is a manifestation of "grace" (WWR1, 391–2; 402–3). In effect, Schopenhauer thought that denial of the will was a "free" act of "grace" because, while in normal action which is governed by the principle of sufficient reason the character always responds to motives, when these principles of reason are superseded, "the individual motives become ineffective" (WWR1, 403). They become so because in the denial of will, there is no longer any character for them to effect! "The character itself can be entirely eliminated by the above-mentioned change of knowledge.... It is not a question of a change, but of an entire suppression of the character" (WWR1, 403). The renunciation of will is the renunciation of the "individual will," and this has earlier been defined precisely as the character. The only entry of freedom then into the moral life of people is for Schopenhauer in asceticism, in which the "denial of the will-to-live" destroys the character, whereupon the motives that were once necessarily subject to the principle of sufficient reason, which impel one to engage in immoral, and even moral conduct, are rendered utterly ineffectual. It is certainly not easy to see how Schopenhauer could make these two conceptions of renunciation, one as a "voluntary act" and the other as an "effect of grace," consistent with one another. Indeed, Schopenhauer, in perhaps one of his exceedingly rare moments of humility, is not timid in conceding this point, referring constantly as he does to denial as a "contradiction" which he cannot unravel.

What is clear from Schopenhauer's thematization of will-renunciation is that the cessation of falsification, the full piercing through *māyā,* is a pre-requisite for its accomplishment. With the full dissolution of the *principium individuationis,* Schopenhauer thinks, the individual will no longer make distinctions even between her own suffering and that of another, in contrast to what he says about actions that are motivated by compassion. When *māyā* is taken away, I no longer even make distinctions between my own will and the wills of others, but see the thing in itself in all its ill-fated glory, as the ground upon which all want, confrontation and consequent suffering rest. No more can one who is opened up to all of this even be content with compassionate assistance to those in need, for the horror of the world has become overwhelming. In one of Schopenhauer's oddest ethical formulations, the ascetic sees into the meaning of "eternal justice" (*ewige Gerechtigkeit*). Normally, those of us deluded by *māyā* seek redress for immoral conduct in the world because of our fixation on individuality. "He," Schopenhauer says describing such a deceived person, "sees one person lying in abundance, pleasure and delights, and at the same time another dying in agony of want and cold at the former's very door" (WWR1, 352). No compensation could be sought according to "temporal justice" for such an apparently unjust state of affairs, for as Schopenhauer says elsewhere, while it would be both illegal and immoral to take food or warm clothing from the poor man in this scenario, it is no way immoral for the rich man not to offer him these, since not offering them does not actively infringe on the poor man's "will" (WWR1, 339). Consolation for this sad situation can only be found by one who sees past the individuality of suffering.

> It becomes clear to the man who has reached the knowledge referred to, that, since the will is the in-itself of every phenomenon, the misery inflicted on others, and that experienced by himself, the bad and the evil, always concern the one and the same inner being, although the phenomena in which the one and the other exhibit themselves stand out as quite different individuals, and are separated even by the wide intervals of time and space. He sees that the difference between the inflicter of suffering and he who must endure it is only phenomenon, and does not concern the thing-in-itself, which is the will that lives in both. Deceived by the knowledge bound to its service, the will here fails to recognize itself; seeking enhanced well-being in *one* of its phenomena, it produces great suffering in *another*. Thus in the fierceness

> and intensity of its desire it buries its teeth in its own flesh, not knowing that it always injures only itself, revealing in this form through the medium of individuation the conflict with itself which it bears in its inner nature. Tormentor and tormented are one. The former is mistaken in thinking he does not share the torment, the latter in thinking he does not share the guilt. (WWR1, 354)

It seems that Schopenhauer has gotten some inspiration in the formulation of this doctrine of "eternal justice" from the *Bhagavad Gītā*, as sentences such as "tormentor and tormented are one" suggest.[22] Atwell has even defended the logical integrity of this notion by saying that it follows coherently from Schopenhauer's prevalent metaphysics of "universal ecologism," or the idea that the will is everything. Atwell reasons that the doctrine of "eternal justice" is merely a logical consequence of the metaphysical thesis that the essence of the world and all things in it is will, for if one accepts this, then it is plausible to conclude that the perpetrator in an immoral act is will and the victim in the same act is also will, making the will both the guilty party and the injured party, paying for all of its crimes (Atwell *Human* 195). The problem with the doctrine however, as Atwell, along with Copleston and Hamlyn before him, has pointed out, is that there really is no basis for saying that, merely because the tormentor and tormented share the same essence, the immoral way in which the former treats the latter is in any way "eternally just" or "justified" (Copleston 146–7; cf. Hamlyn 139–40; Atwel, *Human* 195–7). Schopenhauer does not tell us, nor could he tell us, what it is that is "just" about one man tormenting another from any perspective. Copleston specifically objects to the notion of "eternal justice" by lamenting that the truth of the matter is that, on Schopenhauer's view, no one can be held either responsible or just. The will is transcendent of all moral laws and cannot coherently be "blamed" for anything that happens; the wealthy egoist in the above scenario, as we saw, is not morally liable for failing to feed the poor man as long as he does not infringe on the latter's will; the poor man is left to suffer for a crime that is in no intelligible way his fault (Copleston 147).

Copleston's indictment is a convincing one, for it is quite strange for Schopenhauer to say, as he does at the end of the cited passage: "the tormentor is mistaken in thinking he does not share the torment, the tormented in thinking he does not share the guilt." What Schopenhauer means to say, presumably, is that the tormentor as the thing in itself must share in the suffering he causes himself through the will's "inward conflict," while the tormented as thing in itself must share the guilt, for he is of the same essence as his nemesis. But the individual of the tormentor obviously does not share any of the victim's suffering, for the former is an egoist and is not compassionately sensitive to the poor man's suffering in the first place, and the individual of the tormented is obviously an innocent victim. However much the teaching of "eternal justice" may follow from joining Schopenhauer's falsification thesis to his metaphysics of will, which it in any event seems to, the doctrine is at best grossly mislabeled and as such has understandably offended the moral sensibilities of the critics.[23]

5.2.2 "Nothingness" and the Standpoint of Enlightenment

In his explication of asceticism, an interpretation which characterizes ascetic practice as a "renunciation of will," Schopenhauer anticipates the reader's puzzlement over one final problem. If human experience, or in Schopenhauer's parlance "the world," is to be accounted for in terms of will and representation, how are we to conceive of the experience of someone for whom the principles of sufficient reason that govern representations have been laid aside, and by whom the will has been renounced? Schopenhauer asserts immediately the any positive report of what sort of experience the perfected "renouncer" may have is simply not possible for the philosopher, for the philosopher is committed to the logical order of explanation according to the laws governing concepts and the other principles of sufficient reason. The best anyone could do in an attempt to give any such positive account is to refer to the reports of ascetics themselves, in their descriptions of the "denial of the will," an experience they variously call "ecstasy, rapture, illumination, union with God, and so on" (WWR1, 410).

(WWR1, 410). "It is precisely here," according to Schopenhauer, "that the mystic proceeds positively, and therefore from this point, nothing is left but mysticism" (WWR2, 612). The philosopher's depiction of the perfected experience of the ascetic must remain negative, for when the will has been "freely" denied, all forms of its manifestation, themselves representations, are no longer relevant for discussion. As Schopenhauer puts it, "no will, no representation, no world" (WWR1, 411).

But how is this "negative" exposition the philosopher proposes to give of "mystical" experience or knowledge itself to go forward? In logical terms, every negation is for all intents and purposes only a "relative" negation, a negation of a determinate something that gives us only "a nothingness as privation, or *nihil privativum*" (WWR1, 410). Given the logical impossibility of thinking of an "absolute negation" (*nihil negativum*), we also are unable to represent to ourselves in any satisfying way the experience of "nothingness" the ascetic, we suppose, has ontologically.

> What is universally assumed as positive, what we call *being*, the negation of which is expressed by the concept *nothing* in its most general significance, is exactly the world as representation, which I have shown to be the objectivity, the mirror, of the will. We ourselves are also this will and this world, and to it belongs the representation in general as one aspect of it. The form of this representation is space and time; and so, for this point of view, everything that exists must be at some place and in some time. Then the concept, the material of philosophy, and finally the word, the sign of the concept, also belong to the representation. Denial, abolition, turning of the will are also abolition and disappearance of the world, of its mirror. If we no longer perceive the will in this mirror, we ask in vain in what direction it has turned, and then, because it no longer has any *where* or any *when*, we complain that it is lost in nothingness. (WWR1, 409–10)

From the "point of view" of the philosopher, who carries herself forward according to representation and will, and hence interprets the world through these media, the "abolition" of both will and representation makes it seem as if the world has disappeared, and she shrugs her shoulders at and bemoans the "nothingness" which she is left to somehow conceive in the experience of the ascetic. But, Schopenhauer is quick to add, this "nothingness" that the philosopher believes somehow to be a complete negation of the world as she knows it is really also only a "relative nothing." The "point of view" to which the philosopher is committed is after all only just that, a "point of view," and in like manner, whatever "point of view" the ascetic occupies, even if it be one that does not follow the order of intellect and reason, is still another "point of view." It is not the case, for Schopenhauer, that the ascetic does or could reside somehow in an "absolute nothingness"; rather, Schopenhauer obliquely describes the "mystical state" as one in which "only knowledge remains, the will has vanished" (WWR1, 411).[24] The fascinating and suggestive consequence of this is that, while it may be true that we can simply say no more about the experience of the "renouncer," than otherwise to us his world is a "nothing," the "renouncer" feels the same way about our experience, that in representation and will, we are ourselves caught in a kind of "nothing."

> We have to banish the dark impression of that nothingness, which as the final goal hovers behind all virtue and holiness, and which we fear as children fear darkness. We must not even evade it, as the Indians do, by myths and meaningless words, such as reabsorption in *Brahman* or the *Nirvana* of the Buddhists. On the contrary, we freely acknowledge that what remains after the complete abolition of the will is, for all those who are still full of the will, assuredly nothing. But also conversely, to all those in whom the will has turned and denied itself, this very real world of ours with all its stars and galaxies is—nothing. (WWR1, 411–12)[25]

The falsification thesis makes its final appearance here, in the very last lines of Schopenhauer's presentation of his systematic philosophy. The world of representation is, for those who orient themselves in the world according to its strict principles, the world of *being*. But for those who no longer "know" the world in strict adherence to these principles, the *principium individuationis* is *māyā*, a fabrication, a "nothing." What they know the world to be is, beyond this point, simply not possible for philosophers to communicate. Here, not even the concepts he otherwise cherishes from the classical Indian philosophical tradition, such as *brahman* and *nirvāna*, will be of service.

CHAPTER 6

Two Legacies of Schopenhauer's Appropriation

6.1 SCHOPENHAUER'S STIGMAS

We have seen from the forgoing chapters what effects Arthur Schopenhauer's understanding and appropriation of the notion of *māyā* from the pre-systematic *Upaniṣadic* tradition had on his systematic philosophy. *Māyā* for Schopenhauer was the falsification of our perception of "the world," the taking of the world to be nothing more than a collection of differentiated phenomena and individuals of heterogeneous natures, and as such, it served as his system's "linking" concept, tying his epistemology, metaphysics and ethics together. The falsification of the world's true nature, a unitary and all-pervasive will, was the result of the *a priori* functions of the intellect. But in breaking through these and coming to a realization of will, we understand how it compels individuals to predominantly egoistic conduct, making the world a kind of theater of agonistic conflict. Egoism, based on a fabricated picture of the world, is rendered ineffectual in the morally virtuous person who sees the world aright and responds to others and their respective individual wills with compassion. Though this basic falsification thesis underwent revision and to a certain degree became less significant for his later thought, Schopenhauer's appropriation of *māyā* proved pivotal to the philosophical system built in the first edition of *The World as Will and Representation*.

Commentators who have approached Schopenhauer's relationship to classical Indian thought from a hermeneutic perspective for the past forty years have paid little attention to the systematic use to which Schopenhauer puts the idea of *māyā*. They even discounted, to a predominant degree, the possibility that any idea from the pre-systematic Indian philosophical or religious traditions could have influenced Schopenhauer's own formal philosophical thinking. Although, as this study has shown, this assessment was incorrect, it must also be noted that the logical structure of Schopenhauer's systematic philosophy was not a matter with which these scholars primarily concerned themselves. Extended passages dealing more explicitly with the Indian religious and philosophical traditions in Schopenhauer's *corpus* raise for them interpretive problems much more pressing and general. Schopenhauer, having come at too early a period in the Western reception of Asian thought to fully appreciate the character of the Indian philosophical tradition, subordinates that tradition to his own hermeneutical interests. He views the Indian philosophical tradition with overly Romantic eyes. He believes that Hindu and Buddhist asceticism embody a philosophical "pessimism" that runs counter to the theologically naïve "optimism" of Judaism and Islam. He believes himself to be the inheritor of the *philosophia perennis*, the receiver of the great "mythical" message that can be found in "ancient Indian wisdom," Plato and Christianity, a message that is only fully systematized by him. For these commentators then, rather than having been influenced by Indian philosophical or religious thought, Schopenhauer uses it as a mirror of his own ideas and in this way attempts to legitimate his own historical importance. Rather than elevating the Indian tradition or serving the purpose of enhancing its understanding in the West, Schopenhauer actually stigmatizes it with "pessimistic," "irrationalistic" and "a-historical" themes that plague his own thought. Schopenhauer's legacy in the history of the encounter of the West with Asian thought is thus his epitomization of high Romantic Orientalism.

There are without question highly problematic consequences of Schopenhauer's interpretive treatment of the classical

Indian religious and philosophical traditions that we find for the most part in the works from the second half of his philosophical career. Particularly in the works from the beginning of the 1840's to the end of the 1850's, which include original works and revisions of earlier ones, three stigmatizations of India's religious and philosophical heritage emerge and become progressively more intensely magnified. The first has to do with Schopenhauer's "perennialism," his conviction that the "ultimate truths" that can be attained by the historical phenomena of religion and philosophy are essentially the same from culture to culture. This perennialism, according to the Romantic historiography Schopenhauer too readily adopts, puts Indian Hindu and Buddhist thought at the origin of a rather odd historical continuum that proceeds through Plato, the Christian mystics, Eckhart, Bruno, Boehme and Kant to himself. The second stigma results from what follows from the first; Schopenhauer, standing as he supposedly does at the end of this historical unfolding of philosophy, considers himself specially privileged to be the interpreter of that history. What was before "mythically" and imperfectly represented as the apex of philosophical truth by the *Upaniṣads,* later Vedānta and Buddhism falls to him to clearly and systematically explicate. Finally, Schopenhauer, owing to the anthropological negativism of his own doctrine of the will and the ascetic renunciation it is supposed ultimately to prompt, sees in the Hindu and Buddhist religions a kindred spiritual "pessimism," a tendency to despair at the infinitude of suffering of a godless world, and to represent "salvation" as the "liberation" (*Erlösung*) from such a world. For all their negativism however, Schopenhauer thinks, at least the Hindu and Buddhist traditions do not ultimately philosophically shrink from this, as opposed to the theological "optimism" with which the Western traditions, Judaism in particular, attempt to build their worldviews. These stigmas of Schopenhauer's hermeneutic have a number of pernicious consequences. They first of all make the study of Indian thought valuable, not insofar as the philosophical complexities, innovations, insights and contributions of this heritage are unique and worthy of study in their own historical development, but only inasmuch as it can validate some preconceived and generalized set of tenets that comprise a trans-historical "perennial" philosophy. Secondly, Schopenhauer does not propose to learn from the Indian philosophical tradition nearly as much as he plans to teach it about itself. As the final systematizer of all philosophical truth he fancies himself to be, Schopenhauer believes that the classical Indian religious and philosophical "lifeworlds" only find their full interpretation and explication in his own selective and rudimentary understandings of a few of their respective concepts and practices.[1] Finally, Schopenhauer appropriates the Hindu and Buddhist spiritual traditions, or at least elements from these to his own taste and liking, to articulate a supposed fundamental opposition between these and the religions of Christianity, Islam and especially Judaism. In fact, Schopenhauer does nothing less than use his depiction of Hindu and Buddhist beliefs as a stick with which to beat what he holds to be the naïve spiritual "optimism" of Judaism. The comparative hermeneutic he espouses proposes to elevate the Indian religious traditions in order to denigrate the Semitic ones. This final stigmatization appears frequently in Schopenhauer's late works. No study of Schopenhauer's encounter with Indian thought would be complete or adequate that did not confront directly these aspects of it, and so in the first part of this chapter, we shall deal with each of these in turn.

On the other hand, it would be a mistake to reduce the entirety of Schopenhauer's reception and appropriation of elements of Hindu and Buddhist thought to these obviously regrettable and negative consequences. These arise, as mentioned, in Schopenhauer's late works, namely in the 1841 *Basis of Morality*, the 1844 and 1859 editions of *The World as Will and Representation*, the 1848 revision of his dissertation, *On the Fourfold Root of the Principle of Sufficient Reason* and his 1851 popular work *Parerga and Paralipomena*. It is during these two decades that Schopenhauer's study and knowledge of Asian thought increased a great deal, and when his mention of Hindu and Buddhist ideas became more and more frequent, but at the same time when his "perennialist" and "anti-Judaic" representation of the Indian religious and philosophical traditions crystallized. The first edition of his *World as*

Will and Representation, initially appearing in 1819, did not adopt such perspectives. The treatment of Indian thought in this work is bound up with the systematic development of the falsification thesis, a thesis which, as it turns out, created a legacy of its own in the history of Western philosophy, a new and broad-ranging philosophical orientation that devoted itself to the rethinking of ethical and axiological values based on a mistrust of traditional epistemology and metaphysics. Schopenhauer's appropriation of the notion of *māyā* from the pre-systematic Indian philosophical tradition is instructive in several important respects for those interested in cross-cultural philosophy, for it shows us to what extent and in what ways the venture of understanding and developing ideas across historical and cultural boundaries is a complex, creative hermeneutic process. The present chapter then will examine both of these trends, in an effort to gain a balanced look at the multidimensional legacy of Schopenhauer's encounter with Indian thought. First we will examine Schopenhauer's stigmatizations of the Indian tradition, the perennialism, interpretive privilege and anti-Judaic hermeneutic Schopenhauer espouses in his representations of the Hindu and Buddhist traditions. We will then examine some of the important implications Schopenhauer's systematization of the concept of *māyā* has for the study of cross-cultural philosophy, as well as the new orientation to epistemology his appropriation created, through Nietzsche, in the Western tradition.

6.1.1 Monological Perennialism

Schopenhauer has often been charged with harboring an "a-historicism," discounting the importance of history to philosophical discourse. Indeed many have taken this a-historical tendency of Schopenhauer to be the characteristic mark of his Romanticism as well as what aligns him with the Indian tradition (Glasenapp 495; Gestering 122; Sedler 48).[2] True enough, Schopenhauer's doctrines of the will, aesthetic experience, the superiority of art to history in mediating the nature of human character and consciousness in general leave one with the impression that history is simply dismissed by him. This impression however turns out to be very misleading when one recognizes how often Schopenhauer refers to specific classical and contemporary philosophers he considers either predecessors or antipodes, how consistently he traces and characterizes the development of philosophy from India to Plato and Aristotle, Seneca, the Christian philosophers to the rationalists and Kant, and laments its decline at the hands of the Idealists, what a sharp eye he has for the histories of art and culture. Schopenhauer however did not only consider history to be of the utmost importance to the development of philosophy, a consideration that at any rate could hardly be denied, but also entertains philosophical reflections on history.

For our present purposes, there are basically two characterizations Schopenhauer gives of Indian religious and philosophical history. The first, closely associated with the views of Romantic contemporaries, places India at the beginnings of cultural, intellectual and spiritual history, and even sees India as the birthplace of European language and civilization. This representation of India was advocated by Herder, the Schlegel brothers and Schelling and as a result, was perhaps a predominant view during the German Romantic period.[3] Though it was doubtless known to Schopenhauer as early as 1814, when he first met Friedrich Majer and read Schlegel's *Über die Sprache und Weisheit der Indier*, he does not appear to have adopted this perspective of India himself until the early 1840's. While on the one hand the view of India as the intellectual and spiritual "mother" of Europe, and particularly Germany, purported to elevate the importance of Indological studies, it also had the effect of legitimating Europe as the inheritor of all the "original" institutional, intellectual and religious achievements of the original, pristine "homeland." The second characterization Schopenhauer imputes to the classical Indian tradition, again in a similar manner to Majer and Schlegel but without their commitments to theistic Christian doctrine, was that within its spiritual and philosophical heritage dwelt a "mythical" and "indirect" apprehension of the highest philosophical truths, which in their turn were acknowledged throughout history by the great philosophers of every culture. Indian thought was in this sense the first place where "perennial philosophy" made its appearance. Again, this type of perennialist model, which would have such a thoroughgoing effect on Schopenhauer's later disciple, Paul Deussen, purportedly elevates the classical Indian philosophical tradition by rendering insignificant whatever particular philosophical reflections that were not found to be in accord with the *philosophia perennis*. Therefore I label this strand of perennialism "monological," for it begins with a pre-conceived construct of what constitutes the body of philosophical truth, and proceeds to highlight in a given tradition only that which one believes to corroborate the construct. It does not involve a "diological" openness to another tradition in which one lets the conflicting and diverse claims of that tradition stand.

We find the first portrait of India as Europe's cultural and philosophical birthplace in Schopenhauer's 1840 essay, *On the Basis of Morality*, in the midst of a discussion on Schopenhauer's ethics. The "fundamental philosophical convictions of cultured Europe have undergone a revolution in the last fifty years" because of the (re)introduction of Hindu and Buddhist thought (Schopenhauer BM 45).

> Brahmanism and Buddhism are the most ancient and widespread (of religions), and thus, as regards time and space, the most important of mankind; in fact they are even the original, native religion of our race, which is known to be of Asiatic descent and which once more receives a tardy message from them in its strange homeland. (BM 44–5)

The cultural and even racial heritage of Europe here lies in India, and this is called upon to legitimate Schopenhauer's appropriation of the doctrines of the Hindu and Buddhist traditions. Schopenhauer alludes in the "metaphysical appendix" to *On the Basis of Morality* to the "fundamental view of Indian wisdom" as is found in A. W. Sclegel's translation of the *Bhagavad Gītā* as agreeing with his own ethics of identification (BM 213–14). In the 1848 edition of *The World as Will and Representation*, we find a passage quite similar to what could be found in the works of the man who had first introduced him to Indian thought, Friedrich Majer, half a century earlier. In an attempt to ground his notion of the mere phenomenality of individuality, Schopenhauer writes:

> The conviction here described and arising directly out of the apprehension of nature must have been extremely lively in those sublime authors of the *Upanishads* of the *Vedas,* who can scarcely be conceived as mere human beings. For this conviction speaks to us so forcibly from an immense number of their utterances that we must ascribe this immediate illumination of their mind to the fact that, standing nearer to the origin of our race as regards time, these sages apprehended the inner essence of things more clearly and profoundly than the already enfeebled race, as mortals now are, is capable of doing. But, of course, their comprehension was also assisted by the natural world of India, which is endowed with life in quite a different degree from that in which our northern world is. (WWR2, 475)

This quotation appeals to all the Romantic depictions of India and the authors of the early canonical texts of the *Vedic* tradition; their proximity to the beginnings of history which somehow gives them a more "immediate and direct apprehension" of "the inner essence of things," their "more lively natural southern environment," and so on.[4] In an exceedingly odd and strained contortion, this depiction seeks to elevate the value of the classical Indian religious and philosophical heritage by fixating it in a "primitivism" from which the "already enfeebled races" of contemporary India have in some unspoken way become waywardly separated. India's pristine heritage makes it the archetype of all fundamental religious and philosophical thought and denigrates modern Europe as having lost or disregarded its own roots. At the same time, present-day "enfeebled" India, having fallen under the sway of Islamic and British colonialism, though still following as best it can the tenets of its indigenous traditions, cedes to Europe, its spiritual "child," the privilege of interpreting those traditions and carrying them forward in its philosophical reflection. Wilhelm

Halbfass has argued that Schopenhauer's enthusiasm for India was not aligned with that of the Romantics, for Schopenhauer did not share their "glorification of childhood and yearning for a lost home" (*India* 108). This may be so, but it must also be concluded that the common Romantic depiction of India as the birthplace of Europe, the origin of all language and religious truth, was one Schopenhauer was more than prepared to invoke as a device of legitimization of those doctrines that found favor with him.[5]

It must also be pointed out however that Schopenhauer makes reference to the antiquity and indigenous standing of Hinduism and Buddhism as an argument against the European Christianization of India.[6] Such a project Schopenhauer thought not only pernicious but also futile. Rather than Christianity transforming India, what would actually transpire in the foreseeable future would be a Hindu and Buddhist transformation of Europe that would prompt a second European Renaissance. In an 1844 addition to the first volume of *World as Will and Representation*, while discussing the "denial of the will-to-live," Schopenhauer asserts that this doctrine finds its origins in Indian asceticism and from there finds its way into the teachings of Pythagoras and Plato. He continues:

> Never has a myth been, and never will one be, more closely associated with a philosophical truth accessible to so few, than this very ancient teaching of the oldest and noblest of peoples. Degenerate as this race may now be in many respects, this truth still prevails with it as the universal creed of the people, and it has a decided influence on life today, as it had four thousand years ago. . . . We, on the contrary, now send to the Brahmans English clergymen and evangelical linen-weavers, in order out of sympathy to put them right, and to point out to them that they are created out of nothing, and that they ought to be grateful and pleased about it. But it is just the same as if we fired a bullet at a cliff. In India our religions will never at any time take root; the ancient wisdom of the human race will not be supplanted by the events in Galilee. On the contrary, Indian wisdom flows back to Europe,

> and will produce a fundamental change in our knowledge and thought. (WWR1, 356–7)

This passage is striking in a number of highly conflicting respects. The classical Indians are again referred to as "the oldest and noblest of peoples" while their contemporary descendants are labeled, for a persistently unspecified reason "degenerate in many respects." In his encounter with India, Gestering has posited, Schopenhauer displays his ethnocentricity in his methodological approach to classical Indian thought, uncomprehending of the fact that India was not Europe, that it "behaves culturally in some incompatible manner" (58–9). Schopenhauer, unfortunately, did not mask what ethnocentricity he bore in such subtle ways, but rather displayed it in much cruder racial terms, as he does here. D. W. Hamlyn has detected a deep irony in Schopenhauer's jab in this passage at the "English clergymen" who so ignorantly and callously strive to divest Hindus and Buddhists of their traditional beliefs out of Christian "sympathy" for them, given the preeminent place Schopenhauer gives to sympathy in his own ethics (140–41). Schopenhauer shows also in the quotation a great deal of support for the Brahminical tradition, for it is supposedly the Brahmins who most suffer the insults of the Christian doctrinal onslaught, and ignores, mostly due to his own lack of knowledge, the devotional, theistic strands of Hindu faith. Schopenhauer's enthusiasm about India is an enthusiasm for a certain representation of the *Vedic* and Brahminical "orthodoxy."[7] All this being the case, Schopenhauer vehemently opposes the European attempt to justify colonial rule under any Christian rubric, and is confident that in the end, this attempt will prove to no avail. Schopenhauer may have been far too optimistic about the degree to which the study of classical Indian philosophy would transform Europe, but then again, the passage above may tell us much more about what happened to its European author as a result of such study.

As mentioned above, Schopenhauer's historiography, adopted from the Romantics, fixates the classical Indian tradition in a "primitivism" in order to glorify some of the ancient *Vedic* and Buddhist religious teachings. But then again, only those teachings are valuable that are thought to congeal into a trans-historical and trans-cultural "perennial philosophy." In 1841, Schopenhauer first writes that the *Upaniṣadic* doctrine that all individuality is merely phenomenal and ultimately "illusory" is also the essential teaching of Pythagoras, "the whole philosophy of the Eleatic school," "pervaded the Neoplatonists," constituted "the inspired mysticism of the Sufis," and entered Europe through Scotus Erigina and was carried forward there by Giodano Bruno, Kant and Schelling's "eclectic" synthesis of Spinoza, Kant and Jocob Boehme (BM 207–08). In the 1844 edition of *World as Will and Representation,* this history of the *philosophia perennis* is given in greater length and detail, with Christian mystics such as Meister Eckhart, Blaise Pascal and Angelus Silesius added (WWR2, 612–15). In the same volume, Schopenhauer suggests that the Buddhist and Vedāntic rejection of "extreme" forms of asceticism, their notion that redemption consists in ultimate knowledge and not action, coincides "essentially" with the teaching of Luther that one is saved not by "works" but "faith" (WWR2, 607–08). Nonetheless, ascetic practice is spoken for in all philosophies worthy of that label throughout the world, despite the fact the contemporary Europe holds the truths of these philosophies in contempt. The texts of the *Upaniṣads* and early Buddhist works may stand comfortably with all that has been written by or about the Christian mystics. In fact, anyone who believes the most fundamental Christian teaching to be grounded in its "non-mystical theism" must be, in Schopenhauer's view, mistaken.

> Whoever has read such works, and has compared their spirit with that of asceticism and quietism, as it runs through all the works of Brahmanism and Buddhism and speaks from every page, will admit that every philosophy, which, to be consistent, must reject that whole mode of thought, in that it declares the representatives of it to be impostors or madmen, must on this account necessarily be false. It must truly be a strange madness which, in circumstances and among persons of the widest possible difference, expressed itself with such agreement, and was, moreover, exalted to a principle teaching

> of their religion by the oldest and most numerous races on earth, by some three-quarters of all the inhabitants of Asia. But no philosophy can leave undecided the theme of quietism and asceticism, if the question is put to it, since this theme is in substance identical with that of all metaphysics and ethics. Here, then, is a point on which I expect and desire every philosophy with its optimism to express itself. And if, in the judgment of contemporaries, the paradoxical and unexampled agreement of my philosophy with quietism and asceticism appears as an obvious stumbling block, yet I, on the other hand, see in this very agreement a proof of its sole accuracy and truth, and also a ground for explaining why it has been discretely ignored and kept secret by *Protestant* universities. (WWR2, 615)

Schopenhauer introduces a blurry but fascinating dynamic here. Philosophical perennialism acknowledges of necessity the need to account for ascetic practice and mystical realization, for these supposedly are common to every truly philosophical tradition of the world. The antiquity of the "Brahminical and Buddhist" doctrines, as well as the fact that "three-quarters of all the inhabitants of Asia" ascribe to one form or another of these faiths verifies this. It is on the one hand an amazing stretch for Schopenhauer to believe that "three-fourths of all the inhabitants of Asia" were privileged to the "mysticism" of the *Upaniṣads* or the "esoteric" principles of Buddhism, especially since Schopenhauer had asserted on the very page preceding the above quotation that "actual inner experience . . . is, of course, not accessible to everyone, but comes only to a favored few" (WWR2, 614). He ignores almost completely the theistic and devotional stands of practice within the Asian religious traditions, not to mention how they might compare with Western theistic and devotional practices. Instead, Schopenhauer relies on the antiquity of the "philosophies of quietism and asceticism," their universality, the assumption that a vast majority of the world is actively committed to them, as explanations for the positively conspiratorial rejection of his own philosophy by "Protestant" universities of Europe. Europe here is rooted in the perennial philosophy, rooted through its long-forgotten but newly rediscovered Indian heritage, through its own Christian mystics and increasingly marginalized philosophers, martyrs like Bruno, Pascal and of course now Schopenhauer himself. Europe has gone astray over the centuries owing to a progressively (counterfeit) rationalist commitment to monotheism, creation from nothing, the eternal nature of the intellectual soul and so forth. But Europe will be called back, sooner or later, to the perennial philosophy, probably by India, or more properly, the Europeans who have been reawakened by India. Despite Schopenhauer's articulated desire for "every philosophy to express itself" in the above passage, what is really happening is that his representation of the development of the *philosophia perennis* through the many different cultures of history is speaking for them. "Brahmanism and Buddhism" in this sense are primarily appealed to for their evidentiary value. For the later Schopenhauer, pre-systematic Indian philosophical and religious thought is not the source of inspiration for an important element in his systematic epistemology, metaphysics and ethics, as it was for his early period. Now that the system has long been completed (as well as changed and in Schopenhauer's own view, perfected), what Schopenhauer conceptually owes to the classical Indian tradition is supplemented by how important it is to him that India is a member in the perennialist camp. The later Schopenhauer treats Indian thought (as well as the intellectual and religious productions of other cultures) as evidence for the more grandiose claims of a supposedly tans-historical philosophy. Schopenhauer's perennialism is in this sense monological.

This sort of evidentiary treatment of classical Indian thought is also characteristic of Schopenhauer's references to Vedānta. Idealism, and particularly the Kantian idealism Schopenhauer in part adopts and in part transforms, is said to be the very same epistemological position that India and the rest of "non-Mohammedan Asia," has known for thousands of years (WWR1, 424). Schopenhauer repeats this idea often in his works of the 1840s. The idealism Schopenhauer espouses as its central tenet is that "plurality is only apparent," and what follows from this is that the "inner essence," the "thing in itself" of all things must be one and homogeneous, a tenet Schopenhauer writes in 1841 is precisely the teaching of the *Upaniṣads* (BM 207). In one of his many 1847 additions to his dissertation, *On the Fourfold Root of the Principle of Sufficient Reason,* Schopenhauer asserts that "in India idealism is the doctrine even of popular religion, not merely of Brahmanism but also of Buddhism; only in Europe is it paradoxical in consequence of the essentially and inevitably realistic fundamental view of Judaism" (FR 50-1).[8] In the final edition of *World as Will and Representation* appearing a year before Schopenhauer's death, a very interesting parallelization is found between Schopenhauer's notion that for the "renouncer of will," the everyday world is reduced to a mere relative "nothing" the Hindu notion of *mokṣa* or "liberation," and the early Buddhist attempt to articulate the relationship between *nirvāna* and *saṃsāra.*

> The Buddhists with complete frankness describe the matter only negatively as *Nirvana,* which is the negation of this world or of *Samsara.* If *Nirvana* is defined as nothing, this means only that *Samsara* contains no single element that could serve to define or construct *Nirvana.* For this reason the *Jains,* who differ from the Buddhists only in name, call the Brahmans who believe in the *Vedas, Sabdapramans,* a nickname supposed to signify that they believe on hearsay what cannot be known or proved. (WWR2, 608)

There can be no question that in these passages, Schopenhauer fails to take account of the differences between his own understanding of *māyā* and how he formulates a Kantian falsification thesis out of it, and the classical Vedāntic conceptualization. He does not seem to comprehend how the Māhāyana Buddhists expanded upon the classical Theravāda dichotomization of *nirvāna* and *saṃsāra.* He even obscures the distinctions between Jaina and Buddhist thought. Nonetheless, these citations do tell us something about how significant Schopenhauer's falsification thesis was to his system, and to what extent he was indebted to *Upaniṣadic* and Vedāntic theoretical speculation for that thesis. They also exemplify a more sophisticated comprehension of pre-systematic Indian philosophy than that possessed by any other European philosopher before at least the 1880's, and this won for Schopenhauer admiration and lent him credibility as an interpreter of Indian thought from his contemporaries. It took European Indological studies at least twenty-five years to begin to contravert some of Schopenhauer's assessments of the Indian philosophical and religious traditions, and perhaps an additional forty to sixty years for his overall characterizations of those traditions to be abandoned by European scholars. And so, if Schopenhauer's treatment of classical Indian philosophy is "monological" in the sense that it is his interpretation of the significance of some specific doctrines that was important to him, it must be added that Schopenhauer was one of the very few in the European philosophical community who was talking at all about India, not to mention with India. And he was, with the exception of a few artists like Wagner and Thomas Hardy and a few disciples like Julius Frauenstädt, almost utterly passed over in disregard by the European philosophical scene until the Schulpforta classmates Nietzsche and Deussen shone on him their own spotlights.

Schopenhauer's monological perennialist attitude was not confined to classical Indian philosophy, it also extended to classical Greek and Semitic and even into more recent developments in European thought. It undoubtedly did in part have to do with the Romantic Orientalist enthusiasm for India, and is also understandable in the larger context of the trenchancy of Europe's philosophical self-elevation. It also had a great deal to do with Schopenhauer's own peculiar demeanor. Even the most enthusiastic of Schopenhauer supporters, the late Arthur Hübscer had to concede:

> He was not a diological thinker like the Romantics, like those who tried to find fulfillment in the vibrant exchange of forces and ideas being passed back and forth in the debate halls and strengthened in their creative confrontations. In his view, the dialogue served the purposes of pursuing problems as well as testing and criticizing their solutions. But no philosophical truth was

> ever invented in the course of the interactive thought of the dialogue. (192)

Philosophical truth was for Schopenhauer a matter of observation, study and reflection, but never mere dialogue. And so, monologue was a native element of Schopenhauer's own cultural and personal complexes. But, as mentioned, it also manifested itself in his interpretation of classical Indian thought because, to put it simply, he was one of a few German philosophers of the time speaking of India, and, owing to his total lack of success in the academy and the almost complete ignominy in which his works dwelt until the last ten years of his life, almost no one who could have meaningfully advanced the conversation was listening.

6.1.2 "Myths," "System" and Interpretive Privilege

Schopenhauer, in 1844, made a number of interesting distinctions between philosophy and religion. On the one hand, religion and philosophy for Schopenhauer arise out of the same "metaphysical need" that human beings have, owing to their powers of reflection, to understand their origin, being and the inevitability of their coming death (WWR2, 160). Metaphysics does require that the world be understood "objectively" and "as a whole," but at the same time, "the strongest impulse to philosophical reflection and metaphysical explanations of the world" comes out of the human wonder at the great suffering to which we are destined, and as a result, were it not for such suffering, "it would possibly not occur to anyone to ask why the world exists, and why it does so in precisely this way" (WWR2, 161).[9] Religion, however, turns this need of suffering beings to deal with the hardships of life and the specter of death into belief systems which stress rewards in the afterlife in exchange for faithful assent and ethical conduct, while metaphysics employs the same need to a systematic intellectual attempt to comprehend "that which is hidden behind nature, and renders nature possible" (WWR2, 164). Religion, is in this sense a kind of "metaphysics for the masses," for since so few, in Schopenhauer's view, have time for or are capable of real reflective thinking, religion provides them with a set of beliefs which do not require the sorts of logical and empirical justifications the genuine metaphysician demands.[10] Religion employs myths and stories that purport to mediate metaphysical truth, but they do so, as Schopenhauer says, "*sensu allegorico*" while systematic metaphysics strives to present the truth "*sensu stricto et proprio*" (WWR2, 166). Religion is an allegorical activity in which symbolic structures are applied to represent what are believed to be metaphysical realities, while philosophy is a descriptive discipline that mediates the metaphysical order of things through logically related concepts. The philosopher cannot accept the allegorical symbols of religion, at least not in the literal senses in which the "believers" of a religion accept them, because, first, he is not interested in "belief" but in what can be grounded through "thought," and secondly because of his commitment to, indeed obligation to employ, logical and conceptual language (WWR2, 166–68). The separation between the practice of religion and philosophy is so strict that even attempts to mediate between the two, such as "philosophy of religion," are in their very inception misguided. Schopenhauer calls the philosophy of religion a "strange hybrid or centaur," for it tries to interpret the allegorical representations of religion in a "strict and proper sense" acceptable to the metaphysician, but this very attempt assumes that the philosopher of religion knows the "strict and proper sense" of metaphysical truth to begin with, making the whole interpretive enterprise superfluous (WWR2, 168). As Alfred Schmidt has pointed out in his study of Schopenhauer's philosophy of religion, *Die Wahrheit im Gewände der Lüge*, Schopenhauer is firmly committed to the Enlightenment idea that philosophy should be wholly "independent" of religion, and in fact not only has the resources available to interpret religion, but to replace it (178–80).

Consistent with this belief that philosophy was the proper interpretive medium of religious doctrines, Schopenhauer offers frequent characterizations, from the perspective of his own systematic thinking of course, of various Hindu and Buddhist religious symbols and doctrines. Most frequent among these characterizations, ones that lasted from the very beginning of his encounter with Indian religion until the end of his life, include the following. Shiva, at once the god of destruction and depicted with an erect *lingum*, stands for the eternity of the "will-to-live" throughout the cycle of birth and death (MR1, 181; 371; 440; WWR1, 276; 331; 399; WWR2, 511). He takes the *Vedic* fire sacrifice, as described in the *Chandogyopaniṣad* and by Colebrooke in *Asiatic Researches* as symbolic of the pervasiveness of the metaphysical will's self-sacrifice and as a prolepsis to the ascetic's "denial of the will" (MR1, 286; WWR1, 381–2). He interprets the symbolic significance of the Hindu and Buddhist doctrines of reincarnation alternatively as proof that the individual is a passing, fleeting phenomenon while the will-to-live is eternal, and as evidence that the immoral conduct of human beings ensues from their "intelligible characters" and has metaphysical import (MR1, 389; 487–88; WWR1, 356; 365; WWR2, 480; 502–09; 600–10; 628–9).

The problematic nature of Schopenhauer's distinction between the "mythic" and "symbolic" locutions of religious doctrine and the "descriptive" and logical ones of philosophy comes nonetheless to the fore in his ambivalence over pivotal Hindu and Buddhist terms such as *brahman* and *nirvāna*. Schopenhauer both extols and dismisses these concepts and their philosophical import. For instance, as we saw in the previous chapter, when discussing in 1818 the "resignation of the will-to-live" in the practice of asceticism, Schopenhauer addresses the notion of "nothingness."

> We have to banish the dark impression of that nothingness, which as the final goal hovers behind all virtue and holiness, and which we fear as children fear darkness. We must not even evade it, as the Indians do, by myths and meaningless words, such as re-absorption in *Brahman* or the *Nirvana* of the Buddhists. On the contrary, we truly acknowledge that what remains after the complete abolition of the will is, for all who are still full of the will, assuredly nothing. But also conversely, to those in whom the will has turned and denied itself, this very real world

> of ours with all its suns and galaxies is—nothing. (WWR1, 411–12)

Here, "the Indians" are singled out for castigation because they "evade" the issue of "nothingness" with "myths and meaningless words" such as *brahman* and *nirvāna*. Amazingly, the footnote to this very passage added in 1859 explicates what Schopenhauer is saying by making reference to Izak Schmidt's description of the "highest" teachings of the Buddhist *Prajña-Paramita* literature (WWR1, 412). In the "supplement" to this final section of Schopenhauer's "main work" in 1859, the "resignation of the will" is seen as the ascetic's preparation for death, and along with classical Greek philosophers, Śaṅkara is quoted twice approvingly, and a long discussion of the etymology of the word *nirvāna* following Colebrooke, Schmidt and Hardy is solicited to clarify the "nothingness" that is experienced after the ascetic has renounced the will (WWR2, 508–09). One is left to wonder why the Schopenhauer of 1859 has come to rely on those very concepts from the Vedāntic and Buddhist traditions that the Schopenhauer of 1818 had rejected as useless in an identical context. The same turnabout transpired with regard to Schopenhauer's estimation of the *Upaniṣadic* idea of *brahman*. While the early Schopenhauer had very little use for the term, during the very period in which he was first developing his metaphysics of will, he would later try to show that the word *brahman* was etymologically derived from a Sanskrit root that according to one translation by Max Müller meant "force, will, wish, and the propulsive power of creation" (see Halbfass *India* 111). What could account for these changes of heart, these shifting ambivalences with whether or not to use these important Vedāntic and Buddhist terms?

Various scholars have suggested some general answers to this question. It is tempting to ascribe with Jean W. Sedler Schopenhauer's obsession with these concepts to his "propensity to find corroborations between his own ideas with as many thought systems as possible" (180). Halbfass, citing a number of entries in Schopenhauer's *Nachlass*, concludes that Schopenhauer always takes his own philosophy as the standard of truth and refers to concepts from the Indian as well as other traditions in order to "mirror" his own (*India* 114). The problem with such characterizations is that they attempt to explain Schopenhauer's stance toward the Indian religious and philosophical traditions in too consistent and static a manner. Before the 1830's, in the statements Schopenhauer makes with regard to his relationship to Indian philosophy, he acknowledges at once a special indebtedness to the *Upaniṣads* as well as an obsession with the newness and originality of his system. He admits on more than one occasion that his philosophy would have been impossible had not the *Upaniṣads*, Plato and Kant found their way into his thinking, that those familiar with the *Upaniṣads* are "best of all prepared" to receive his philosophy, and yet at the same time "each of the individual and disconnected utterances that make up the *Upanishads* could be deduced as a consequence of the thought I am to impart, although conversely my thought is by no means to be found in the *Upanishads*" (WWR1, xv–xvi). This is in itself relatively unproblematic, inasmuch as Schopenhauer is telling us that while the *Upaniṣads* counted as one of his inspirations, his philosophy is different from what they espouse, and while his doctrines could be connected with certain of their "disconnected utterances," they do not contain his system, which in itself is unique. But as Schopenhauer becomes more obsessed with his philosophical legacy, an obsession which increases in intensity from the 1830's to the 1850's, no doubt partly as a result of his continuing obscurity in the European philosophical scene, his espousal of perennialism grows more and more committed. One finds frequently repeated insistences in his works after 1830 that he, Plato, Kant, the Christian mystics, and "ancient Indian wisdom" all "teach the same," that while his doctrines of ethics and metaphysics seem counterintuitive to contemporary European scholars, they are "in agreement" with the teachings of the "oldest and noblest of all races" whose religions are believed in by the "majority" of people in the world. Schopenhauer does in these instances rely on the antiquity of Indian philosophy, on the sheer number of worshippers who ascribe to the doctrines of India's native religions, on the usefulness of Hindu and Buddhist concepts to reveal metaphysical truths which most Western religious and philosophical ideas do not have access to, and so by validating these ideas, he validates his own system. Part of Schopenhauer's early subordination of ideas from classical Indian religion and philosophy to his own and his enthusiastic advocacy of these same ideas later in his life has to do with his increasing anxiety over the course of four decades that his philosophy was almost completely ignored. Validation from antiquity turned out to be much easier for Schopenhauer to obtain and find comfort in than validation from his contemporaries. After his works finally did become popular in Europe in the 1850's, this tendency to strengthen his legacy through the alignment of his philosophy with "as many thought-systems as possible" only became more pronounced. As Schopenhauer's familiarity with classical Indian thought increased during this period, so did his illustrations of the kinship between Hindu and Buddhist doctrines and his own philosophy.

But if one were to insist on a more fundamental and consistent reason for Schopenhauer's ambivalence over the philosophical viability of ideas from the Indian religious traditions, a good candidate would be his belief outlined above that the method of philosophy was superior to religious faith. It must be remembered that Schopenhauer's acquaintance with Indian philosophical reflection was almost entirely restricted to, and in any event was thematically focused on, the pre-systematic period, before the flowering of the *darśanas*. Schopenhauer had no real knowledge or appreciation of classical or new Nyāya logic, Vaiśeṣika ontology, the Grammarians' philosophy of language, the Buddhist phenomenalist, logical or epistemological systems, not even the sophisticated formulations on consciousness developed by the sects of Vedānta's great commentarial traditions. Late in his life he gained some familiarity with classical Sāṃkhya, Vaiśeṣika atomism, the Buddhist *Prajña-Paramita* literary corpus and Śaṅkara's *Brahmasūtrabhāsya,* but this did little in the way of changing the overall characterization of Indian thought he had formed over the decades. For Schopenhauer, the single most valuable element of Indian philosophy was the notion of *māyā,* and apart from this, the paramount "mystical" doctrines as well as the widespread devotional religious practices of Hinduism and Buddhism were connected with the "mythological" orientation of these heritages. In the end, these concepts simply did not perform what was required of genuinely philosophical reflection. Myth was truth borrowing the clothing of fables in order to be communicated to the masses (Schopenhauer WWR2, 629). This perception, that the philosophy of the Hindu and Buddhist traditions was inextricably "mythological" and seamlessly attached to the doctrines of salvation (*mokṣa*) of these respective religions, was not only practically universally adopted in Europe for almost one hundred years after Schopenhauer's death, but was actively promoted by the majority of twentieth century neo-Vedāntins as the fundamental distinction between Indian and Western thought. This was not due only to Schopenhauer, for this generalization was also adopted in different manners by Hegel, Schelling, the Schlegel brothers, Nietzsche, Deussen and even Husserl, but certainly the generalizations he laid down were influential.

While Schopenhauer may to a certain extent be excused for these blanket characterizations in mind of his unfamiliarity with the Scholastic *darśanas*, there remains something highly suspect about his sharp dichotomization of the "philosophical" and "religious" approaches to metaphysics, especially when one considers what he has to say about "mysticism" or "direct inner experience." When it comes to communicating the nature of what is realized in "mystical experience," Schopenhauer consistently maintains that philosophical language is no better off than mythological or religious language. In the first edition of *World as Will and Representation* in 1818, Schopenhauer tells us that the farthest philosophical language can go in describing the state of the ascetic's "resignation of the will" is to characterize it negatively as "relative nothingness"; it cannot be called "knowledge" in any coherent sense, because every form of knowledge with which we are familiar is marked by the correlativity of subject and object (WWR1, 410). If one were to insist on a positive account, one could only refer to the descriptions of the ascetics themselves, as "ecstasy, rapture, illumination, union with God," the last of these terms being one which Schopenhauer would never philosophically accept as a metaphysical truth (WWR1, 410). Precisely where the linguistic and epistemological "rupture" supposedly occurs in "mystical" states of "renunciation," the whole basis Schopenhauer gives for the supposition that the "strict sense" of metaphysical language is superior to the "allegorical sense" of mythological language collapses. This situation remains the same for the second and third editions of *World as Will and Representation*. There, he writes that even though the metaphysician and mystic are distinguished by their methodological "starting points," the mystic beginning with "inner experience" and the metaphysician delving into "outward observation," they are both found *almost* silent before the "renunciation of will," with Hindu worshippers in dimly lit temples chanting "*Om*" and metaphysicians talking obliquely of "nothingness" (WWR2, 611–12). Indeed, Schopenhauer even feels moved to concede at this point that, as philosophers, "we" run into "the limitation of our point of view" when we attempt to describe the ascetic experience, while this is exactly where the mystic can proceed positively (Ibid., 612). Now, there is obviously no problem in Schopenhauer's wish to adopt the philosophical method he believes best suited to his purposes, and leave "mythology" and "mysticism" to others who presumably have less serious concerns than the "strict sense" of truth. But Schopenhauer, as we have seen above, has gone farther. He has maintained that the philosopher's recourse to the logical and empirical structures of conceptual thought is a superior approach to metaphysical inquiry than the allegorical approach of religion, and as a result, philosophy, specifically systematic philosophy, holds interpretive privilege over the discourse of religion. This very fact legitimates often in his own mind his prerogative to explicate for his readers the "actual" metaphysical import of various Hindu and Buddhist symbols, doctrines and religious practices. But this whole line of argument is canceled suddenly when Schopenhauer confronts "mysticism." Schopenhauer did not proffer a sophisticated enough philosophy of language to buttress the radical separation he suggested between systematic metaphysics and religion in any event, for why should we believe "strict" conceptual language superior to "allegorical" religious language in the discipline of metaphysics when neither can adequately communicate the "direct" realization of metaphysical truth in the end? If philosophy is in fact to be preferred to religion as the more trustworthy explication of metaphysics, indeed if philosophy can tell us what religious beliefs "really" mean, this is not adequately justified anywhere by Schopenhauer. It may even be said that, once the metaphysical cards were laid on the experiential table, these suppositions didn't even satisfy the philosopher himself.

6.1.3 A Pessimist's Comparative Hermeneutic

The oddest, and by far the most problematic manner in which Schopenhauer represents the classical Indian religious and philosophical traditions is found in his shifting juxtapositions of these to the religions of Christianity, Islam and especially Judaism. The basic dichotomy runs thus: the Semitic, monotheistic religious traditions, Islam and Judaism, are "realistic," in as much as they believe in an objective world created by God, and "optimistic" insofar as they posit that the world has a teleological purpose connected with historical salvation and redemption by God. The Indian religious traditions, on the other hand, are "idealistic" in the sense that they hold the world to be a merely phenomenal, though eternal appearance, and "pessimistic" inasmuch as they represent release from the world of suffering through renunciation as salvation. Schopenhauer, it turns out, spurns "realism" as a philosophical position, and holds "optimism" in vehement moral contempt for its failure to take due stock of the suffering of the world, and as a result, the Indian religious traditions are held in much higher esteem by Schopenhauer. Christianity, although in some respects a theological "sect" of Judaism, burdened as it is by the "realism" of the latter's doctrinal heritage, is in essence "pessimistic" as is witnessed by its tenets of original sin and its placement of human suffering and other-worldly salvation at the center of its concern. Christianity has "Indian blood in its veins," is somehow of partly Indian origin, and interpreted correctly, is a "true" religion. The hermeneutic Schopenhauer uses to compare and assess religious traditions is his unique measure of a given religion's "optimism" or "pessimism."

Schopenhauer's philosophy is of course most frequently associated with pessimism, and his employment of pessimism as a comparative hermeneutic has been found by a few scholars to be the most pernicious manifestation of his anti-Semitism and general cultural naiveté. Gestering thinks that the major legacy of Schopenhauer's encounter with Indian thought was his association of it with his own brand of pessimism (35). Schopenhauer tries, according to Gestering, to solve all cultural problems with his notion of "denial of the will-to-live," and this kind of unreflectivity leads him to entirely fail to notice that his assessments of Indian religion reflect "axiological principles inherited from his own culture" (58). Schopenhauer's unrelenting focus on concepts of "anthropological negativity" causes him to so obsessively fixate on the Buddhist emphasis on suffering or Hindu notions of "renunciation" that he treats India as if it needs "no hermeneutic," and this treatment proves just how "ethnocentric" Schopenhauer really is (Gestering 59).[11] J. J. Clarke has taken note of the fact that Schopenhauer's hermeneutic of pessimism compels him to use Indian thought to "drive a wedge between Christianity and Judaism" (68). India is the tool with which Schopenhauer, on his own terms, validates the Christian tradition and denigrates the Jewish.

To focus exclusively on Schopenhauer as, to use Fredrick Copleston's phrase, "the philosopher of pessimism" and thus to treat his association of Indian religious thought with this pessimism as the overriding legacy of his encounter with India is again to make too static and total those characterizations. No such labels as "pessimistic" or "optimistic" are applied by Schopenhauer to any religious or philosophical system in the first edition of his "main work": these words appear nowhere in Schopenhauer's writing until the *Nachlass* of the late 1820's (Atwell *Human* 146). Occasional reference is made to pessimism in the 1844 edition of *The World as Will and Representation,* but not until the 1850's did the terms "pessimism" and "optimism" come to be used with any consistency (Atwell *Human* 146).[12] Like his attachment to perennialism then, Schopenhauer's categorization of philosophies and religions according to these labels became important to him only in the last two decades of his life, and only systematically so during the last ten years.

This qualification, however, does not help make much sense out of the comparative hermeneutic Schopenhauer ends up thematizing and applying. He articulates the hermeneutic in the following way:

> I cannot, as is generally done, put the *fundamental difference* of all religions in the question whether they are monotheistic, poly-theistic, pantheistic or atheistic, but only in the question whether they are optimistic or pessimistic, in other words, whether they present the existence of this world as justified by itself, and consequently praise and commend it, or consider it as something which can be conceived only as the consequence of our guilt, and thus really ought not to be, in that they recognize that pain and death cannot lie in the eternal, original and immutable order of things, that which in every respect ought not to be. The power by virtue of which Christianity was able to overcome first Judaism, and then the paganism of Greece and Rome, is to be found solely in its pessimism, in the confession that our condition is both exceedingly sorrowful and awful, whereas Judaism and paganism were optimistic. (WWR2, 170)

The testing of a philosophical system can also be done through this hermeneutic, for as Schopenhauer reminds us, metaphysics begins with the "wonder" or "astonishment" at the world's existence, and matures through the astonishment at the amount and degree of suffering and evil in the world (WWR2, 170; 172). For this reason, he considered Spinoza's idea that this was "the best of all possible worlds" not only logically odd, but morally pernicious, for it divested the ethical consequences of evil of their real significance. Schopenhauer believes that "the world" is "the consequence of our guilt," presumably since we are manifestations of the will-to-live which compels us as individuals to egoism, and from an ethical point of view, really "ought not to be."[13] But the issue of whether a philosophy "praises" or "condemns" the world betrays its total unreliability as a hermeneutic criteria of religious comparison already in the instant passage. Schopenhauer displays an amazingly naïve "historical sense" by insisting that Christianity achieved its cultural and political ascendancy in its first four centuries of existence "solely" by virtue of its pessimism, along perhaps with the unspoken hope that his philosophy would achieve similar acclaim throughout the world in the future for the same reason. A very strange wish.

The hermeneutic of optimism and pessimism was conceived by Schopenhauer, as mentioned above, in several ways. There was a metaphysical component to the hermeneutic as well as an ostensibly ethical one. On one occasion, Schopenhauer thematized the metaphysical component of the hermeneutic simply with respect to his metaphysics of will, writing that optimism was the "unwarranted self-praise of . . . the will to live," while pessimism was the "denial" of this will, as is found in "Brahmanism, Buddhism, and also genuine Christianity" (WWR2, 584). This component however had a wider scope than this, appealing to the connection of realism and monotheistic creationism as opposed to idealism, atheism and the mere phenomenality of the world. In the 1848 edition of *The Fourfold Root*, Schopenhauer claims:

> It is positively scandalous how, even today in the works of German scholars, religion and theism are usually regarded without more ado as identical and synonymous, whereas religion is related to theism as a genus to a single species. In fact only Judaism and theism are identical. Therefore all races who are not Jews, Christians or Mohammedans are stigmatized by us with the common name of heathens. Because of the doctrine of the Trinity even Christians are reproached by Mohammedans and Jews with not being pure theists. For whatever anyone may say Christianity has Indian blood in its veins, and thus has a constant tendency to be rid of Judaism. Kant's *Critique of Pure Reason* is the most serious attack ever made on theism, and this is why the professors of philosophy have hastened to put his work on the shelf. If it had appeared in Buddhist countries, then ... one would have perceived in it nothing but an edifying treatise on

> the more thorough refutation of its heretics, and the more salutary confirmation of the orthodox doctrine of idealism, namely that of the merely apparent existence of this world that is presented to our senses. (FR 187)

Schopenhauer begins this point by critiquing a pervasive tendency in Romantic scholars who had engaged with the Indian tradition, namely Herder, the Schlegel brothers, Schelling, and even Friedrich Majer, to find in the religious traditions of Indian antiquity a "pure, original monotheism" from which the Christian tradition had become separated through its centuries of theological development. This "monotheistic prejudice" had began to corrupt, in Schopenhauer's view, newer translations of the *Upaniṣads* by Poley, Röer, Colebrooke and even Rommohan Roy, for despite the facts that they were made directly from Sanskrit and many of the "late" *Upaniṣads* make frequent reference to a single "God," Schopenhauer believed that these translations falsely projected "Jewish theism" into these scriptures (see BM 207; PPII 348; WWR1, 486). Schopenhauer was convinced that Christianity and Islam were, inasmuch as they ascribed to monotheism, "sects of Judaism" and had created in Europe the pretension that genuine religion was as such monotheistic, even though these three traditions squabbled amongst themselves and one another over how to theologically formulate that commitment. Christianity, however, was somehow partly exempt from these errors, for its doctrine of the Trinity was one of the signs that it had "Indian blood in its veins" and thus always exhibited a tendency to "be rid of Judaism."[14] One of the important components of Indian religion that helps undermine this "Jewish monotheism" is idealism, which proves the world to be merely an epistemological phenomenon "presented to our senses." In an interesting piece of hermeneutic speculation, Schopenhauer imagines that while modern German professors reject Kant out of their theological and religious beliefs, Kant's idealist assault on theism would be received favorably as "orthodox" in "Buddhist countries." The "realist" view of Jewish theology posits that God created an objective world, but the logical consequence of a doctrine of creation *ex nihilo* is that Judaism can have no "doctrine of immortality," whereas "Brahmanism and Buddhism," along with Christianity, which "is Indian in spirit, and therefore, more than probably, of Indian origin, although indirectly, through Egypt," can espouse that the fundamental nature of the human being is with that of all other things, eternal, even though individuals are born and die (WWR2, 488). This equips Hinduism, Buddhism and "Indian Christianity" with a much greater capacity to reconcile their worshippers to death than Judaism and "Jewish-European Christianity" possess (WWR2, 463).[15] These arguments are combined with Schopenhauer's earlier arguments in support of idealism and against realism in order to buttress the superiority of Christianity and the Indian traditions over Judaism.

This truth of the metaphysical view of the world endorsed by Hinduism, Buddhism and Christianity over Judaism is for Schopenhauer supplemented by their ethical superiority as well. "The innermost kernel and spirit of Christianity is identical with that of Brahmanism and Buddhism; they all teach a heavy guilt of the human race through its existence itself, only Christianity does not proceed in this respect directly and openly, like those more ancient religions" (WWR2, 604). While the Hindu and Buddhist religions have at their center doctrines which prove that the desires of the phenomenal world are deceptive and lead to suffering, and that the proper orientation toward the unitary metaphysical essence of all beings is compassionate identification with others and will-renunciation, Christianity's approach is more metaphorical. It pictures "original sin" as coming from the guilt of the first human couple, with Christ serving as the divine example of compassionate love and renunciation. All the same, the Christian myth makes the same point about the evil of worldly existence and the necessity for transcending it as the Indian religions do, it contains their "kernel."

> However it may be in other respects, that (verse) "All is very good" in the Old Testament is really very foreign to Christianity proper, for in the New Testament the world is generally spoken of as something to which we do not

> belong, which we do not love, the ruler of which, in fact, is the devil. This agrees with the ascetic spirit of the denial of one's self and the overcoming of the world. Like boundless love of one's neighbor, even of one's enemy, this spirit is the fundamental characteristic which Christianity has in common with Brahmanism and Buddhism, and which is evidence of their relationship. (WWR2, 624–5)

The words of God in Genesis after he had created the world, "it is very good," are the cornerstone for Schopenhauer of Jewish "optimism."[16] The world is good, it is meant to be good, and it is the mission and destiny of the Jewish people in history to be safeguarders of that goodness as a witness to the benevolent God of creation. Schopenhauer claims that in Christianity, Europe relearned "what all of Asia" knew long before, that worldly life is evil, ephemeral and burdened by suffering and injustice, and was as a result completely transformed (WWR2, 627). Hinduism and Buddhism are religions that teach that release from the world of birth and death, not a historical progression to moral perfection as in Judaism, is the only road to true salvation, and in this lies their pessimism (WWR2, 628).[17]

An entirely separate study would probably be required to unravel all of the generalizations Schopenhauer makes with regard to Judaism, Islam, Christianity, and the Hindu and Buddhist traditions with the comparative hermeneutic he employs, and I will not attempt to solve Schopenhauer's extremely problematic characterizations of these traditions here.[18] Our immediate concern is how this "pessimist's hermeneutic" is used to pit Christianity fundamentally against Judaism through the former's purported origination from Hindu and Indian Buddhist thought, and to identify the Indian religious traditions by their "pessimism." As to the first point, Clarke's observation is certainly accurate, that Schopenhauer uses Indian thought to "drive a wedge between Christianity and Judaism" (68). Just as above, where Indian philosophical thought was solicited as evidence to verify the tenets of the *philosophia perennis*, or more properly Schopenhauer's representation of those tenets, here the Hindu and Buddhist traditions, constructed as monolithic entities with hardly any distinction between them, are aligned with Christianity in the most tenuous, obscure and arbitrary fashions against Judaism, which is itself treated as a religious monolith. It is completely unclear, in any of these cases, how idealism logically implies a pessimistic worldview, for this was not the conclusions either Kant or Hegel came to. It is even more curious how idealism must entail atheism, since Schopenhauer's near and actual contemporaries, Berkeley, Kant, Jacobi, Reinhold, Fichte, Schelling and even Hegel all held their own unique brands of religious faith. Theism can be and has been attacked or supported on realist, empiricist, nominalist, solipsist, skeptical and idealist grounds, and so it is at least problematic to say how any particular ontological position could decide the matter of theism with any logical necessity either way unless it had done so *a priori*. This is perhaps what Schopenhauer could have but failed to learn from the Kantian antinomies, instead of taking them as outright refutations of the monotheistic position. It is also what could have been gleaned from early Buddhist skepticism, but again what Schopenhauer took from Buddhism was the implication that, because the Buddha remained silent on questions concerning God's existence, this silence constituted denial. One could ask conversely how realism necessarily leads to the conclusion that God exists, or that creationism must presuppose a realist ontology, for had not Berkeley fit God's existence into a different ontological picture? To say that the *Upaniṣads* and Vedānta in general, taking into account its Advaita, Dvaita and Viśiṣtadvaita interpreters, espoused an idealistic atheism is of course also in gross contradiction to the facts, not to mention the whole religious matrix he abstrusely referred to as "Hinduism." Again, as a philosophical thinker interested in building a system, Schopenhauer is at liberty to attempt to find his own positions on these matters. But to take those solutions and convert them into a hermeneutic that receives every true idealism as atheistic and every consistent realism as monotheistic, and considers every available departure from this as an aberration of some kind, is to be not merely historically naïve, but willfully historically blind. It is not the case, as we have seen, that Schopenhauer was "a-historical," but it must be conceded that in this case the historical judgments he made about the world's religious traditions and their various philosophical positions were woefully inadequate. Schopenhauer, in his late works, is not concerned with these facts. He has found what to him must have seemed an ingenious interpretation of Christianity that grounded it in the spiritual soil of India, an interpretation which not only "saved" the better parts of Christianity and made the study of Indian thought that much more important to Europeans, but also showed up Judaism and its heritage to be a religious impostor in Europe. Those scholars who defend Schopenhauer against the charges of ethnocentricity have not considered these implications of his hermeneutic of pessimism at all.

Turning briefly to the notion that the religious traditions of India are fundamentally and uniquely pessimistic, this is again a gross generalization that takes very little of the Hindu and Buddhist traditions into account. But let us take into consideration merely those reasons Schopenhauer cites for labeling these religions "pessimistic." Indeed, the formula for *mokśa* in the general scheme of the *Upaniṣadic* and post-*Upaniṣadic* representation, as well as that of the later *darśanas,* sees salvation as release from the world of rebirths, where ignorance and false desire entrap one according to the law of *karma*. It is also accurate to say that escape from the cycle of rebirth or *saṃsāra,* the cessation of the inevitable suffering of causal existence, was the basic model of liberation in the various strands of the Indian Buddhist tradition. Achieving these goals, according to Schopenhauer's characterization, requires that the "will-to-live" be renounced, and with it all hope for historical or moral progress and lasting happiness "in the world." Given this very general picture, it would perhaps be understandable if we were to encounter those who would consider such models of salvation "pessimistic," but we would then be entitled to ask *who* would consider them so, and *for what reasons*. Maybe a materialist who believed the ultimate aim of life (*puruṣārtha*) was to enjoy the hedonistic acquisition and possession of wealth would find these formula for salvation unappealing. But Schopenhauer (at least philosophically) does not advocate hedonistic materialism. Perhaps a monotheist who is convinced the world is a praiseworthy place and dedicates himself in whatever ways he can to its improvement and looks forward to an eternal life with God would find these Indian religions, depending on how much he knew about them, too dark for his spiritual temperament. But Schopenhauer (at least philosophically) was an ardent atheist who thought the world was not morally improvable, neither did he believe in the notion of an individuated, rational eternal soul. Far from it, Schopenhauer thinks that the "will-to-live" as it manifests itself in a world of individuals wreaks such havoc that it would be better for the world to have never existed, which is not, despite Schopenhauer's insistence, thematized in either the Hindu or Indian Buddhist tradition. Given this, one is at a loss as to why *Schopenhauer* feels compelled to label these religions "pessimistic." Would it not make more sense to feel as if, insofar as the Indian religious traditions offered *mokśa* at all from a world seen as so irredeemably terrible, they were rather "optimistic?" The only truly pessimistic philosophy in the scenario Schopenhauer specifically gives would seem to be one that offered human beings no relief at all from the suffering of a godless world, or fancied that they were bound to be reborn eternally into it, something like the fate of Sisyphus or Nietzsche's Zarathustra.

The assessment as to whether something should be taken optimistically or pessimistically is in its most common levels psychological or attitudinal, and in its most sophisticated, axiological and aesthetic. In either case, the judgment is personally subjective. In order for me to be pessimistic about a state of affairs, I must either believe that it will turn out badly for me or others, or have in mind a preferred outcome or state of affairs to which the one present does not or cannot measure up. This is what is hermeneutically odd about comparing religious traditions in general as to whether they are optimistic or pessimistic, for in order to be confident that such a standard can be applied successfully and agreed upon, one would have to assume that a preferred state of affairs, in this case, a model of salvation, is held in common. This is a dubious, and indeed impossible assumption for a historical hermeneutic of comparing religions. But this project goes awry even for

Schopenhauer, who compares different models of salvation, and then comes to completely illogical conclusions as to which ones are optimistic and pessimistic consistent with the metaphysical positions he embraces. The metaphysical doctrine he embraces implies as the preferred state of affairs "will-renunciation," and this is precisely what he finds to Hinduism, Buddhism and Christianity, and still he calls them pessimistic.[19] Schopenhauer takes a poorly formulated hermeneutic and makes it ludicrous. But unfortunately, it went even beyond this. By stigmatizing the Indian religious and philosophical traditions with the label of "pessimistic," a label that stuck with Phillip Mainländer, Edward von Hartmann, Nietzsche and Deussen, Schopenhauer did perhaps at least as much to detract from the perception of these traditions in the West as he did to advance it, caused more philosophers to dismiss India or be misled by these characterizations of its antiquity as he did to inspire others to its serious study. In short, Schopenhauer's stigmatizations of India undermined its understanding and reception in Europe at least as much as his enthusiasm and philosophical idealization of classical Indian thought opened new doors to it.

These stigmatization of the classical Indian religious and philosophical traditions perhaps make it understandable that Schopenhauer has been passed over in ambivalence or dismissed entirely by Indian philosophers in the twentieth century. His lack of both broad and detailed knowledge of the Indian philosophical tradition, especially as it exhibited itself in the centuries of sophisticated epistemological, metaphysical and linguistic argumentation among the *darśanas,* combined with the inaccurate generalizations and obfuscations he made of what he did know, does not make Schopenhauer a tenable interpreter of Indian thought for the end of the twentieth century. Even were we to grant that in terms of the progress of Western scholarship in the first half of the nineteenth century, Schopenhauer's attitude and dedication to the study of Indian thought were admirable for his time, little use can be made of his depictions of the Hindu and Buddhist traditions today. This has led, in certain respects understandably, to the same disregard of Schopenhauer to pervade in contemporary reflections on cross-cultural philosophy. For some Western scholars who have taken up this field, such as Gerald James Larson, Schopenhauer's "exuberant affirmation of matters non-European is clearly a case for the psychoanalyst" and not the comparative philosopher (7–8). To stop here however, as was mentioned above, would be to limit the results of Schopenhauer's encounter with the classical Indian tradition to what he wrote about it mostly in the last ten to fifteen years of his philosophical career, and to totally disregard the significance of his appropriation of the concept of *māyā,* and his systematic incorporation of that concept. The legacy of this appropriation, created largely during the first part of his philosophical reflection that culminated in the first edition of *The World as Will and Representation* in 1819, has important consequences for contemporary reflections on cross-cultural philosophy. I shall therefore conclude the present study with some reflections on this other legacy and its implications

6.2 SCHOPENHAUER'S APPROPRIATION AND CROSS-CULTURAL PHILOSOPHY

As was presented in the Introduction, the relatively new field of cross-cultural philosophy has been over the last several decades greatly concerned with the large-scale methodological problems of whether or not philosophizing across cultures is feasible or even possible. Questions have even been raised as to whether, and the case aggressively made that, "philosophy" is a specifically Greek and derivatively European historical-cultural phenomenon by twentieth century thinkers who are themselves deeply at odds about the practice and value of philosophy. These questions are certainly pressing and important. Can one think and understand across historical and cultural boundaries in ways that make possible expansive and constructive philosophical reflection, or are such attempts ill-conceived in the first place owing to the radical differences between cultures, their divergent self-understandings, and the irreconcilable linguistic, religious and intellectual activities in which they participate? Is reflection about the "philosophical" ideas and concepts of another culture always hermeneutically and politically determined by one's own culture so completely that those reflections betray only one's own pre-understandings and historically conditioned interests? While careful methodological consideration must be given to these large questions, partial answers to them must be sought in the context of concrete investigations of those thinkers and periods in which cross-cultural philosophy was attempted. As J. N. Mohanty has written, albeit in a somewhat different context than the one in which the present project was conceived:

> At one extreme we have the universalist, the essentialist, who holds that rationality must be the same everywhere, that philosophy and science could not, in their essence, be touched by local differences. Strip them of their cultural externalities, they come out as the same sort of enterprises. At the other extreme we have the familiar relativist (whose number and variety today are beyond count), who holds that the very concepts of "rationality" and "truth" in "science" and "philosophy"—as applied to culturally diverse communities—are not only different, but at least sometimes radically different, which would amount to saying that Indian and Western philosophy are not only different philosophies but, as philosophies different, i.e., the very sense of "philosophy" differs from one to the other so much that to use the same word for both is just misleading. I can only briefly state my reasons for rejecting both. Show the relativist that a particular thesis in an Indian philosophical system is just the same as one in the West, his response would be: that semblance of identity is your own making, you have abstracted the thought from its context and made it appear that way. This is an *a priori* argument that no evidence can refute. The essentialist is no better off. Show him that two seemingly identical theses are really different in significant ways, he will say those differences are extrinsic, context-sensitive, and do not affect the essence. ("Interpreting" 215–16)

The results of actual studies of thinkers who have attempted to interpret and construct theories across cultural and historical boundaries, and not merely a set of arguments on principle, are necessary in any assessments as to the possibilities and limits of cross-cultural philosophizing as it has been tried. Schopenhauer, as one of the only thinkers in the history of the Western tradition who attempted to make systematic use of an idea he appropriated from the Indian philosophical tradition, provides an interesting and instructive case study for the cross-cultural philosopher. Without being able to delve very far or with great detail into the complex theoretical arguments in the field of cross-cultural philosophy, I would like to suggest some of the implications of Schopenhauer's systematic appropriation of the *Upaniṣadic* and Vedāntic notion of *māyā* that are relevant to the ongoing discussions in this discipline.

First, and perhaps most basically, *cross-cultural philosophizing is a broad-ranging historical activity of which Schopenhauer is only one of the more recent participants*. This point may seem trivial but is actually, given the skepticism as to whether cross-cultural philosophy is at all possible voiced in the twentieth century, quite significant. Much attention has been paid in this century to defining "philosophy," its content, concerns, scope and especially the role it has played in the context of European cultural, institutional and political history, and in this fashion delimiting it in one way or another to the European context. Nineteenth and twentieth century histories and historiographies of philosophy, as Wilhelm Halbfass has shown in some detail, identified the uniqueness of European philosophy to lie in its concentration on purely theoretical interests as well as its freedom from the soteriological interests of religious dogma, characteristics which distinguished it from Indian "philosophy," in which practical and soteriological concerns were at best intermingled with, and at worst dominated over, purely theoretical and logical pursuits (*India* 157).[20] This assessment seems to have had a great effect on Edmund Husserl, who thought that the discipline of pure *theoria* was the special province of Greek and European philosophy, and that this made it simply inappropriate to speak of Indian or Chinese "philosophies." Beginning with Heidegger, however, different assessments, which ironically led to the same conclusion that philosophical activity proper was the unique production of the West, were made of Greek and European philosophy, that they were consumed by the search for "Being," that they involved the ill-conceived project of essentialist, objectifying and universalist metaphysics, and that the rejection of such thought was the key to the inauguration of truly pluralistic thinking. In a recent essay entitled "Heidegger and Indian Philosophy," Joseph O'Leary has written:

> If Heidegger had embarked on a dialogue with India, he might have been as unwilling to talk about being as he was when in dialogue with theology, or with Japan. This is perhaps less an "exclusion" than a sense that, however fruitful inquiry into the ontological aspect of Indian thought may be, we need to get beyond this if the Indian "great beginning" is to put us in question in light of its own foremost concerns. . . . Heidegger is the opposite of a Eurocentric imperialist, for his awareness of the historical contingency of Western ontology clears the path to a radical pluralism of what he calls the "great beginnings. . . ." His discovery that Greek ontology is but a province of thought makes him a pluralistic thinker in principle, not a provincial one. To stress the commonalities between India and Europe to the point where these differentiations are flattened out is to regress from this diological openness. (179–80)

Another recent representative of the notion that cross-cultural philosophizing is more or less impossible has been Richard Rorty. He has asserted that, since the historical "needs" of various cultures are incommensurate with one another, only an act of "imaginative recontextualization" could make those different needs and the concepts that arose out of them equivalent (Rorty 332–7).

The notion that philosophy is a specifically Greek and derivatively Western intellectual pursuit and thus to preclude the possibility that cross-cultural philosophy is possible results for the most part from three factors: an arbitrarily and parochially refined definition or definitions of what philosophy is, a historiographical interpretation of the role of philosophy in European history that leads to indefensible historical conclusions, and misleading characterizations of what the activity of philosophizing across cultural boundaries consists in. Philosophy was thought by its early twentieth century Western historians as well as Husserl to be a uniquely theoretical and non-religious activity, judgments obviously too narrow to account even for the role philosophy played in the West for so many centuries as the "handmaid" of theology, as couched in metaphorical parables and aphoristic analogies by thinkers from the Pre-Socratics and Plato to Kierkegaard and Nietzsche. Much less did they take into account the Indian *darśanas* and their own institutional scholastic establishments. In the second half of the twentieth century, philosophy has been defined according to the Heideggerian and deconstructionist characterizations as the series of objectifying and essentialist metaphysical inquiries into "Being," and Asian "ways of thinking" have been praised for their difference and divergence from the obsession with such inquiries. Despite the fact then that early twentieth century philosophers took an inordinate and exceptionalist pride in their discipline, while later twentieth century hermeneuticians and deconstructionists felt an inordinate and exceptionalist shame in the tradition they had inherited, both reached the conclusion that philosophical thought is uniquely Western, and however sophisticated patterns of intellectual reflection develop in other cultures, they cannot be characterized as philosophical reflection. One wonders what could possibly be "pluralistic" about such a conclusion, especially given the self-preoccupied and inadequate conceptions of philosophy out of which it arose in these cases. One wonders what necessitates such a persistent parochialism about the definition of "philosophy" when historical investigations of what roles it has played in the history of European culture itself, not to mention the Indian, Chinese, Japanese, Islamic or African, could prove such delimitations unacceptable. Philosophy, as broad-ranging reflection on the world, its origin and constitution, how human beings come to know, what language is, what moral and immoral behavior is, what is useful and what not, what the aims of life ought to be and what not, has been pursued in too many different media and for too many different thematized purposes even in the history of Greek, Semitic and European cultures to justify such neat, exclusively theoretical or metaphysical delimitations.

Schopenhauer was a cross-cultural philosopher because he attempted to think in and through philosophical concepts he understood from another tradition, albeit seen through his own cultural lenses. This pursuit was hardly inaugurated with him, for we have throughout history numerous attempts of this kind. The intellectual interaction between Greeks and Indians during and after the Alexandrian period, which we know occurred but about which we know little, is one outstanding example. Another is the transmissions of Buddhism from its native Indian soil to China through the translations and unique systems of persons such as Kumārajiva and Xuanzang, and from there to the other cultures of East Asia. A third could be taken to be the merging of early Semitic Christianity with Greek and Roman philosophical and religious thought, which for centuries produced the various and competing Christian creeds. But one need not go nearly so far, for it would be difficult to show, as Rorty has proposed, that Heidegger was necessarily responding to the same cultural "needs" as were felt by Pythagoras or Plato, or even Kant and Hegel for that matter, but this did not prevent him from developing a new philosophical understanding of these thinkers. The practice of philosophizing across cultures is not something that it is feasible to decide as to its impossibility *a priori*: such a conclusion would in any event be historically suspect, just as an *a priori* conclusion as to its universal possibility would be historically naive. Cross-cultural philosophy has, under a variety of cultural circumstances of interrelation, tended to happen, and it is only after it happens in a particular instance that others are able to reflect on the viability of the theories and conclusions that resulted from it. But what must be remembered is the fact that all philosophical activity, and in particular cross-cultural reflection, involves conceptual understanding that is always hermeneutic in nature. The failure to recognize this leads to thoroughly misleading notions of what cross-cultural philosophy involves. The undertaking of the attempt to understand and interpret across cultural boundaries has never, and hermeneutically could never, involve a perfect duplication of a concept or theory from one historical period and cultural space to another, coupled with a fixed set of criteria enabling us to interpret them as their "originators" did. Cross-cultural philosophy involves conceptual appropriation, the success of which is always open to reassessment, critique, deconstruction, correction or, as the case may be, the development of a whole new set of thematized concepts or philosophical trends in a culture in which these new ideas and paths of thought had not been trodden before. Schopenhauer in this sense belongs very much to the history of cross-cultural philosophy. His understandings of the classical Indian religious and philosophical traditions, as we have seen above, merit critique, and many of his conclusions to be sure are of no use today. But in his philosophical appropriation of the notion of *māyā* and systematic development of that notion into a thesis of falsification that had epistemological, metaphysical and ethical implications, Schopenhauer made a unique contribution to the history of modern European philosophy and even modern Indian thought.

Secondly, *in his initial philosophical encounter with the presystematic Indian tradition, Schopenhauer did not appropriate an entire "conceptual scheme," but a concept*. Karl H. Potter once argued against the thesis, proffered by Quine, that in order to translate concepts across linguistic and cultural boundaries, one would have to be familiar with and be able to translate accurately the entire "conceptual scheme" of a language, otherwise the whole business of translation and cross-cultural understanding must be admitted to be at best indeterminate.[21] Potter pointed out that the holism of such an argument is difficult to adopt, for even those who share the same language do not have entirely overlapping "conceptual schemes," but this does not make communication and understanding impossible in a shared language, and so it is not necessary to suppose this is the case between different languages (19-24). Potter's arguments were mostly concerned with the human sciences such as history, cultural anthropology and descriptive comparative philosophy, but I would like to expand on this point as it relates to creative cross-cultural philosophical thought, Schopenhauer's case being the one in focus. It is very doubtful that any philosopher, with the possible exception of Hegel, to a lesser extent Heidegger, and maybe some of the classical Indian grammarians, believed that he or she was assuming the entire conceptual scheme of a language in order to give it a thoroughgoing explication. More frequently, philosophers deal with certain concepts, arguments, and certainly "worldviews" which they for various reasons believe to be of particular importance, with the intention of refining or redefining these in order to found or establish some putatively "universal" truths. These "universal" propositions are supposed to be true of any place and time with respect to a certain set of phenomena, whether it be language, knowledge, logical relations, metaphysics, morals and so on, but they are not thought to be truths about every thing. In other words, philosophers deal in concepts, not in the entire "conceptual scheme" of a language. In appropriating the concept of *māyā*, Schopenhauer certainly does not adopt, nor does he pretend he is adopting, the entire "conceptual scheme" of the Sanskrit philosophical tradition, and in fact he does not even adopt the entire "conceptual scheme" of *māyā* that we find in the *Upaniṣads* or the centuries of Vedāntic commentary on them. He does not understand *māyā* as *adhyāsa*, *nirmāṇaśakti* or *āvaranaśakti* in the technical senses in which those terms were employed by the Vedāntins. He thematizes it as the *principium individuations*, the forms of sensibility of time and space whereby a homogeneous and unitary metaphysical will becomes manifest through the intellect as a world of heterogeneous individuals and things. This being admitted, his general understanding of the concept is strikingly adept, as he like the Vedāntins thinks *māyā* to be the spontaneous function of the intellect (*Verstand*, *buddhi*) that organizes, individuates and apprehends perceptions, which is to say that for both Schopenhauer and Advaita Vedānta, *māyā* is what makes the world appear to consciousness.[22] Furthermore, it is what makes the world appear to consciousness falsely, as what it really in essence is not, even though Schopenhauer's and Vedānta's metaphysics differ vastly. Given the fact that the only help the early Schopenhauer had in his understanding of *māyā* was that of Duperron's translations and appendices, with no recourse to any of Vedānta's commentarial literature, this is all the more extraordinary. Schopenhauer appropriates the idea of *māyā,* weaves it into a falsification thesis in a philosophical vocabulary more familiar to him, and systematizes the idea in such a way as to connect epistemology, metaphysics and ethics. It is in this conceptual appropriation that the *Upaniṣads* were as much a philosophical "influence" on him along with Plato and Kant: he interprets and reinterprets within their various concepts, and not globally between Greek, Indian and German "conceptual schemes."

Third, *Schopenhauer's encounter with the classical Indian tradition was both historically conditioned and creative.* As mentioned in the opening chapter, Schopenhauer's initial discovery of India resulted in a hermeneutic appropriation that had measurable consequences for his own philosophy. It was of course Gadamer who took over the early Heideggerian ontological orientation and developed it into a historical hermeneutic, which sees such phenomena as the effectiveness of historical consciousness (*wirkungsgeschichtliches Bewustsein*). This meant that the significance of a text to an interpreter is certainly historically conditioned by the interpreter's own cultural and historical setting, the methods that history validates as the proper ways to receive and explicate a text and so on. But on the other hand, this process also prompts the interpreter to question the texts before her in new ways, to develop new "understandings" of the text's content or subject matter. Many who have devoted attention to Schopenhauer's reception of pre-systematic Indian thought have suspected, as we have seen above, that this reception was so comprehensively colored by the German Romantic approaches to India that prevailed in the early nineteenth century that Schopenhauer's case can be reduced to the Orientalist tendencies of that period. The whole business of "comparative philosophy," before and after Schopenhauer, whether it has been devoted to emphasizing similarities or differences between cultures, or explicating ideas from one culture in another, has historically been dominated by the interpretive standards of the politically privileged cultures, as Daya Krishna has insisted.

> Comparative studies are not just comparisons. The are comparisons between societies, cultures and civilizations. Across the boundaries defined by the "we" and the "they," the world of comparative studies is invariably an attempt to look at what, by definition, is "another reality" from the viewpoint of that which is not itself. The contradiction lying at the very foundation of comparative studies is sought to be glossed over by the appeal to the universalism of all knowledge, and the identification of the knowledge with the privileged "us" from whose view-point all "other" societies and cultures are judged an evaluated. The roots of this privileged position have generally lain in the political and economic power of the society of which the viewer happened to be a member. The anthropological studies from which most comparative studies have arisen were, by and large, an appendage of the extension of some western European countries' political and economic power over the globe for the last three hundred years or so. (Krishna 71–2)

There can be no question, as we have discussed in detail in the first part of this chapter, that Schopenhauer makes global "comparative" generalizations about the classical Indian religious and philosophical traditions and their relevance to Europe that were reflections of early Romantic Orientalism. Again, it must be remembered, Schopenhauer's appropriation of *māyā* was at the same time the emphasis of a concept that was not important to the German Romantics who became captivated with ancient India. Granted, the association of Kantian idealism with the *Upaniṣads* did have a European precedent in Duperron's appendices to his *Oupnek'hat*, but it was only Schopenhauer who pursued and developed this association systematically through his understanding of *māyā*. Schopenhauer's early encounter with the Indian tradition then was not limited to intellectually responding to the Romantic Orientalist interpretive "needs," "privilege" or "power," but also helped him to formulate a philosophical system that was an effect of his own peculiar creativity. While such creativity may not necessarily be generalizable to every cross-cultural philosophical encounter, it is a mark of hermeneutic understanding and appropriation as both Gadamer and Riceour conceived it.

Finally, *Schopenhauer's appropriation of the notion of māyā, and his thematization of an epistemological falsification thesis around that notion, created, almost invisibly, a new orientation towards epistemology in the Western tradition.* Halbfass and Clarke have praised Schopenhauer's unique brand of Orientalism in that Schopenhauer employs Indian thought towards a critique of traditional Western theology, metaphysics, and "objectifying" ways of conceptualizing the world (Halbfass *India* 120; Clarke 69). This achievement however was supported by Schopenhauer's falsification thesis. This thesis, and variations on its theme, created an entirely new orientation to epistemology in the Western tradition. To characterize this orientation generally, as to do so in detail would go beyond the purview of this dissertation, it may be said that a great deal of philosophical effort in the Western tradition, going back to Plato and Aristotle, had been devoted to discovering what powers knowledge possessed, how successfully knowledge, whether rationally or empirically derived, could mediate to us the true order and being of things, and what virtues accrued from the dedicated pursuit and acquisition of knowledge. Beginning with the empiricists, Locke, Berkeley and Hume, and running through the rationalism of Descartes and the idealism of Kant, different methods of investigation were adopted that were meant to discover alternatively the basis of human knowledge, upon what sorts of cognition it was built, and what its inherent limitations might be. With his falsification thesis, however, Schopenhauer takes what amounts to a radically new step in the history of Western thought, for although he does inquire into what sorts of powers knowledge possesses, as well as into its transcendental limitations, he also finds that knowledge, by its very nature and character, actively fabricates, distorts and even "covers over" the true, inner nature of the world with "the veil of *māyā*." Knowledge is not an independent faculty that stands as the distinctive virtue of human existence, it is rather for Schopenhauer subordinate to will, and is compelled by the will of the individual to represent the world in accordance with the individual's own desires.[23] This legacy is picked up by Nietzsche, who consistently referred to knowledge as a "fabrication," a "lie that made life possible," a function of the "will to power."[24] Of course, in his middle and later works, Nietzsche tried to distance himself from Schopenhauer's metaphysical interpretation of will, and indeed suggested that the many different wills of each individual were based on the dynamics of interpretation.[25] But the Schopenhauerian notion of falsification can be seen as a major theme from the beginning to the end of Nietzsche's philosophical career. This legacy has found its way even into late twentieth century thought, though by then reworked and employed to different ends, in the works of Foucault, who raises pivotal cultural and ethical issues by decrying traditional Western systems of knowledge that are in the end driven to and by "power."[26] The other consequence then of Schopenhauer's encounter with the pre-systematic Indian philosophical tradition, his appropriation of the notion of *māyā* as a thesis of falsification, and the epistemological, metaphysical and ethical implications of that thesis, is a quite influential change in the orientation of an entire strand of Continental philosophy towards knowledge, its powers and its value. Through Schopenhauer, and as such surely in a transformed manner, elements of the Vedāntic and early Buddhist treatment of knowledge and its powers of fabrication and deception work long-term effects on the Western philosophical tradition, although, again as a result of Schopenhauer's presentation, as well as the relegation of Schopenhauer's work once more to relative obscurity after Nietzsche, they do so almost invisibly.

In Schopenhauer's reception of the idea of *māyā,* his formulation of that idea into a full-fledged thesis of falsification, and his making that thesis a linking concept of his system, bridging epistemology, metaphysics and ethics, both the historical limitations and the creative impulses of a constructive thinker show themselves. Schopenhauer is a cross-cultural philosopher not in the manner of a bland and "objective" comparativism, in which ideas are treated simply as the results of cultural sedimentation and measured against one another in order to determine their mere similarity or difference. Even those who believe themselves to be participating in a merely "comparative" discipline of examining religion or philosophy are often blind to the fact that one does not merely compare with hermeneutic arbitrariness, but under the banner of some overriding interest that makes the comparison in question significant, the truth of those ideas being compared for instance, their falsity, their relevance, their manifestation of divergent cultural values, even the masked glorification of the culture of the one doing the comparing. For all of his stigmas, faults, misunderstandings, and shortcomings, Schopenhauer was not blind to this dimension of his encounter with classical Indian religion and philosophy, for he understood perhaps more acutely than most philosophers who preceded him in his tradition that all thought is value-laden. He proceeded to highlight and build upon those concepts he learned from the Indian tradition that he believed were philosophically useful, and either curtly rejected, relented to pursue or ignored the rest. A great, and generally under-appreciated, degree of his significance lies in the fact that, in the pursuit of constructive philosophy, Schopenhauer believed that the classical Indian tradition had much to say, and in this he was certainly far ahead of his Romantic and Hegelian times. And yet, having done much to awaken the West to another great intellectual and spiritual heritage, Schopenhauer can be safely left to nineteenth century Europe as one who convinced himself that Indian philosophy, and what it had to contribute to the ongoing discovery of knowledge, ought to be heard only through his own voice.

Endnotes

Chapter 1

[1] For Nietzsche's interpretation of Manu, see *Twilight of the Idols,* 188–91.

[2] This seemed to echo Schopenhauer's own belief that he had brought to a definitive end the age-old debate in Western philosophy between idealism and realism (see Schopenhauer, "*Skitze einer Geschichte der Lehre vom Idealen und Realen.*" [PPI 9–17]. In the citations of this book, Schopenhauer's works will be abbreviated thus: BM = *On the Basis of Morality;* FR = *On the Fourfold Root of the Principle of Sufficient Reason;* FW = *On the Freedom of the Will;* GB = *Gesammelte Briefe;* HN = *Der handschriftliche Nachlass;* MR = *Manuscript Remains;* PP = *Parerga und Paralipomena;* WN = *On the Will in Nature;* WWR = *The World as Will and Representation;* while numbers appended to these citations indicate the volume numbers of the work quoted. Note: All translations into English of quotes from German, Latin or Sanskrit, unless included within a cited text or otherwise indicated, are my own.

[3] Mockrauer's views on the ideal cultural exchange between India and the West are relevant to his interpretation, thinking as he did that Europe should be the "protector of Indian culture" (22); offering its own scientific and technological achievements (19–26), while itself benefiting from India's spiritual wisdom.

[4] Hacker identifies some basic differences between Schopenhauer's and Vedānta's views of the person, among which are the former's "monism of will" as opposed to the latter's "monism of consciousness" (277) as well as the former's final irreducible dualism between will and intellect as opposed to the latter's stricter monism of cognition (279). These are issues to which we shall return.

[5] Perhaps even the most charitable reading could only grant that Schopenhauer belongs to a group of nineteenth century German thinkers "whose enthusiasm or attention did not match their knowledge of the philosophical literature" (Mohanty "Between" 164).

[6] This hackneyed method of thematic classification still enjoys a place in more recent works on Schopenhauer and Buddhism. Most nota-

ble in this regard is Dorothea Dauer's short book *Schopenhauer as Transmitter of Buddhist Ideas*. This book made an attempt to show how Schopenhauer's philosophy fit into the scheme of the "Four Noble Truths" taught by Gautama Buddha with little regard for the systematic contexts either of those concepts it extracts from Schopenhauer or those of various strands of Theravāda and Māhāyana Buddhism which are mentioned. Important distinctions between Vedānta and Buddhism are blurred (13–14), Schopenhauer's rejection of an "intellectual soul" and the Buddhist doctrine of anātman are pronounced the same (17) and Schopenhauer is said to be in agreement with the ancient Hindus in believing in "the cyclic or repetitive concept of time" (30). Dauer concludes that, "while each point of Buddhist philosophy finds its counterpart bearing a more or less similar connotation in the system of the German philosopher" (35), the latter refused to acknowledge Buddhism as his major intellectual inspiration because of psychological "repression" (9).

[7] Historians of Western philosophy have more and more taken this view. See for example the section dedicated to Schopenhauer in W. T. Jones, 144–157.

[8] The three aspects of Orientalism according to Edward Said's groundbreaking *Orientalism* are first the academic study of the Orient, second the positing of a fundamental "ontological and epistemological distinction" between "Orient and Occident . . . East and West" and finally the establishment of a "discourse" which is manufactured ultimately for the intellectual "construction" and political "domination" of the Orient by the West (2–3). Schopenhauer of course clearly is an Orientalist in the first sense and to some degree in the second, though he was vituperative in his condemnation of European attempts to dominate the "Orient," and in particular the "missionary" justification given for such attempts. However, even with these considerations in mind, Schopenhauer's life did not exceed that "first two thirds of the nineteenth century," when "at no time in German scholarship . . . could a close partnership have developed between Orientalism and a protracted, sustained national interest in the Orient," even though German Orientalism during this time, due to its indebtedness to British Orientalist scholarship, exhibited "a certain intellectual authority over the Orient within Western culture" (Said 19). But Said clearly considered Schopenhauer an Orientalist in the sense that, with the other Romantics, he only appreciated India for the "intellectual" and "spiritual Renaissance" it held open before Europe as a counter-pole to traditional European philosophical doctrines (115). This suggestion is taken up and assessed in different ways by Gestering, Halbfass and Clarke, as we shall see below.

[9] Sedler emphasizes Schopenhauer's understanding of the doctrine of guilt and *karma* (170–1), his notions of desire and suffering which are so "astoundingly close" to those of Theravāda Buddhism (190) as well as his agreement with Buddhism that there is no "soul" or individual consciousness which survives death, necessitating a this-worldly salvation (205). Schopenhauer also shares, not insignificantly according to Sedler, an "a-historicism" with the thinkers of the classical period in India (122).

[10] Schopenhauer's many references to the kinship of his thinking with figures as disparate as Plato, Kant, the authors of the *Upaniṣads* and Eckhart supports this contention.

[11] This very suggestive observation seems corroborated by the stress Schopenhauer placed on art as a temporary escape from the will, which so closely resembles Kant's notion of the disinterested contemplation of aesthetic judgment (Desmond 101–22).

[12] See also HN 5: 324; 341ff.

[13] In one of the appendices to his translation of the *Oupnek'hat* entitled *De Kantismo*, Duperron wrote that the return of human beings to a reflection upon their own inner nature was what Kant and the *Upaniṣads* emphasized most.

[14] Halbfass argues that Schopenhauer in no way shared the common Romantic interest in returning to the lost cultural and spiritual origins of Europe thought to lie in particular in India (*India* 108).

[15] The two foremost contemporary German commentators on Schopenhauer, the late Rudolph Malter and Volker Spierling, never refer to Schopenhauer's acquaintance with Indian philosophy.

[16] Naegelsbach's argument is a very sophisticated one, and we shall return to it again in detail later.

[17] While Schopenhauer appears to espouse the Romantic idealization of the Indians as the "oldest and noblest of peoples" (Glasenapp 489) and certainly believes with the Romantics that the Christian religion has its spiritual roots in India (Ibid., 492), he thoroughly rejects the idea that India is the land of pure and lost beginnings of Western and particularly German culture (Halbfass *India* 108).

[18] See Halbfass *India* 120 and Clarke 68–9.

[19] Schopenhauer is fond of comparing the structure of his system to a living organism in which each part supports the functioning of all the others (WWRI, xii).

Chapter 2

[1] Interestingly, this advice according to Schopenhauer, included the insistence that he not study Spinoza and Aristotle, advice it seems he did not strictly follow given the mention of both in his notes from the period. Rüdiger Safransky speculates that Schulze's advice to study Plato and Kant was based on the fact that contemporary philosophy was striving toward a new, comprehensive metaphysical description of the world like Plato once gave, that now would start from Kantian principles (105).

[2] In his introduction to these transcribed lectures, Arthur Hübscher tells us that it was Fichte's penchant to demand that his students merely listen to his lectures without being allowed to take continuous notes, rather he believed they should be intent on the lectures, reflect on them and then transcribe them "in a way suitable to their nature." Hübscher observes; "Fichte's method of stimulating the student to form his own ideas confronted Schopenhauer with a new problem. His transcripts throughout enable us to perceive his collaboration with the lecturer and to a great extent bear the stamp of his way of thinking. In the emphasis on particular trains of thought and in the neglect of others, in the special way of summarizing into a concise extract, they show us a thoroughly independent molding of the subject matter presented by Fichte" (MR2, xv). We can see how, from the very beginning of his philosophical career, the peculiar way Schopenhauer selectively interpreted the texts he read was ingrained in him, perhaps for the first time, by Fichte's lecturing style.

[3] See Malter's *Der eine Gedanke: Hinführung zur Philosophie Arthur Schopenhauers* 1988 and Atwell *Character* 18–32.

[4] See Atwell *Character* 25–26.

[5] Schopenhauer took two lectures from this universal historian of commerce, trade, politics and science, one in the Fall of 1809 on "History of the European States from the Barbarian Invasions to the Most Recent Times," which coincided with a book he published on the same topic that year, and an 1811 lecture on "Ethnography" (MR2, vii–ix; xiii; 3–4). Interestingly, the man who first introduced Schopenhauer to the *Upaniṣads*, Friedrich Majer, met with Heeren and L. T. Spittler weekly in 1796 in group study meetings to discuss, among other things, Indian history when he himself went to Göttingen (Merkel 160).

[6] App, "Notes and Lectures by Schopenahuer Related to Vols. 1–9 of the *Asiatick Researches.*" *Schopenhauer Jahrbuch* 79, 1998, 11–33. As App points out, Schopenhauer would put these lecture notes and journal references to frequent use five to six years later during the formation of his system, as we shall also see below.

[7] *Oupnek'hat: Secretum Tegendum*. 2 vols. Agentorati, Paris, 1801–2. These volumes contain translations of fifty *Upaniṣads* and a number of commentarial appendices. They were not made directly from Sanskrit, but rather into Latin from the 1657 Persian translations of Dārā Shukh, the great grandson of the Mogul emperor Akbar (1542–1605), which he likewise entitled *Sirr-I Akbar* or "The Great Secret." Shukøh was also a universalist In a preface to his translations, he claimed that the *Upaniṣads* were the original texts espousing monotheism, and that they were followed in this doctrine by the Torah, the Psalms, the Gospels and finally the Koran, a belief for which his brother Aurangzeb ordered his execution two years after his translations were completed (see Halbfass *India* 34). Max Müller, who did his own translations of the *Upaniṣads* into English in the late nineteenth century, called Duperron's renderings "awful" and thought Rommohan Roy's far superior (417). Schopenhauer however continuously rejected newer, direct translations as being "infected" with monotheism and praised Duperron's translations as "the most rewarding and elevating reading, excluding the original text, possible in the world. It has been the consolation of my life and will be of my death" (PP1, 348).

[8] Schopenhauer did not think highly of these memoirs, but cited them several times in his main work (see WWRI, 384, 388).

[9] App, "*Schopenhauers Begegnung mit dem Buddhismus*." in *Schopenhauer Jahrbuch* 79, 1998, 35–56, 38.

[10] Krausse was apparently much more existentially involved with his studies of the Indian philosophical tradition than was Schopenhauer. He was known to teach small groups about Indian meditational techniques. His conjectures about compassion as embodied in classical Indian theories of metaphysics may have had a great impact on Schopenhauer, whose "*tat tvam asi*" ethic, as Hacker called it, we shall examine in more detail later.

[11] App has dramatically corrected previous scholarship on Schopenhauer's early familiarity with Buddhism in his two papers in the 1998 *Schopenhauer Jahrbuch*.

[12] This conclusion would require revision were consideration to be taken of how much Schopenhauer read and annotated on Indian thought during these years, as we have seen.

[13] Of course the entries directly dealing with Kant in the notes of this year exceed in length any of those dealing with Indian ideas, whose discussion is never as sustained.

[14] As we saw in the preceding chapter, J. I. Gestering has made a compelling case for this. This work will not enter into the interesting debate that has emerged in recent years as to whether any such term as "pessimism" can philosophically describe Schopenhauer's system. The

two sides of this argument have been well laid out by Bryon Magee (13–14) and John E. Atwell (*Human* 143–79).

[15] Schopenhauer admits in this note of early 1814 of having difficulty explaining the Platonic Ideas *vis-à-vis* concepts, for while for instance there can be a concept of zinc, there can be a Platonic Ideas only of organic bodies and crystals. "The Platonic Idea is the identical in many individuals which is left over simply after their diversity is abolished which is to be attributed to the forms of the phenomenal appearance of the Platonic Idea, to time and space. . . . The concept would be that which unites more than time and space separate, thus also the transcendental diversities" (MR1, 194).

[16] To this claim he adds the interesting point that, while individuals or particulars are transitory, "transitoriness" belongs to the Platonic Idea, which is supposedly itself outside time. How a temporal category can be attributed to an atemporal reality is just one of the many continuing problems of Schopenhauer's conception of the Ideas.

[17] This notion of relation is retracted by 1817, when he notes that contemplation of the Ideas is free from all relation, but this presents its own problems. In that year, he enters in his manuscripts an almost totally incomprehensible note; "The (Platonic) Idea is not only outside time, but also outside space; for the forms of things and of living individuals change in the same way, but the (Platonic) Idea they express remains the same. It is the innermost essence of the impression produced by the intuitive perception of the forms, and it can be the same, in spite of the great difference of the spatial relations of the form" (MR1, 524–5). Schopenhauer insists that essences of forms are not conceptualized but intuited "purely," that is, apart from spatio-temporal relations. These are not pure intuitions of time and space in the Kantian sense, but rather pure intuitions of a non-spatial, nontemporal form, which goes against all the Kantian premises concerning intuition to which Schopenhauer ascribes. The idea is incomprehensible and does not appear in Schopenhauer's published works, but it does bear witness to the difficulty of making much epistemological sense out of the Platonic Ideas as Schopenhauer conceives them.

[18] The parallels with the Kantian aesthetics of "disinterest" are clear here; see Desmond 103–107.

[19] See Henrich's essay "On the Unity of Subjectivity" 17–55.

[20] In the notes of 1812 to 1815, this notion of "pure consciousness" or "pure subjectivity" was thematized by Schopenhauer as the "better consciousness." Rüdiger Safransky has contended that *The World as Will and Representation,* though it never mentions the "better consciousness," is an explication of the notion as it is spelled out in the note-

books of the formative years of the system (152). There is no doubt that "the better consciousness" occupies a central role in Schopenhauer's early philosophical thinking, for he speaks of it as the genius of theoretical reason and the moral legislator of the practical, the essence of holiness and salvation, as transcending the empirical world, as the denial of the empirical world in reverence to the Platonic Ideas, the "good will," the ultimate existential choice between the finite and the eternal and so forth (MR1, 23–4; 46; 72; 74; 189–92; 98; 120). It is the idea from which the notion of "pure subjectivity" or "pure knowing" first emerges and is, as Safransky maintains, what originally sets Schopenhauer's philosophy the task of explaining epistemology, metaphysics, aesthetics, ethics and "mysticism" as a "hermeneutics of existence" (132–3; 139; 213–14). However, the notion of the "better consciousness" completely disappears from Schopenhauer's notebooks after early 1815 and is never mentioned in any of the published works. This happens, I believe, due to the more "pessimistic" outlook Schopenhauer derives from his metaphysics of will, with which he could never harmoniously reconcile the "better consciousness." Therefore, while Safransky is certainly right to emphasize its formative role in Schopenhauer's early thinking, the fact that it is completely eliminated from Schopenhauer's reflections after early 1815 and hence is never employed in Schopenhauer's systematic philosophy renders untenable Safransky's belief that the "better consciousness" always is the underlying support of that system, and so I have chosen not to highlight it in the presentation of major themes from the *Nachlass* in this chapter.

[21] Schopenhauer's beliefs about concepts are much more characteristically empiricist than idealist, for he believes concepts are the results not of *a priori* applications of categories to perceptions (Kant) or progressively all-encompassing movements of the thinking of Spirit (Hegel), but rather more in the manner of Locke or Hume, he considers concepts to be "abstractions." He also believes concepts to be coextensive with words; that is to say, he holds intuitive perception to be prelinguistic, but all thought to be linguistic (FR 148–9).

[22] Schopenhauer showed more than an empiricist mistrust of abstract conceptual thought. He writes in 1815; "The perception of real objects does not compel anyone to form concepts from them, only that man does this who is compelled to do so by some interest and hence by a motivated act of will" (MR1, 299). This doctrine is a bit puzzling, for while concepts are supposed to be "arbitrary abstractions" of qualities isolated from perceptual cognitions, motivation is said to precede these abstractions, but if that were the case, Schopenhauer should not call the abstractions arbitrary. In any event, Schopenhauer has with this idea turned the

traditional idea that will is subordinate to reason completely on its head: for him, concepts and hence reason are subservient to will. His mistrust of reason as a guide to morality is already well-defined in 1813, when he writes against the Kantian categorical imperative, "the faculty of reason is not the light shining from heaven, but only a signpost set up by ourselves and directed to the chosen goal, that it may show us the direction when the goal itself is concealed. But we can just as easily point it to hell as to heaven" (MR1, 59).

[23] In the second edition of his dissertation published in 1847, Schopenhauer makes some significant adaptations of his original thoughts on this matter in accordance with a metaphysics of will which did not exist when he first wrote the dissertation. For the later Schopenhauer, will is not a class of objects as it was in the dissertation.

[24] This argument also bears the stamp of Kantianism. Kant has posited that every act of free will breaks the chain of merely phenomenal causal necessity, for choices were not explicable in terms of the *a pirori* necessities which hold good for representations. The will is one, undifferentiated and transcendentally (though not phenomenally) free for Schopenhauer for this very reason; that it does not fall within the bounds of space, time and causality. He writes in 1814; "The same object is given to us in two quite different kinds of knowledge, and only quite empirically do we know it is the same object. From the consciousness of my body's movements in consequence of my will, I can never construct *a priori* the shape of this body, but I must obtain such shape through external intuitive perception. And from the knowledge of my body which has been gathered through intuitive perception, with my senses and understanding, I can never understand where its movements come from. In the latter kind of knowledge the body now appears entirely as an object of the first class and under the dominion of the law of causality. But with every arbitrary movement the law is abolished and this for us remains an eternal miracle in so far as we are left in this kind of knowledge" (MR1, 171). The argument is quite plainly much more Kantian than Fichtean; for Fichte the striving (*Streben*) of an ever spontaneous consciousness to know itself through a self-imposed *Hemmung* in the representations of intuition does not incorporate bodily activity, and so cannot really be considered a precursor to Schopenhauer's notion of will.

[25] As we shall see when we examine Schopenhauer's systematic ethics, the epistemological distinction between self and other does not disappear in the compassionate person, rather the distinction is maintained, though the compassionate person does not act according to it. Rather, she acts with the reflective knowledge that the world is at bottom one undifferentiated will, and so comports herself to the suffering other

as if those sufferings were her own. What Chansky has said of the Platonic Ideas also applies when it comes to Schopenhauer's epistemology, metaphysics and ethics of compassion; the principles of knowledge are not abolished for the compassionate, rather they no longer serve as guiding principles for their conduct.

[26] Halbfass considers the concept of *brahman* "Schopenhauer's most important Indian point of reference" (*India* 119). I tend to think, given Schopenhauer's early and repeated rejections of the notion as meaningless and "too mythological," these later attempts to align it with his central metaphysical doctrine of will were more or less *ad hoc*. *Māyā* is much more central to his own philosophical framework.

[27] Almost four decades later, Schopenhauer judges the Sāṃkhya system by this standard, saying that its dualism between *puruṣa* and *prakṛti*, spirit and matter, is precisely its point of departure from "the *Vedas*" (PPII, 350). Schopenhauer wrote nothing of the more objectively realistic Nyāya-Vaiśeṣika with which he was nonetheless familiar. Schopenhauer would seem to make a distinction of "orthodoxy" and "heterodoxy" within the *darśanas* between those which were subjectivistic and objectively oriented, a distinction Deussen elaborated more fully later between Vedānta and Sāṃkhya.

[28] The Vedāntins themselves would interpret such passages in the light of their ideas of *pariṅāmavāda* and *satkāryavāda*, the cosmological "doctrine of evolution" based on "the pre-existence of the cause in the effect." Even Śaṅkara does not revert to subjectivism in order to explain *pariṅāmavāda*, but rather offers a cosmological explication of such passages (see his *Upadeśasāhasrā*, II, 1: 18–22).

[29] Kant left no room for his epistemology to be construed as implying an illusionism of any kind. He wrote in the 1787 or "B" edition of the *Critique of Pure Reason*; "When I say that the intuition of outer objects and the self-intuition of the mind represent the objects and the mind, in space and time, as they affect our senses, that is, as they appear, I do not mean to say that these objects are a mere *illusion*. For in an appearance the objects, nay even the properties that we ascribe to them, are always regarded as something actually given. Since, however, in the relation of the given object to the subject, such properties depend upon the mode of intuition of the subject, this object as *appearance* is to be distinguished from itself as object *in itself*" (88). He continues, "it would be my own fault, if out of that I ought to reckon as appearance (*Erscheinung*), mere illusion (*Schein*). That does not follow as a consequence of our principle of the ideality of all our sensible intuitions—quite the contrary. It is only if we ascribe *objective reality* to those forms of representation, that it becomes impossible for us to prevent everything being thereby trans-

formed into mere *illusion*" (89). Kant does not believe his doctrines imply an illusionism, for in order for that to be the case, one would have to know what the thing-in-itself was like and then distinguish it from the representation so that one could show how the former was a falsification of the latter. He does not, however, believe things-in-themselves are knowable, and so no illusionism would be warranted. Schopenhauer of course rejected the 1787 "B" edition and thought the first edition more accurately represented Kant's position; he even convinced Schubert and Rozenkranz to confine their 1835 edition of the *Critique* to the 1781 manuscript to the exclusion of the "B" edition. The reason an "illusionism" becomes possible for Schopenhauer's philosophy was that, in his early career, he believed that he had found the nature of the thing-in-itself, will, and thus could show how representations falsified it, and moreover, he thought human beings normally orient themselves in their would by doing exactly what Kant above said was a condition of rendering everything into an illusion, namely attributing objective reality to "non-substances," mere forms of human sensibility.

30 In the *Vedic* hymns, this power is attributed to Indra and in the early, middle and late *Upaniṣads* to Iśvara's manipulation of unconscious matter, or *prakṛti*; see *Rig Veda* VI, 47:18 and *Bṛihadāranyaka Upaniṣad* II, 5:19, "*rūpam rūpam pratirūpa babhāva tad anya rūpam praticaksanāya; indro māyābhiṣ puru-rūpa iyate, yuktā hy asya harayaṣ śata daśa iti*" (qtd. in Radhakrishnan *Principle* 207). *Śvetāśvatara Upaniṣad* refers to God as the "magician" (*māyin*) whose production is "nature" (*prakṛti*). The *Bhagavadg Ātā* also refers to *māyā* in this sense, with Krishna claiming in several places that his divine *māyā,* composed of nature's qualities, is difficult to escape for those who do not abide in him (VII: 14, in Radhakrishnan and Moore 127). Rāmānuja understands *māyā* in this vein as well. These theistic conceptions of *māyā* were certainly not those Schopenhauer would have approved of. Interestingly, another understanding of *māyā* exists in *Upaniṣadic* thinking, which takes it to be a kind of intended verbal deception, "saying one thing and doing another," as Śaṅkara says, "*māyā nāma bahir anyathāmānam prahāsyainyathaiva kāryaāṃ karoti sa māyā mithyācāra-rūpā*" (qtd. in Radhakrishnan *Principle* 655). This technique of verbal deception was conceived to be at times politically useful.

31 See Śaṅkara's *Brhamasūtrabhāsyam,* I, 4:3 (in Radhakrishnan and Moore 515).

32 See Bina Gupta, 59–60.

33 In the *Gītā,* Krishna encourages Arjuna to participate in the battle against his kinsmen, since "he who thinks the self a slayer and he who thinks it slain are both uncomprehending; it does not kill, nor is it killed" (2:19 qtd. in Radhakrishnan and Moore 108). Hacker was in any

event correct when he cast this doctrine in the light of Krishna's all-embracing nature, so that self and other are not one in an abstract metaphysical sense, but one in Krishna as a personal deity.

Chapter 3

[1] The bravery exhibited by Schopenhauer in singling out his philosophical opponents by name certainly had much to do with his separation from the academic community, which was permanently effected in 1831 after leaving the faculty of Berlin University, for before that time his was noticeably more careful and humble in addressing his living contemporaries, though he became progressively more bitter and vituperative as his own work suffered year after year with inattention (see Safransky, 159, 252, 278). Nonetheless, Hegel's works apart from the *Histories* are conspicuous for their reticence in mentioning the name of the philosopher who Hegel is criticizing, even on those rare occasions when it is obvious who is under fire for holding one doctrine or another. This is the serious qualification that needs to be made to the common stereotype that Schopenhauer was an a-historical perennialist when it came to philosophical truth, while Hegel held the view that philosophical truth develops through and is fulfilled in history. This dichotomy is very misleading. Schopenhauer may have believed that truth was true in all times and places while Hegel held the *Begriff* to be dialectically mediated through the historical process. But Schopenhauer acknowledged the importance of historical philosophers as well as the development of philosophy through them by calling attention to the works of individuals and works in the histories of different philosophical traditions, while Hegel's penchant to leave the names of those individuals out of his polemics brings to the fore that a-historical strand in his thought that historical individuals were incidental to the phenomenology of Spirit. The two philosophers, that is, fundamentally disagree on the *telos* of history philosophically, but they are not as far apart as is often thought on the intimate relationship between history and philosophy.

[2] See also Halbfass *India* 113–17.

[3] This is still a prevalent view in scholarship of the Vedānta daršana, See Bina Gupta *The Disinterested Witness* 1998.

[4] This is also perfectly in line with Vedāntic exegesis. The epistemological teachings of Śaṅkara and his centuries of Advaita commentators presented a theory of cognition wherein, while the transcendental self *(ātman)* was the condition of all knowledge, perceptions depended upon the interaction of physical phenomena, such as the mind (*buddhi*),

sensory impressions (*pratyayas*) and matter (*prakṛti*). This transcendentalized Sāṃkhyan model of cognition in summarized nicely in Sengaku Mayeda's introduction to his translation of *A Thousand Teachings: The Upadeśasahāsri* 33–40.

[5] *îadṛśto dṛśtā, aśrutaṣ śrutā, amato mantā, avijñāto vijñātā, nānyoítoísti* III, 7:23 (qtd. in Radhakrishnan 1993, 229). In an 1847 addition to the 1813 manuscript of his dissertation, *On the Fourfold Root of the Principle of Sufficient Reason*, Schopenhauer explicitly draws attention to the fact that he has the *Bṛhadāranyaka Upaniṣad* in mind here when he cites it (III, 7, 23) in support of this very doctrine of subject object correlativity (FR 208). This is also a formulation from the beginning of the *Kena Upaniṣad*, which describes Brahman as "that which is not seen by the eye, but that whereby the eye sees," (*ìyac cakṣuṣā na paśyati yena cakṣūṁṣI paśyatiī* I:7, qtd. in Radhakrishnan *Principle* 583). Schopenhauer makes numerous allusions to passages from the *Bṛhadāraṅyaka* when discussing representation theory, as when he pictures Kant's notion of a unitary consciousness in which "all representations are ranged as pearls on a string, and by virtue of ... the 'I think'" which is "the thread of the string of pearls" (WWR2, 251). This may come from *Bṛhadāraṅyaka*'s motif of Brahman as the "inner controller," "the thread on which the world is strung" and that which "knows everything" (III, 7:2-4 in Radhakrisnan *Principle* 225–26). Of course, as we saw in the last chapter, these passages were mediated for Schopenhauer's understanding through the Kantian interpretations of their translator, Anquetil Duperron, supra, 74–75.

[6] Supra, 79–82.

[7] These factors do however play a large role in Schopenhauer's representation theory, as we shall see below.

[8] See the *Critique of Pure Reason* 88–89.

[9] There is a certain temptation here to assess Schopenhauer's appropriation of *māyā* with respect to the Advaitic thematization of this concept. Śaṅkara and his commentators make *māyā* synonymous with technical epistemological terms such as *avidya* or *adhyāsa*, but such comparisons would not yield much, since these terms describe how the unqualified and timeless "self" or *ātman* becomes confused with the objects of the empirical world. On the other hand, the Advaitic theory of error or perceptual illusion, the "indeterminability theory" (*anirvacaniya-khyāti*) exhibits some of the paradoxicality of certain kinds of representations discussed here. We often are mistaken about what an object is; the prototypical example given by Indian epistemologists is of course mistaking a rope for a snake. The theory of "indeterminabilty" says that the status of the object about which we were mistaken cannot be shown to be nonexistent, for we did see it, but neither can it be shown to exist, since the

object we thought we saw was not there. The snake we thought we saw, according to Advaitins, cam neither be said to exist or not exist, and so its ontological status as an "illusion" (*khyāti*) is "indeterminable" (*anirvacaniya*). This theory is of course quite different from the paradoxicality of representations Schopenhauer explains, for the latter speaks more of representations as such, whereas the former theory attempts to clarify the nature of perceptual error.

[10] Supra, 56-7. This thesis maintained an important status throughout Schopenhauer's *Nachlass* from 1812 to 1818; see MR1, 26-27, 61, 228, 237. The idea that every representation consists of a subject and object as correlates was first identified as a fundamental part of Schopenhauer's epistemology by Johannes Volkelt, *Arthur Schopenhauer: Seine Persönlichkeit, seine Lehre, sein Glaube* 89–101.

[11] Kant's position here is indeed difficult to ascertain. It doesn't seem as if he is espousing the view that apperception unconditionally obtains in all cognitions, but rather that it is possible for any cognition to be apperceived. Then again, the entire thrust of Kant's transcendental idealism is to ascertain what makes experience possible, and to establish that means to uncover what is both actual and necessary in the constitution of experience. If the transcendental unity of apperception is possible, then upon transcendental considerations, it is a necessary element of any experience properly so called. This problem cannot be solved in the present context, though it is not difficult to be sympathetic to Schopenhauer's confusion on this issue.

[12] One of Schopenhauer's most frequent and derisive criticisms of Kant is that he persistently defined the perceptual process in terms of thinking. He accused Kant of believing causality to be a reflective concept and thus making sensation a *de facto* conceptual process (FR 116–7), of making a conceptual object (the thing in itself) the ground for perceptions (FR 233–5; WWR1, 442, 444), of making abstract concepts rules for perception (WWR1, 431; 447–8), of introducing "objects" into sensation when these could exist only for intuition (WWR1, 438–9), of construing concepts as the most essential elements of knowledge (WWR1, 474–5). In his own epistemology, Schopenhauer attempts to delimit the faculties clearly; there is sensation in which there is no objective content but only a local, specific feeling beneath the skin (FR 76–7; WWR1, 19–20), intuition as the application of time, space and causality to sensations and thus making them objects for a subject (FR 78; 82; 86–94; 130; WWR1, 11–12; 21) and reason as abstracting or isolating certain qualities of perception and forming useful abstract concepts (words) out of them in order to think many particulars through them (FR 146–51; 171; WWR1, 39–41; 45). But Schopenhauer's own construction of a faculty psychology has proven

highly problematic as well. He says for instance that the understanding draws an "immediate and intuitive inference" that an external body causes sensations, leaving it unclear as to how the understanding can infer anything, that being the job of reason (FR 82; WWR1, 439). He claims the understanding constructs bodies by interpreting sensations "geometrically," whereas later he thought all applied mathematics to be conceptual (FR 86–94; WWR1, 54–7). Though he insists that concepts depend for their material on perceptual data, in the manner of the empiricists, he leaves unexplained how specific qualities are present in representations in order for conception to abstract some and "drop" others (FR 146–7; 150–1; WWR1, 10–11). There is a consensus in Schopenhauer scholarship that Schopenhauer's own faculty psychology is burdened by the attempt to apply an empiricist theory of concepts to an idealist model of perception, as well as by irreconcilably separating sensation, perception and conception due to his fear that Kant had associated them too closely (see Hamlyn 19–20; 43–6; Malter "*Abstraktion*" 270–1; Janaway 159–63; 165–6; Gardiner 107, 113.

[13] See Atwell *Character* 193, note 15.

[14] D. W. Hamlyn has pointed out nicely how problematic this account is, for it leaves completely unclear how the understanding can apply time, space or causality to sensations since sensations carry with them only a temporal determination. If the understanding attributes a cause to sensations, it has no way of knowing what kind of cause to attribute; if the understanding makes spatial determinations of what is sensed, it has no way of determining how to attribute them since sensations are supposedly not spatial (Hamlyn 19–21). The principle of sufficient reason, on Schopenhauer's account, may provide the form of one object's connection with another, but it has no way to provide the details of the connection (Hamlyn 21). Hamlyn suggests that Schopenhauer lands himself into this unfortunate consequence by trying to justify his idealism through a deficient empirical model of perception (45–6). Schopenhauer, as we shall see later, tries to solve this problem decades later through what I shall call "brain idealism," but even that solution turns out to be inconsistent with his ontology.

[15] Hamlyn also critiques Schopenhauer's notion of concepts. "If," Hamlyn writes, "abstraction is a cognitive act it must work on what is already known in the perceptual instances, but if something is indeed known in them they must surely presuppose already some concept of the object perceived. How then is that concept obtained? On the other hand, if the abstraction is not a cognitive act of that kind, but the concept comes into being, so to speak mechanically, it remains quite obscure what principles govern the selection of instances in such a way that they give rise

to the concept" (23). Once again, these ambiguities seem to result from Schopenhauer's efforts to retain theoretically attractive facets of both idealism and empiricism in his own epistemology. Schopenhauer did not accept Kant's notion of concepts as *a priori* and synthesizing the data of intuition, for that account associated too closely perception and thinking. Schopenhauer was an advocate of the empiricist dictum "*nihil in intellectus nisi prius in sensu,*" but wedding that principle to an idealist doctrine of *a priori* formal knowledge resulted in a doctrine of conceptual abstraction that did very little in the way of describing how abstraction occurs. Despite all of this, Schopenhauer's doctrine of conceptual abstraction was very important to him, for it established the primacy of perceptual knowledge over abstract knowledge (WWR1, 35–6; 45; 56; 474–5) and allowed him to conclude that concepts and reason were at the behest of will (FR 150; 215; WWR1, 83–6).

16 The "material mode" of speech is juxtaposed by Carnap to the "formal mode." Material reference was made of objects of experience, formal reference to "linguistic objects" which had their content in language only and not what Carnap called the "thing-world." I will not go into an elaboration about this interesting distinction here, as it is outside of my present purposes. It was in any case a distinction made before, first hinted at by Neurath, and proposed to dissolve most of the traditional metaphysical problems by establishing that these problems had nothing to do with material reference, but only with formal reference; see Carnap *The Logical System of Language* 289–98.

17 This kind of objection reminds one strongly of Nietzsche's suspicion that the belief that subjects and objects really existed in a relationship that resulted in knowledge was really only a "faith in grammar."

18 Determining the modes and conditions of the "mind dependence" of objects is precisely the method of Kantian transcendental idealism, according to Henry E. Allison 6–10. It is also, by Schopenhauer's estimation, what Berkeley's and Kant's doctrines have in common; see WWR2, 8 and Janaway 53–67.

19 In an 1847 addition to his dissertation, Schopenhauer responded to this very objection by claiming that we can know reflectively about the subject and its modes of knowledge by "inference." "With regard to the necessary correlative of those representations as their condition, namely to the subject, those powers are abstracted from the representations. Consequently they are related to the classes of representations precisely as the object in general is to the subject in general" (FR 209).

20 This fact has led Hamlyn to question how many "things" there are in Schopenhauer's ontology; Schopenhauer has himself suggested there are two, will and representation, but given the fact that the subject

of knowledge and the Platonic Ideas lie outside the principle of sufficient reason also, should they be counted as other "things" (104). As it turns out, this problem seems resolved by the fact that Schopenhauer believed the subject and the Ideas to be an aspect and a mode of representation respectively. It is Janaway who draws a more fruitful question from this coincidence of subject and thing in itself as outside the realm of objective representation, namely the question of self-knowledge and what role the self plays in the world (3–4; 17).

21 Schopenhauer gives an account of everyday perceptual illusions which remains the same throughout his works, according to which illusion happens when the understanding attributes the incorrect cause to an intuitive perception, with illusions of the understanding contrasted from logical errors of reason; reason can make us aware of our illusions, but phenomenologically cannot make the illusion appear correctly (FR 103–4; WWR1, 24–5). The stock examples Schopenhauer uses for perceptual illusion are the stick that looks bent in water and the moon appearing larger at the horizon than at its zenith. Again, this account suffers from the problem of how the understanding can "attribute" or "choose" among causes when it supposedly has no logical powers. Schopenhauer's suggestion that the intellect learns which causes to attribute from experience to its perceptions, while in itself satisfactory, does not conflate well with his idealism (FR 104). Schopenhauer adds however that conceptual errors are much more pernicious to human beings than perceptual illusions, for while a perceptual illusion may only last a few moments, an error of reason can deceive decades, centuries, millennia of human cultures (WWR1, 35).

22 Copleston's argument makes Schopenhauer into much more of a reductionist than he actually was, and totally ignores a distinction Schopenhauer makes which for expositional purposes Copleston was willing to recognize, namely that representational knowledge, though mediate, was only one kind of knowledge, whereas knowledge of the will was supposedly immediate. More on this below.

23 The philosophical theories of *khyāti*, "perceptual error" or "illusion," were discussed by all the different schools of Indian philosophy, the realist Nyāya as well as the anti-realist Buddhists and Vedānta. These theories are to be distinguished from the linguistic theory of falsification in Buddhism and the axio-ontological theory of falsification in Vedānta. The only school of Indian thought for which "illusionism" may have been an ontological position was the Buddhist Vijñānavāda, and in fact this latter has even been compared to Schopenhauer's philosophy by Bryan Magee (340–44). Nevertheless, a distinction between a theory of falsification and illusion is necessary for clearing up many miscon-

ceptions about Indian philosophy, some of which Schopenhauer to a certain degree initiated in the West.

[24] One may try, as the *Māṇḍūkya Upaniṣad* and its famous commentator Guaḍapāda did, to distinguish in some way the "outer" objects of waking life with the "inner" ones of dream on the basis that the latter are "self-luminous" while the former are "illuminated from without," but since the later Vedāntins will argue that all consciousness has as its necessary condition the self luminous *ātman*, even these are somewhat blurred. Schopenhauer will himself come to say that while dreams and waking life are distinguished in terms of their material, the material for dreams comes from the "internal" imagination and for waking life from sensation, both kinds of experience are formally alike insofar as they are representational.

[25] One will recall Kant's argument from the first edition of the *Critique of Pure Reason* in this context, which posits that it is the mind with its transcendental rules of objective constitution that creates nature, not nature with its transcendent absolute laws that constitutes the mind.

[26] While arguing here against Schopenhauer's characterization of science with the suggestion that Schopenhauer does not take account of its predictive function, Gardiner elsewhere rebukes Schopenhauer's contention that these efforts to make nature predictable shows that science is basically a practical and not primarily a theoretical endeavor. Science does after all, Gardiner writes, satisfy merely intellectual curiosity (141–3).

Chapter 4

[1] Supra, 35; 37–8; 77; 79; 84–6.

[2] Schopenhauer's consideration of the importance of language did seem to exceed the estimation of language by the other Idealists at any rate. In his dissertation, he refers to language as that medium of "arbitrary signs" whereby reason reduced the world of perception into fixed universal concepts, and so to master language was for him to master "the whole machinery of reason" (FR 148–9). He often points out, as he does in the first edition of *The World as Will and Representation*, that the same word is used in Greek and Italian for both speech and reason, *logos* and *il discrsio*, while in German, the term for "reason," *Vernunft*, is etymologically related to the verb *vernehmen*, which connotes understanding words (WWR1, 37). He also points out that language is how whole civilizations cooperate and how science, religion and culture are disseminated (ibid.). In an emendation to his "Criticism of the Kantian Philosophy" in

the first volume of his "main work," Schopenhauer responds to the idea of S. Stern that language and grammar govern even perception. Schopenhauer suggests that logic itself is based on grammar, that the Aristotelian table of judgments could be derived from the grammatical relationships of the substantive, predicate and copula in a proposition, which are the fundamental constituents of language as such, and thus all languages (WWR1, 477–80).

[3] Commentators have attempted to find precedent for Schopenhauer's metaphysics of will. Christopher Janaway believes these precedents can be found mostly in Kant and Fichte. With respect to Kant's third antinomy, Schopenhauer's metaphysics of will is an offshoot from Kant's notion of "radical initiation," or the willed, spontaneous action giving birth to a new causal series without being a cause itself (Janaway 85–7). As regards Fichte, the will metaphysics is meant to resolve a problem in Fichte's *Sittenlehre,* which depicts the knowing self as necessarily knowing itself as willing and not knowing (Janaway 131–2). Before Janaway, Gardiner found Schopenhauer's ideas on the identity of will and body to be derived partly in adoption of and partly in criticism of the French physiologist Maine de Biran (156–7). While Schopenhauer did not read Maine de Biran until well after the publication of the first edition of The World as Will and Representation, Schopenhauer freely admits of his indebtedness to Kant in his reflections on the will and its freedom (WWR1, 612; WWR2, 162), and the obvious effects Fichte's thoughts on the will had on his own philosophy can be seen from his notes on Fichte's lectures of 1811 and 1812 (MR2, 16–233; 392–417).

[4] Indeed, in the second edition of *The World as Will and Representation* of 1844, Schopenhauer adds to this section the qualification: "the knowledge I have of my will, although an immediate knowledge, cannot be separated from that of my body. I know my will not as a whole, not as a unity, not completely according to its nature, but only in its individual acts, and hence in time, which is the form of my body's appearing, as it is of every body. Therefore the body is the condition of knowledge of my will. Accordingly, I cannot really imagine this will without my body" (WWR1, 101–2). The perspective is taken up fully in the second volume of the second edition and we shall deal with it in detail below. It is on this point that the philosophy of the early Schopenhauer is to be distinguished from that of the latter in one of the clearest ways, and shows how misleading is the common tendency to take Schopenhauer at his word that his philosophy was basically homogeneous throughout his career.

[5] Schopenhauer was never unaware of the theoretical difficulties of his position. He claimed that the truth of the will's identity with the

body could only be obtained through the peculiar "double knowledge" we have of our bodies (WWR1, 103), called this truth "the miracle *par excellence*" and acknowledged that the relationship of the will to the body could not really be explicated through "the reference of an abstract representation to another representation" (WWR1, 102). As it is for Schopenhauer beyond the capacities of both religious and philosophical language to adequately characterize the relationship of the will to the body, Schopenhauer's whole metaphysics takes on all the marks, and weaknesses of, an apophatic belief.

[6] In his *Brieftasche* from this year, we find such notes as the following: "To recognize the thing in itself is a contradiction because all cognition is representation, whereas the thing in itself means the thing to the extent that it is not." "Just because the will is the most immediate phenomenon of the thing in itself, it evidently follows that if the remaining phenomena of the thing in itself were brought to us equally close, i.e., if their cognition were raised to the same degree of clarity and immediacy as our will, they would present themselves just as the will does in us. I am therefore entitled to state that the inner essence of every thing is will, or that will is the thing in itself" (qtd. in Safransky 267).

[7] Atwell raises a serious doubt about this. He believes that Schopenhauer cannot draw the analogy that we know our own bodies from one aspect like we know "other bodies," other "representations" in the first place. The knowledge of my own body and of external objects may be as different representations different from the start, for the whole thrust of the argument is that the body is never known only as a representation (Atwell *Character* 86–7).

[8] Schopenhauer's philosophical works and lectures had been singularly unsuccessful and had gone almost completely without notice among his contemporaries up to this time. Upon being hired to the philosophical faculty in Berlin in 1819, Schopenhauer asked the dean to schedule his lecture on "The Essence of the World," at the same time as Hegel's. Hegel actually cordially attended Schopenhauer's inaugural lecture on "Motive," and the two engaged in a brief confrontation during this lecture, but to no avail. Hegel's lecture that semester attracted in excess of two hundred students, while Schopenhauer's only drew five (Safransky 252). For the entirety of the 1820's the lectures Schopenhauer proposed in Berlin got no registered students, and his *opus, The World as Will and Representation,* sold few copies and elicited a mere three unenthusiastic reviews by Johan Friedrich Herbart, Jean Paul and Ludwig Tieck. According to Safransky, Schopenhauer's lectures were unpopular mainly because his constant approbation of Kant and the classical philosophers and his dismissal of the post-Kantian idealists made his

thought seem outdated, and his aesthetics and ethics were too a-historical, pessimistic, "too Indian" to be relevant to contemporary discussions (260–2). During the decade, Schopenhauer, literate in seven languages and actively competent in five of them, proposed several translation projects, notably of Kant into English and Hume into German, and while these failed, he did translate his own dissertation into Latin and the ethical maxims of the Spanish writer Gracian into German. The work *On the Will in Nature* did nothing for Schopenhauer's fame; five hundred copies had been printed of the original edition, and one year later, only one hundred twenty five had sold (Safransky 293–4). With the exception of an essay he wrote, *On the Freedom of the Human Will*, which won a prize from the Norwegian Society for Learning in Trondheim in 1839, Schopenhauer's published philosophical works dwelt in ignominy until he began composing more "popular" works such as the *Parerga und Paralipomena* in 1851, when from that point until his death in 1860, Schopenhauer enjoyed some measure of philosophical "fame."

[9] This is another disagreement which has persisted among Schopenhauer scholars for decades, namely, the issue of whether his epistemology was not fundamentally physiological from the start, or whether he was basically a Kantian idealist who eventually became inclined towards the physiological model of representational knowledge found in his later works. Alfred Schmidt maintained that Schopenhauer was originally a Kantian, later leaned toward materialism and then ended up trying to reconcile the two accounts (see "*Schopenhauer und der Materialismus*" 52–3). Christopher Janaway believes that both accounts, the idealistic and physiological, were always intertwined in Schopenhauer's thought, from beginning to end (81–2). John Atwell chimed in on this debate with the suggestion, based on textual considerations, that Schopenhauer was not a Kantian until his later works, specifically the works of the 1840's (*Character* 75–6). The textual evidence, both of Schopenhauer's notes and his published works, seems to suggest that both Kantianism and physiological accounts of knowledge played roles in his early and late works. But there are two basic reasons why it is reasonable to conclude that Schopenhauer's interest in the physiological picture of the intellect was subordinate to his idealistic leanings. From his dissertation and 1816 essay on *Vision and Colors* all the way to his 1844 and 1859 editions of *The World as Will and Representation*, Schopenhauer never used the Kantian model of knowledge to establish his physiological picture of the intellect, but rather he employed arguments from physiology to prove to a broad audience that the Kantian notion of *a priori* forms of knowledge was the most viable epistemological viewpoint. Schopenhauer's self-admitted early preoccupation with Kant discounts Atwell's

charge that Schopenhauer was not at the beginning a Kantian (see WWR1, xiv). Secondly, while his physiological ruminations in his early writings never had much consequence for his metaphysics in the works preceding the 1830's, in the books after the mid 1830's, Schopenhauer's physiological studies had a profound effect on making his ontology more realistic. In any event, Schopenhauer stands between the two strands of idealism in the nineteenth century, one strand of which is represented by the purely epistemological approach of Reinhold, Fichte and Schelling, and the other strand of a more cognitive approach represented by Helmholz.

[10] Supra, 103–16.

[11] This subject-matter correlativity thesis which resulted in Schopenhauer's attempted synthesis between idealism and materialism was very important to his later philosophy. At the end of the first essay of the second edition of *The World as Will and Representation*, entitled "On the Fundamental View of Idealism," Schopenhauer composes a dramatic dialogue between "The Subject" and "Matter," which begins with the two arguing over which one is responsible for the creation of the other, and ends with the two agreeing that they are co-equal partners in representational knowledge (WWR2, 17–18). Schopenhauer admits of taking for his inspiration of this composition a thirteenth century drama by Krishna Mishra entitled *Prabodha-candra-udaya*, or "The Rising of the Moon of Knowledge." Schopenhauer takes another metaphor from the Sāṃkhya tradition in this work to describe the relationship between the matter and the subject, namely that of "a strong blind man carrying a sighted lame man on his shoulders" (WWR2, 209). It is interesting that the interaction in knowledge between the self or subject of knowledge (*ātman*) and the "material but inert" mind (*buddhi*) and matter (*prakṛti*) is also insisted upon by the epistemologists of the Vedāntic tradition.

[12] It will be remembered that Janaway has rebuked this argument, saying that if we can have no determinate knowledge of the thing in itself, we could have no way of figuring out which phenomenon is its nearest relative (197). Schopenhauer's justification for saying this is that, while all other phenomena are known according to space, time and causality, and the thing in itself can be known according to none of these forms, so the will must be the closest relative to it because it is known only according to time and not space or causality. But if Schopenhauer thinks, as he did in the first volume, that "pain" or "pleasure" are immediate affections of the will, it would be plausible to suppose that space applies to it too, for pain and pleasure are often localized in the human body.

Chapter 5

[1] A number of major commentators have adopted in one way or another Nietzsche's reduction of Schopenhauer's ethics to the idea of "world-renunciation" and found it problematic. Frederick Copleston concluded that since Schopenhauer's vision of the will, the ground of all things, was at best amoral and at worst positively evil, the idea of spinning any ethical system from this metaphysics of will was ill-conceived from the beginning (143). Schopenhauer's characterization of the world as doomed to contest and suffering because of will does not, for Copleston, confer on the world any moral significance, but might make us hate it and want to find a way out of it (148). Nietzsche's view was surely a peculiar one for the Jesuit scholar Copleston to adopt, since Nietzsche found in Schopenhauer's moral doctrines a "resurrection" of the teachings of Christianity, a resurrection Nietzsche found contemptible (Nietzsche *Twilight* 26). Copleston, for his part, believed that Schopenhauer's ethics was derived primarily from the ethically "passive" Hindu and Buddhist traditions, and this put it in stark contrast to the ethics of Christianity which was, unlike Hinduism and Buddhism, "a religion of life" (179). While for the most part the evaluative judgments of Schopenhauer's philosophy as "life-denying" have disappeared from the secondary literature, the notion that his system of metaphysics was basically inspired by ethical considerations is still prevalent. In his final book on Schopenhauer, John Atwell wrote: "No one asks about the 'essence' of the world, no one poses the question 'what is the world ultimately or at bottom?' without a special reason. Something must be regarded as troubling, disturbing, mysterious or puzzling about 'the world' if one is to seek that which would resolve 'the riddle of the world.' . . . So Schopenhauer might have explicitly urged his reader to reflect upon life and the world, convinced that if the reader does so, he or she will realize that suffering permeates the whole of conscious existence, upon which he or she will very likely wonder what can possibly explain this fact, this 'riddle of the world.' It is this very wonder that, for Schopenhauer, constitutes the metaphysical thrust" (*Character* 16).

[2] Curiously, Atwell finds later in his *Schopenhauer: The Human Character*, one of Schopenhauer's most important contributions to ethical theory to have been his proof that actualism is not inconsistent with the ascription of moral responsibility in the first place. Even if one were to believe, as an actualist does, that agents are nothing besides the deeds they in fact perform, and that the agent's various acts are causally determined and not subject to choice, this in no way hinders us from making moral descriptions of their actions as laudable or pernicious, nor does it

prevent us from realizing that since a certain individual performed an act of moral worth, they are morally responsible for it. What we cannot do on an actualist view of agency is formulate an imperative theory of ethics, prescribing a set of moral "oughts" for agents whose actions are in every case determined. But we can nonetheless morally characterize actions within an actualist position (see Atwell *Human* 67–73). This should have implied for Atwell that Schopenhauer's attempted synthesis of actualism and causalism was superfluous, since Schopenhauer really had no theoretical need for a causalist story to provide for moral responsibility. Atwell, however, appears not to have been aware of this consequence.

[3] Schopenhauer, in addition to conceiving of his ethics as metaphysical, thought his method for approaching ethics could take on only a descriptive, and not an imperative stance. Ethics can describe and characterize how human beings behave, but since the will is not subject to the conditions of knowledge set by space, time and causality, philosophy cannot prescribe for this "free" will "oughts" by which it should conduct itself (WWR1, 272). Schopenhauer goes out of his way to insist repeatedly that his ethics is metaphysical and descriptive, but not prescriptive, that is to say, not a theory of moral principles, but of the basis of moral conduct. "Philosophy can never do more than interpret and explain what is present and at hand; it can never do more than bring to the distinct and abstract knowledge of the faculty of reason the inner nature of the world which expresses itself intelligibly to everyone in the concrete, that is, in feeling. It does this, however, in every possible relation and connection and from every point of view. . . . The point of view given and the method of treatment announced suggest that in this ethical book no precepts, no doctrine of duty are to be expected; still less will there be set forth a universal moral principle, a universal recipe, so to speak, for producing all the virtues. Also, we shall not speak of an *'unconditioned ought,'* since this involves a contradiction. . . . The will is not only free, but even almighty; from it comes not only its action but also its world; and as the will is, so does its action appear; so does its world appear; both are its self-knowledge and nothing more. The will determines itself and therewith its action and its world also; for besides it there is nothing and these are the will itself. . . . Our philosophical attempts can go only so far as to interpret and explain man's action, and the very different and even opposite maxims of which it is the living expression" (WWR1, 271, 272). Again, in a brief discussion on the two ultimate alternatives for the will as it inhabits every individual, namely "the affirmation or denial of the will to live," Schopenhauer stresses the role of ethics as describing the alternatives without prescribing which one should be taken in any given

case. "Affirmation in its different degrees on the one hand, and denial on the other . . . both start from *knowledge,* though not from an abstract knowledge expressing itself in words, but from *living knowledge,* expressing itself in deed and conduct alone." . . . To exhibit both and to bring them to the distinct knowledge of the faculty of reason can be my only aim, and not to prescribe or recommend the one or the other, which would be as foolish as it would be pointless (WWR1, 285). And so, to return briefly to Nietzsche's evaluation of Schopenhauer's ethics, we may say that, while Nietzsche may have been inaccurate in judging the moral system of Schopenhauer to have been conceived in an imperative context, he was right in emphasizing the centrality of ethics to Schopenhauer's thought, and lends some credence to the suspicion that Schopenhauer's goal was to make his metaphysics an extension of his ethical sensibilities.

[4] This chapter does not deal primarily with Schopenhauer's broad-ranging attacks on Kant's ethical doctrines, but these are significant, insightful and reveal Schopenhauer's immersion in Kant, and so these criticisms deserve mention. His first general objection to Kant is that he equates the good life with the rational life by making the categorical imperative a universal rule to which every thinking being would assent. The good man, however, according to Schopenhauer, often does things which are irrational, as when a rich man gives away all he possesses or a patriot sacrifices his life for an ungrateful nation, while the man who selfishly guards all his possessions to prepare for a happy life and the calculating tyrant, while being perhaps morally deplorable, act in eminently rational ways (WWR1, 515–6). The second broad objection maintained that Kant wished to legitimate his moral philosophy on transcendental grounds through a false parallelization of his ethics with his epistemology. In the area of epistemology, Kant held that the *a priori* was that which made all experience possible, while in the ethical sphere, the *a priori* could establish how all merely ought to behave, rather than how people actually can behave in such and such ways (BM 64). In addition, while in epistemology, *a priori* rules were restricted to the phenomenon, in ethics they were supposed to take us as near to the thing-in-itself as it was possible to go (BM 65). In detail, Schopenhauer thought that Kant's ethics of "ought" was based through and through on egoistic motives, for one only assents to an ought out of concern for some sense of reward or punishment (BM 55), while the categorical imperative, in its demand for universal acceptance, means that those who assent to it want not only to practice virtue, but also enjoy it (BM 89–91). Kant's notions that human beings were of "unconditional worth" and should be treated as "ends in themselves," though they have a nice rhetorical ring, are also flawed, for

"worth" can only be determined in concrete circumstances with respect to particular people, while the idea of "end" can only be spoken of with regard to some specific intent or other (BM 95). Finally, the categorical imperative of Kant is not really a foundation of ethics, which explains how deeds of moral worth are possible, but is really a principle of conduct prescribing certain types of behavior that only masquerades as a foundation for ethics because of its merely formal and not empirical content (BM 73–4). A merely formal principle cannot, in any event, have any effect on the conduct of human beings; any such effect must be sought for in the living moral character of the experiences in which people actually find themselves (BM 75). We shall encounter a few other critiques of Kant as they are in various ways relevant to the following discussion.

[5] Schopenhauer believes the primary proof for this can be found in Kant's proposed solution to the third Antinomy in the "Transcendental Dialectic" of the *Critique of Pure Reason*. The thesis that there must be freedom of action within the causal nexus of nature does not really contradict the antithesis that there is no freedom in nature, but only strict causal determinism (Kant 409). While phenomenally, all acts are determined through *a priori* rules of causality, "the power of transcendental freedom" can be found to initiate a new series of actions without having itself been caused, whenever I will a certain act, like stand up from my chair (Kant 414). This argument, while it is not very convincing, was for Schopenhauer the precursor to the separation of the intelligible and empirical character in Kant's thought, with the empirical character determined by the principle of sufficient reason of motivation (FR 210–14), and the intelligible character enjoying transcendental freedom as it was not bound by space, time and causality. Even though Schopenhauer viewed this distinction by Kant to have been "the point where Kant's philosophy leads to mine, or mine springs from his as its purest stem" (WWR1, 501), Schopenhauer's conceptions of transcendental freedom and the intelligible character differ widely from Kant's. This difference is not one of which Schopenhauer is unaware, for he notes that in the intelligible character, he recognized the ultimate nature of human beings to lie in their willing, whereas Kant never became conscious of this, at least not explicitly conscious (WWR1, 502; 505). "Kant, however, whose merit in this regard is especially great, was the first to demonstrate the coexistence of . . . necessity with the freedom of the will in itself, i.e., outside the phenomenon, for he established the difference between the intelligible and empirical characters. I wholly support this distinction, for the former is the will as thing-in-itself, insofar as it appears in a definite individual in a definite degree, while the latter is this phenomenon itself as it manifests itself in the mode of action according to

time, and in the physical structure according to space" (WWR1, 289). Kant's contrast of the intelligible and empirical characters is thus for Schopenhauer "among the most admirable things ever said by man" (WWR1, 505).

[6] John Atwell even proposed that Schopenhauer's understanding of the intelligible character influenced his account of natural science. Just as the empirical human being can be explained with reference to his or her empirical character, so the interactions of phenomena can only be explicated in terms of natural forces (Atwell *Character* 70). Were it not for natural forces and the intelligible character, our explanations of the world would be reduced to natural phenomenalism, according to which we can give no systematic account of natural phenomena, and "human phenomenalism," which offers no explanation of the moral significance of actions, respectively (*Character* 70). Atwell's thesis is perhaps the newest formulation of Nietzsche's charge that in Schopenhauer, what we have is not really a metaphysical ethics, as Schopenhauer intended, but an ethical metaphysics, that is, an account of what the world is that is first inspired by ethical considerations. This kind of explication of Schopenhauer has always been appealing. But in a certain sense, the present chapter is an argument that is opposed to this interpretation, in its attempt to make the case that Schopenhauer's proposed basis for morality followed from his epistemological and metaphysical thought.

[7] Atwell finds this argument particularly impressive. He invents a dictum for the idea that Schopenhauer is resisting; "responsibility implies avoidability." This dictum can be used in one of two ways, either to impute moral responsibility to someone by saying that they could have chosen differently, or to absolve someone of responsibility by somehow establishing that they could not have acted differently. What Schopenhauer maintains is that, the only way a particular agent can avoid acting in the ways he actually does is for that agent to have been a whole different person, a whole different "type" of person, that is, to have had a wholly different character when presented with a moral dilemma. To say that the agent performed a certain act owing to his character is to maintain that an agent's particular contribution to a deed is what gives it moral significance. For Atwell, this line of argumentation is entirely defensible and in fact refutes the supposition that "responsibility implies avoidability" (see Atwell *Human* 45–8). Schopenhauer himself saw the importance of this argument as its putting down the idea of Descartes and Leibnitz of a "*liberum arbitrium indifferentiae,*" or a completely free will that was subordinate to the intellect and could choose its alternatives freely in accordance with the intellect's dictates. For Schopenhauer, the reverse is the case; the intellect is subordinate to and an instrument of the

will, and is ignorant of the inclinations of the intelligible character until those inclinations became manifest through the acts of the empirical character (see Schopenhauer, WWR1, 290–3).

[8] Atwell makes Schopenhauer's arguments more contemporary by associating this strand of thought with "environmental determinism," a position which holds that every element of the personality and character is shaped by environmental factors, rendering a person's deeds in one way or another traceable to the influence of his or her surroundings (see Atwell *Human* 23–4).

[9] It is interesting that this theory does not change from the first edition of *The World as Will and Representation* to the second, even though, as we saw in the preceding chapter, Schopenhauer's thoughts on the will as thing in itself did undergo revision during the intervening period. While the will was the unchanging thing in itself in the first edition of 1819, it had become the thing in itself as it appeared in time in the edition of 1844. However, the conception of the intelligible character remained relatively unaltered, with the one exception that Schopenhauer attributes to it one additional quality in the second edition. In addition to being fixed, unique and unalterable as it was said to be in the first edition, the intelligible character becomes in 1844 "inborn," or inherited from one's parents. This has all kinds of fascinating consequences for Schopenhauer's thoughts on the metaphysical import of sexual love (see Schopenhauer, WWR2, 517–67).

[10] D. W. Hamlyn raised an objection to Schopenhauer's notion of motives that was along these lines. Taking issue with Schopenhauer's belief that human beings do not undergo any change of character, Hamlyn wrote: "He appears to think that the basis for the claim lies in the fact that there must be a single nature to a human being if there is to be a constant response to motives, as implicit in the dictum '*operari sequitur esse.*' But even if that implies that a human being must be born with some nature, it may be concluded that that nature remains constant only if the response to motives remains constant. It does not appear however that this is a necessary implication of the principle of sufficient reason as applied to motives. It would follow only if, given that something is a motive, it must always be so; but that is the very point at issue" (Hamlyn 129). As stated, Hamlyn's point is somewhat unclear. He seems to be accusing Schopenhauer of making use of a viciously circular argument that makes the following two claims: a motive is a motive only with respect to a human character that responds to it in a consistent manner, and a human character is constant and unalterable only because a given motive is always a motive for it. These claims attempt to gain their force through the circularity of their respective definitions, but apart from this, offer no

evidence why either motives or character should be considered constant. I add to this point merely that no such evidence that could lend credence to either claim could possibly be solicited, given the transcendental vocabulary in which Schopenhauer has clothed the notion of intelligible character.

[11] He does however discuss related issues in the first edition. His says that persons of distinctly different moral types are driven by more or less vehement forces of willing, ranging from passionate to indifferent to bored (Schopenhauer, WWR1, 322). Interestingly, Schopenhauer's readings of Colebrooke's translations of the *Gītā* lead him to compare these various "poles of willing" to the *raja, sāttva* and *tama guṇa*s of the person as pictured in the Sāṃkhya system of classical Hindu thought (WWR1, 321). He speaks of the degree of the person's moral wickedness as corresponding to the extent to which they affirm their own wills beyond the bounds of their own bodies at the expense of others, as in sexual misdeeds and violence (WWR1, 327–8). He even defines "right" and "wrong" behavior along these lines, saying that since the body is "the boundary of the will," any act that affirms the will beyond the body that encroaches on another's will is "wrong," while any "right" action is one that does not violate the "boundaries" of another's will (WWR1, 339). In the second edition of 1844, after his thematization of "bad," "just" and "good" character in the 1841 *Basis of Morality*, Schopenhauer attempts to align his notion of the "bad" person with the degree of willing present in him along with the degree of his commitment to the *principium individuationis* (WWR1, 362–3). But Schopenhauer's early thoughts in the first edition of his "main work" on *ennui* or "boredom," his idea that the person who does not constantly will is bored, and that what we normally think of as happiness is actually boredom, recede into unimportance in his later systematic works (WWR1, 312).

[12] One of the fascinating implications of these ideas is relevant to Schopenhauer's thoughts on suicide, which he himself did not appear to recognize. As is well-known, Schopenhauer believed suicide to be an "unenlightened" solution to the problem of human suffering, an egoistic attempt to eliminate personal suffering that was not informed by the knowledge that all willing beings suffer and a knowledge that one should try to eliminate it by wiping out the transcendental cause for suffering rather than the personal symptoms, as it were (see WWR1, 398–402; WWR2, 463–509; PPII, 244–57; 275–77). But in addition to all this, according to Schopenhauer's ideas on these three fundamental motives of human behavior, while we can wish for our own happiness, another's suffering or another's happiness, we cannot wish to do harm to ourselves. The motivations to commit suicide are for Schopenhauer certainly

egoistic, they intend the cessation of one's own suffering and perhaps to make others feel badly about one's death, but they are not immoral, for a person who kills himself intends no positive harm, either to himself or others. One may question whether it is indeed impossible to wish to do harm to oneself. But this implication raises the larger issue which we will confront in much greater detail in our discussion of Schopenhauer's doctrine of compassion. Schopenhauer considers the moral worth of acts to lie for the most part in their intent, and not in their result. Thus, it is for Schopenhauer morally irrelevant whether suicide or any other act actually does harm to people, the moral issue lies merely in whether or not the intent to do harm was present in the agent. This is, as we shall see, one of the greatest weaknesses of Schopenhauer's ethics.

13 This is the one major disjunction between Schopenhauer's metaphysics and ethics which has gone completely unnoticed by Schopenhauer's commentators. As we saw in the previous chapter, Schopenhauer considered metaphysics to be an explication, not of the "how, why or wherefore" of existence, but of the "what" only. Metaphysics was for him a philosophical explanation of what the world is in essence, not a causal explanation of "grounds and consequents." Schopenhauer, as we also know, held it as his greatest achievement to have created a metaphysics that had ethical import, an ethics that had metaphysical foundations. This he indeed tried to do through the falsification thesis, as we shall see. But here, Schopenhauer defines the fundamental task of ethical thinking to be a discovery not of the "what" of morals, but the "why and wherefore," the "ground." This is perhaps understandable given that ethics is a theoretical activity which concerns itself with the moral worth of actions, all of which must be thought of as being "caused" or having a "ground." But this would also mean that there should be an irreconcilable discord between Schopenhauer's methods of doing metaphysics and ethics, a discord which neither he nor any of his critics, has taken any account of.

14 This catalog Schopenhauer makes of Western philosophy is typical of his later thought, as we shall have further occasion to see in the next chapter. It also demonstrates to a certain degree Schopenhauer's superficial, or perhaps more accurately uncomprehending reading of Hegel as well as his naïveté on the problems of political and social philosophy, to which Hegel most contributed. For Hegel, of course, the State was not the originator of morals, but *Geist*, which was the "social spirit" which transformed the ethos of a given society through history. Schopenhauer simply takes no measure of the moral dimensions of the State in his own thought, beyond his convictions that the State was committed to the safeguarding of the rights of security and property (see WWR1, 334–

50). Christopher Janaway has complained that Schopenhauer's conception of political freedom within a society was totally inadequate, for it held such freedom to be a people's unrestricted allowance to follow its own laws, and did not deal with how societies diminished people's rights through legalistic means (231). Nonetheless, Schopenhauer's admonitions that even completely law-abiding societies could still lack all virtue (WWR1, 369) and his contempt for the idealization of the State in Kant and Hegel as the functionary of social moral progress (WWR1, 344–5) are noteworthy.

15 Schopenhauer seems at times at odds with himself on this issue. In a discussion of regret or repentance (*Reue*), Schopenhauer says that we never repent for what we will or desire, but only for what we have actually done (WWR1, 296–7). He proclaims that the human being knows herself most clearly through her deeds, not through wishes or feelings, since the character is revealed clearly in its actions (WWR1, 300). He derides the history of Christianity as belying the "high" moral principles it preaches, citing the Inquisition, Reformation massacres, the Crusades and even the Christian legitimization behind the decimation of the Native American peoples and African slavery, saying "while everyone in his own mind believes his faith strong, the deed is the hard touchstone for all our convictions" (BM 171). These comments seem to be suggesting, in language that is more or less unambiguous, that the ethical significance of a deed resides in the deed itself, and that the character should be judged through it. But it is just as clear that he also believes that actions attain their moral worth through the intentions with which they were performed: "We can hardly ever pronounce a correct moral judgment on the actions of others, and rarely on our own. The deeds and ways of acting of an individual and of a nation can be very much modified by dogmas, for example, or customs. In themselves, however, all deeds (*opera operata*) are merely empty figures, and only the disposition that leads to them gives them moral significance" (WWR1, 369). Schopenhauer's position on this issue appears to alternate depending on which of his moral teachings he is talking about. When attempting to show how we can know the moral content of our intelligible character, he emphasizes the deed as the compass of self-knowledge, and when discussing how we are to morally assess a person, we should not do so by her deeds, but by her intentions. For Schopenhauer's system, unfortunately, such inconsistencies were often passed over by the philosopher himself as if they were fortuitous conveniences.

16 We can recall that this description strongly echoes Schopenhauer's earlier characterization of the solipsist, or "theoretical egoist." "He must assume that this one object is essentially different from all oth-

ers; that it alone among all objects is at the same time will and representation, the rest, on the other hand, being mere representations, mere phantoms. Thus, he must assume that his body is the only real individual in the world, i.e., the only phenomenon of will , and the only immediate object of the subject. . . . Other objects (are) considered as mere *representations. . . . Theoretical egoism* . . . regards in this way as phantoms all phenomena outside its own will, just as practical egoism does in a practical respect; thus in it a man regards and treats only his own person as a real person, and all others as mere phantoms" (WWR1, 104). It seems clear that practical egoism, according to Schopenhauer, has its roots in some form of theoretical egoism, and so the latter results in a position which, though supposedly logically irrefutable, leads to madness and moral perversity. John Atwell believed that the beliefs of the egoist and the solipsist do not exactly coincide in Schopenhauer, though his reasons for maintaining this were sketchy and not compelling (see Atwell *Human* 120).

[17] Again, those interested in contrasting Schopenhauer's understanding of *māyā* with the original Vedāntic thematization may take their start from here. Schopenhauer believed that *māyā* was an effect of the *principium individuationis,* the transcendental forms of perception, space, time and causality, without which nothing could appear as a discrete phenomenon in a particular place and as a constituent in the causal process. Through this process, we take things in our experience, ourselves primarily among them, to be heterogeneous, that is, each with their own unique, fundamental natures. This way of "taking" things (*Wahrnehmung*) according to the dictates of the *principium* only gives us a fabricated, falsified picture of the world, others and ourselves. For Śaṅkara, on the other hand, according to the famous and definitive *adhyāsabhāsyam* at the opening of the *Brahmasūtrabhāsyam, māyā* is equated with the transcendental error of "superimposition," or *adhyāsa*. According to this theory, the characteristics of the "eternal," "changeless" and "knowing" "self" (*ātman*) are superimposed upon the activities of the empirical "ego" (*ahaṃ*), and vice-versa, so that they become wrongly identified with one another. The process involves the following. When we say for instance "I know" (*jñami*), we wrongly attribute knowledge to the merely empirical mind (*buddhi*) by associating the psycho-physical activity of perception (*upalabdhi*) which takes place in the "brain" (*manas*) with real subjective apprehension (*dṛṣti, avabhoda*), which only occurs by virtue of the "self-luminosity" (*svayaṃprakaṣātva*) of *ātman*. When we claim moral agency by saying "I do" (*karomi*), we fallaciously attribute activities of the body to the "changeless" (*kūṭasthā*) self. When we identify ourselves through bodily qualities (*dharmāḥ*) or emotional states, as when we say "I

am old" or "I am a man" or "I am happy," we erroneously project those changing empirical qualities onto the *ātman,* which is an "eternal substrate" (*nityadharmin*). For Schopenhauer then, *māyā* is heterogeneous empirical plurality that is taken to be exhaustively constitutive of the world, while for Kevalādvaita, *māyā* is in effect incarnate, empirical existence that is taken to be exhaustively constitutive of selfhood. On close examination, these two conceptions of *māyā* are in their details dissimilar. This is borne out by the dissimilarity of their respective notions of what the "thing in itself" is; as Schopenhauer would think it incomprehensible that any conception of "selfhood" could apply to the transcendental realm, while for Vedānta, any notion of a transcendental "will" could be nothing but nonsense.

[18] Supra., 56–7; 103–16.

[19] The formula "*tat tvam asi*" finds its best known and most significant expression in the sixth chapter of the *Chāndogyopaniṣad*. There, Uddālaka Āruṇi is instructing his son Svetaketu on the nature of *brahman* and the identity that Svetaketu and every individual shares with this unitary, eternal ground of existence. "*Sa ya eṣo'ṇimā aitad ātymyam idaṁ sarvaṃ, tat satyam, sa ātmā, tat tvam asi, svetaketo, iti*" (*Chāndogyopaniṣad,* VI: 12:3, 13:3, qtd. in Radhakrishnan *Principle* 462; 463).

[20] It should be noted that, while Kolenda uses this as a general indictment of Schopenhauer's ethics, what he seems specifically to have in mind are Schopenhauer's contentions that one should renounce and not affirm the "will-to-live" if one can, for the will-to-live causes only suffering, and any truly enlightened being should shrink from doing this. We shall discuss this problem in more detail shortly. While more relevant to that particular issue, Kolenda's objection would still be misguided. Schopenhauer does not take himself to be recommending to the reader which course of action the reader should take with respect to will-affirmation or will-denial, for he considers such recommendations futile anyway. Each person's character and the quality of their knowledge will decide that issue, for Schopenhauer, and not anyone's recommendation (WWR1, 271–2; 285; 374). Even if Schopenhauer were suggesting or recommending one course of action or the other through his labeling of denial as being "more virtuous and holy" than affirmation, this would not entail, as Kolenda charges, that his view is "a view from nowhere," for according to Schopenhauer, the ascetics "viewpoint," however valuable, is still, like the affirmer's, only a viewpoint. We will discuss this below as well.

[21] "Denial of one's own body exhibits itself as a contradiction by the will of its own phenomenon. For although here also the body objectifies in the genitals the will to propagate, yet propagation is not willed"

(Schopenhauer, WWR1, 334). Passages such as this give one the impression that, intriguing as Schopenhauer's assertions concerning the "renunciation of will" are, they arise from a conflation of two different senses of the word "will" as he employs it. The first is the metaphysical sense, for which "will" is the thing in itself, and the second is the common, volitionist meaning of willing something. Schopenhauer did not think these senses should be confused, though he himself appears to have done just that in this instance.

[22] One recalls the teaching of Krishna to Arjuna before the great battle between the Pāndavas and Kauravas in this work, "he who thinks the self a slayer and he who thinks it slain, neither comprehend; it neither slays nor is slain" (*Bhagavad Gītā,* II:19, in Radhakrishnan and Moore 108). Of course the doctrinal context here is more theistic in nature, as Krishna is the universal divine essence and teaches Arjuna that, since everyone shares in his eternal, divine nature, no individual is really harmed by a war. Nonetheless, a similar moral issue arises in this context with the one relevant to Schopenhauer's notion of "eternal justice," namely how the eternal nature of Krishna, from whom all beings come and to whom they return, suddenly renders war moral. Schopenhauer, at any rate, persists in evoking vocabulary and symbols from the classical Indian tradition to support his doctrine of "eternal justice." He calls to mind once again the *Upaniṣadic* formula "*tat tvam asi*" to illustrate that all individual beings, the inflicter of suffering and afflicted, are both will, and the notion of *karma* and rebirth is called upon to symbolize the significance of the deed attaching to the transpersonal will (WWR1, 355–6).

[23] Nietzsche's Zarathustra, that model of life-affirmation, who supposedly stands at the opposite pole from Schopenhauer, satirizes the doctrine of "eternal justice" with a psychological twist. "*The Sprit of Revenge,* my friends, has so far been the subject of man's best reflection; and where there was suffering, one always wanted punishment too. For punishment is what revenge calls itself; with a hypocritical lie it creates a good conscience for itself. Because there is suffering in those who will, inasmuch as they cannot will backwards, willing itself and all life were supposed to be-a punishment. And now cloud upon cloud rolled over the spirit until eventually madness preached, 'Everything passes away, therefore everything deserves to pass away. And thus too is justice, this law of time that it must devour its children.' Thus preached madness. 'Things are ordered morally according to justice and punishment. Alas, where is redemption from the flux of things and from the punishment called existence?' Thus preached madness. 'Can there be redemption if there is eternal justice? Alas the stone *It Was* cannot be moved: thus all punishments must be eternal too.' Thus preached madness. 'No deed can

be annihilated: how could it be undone by punishment? This, this is what is eternal in the punishment called existence, that existence must eternally become deed and guilt. Unless the will should at last redeem himself, and willing should become not willing.' But, my brothers, you know this fable of madness. I led you away from these fables when I taught you 'The will is a creator'" (Nietzsche *Thus* 140).

24 One is left to wonder at this point, what kind of knowledge this could be, as Schopenhauer left no place for such a special mode of knowledge anywhere else in his system, much less room in his ontology for anything besides will and representation that could be known. This has perplexed commentators for the last several decades. Patrick Gardiner found it almost an affront that Schopenhauer was attempting to explain anything in "mystical" terms given Schopenhauer's oft-repeated commitment to Kantianism (300). Janaway, in a much more meaningful objection, wondered how Schopenhauer could at this point be suggesting that will, having been subjectively renounced by the ascetic, no longer has any relevance to philosophical discourse, since he seems to have heretofore gone to a lot of trouble to prove that will is the ground of all existence (284). Julian Young and John Atwell took the view that the reason Schopenhauer thought this was acceptable was that he never believed the will to be the "thing in itself" in the first place. For Young and Atwell, the explicit position of Schopenhauer in 1844, that the will was the "nearest and clearest appearance" of the thing in itself, was in fact always Schopenhauer's metaphysical doctrine, even in the first edition of *World as Will and Representation* in 1818. They even conjectured that, if Schopenhauer really did believe the will to be the thing in itself, then no salvation from the will, not even its subjective renunciation, would be possible, since will would in this case still be the ground of existence (see Young 34–5; Atwell *Character* 171). Gardiner's objection is actually not so serious, for as we have seen time and time again, Schopenhauer was not, even by his own self-report, as strict a Kantian as Gardiner perhaps imagined him to be. I have already outlined in the preceding chapter my view that Young and Atwell are more than likely mistaken in their proposal that Schopenhauer never thought the will to be the thing in itself, for this is just as explicitly the position the first edition of *World as Will and Representation* as the explicit position of the second edition is that the will is the "most direct phenomenon of the thing-in-itself." I share in the end Janaway's incomprehension of Schopenhauer's distinctly unique brand of "mysticism," for which instead of seeking union with the thing in itself, in this case the will, one renounces it but still remains, in some sense, that very will. The position is simply odd, and Schopenhauer, perhaps him-

self somewhat uncomfortable with it, appears to me to be consciously and intentionally oblique when dealing with this topic.

25 In a somewhat incongruous footnote to this text, Schopenhauer cites I. J. Schmidt's early commentaries on the Māhāyana Buddhist *Prajña Paramita* literature, and says that the state of the ascetic is one that is "beyond all knowledge" in the sense that it transcends the subject-object correlativity that is the fundamental form of representational knowledge. The note seems strange since in the same passage he denounces the "myths and meaningless words" both Hindus and Buddhists use to describe "ultimate realization." We will discuss this more in the following chapter.

Chapter 6

1 Though Schopenhauer's appraisal of the value of the Indian tradition differs from that of the early Hegel in many ways, the two antipodes do appear to share the assumption that Indian thinking can find its fulfillment only in Europe, that the importance of Indian thought lies in what it contributes to European self-realization. It will be remembered that in his early *Phenomenology of Spirit,* Hegel aligns the Romantic philosophy of Schelling and his contemporaries who admired Indian religion with the thought of that culture, and labels all three "vacuous absolutisms." The Absolute is empty and completely indeterminate: "To pit this single insight, that in the Absolute everything is the same, against the full body of articulated cognition, which at least seeks and demands . . . fulfillment, to palm off its Absolute as the night in which, as the saying goes, all cows are black—this is cognition naively reduced to vacuity" (9). In his later *Lectures on the Philosophy of Religion,* Hegel explicitly identifies both Hindu and Buddhist absolutism as "religions of substance," "abstract unity without determination," "substance without subjectivity" (see Halbfass *India* 89). The full embodiment of subjectivity is to be realized in the completion of *Geist* that unfolds through the Western philosophical tradition. While philosophy may have found its beginnings in India then, for Hegel, it must ascend to genuine absolute knowledge in Europe. Essays by Colebrooke appearing in 1825 and 1826 on Sāṃkhya and Nyāya-Vaiśeṣika, and another on the *Bhagavad Gītā* impressed Hegel enough to write in his *Lectures on the History of Philosophy* that "genuine philosophical systems" existed and developed in India beyond the confines of "religious thought" (qtd. in Halbfass *India* 97). But for most of Hegel's philosophical career, as Halbfass says, "his European horizon transcends all Asian horizons. Asian thought is comprehensible and in-

terpretable within European thought, but not vice versa. The question of an adequate standpoint for the evaluation and comparison of different cultural traditions has been decided by the course of history itself, and it has been decided in favor of Europe. European thought has to provide the context and categories for the exploration of all traditions of thought" (*India* 96). Halbfass contrasts Schopenhauer's reception of the Indian tradition to Hegel's, in the sense that Schopenhauer, rather than asserting the superiority of Western thought, appropriates it in order to marshal a radical critique of traditional Western religions and "objectivist" thinking (*India* 120). Indeed, Schopenhauer does not make any explicit case for the interpretive privilege of Western thought over Asian, and in fact attempts to suggest in many places that the West has much to learn from the Indian tradition, as we shall see. However, by representing himself as the interpreter of the Indian religious and philosophical heritage, Schopenhauer in his own way "envelopes the Indian horizon within his own."

2 Schopenhauer's German-language biographers have especially emphasized the "a-historicism" of his philosophy. Arthur Hübscher attributed the unpopularity of Schopenhauer's first edition of *World as Will and Representation* to its "untimely" a-historical doctrine of will in the midst of Hegel's historicism (191). While Hegel's historical progressivism was an outgrowth of earlier Christian "stage theories" of history (like that of Joachim of Floris) as well as Enlightenment thought, and ultimately led to both the justifications of Bismarck's and Hitler's Reichs and Lenin's Revolution, Hübscher sees Schopenhauer's view of social, political and historical life as having its foundations in Geothe, and that where his assessment of history did not explicitly characterize it as in decline, did regard it as an accidental appearance of will (see Hübscher 195–223). A similar perspective is adopted by Rüdiger Safransky (252–63). Safransky even goes so far as to explicitly say that one of the reasons that Schopenhauer's Berlin lectures, which he scheduled deliberately during the same hours as Hegel's, were so famously unsuccessful was that, next to Hegel's mature logic and historicism, "Schopenhauer's pessimism and denial of the world . . . sounded mystical, and too Indian" (261). The supposition that Schopenhauer and classical Indian thought share "a-historical" traits may as it turns out not only be a superficial view of Schopenhauer, but of classical Indian philosophical reflection as well. J. N. Mohanty has pointed out that, while it may be true that classical Indian thought held essentialist views of consciousness and values represented as unchanging, and these made a philosophical concern with history absent, this does not mean that time and history were unimportant for Indian thought ("Interpreting" 303–7). In fact, *itihāsa* or "history" was not only valued as the traditional means for communicating

"eternal values" through "story" and "chronicle," there were a number of provincial chroniclers in Indian history who had both "historical sense" and interpretive methods (Mohanty *Reason* 188–90). It must also be noted the Indian philosophers of the twentieth century (some of whom were greatly influenced by Hegel and Heidegger), have favored historical approaches to the classical scriptural traditions (Daya Krishna), hermeneutic stances toward the modern reception of classical Indian thought (Jarva Lal Mehta) and have developed fully teleological historical worldviews (Aurobindo Ghose). Halbfass has aptly noted that one of the reasons for the lack of attention paid to Schopenhauer by twentieth century Indian philosophers has been precisely his anti-Hegelian disregard of the importance of history to philosophy (1988, 120).

3 See Halbfass *India* 68–83.

4 The Romantic historian Görres wrote at the beginning of the nineteenth century what was to become over the next several decades a common characterization: "And do you know the land where infant mankind lived its happy childhood years, here stood the pillars of fire in which the gods descended to their darlings and mingled in their spirited play? . . . Towards the Orient, to the banks of the Ganges and the Indus, it is there that our hearts are being drawn by some hidden urge,—it is there that all the dark presentiments point which lie in the depths of our hearts, and it is there that we go when we follow the silent river which flows through time in legends and sacred songs to its source. In the Orient, the heavens poured forth into the Earth. . . . In the primitive cultures of this earth, the original force must still appear undivided; in them, everything muse be contained in the same homogeneity which would later become separated into the various camps" (qtd. in Halbfass *India* 73–4).

5 At one point, Schopenhauer calls the "newest" world religion of history, Islam, its worst, based on the "wretched book, the *Koran*" which "inspires them to bloody wars and the most extensive conquests," in which Schopenhauer is unable "to find . . . one single idea of value." This is then compared to "Brahmanism," whose "Rishis" were "considerably nearer to the beginning of the human race and to the original source of organic nature," giving them "a more genuine disposition of mind" which offered them "a purer and more direct apprehension of the inner essence of nature" and allowed them "to satisfy the need for metaphysics in a more estimable manner." These sages who composed the *Vedas* and *Upaniṣads* were "almost superhuman" (WWR2, 162).

6 European, and specifically Protestant Christianity is what Schopenhauer laments when he decries contemporary attempts to Christianize India. In addition to the fact that, according to second century Christian texts, the religion had traveled to southern India long before it

ever reached Europe, Schopenhauer believes that Christianity, witnessed by its fundamental "pessimism" about the world and its evil, carried in its inception Indian influences. "Christianity," Schopenhauer asserts, "has Indian blood in its veins" (FR 187). We will return to other aspects of Schopenhauer's complicated attempts to distinguish and relate Christianity to classical Indian thought below.

[7] Schopenhauer explicitly articulates distaste for the poetic and dramatic productions of Sanskrit literature, and the theistic devotional backgrounds out of which they arose. He also expresses dislike for the dualistic Sāṃkhya system and holds it to be an unorthodox leave-taking from the *Upaniṣadic* doctrine of *brahman*. Though he does consider *Vedic* ritual and polytheism "primitive," he idealizes in the highest praise the *Upaniṣads*, which he considers to embody the real philosophical content of the Brahminical tradition (see PPII 346–51).

[8] Again, we will return to Schopenhauer's juxtaposition of Jewish and Indian religious thought below in detail.

[9] This notion that metaphysical reflection arises out of suffering strikes many as a very Buddhist-like one. Schopenhauer writes to this end in the 1859 edition of *World as Will and Representation*: "If I wished to take the results of my philosophy as the standard of truth, I should have to concede to Buddhism pre-eminence over the others. In any case, it must be a pleasure to me to see my doctrine in such close agreement with a religion that the majority of men on earth hold as their own, for this numbers far more followers than any other. And this agreement must be yet the more pleasing to me, inasmuch as in my philosophizing I have certainly not been under its influence. For up till 1818, when my work appeared, there were to be found in Europe only a very few accounts of Buddhism, and those extremely incomplete and inadequate, confined almost entirely to a few essays in the earliest volumes of the *Asiatic Researches*, and principally concerned with the Buddhism of the Burmese. Only since that time has fuller information about this religion gradually reached us, chiefly through the profound and instructive articles of that meritorious member of the St. Petersburg Academy, I. J. Schmidt, in the records of his Academy, and then in the course of time through several English and French scholars, so that I have been able to furnish a fairly numerous list of the best works on the religion in my book *On the Will in Nature* under the heading 'Sinology'" (WWR2, 169). This list is given in a footnote from the 1840's edition in which Schopenhauer comments on St. Petersburg Academy works that are mostly on Tibetan Vājrayāna Buddhism, and as his own comments make clear, Schopenhauer considered Vājrayāna a Chinese school (see WN 130–31). Referring to an essay by Spence Hardy, Schopenhauer counts the number of practicing Buddhists

in Asia to be 369 million, and hence believes Buddhism to be the most widely practiced religion in the world (WN 131–32). Schopenhauer felt it necessary to clarify in the quotation from 1859 above that he had not been influenced in his systematic thinking by Buddhism, as a result of some 1856 correspondence with Adam von Doss (see GB 383–85). Given the extent to which Schopenhauer documents the growth of his familiarity with Buddhism over the years, we may trust his words in this case that the agreement he found between his own thought and Buddhism struck him as a "wondrous coincidence" (GB 384). At the same time, Schopenhauer actively pursued these "agreements." In the aforementioned section on "Sinology" in *On the Will in Nature,* Schopenhauer attempts to align his doctrine of the will as the ground of all natural phenomena with what he knew of the philosophy of the twelfth century Neo-Confucian commentator Zhuxi (see WN 136–7). He closes these parallelizations with the familiar disclaimer: "The fact that my fundamental idea is independent from this Chinese authority is established by the reasons stated. For I hope to be believed when I state that I have no knowledge of the Chinese language, and that in consequence I am unable to draw ideas for my own use from original works in Chinese which are unknown to others" (WN 137).

10 Schopenhauer writes: "Why should a religion require the suffrage of a philosophy? Indeed it has everything on its side, revelation, documents, miracles, prophecies, government protection, the highest dignity and eminence, as is due to truth, the consent and reverence of all, a thousand temples in which it is preached and practiced (*sic.*), hosts of sworn priests, and, more than all this, the invaluable prerogative of being allowed to imprint its doctrines on the mind at the tender age of childhood, whereby they become almost innate ideas. With such an abundance of means at its disposal, still to desire the assent of wretched philosophers it would have to be more covetous, or still to attend to their contradiction it would have to be more apprehensive, than appears compatible with a good conscience" (WWR2, 166). Schopenhauer, in passages such as these, displays rhetorical skills equal to those of Rousseau, and as a result is almost unanimously held to be, along with Nietzsche, one of the greatest literary talents among otherwise hard-to-read German philosophers.

11 To other scholars, the suggestion that Schopenhauer was "ethnocentric" would be odd. For J. W. Sedler, Schopenhauer's openness to Asian thought and religious traditions shows that he was remarkably free from European, and specifically German, prejudices of cultural predominance (82). Halbfass has suggested that Schopenhauer's appropriation of Indian religious and philosophical ideas, rather than being ethno-

centric, results in the marshaling of a radical critique of traditional European thought (*India* 120). Clarke, who concurs with Halbfass on this point, rejects the accusation that Schopenhauer, by attacking the Jewish religious tradition with Orientalist ideas, was a racist, for he nowhere writes anything derogatory of the Jewish people or Jewish ethnicity, but merely rejects his perceptions of their religious orientation (191–2). In order for Schopenhauer to be a racist, for Clarke, one would have to equate rejection of Jewish religious beliefs with anti-Semitism. In his biography of Schopenhauer, Safransky recounts several incidents during Schopenhauer's ventures through Amsterdam with his parents in 1803, one in which he first encountered statues of the Buddha and laughed, another in which he attended a Jewish service at a synagogue and was amused by the singing, and still a third where he ridiculed a Protestant service (42–43). Safransky uses these events to illustrate that Schopenhauer was not a "malicious" anti-Semite, but treated all religious phenomena for much of his life "with the same disrespect" (43).

[12] This does not necessarily imply, Atwell is quick to add, that Schopenhauer was not a pessimist much earlier than the 1850's. It was in 1811 that Schopenhauer announced to Wieland in Vienna his intellectual mission by saying that life was a difficult or tricky (*missliche*) thing, and that he intended to spend his life reflecting on it (Atwell *Human* 147). In an 1855 letter to Frauenstädt, Schopenhauer announced that his pessimism had taken shape between 1814 and 1818, which itself was a bright period in Germany, right after its liberation from Napoleonic France (Atwell, *Human* 147.). There is also his often-quoted 1832 recollection of the trip he took with his parents through London in 1805, during which he first beheld the horrors of prison and poverty: "In my seventeenth year, without any learned school education, I was gripped by the misery of life as Buddha was in his youth when he saw sickness, old age, pain and death. The truth that spoke out from the world loudly and clearly soon overcame all the Jewish dogmas impressed on me, and my conclusion was that this world could not be the work of an all-loving Being, but rather that of a devil, who had brought creatures into existence in order to delight in the sight of their sufferings" (qtd. in Safransky 41). It is here that we first find the dichotomy between Indian and Jewish religious thought that would become a major theme in the late 1840's and 1850's.

[13] There is no room here for an involved discussion of the ongoing issue in Schopenhauer scholarship as to whether there can be any such thing as "philosophical pessimism." The best review of the literature and arguments can be found in Atwell's *Schopenhauer: The Human Character*. Atwell notes that while Continental and Russian scholars are predominantly focused on Schopenhauer as a pessimist, British scholars

who take their starting points from the analytical tradition such as Patrick Gardiner, D. W. Hamlyn and Bryan Magee have rejected the notion that a philosophical system as a presentation of purported "facts" could evaluate those facts as optimistic or pessimistic (Atwell *Human* 145). Copleston for his own part thought that any philosophy, whether it was one of "life-denial" as Schopenhauer's or "life affirmation" as Nietzsche's, was pessimistic if it concluded that "life has no ultimate meaning" (Atwell *Human* 143). A drawn out weighing of the issues led Atwell to the conclusion that Schopenhauer's philosophy was a pessimistic one because it logically entailed that the world we live in is the worst of all possible worlds, because it holds as a metaphysical axiom that suffering fundamentally pervades conscious life, and therefore a world without conscious life would be preferable to a world with it (*Human* 169–72). This is presumably where Nietzsche parted with Schopenhauer in his "tragic optimism" of "life affirmation," for which "a human world with all its evil" was preferable to a nihilistic philosophy that endorsed "will-resignation" (*Human* 172). I shall return to this issue of the viability of labeling a philosophy "pessimistic" or "optimistic" as it is relevant to the discussion below.

[14] This was only one of the signs of the fundamental divide between Christianity and Judaism Schopenhauer repeatedly emphasizes, and we shall visit more below. A further reason for Schopenhauer's suspicion that Christianity was of Indian origin had to do with the historical theories supporting it among the nineteenth century Romantics. Schopenhauer adopted the view of Friedrich Majer that elements of Indian thought had found their way to Egypt long before the birth of the Christian religion, and the formation of the latter had much to do with the proximity of Buddhist missionaries, Greek sages and early Christian communities in Egyptian cosmopolitan cities like Alexandria (see Halbfass *India* 73; 356). J. J. Clarke has recently reiterated the many historical contacts between India and the West, from the Buddhist missionary ventures to the West sponsored by King Aṣoka to Alexander's military campaigns into and philosophical encounters with India. Buddhist monks were known to the Hellenic and Roman worlds, and many abstract similarities do exhibit themselves between Christian and Indian "mythologies," and while "evidence is flimsy" and "direct lines of influence are difficult to trace," enough points of contact and mythological and even ritual similarities exist to make room for the speculations of the Romantics (Clarke 37–8).

[15] In the 1859 edition of the first volume of *World as Will and Representation*, Schopenhauer analyzes Christianity into to distinct and separable parts. "Christianity is composed of two very heterogeneous ele-

ments. Of these I should like to call the purely ethical element preferably, indeed exclusively, the Christian, and to distinguish it from the Jewish dogmatism with which it is found. If, as has often been feared, and especially at the present time, that excellent and salutary religion should completely decline, than I would look for the reason for this simply in the fact that it does not consist of one simple element, but of two originally heterogeneous elements brought into combination only by means of world events. In such a case, dissolution would necessarily result through the breakup of these elements. . . . Yet after this dissolution, the purely ethical part would still be bound always to remain intact, because it is indestructible" (WWR1, 387–88). After a brief discussion of the Hindu scriptural traditions and ascetic practices, Schopenhauer declares that the readings of biographies of a Christian and Indian saint side by side would yield agreement and harmony, and that "Christian mystics and teachers of the Vedanta philosophy" would be united in spurning "optimistic shallowness and dullness" (WWR1, 388–89). It will be remembered that it was common among Enlightenment thinkers, particularly those of France and England who Schopenhauer held in incomparably high esteem, had begun the call for the abandonment of the doctrines of Christian faith but a retention of its moral teachings. Schopenhauer inserts into this Enlightenment fissure of Christianity the notion that the expendable dogmatic element of this religion was Jewish in origin, while its morality and asceticism were Indian.

16 There is one thing, Schopenhauer claims, that "reconciles" him to Judaism, and that is the myth of the fall, a witness to human guilt and the suffering they impose upon themselves as a result of this "original" guilt. But this is not even an element native to Jewish thinking proper, for this was taken from the moral dualism of Zoroastrianism (WWR2, 580). The myth of the fall provided the place where "the stem" of Christianity, Indian thought, could be "grafted" onto a religion otherwise ruled over by Jewish monotheistic dogmatism (WWR2, 605).

17 Schopenhauer aligns optimism with theism and pessimism with "mysticism" closely in his comparison of the world's religions. He even distinguishes Sufism, for which he admits great admiration, from Islam on the basis of its mystical orientation as opposed to the strict monotheism of orthodox Islam (WWR2, 605).

18 Barbara A. Holdrege's outstanding recent study, *Veda and Torah: Transcending the Textuality of Scripture* goes a long way toward undermining the superficial dichotomies generations of comparative religion scholars since Schopenhauer have been prone to make between the Jewish and Hindu traditions The brahminical and rabbinic traditions both are constituted, as she says, as "textual communities" by their scriptural

traditions, the respective cosmologies of which give metaphysical, ritualistic, ethical and social order to their traditions as well as legitimate the roles of the "cultural elites," the interpreters of these scriptural heritages (Holdrege 2). She believes that the structural similarities of these traditions and their social implications are much more fruitful areas of comparison than the doctrinal and ritual differences between these traditions, which themselves have always tended to be overgeneralized.

[19] One is reminded of Nietzsche's sarcastic comment in *Jenziets von Gut und Böse* when discussing Schopenhauer's attempt to find a basis for moral conduct: "Schopenhauer, though a pessimist, *really* played the flute. Every day, after dinner: one should read his biography on that. And incidentally: a pessimist, one who denies God and the world but *comes to a stop* before morality—who affirms morality and plays the flute—the *laede neminem* (harm no one) morality—what? is that really—a pessimist?" (*Beyond* 99). One is reminded also of the story that when, on one occasion, Schopenhauer was asked why he espoused a philosophy of "will-renunciation" but was himself so decadent, he responded: "I have taught about sainthood, I myself am no saint." What this suggests is that Schopenhauer did not have the aesthetic sensibility of a pessimist, and this may explain the strange way in which he conceives this hermeneutic. Nietzsche, it should be noted, more or less accepted Schopenhauer's comparative judgments, calling Schopenhauerian, Buddhist and Christian thought both "pessimistic" and "nihilistic." However, he also was aware of the pernicious consequences of such a "pessimist's hermeneutic." He derides Wagner, Schopenhauer's aesthetic disciple, for the "hatred of the Jews" Schopenhauer helped strengthen in him and who overlooked the Jewish origins of Christianity, to which both were devoted through Buddhism (*The Gay Science* 154–55). Nietzsche did not, however, believe that Schopenhauer would have had anything to do with German nationalism, for as he put it: "Everything else that one sees in the foreground—our bold politics and our cheerful fatherlandishness which resolutely enough consider all matters with a view to a not very philosophical principle (*'Deutschland, Deutschland, über alles'*), which means *sub specie speciei* (from the point of view of the species), namely the German species, bears emphatic witness of the opposite. No, the Germans of today are *no* pessimists. And Schopenhauer was a pessimist, to say it once more, as a good European, but *not* as a German" (309–10). After the unification of the German states into a nation under Bismarck, Nietzsche was no longer willing, as he was in his earlier works, to refer to Leibniz, Kant, Hegel, Heine and Schopenhauer as "German" achievements, but as "European" ones. Only after this event, according to Nietzsche, did the general European sentiment of "hatred of the Jews"

turn into a platform upon which German nationalists, among whom were his sister and brother-in-law, were all-too-willing to stand.

[20] For a sampling of these histories, see Halbfass' *India and Europe* 145–59.

[21] This argument is to be found in the second chapter of Quine's *Word and Object* 28–60.

[22] In his study of Schopenhauer's encounter with classical Indian thought, Gestering thought that Schopenhauer's understanding of *māyā* was quite different from that of Vedānta, since for the former *māyā* was of subjective origin while for the latter it was a cosmic, ontological principle, given its relation to *brahman* (43–4). This is true with respect to some of the Vedāntic argumentation concerning *māyā,* particularly in Rāmānuja's attacks on Śankara's Advaita, but it leaves aside the epistemological understanding of *māyā* which developed in the Vedāntic tradition, with which Schopenhauer's thematization has decidedly more in common.

[23] Schopenhauer himself recognized that his philosophy radically departed from the traditional view that reason represents the distinctive and highest feature of human existence, as with him, reason is subordinate to will. This is universally recognized and acknowledged by Schopenhauer's commentators as well. For those scholars interested in Schopenhauer's hermeneutic relationship to classical Indian thought, this ascendancy of will over reason is another characteristic that places Schopenhauer within the Romantic movement (see Sedler 75; Gestering 33–5; Clarke 68–9).

[24] In his first work, *The Birth of Tragedy,* Nietzsche explicitly aligns his conception of the Apollinian in classical Greek art with Schopenhauer's notion of *māyā,* and his idea of the Dionysian with that of the Schopenhauerian "will" (35–6). In *The Gay Science,* after Nietzsche had rejected the metaphysics of will argued for by Schopenhauer, he can still be found saying that "bodies, lines, planes, causes and effects, motion and rest, form and content" are actually merely "articles of faith," and "errors" that are "conditions of life" (177). In *Beyond Good and Evil,* Nietzsche writes: "We are fundamentally inclined to say that the falsest judgments . . . are those most indispensable for us, that without accepting the fictions of logic, without measuring reality against the purely invented world of the unconditioned and self-identical, without a constant falsification of the world by means of numbers, man could not live—that renouncing false judgments would mean renouncing life and a denial of life" (12). The nature of Nietzsche's falsification thesis has been transformed from Schopenhauer's, in that for Nietzsche, our ordered experience is an epistemological fabrication of what the bare senses reveal to us

as constant flux and change (see *Twilight of the Idols* 46). Maudmarie Clark has suggested that Nietzsche's falsification thesis is put to rest by his later perspectivism (137). To be sure, Nietzsche envisioned falsification more as a conceptual than a perceptual process, as she points out, but Nietzsche does retain shifting senses of falsification in his works. I do not have the time to go into the details of this problem here. But this revisioning of epistemology as falsification in Nietzsche and all those influenced by him, owes much to Schopenhauer and his understanding of *māyā*.

[25] As early as *The Gay Science*, Nietzsche opposes Schopenhauer's doctrine that the will lies at the root of representation, as in the following passage: "Against him I posit these propositions: First, for will to come into being an idea of pleasure and displeasure is needed. Second, when a strong stimulus is experienced as pleasure or displeasure, this depends on the *interpretation* of the intellect which, to be sure, generally does this work without rising to our consciousness: one and the same stimulus can be interpreted as pleasure or displeasure" (184). This notion, that interpretation determines will, is developed in *On the Genealogy of Morals* into his theory of perspectivism, and in his late notes he makes this perspectivism again a function of "the will to power." Again, we see how influential Schopenhauer's basic themes were for Nietzsche throughout his writings, for the interaction between intellect and will and the "ultimate choice" of whether to "affirm" or "deny" life are couched from his early to late works in Schopenhauerian vocabulary.

[26] In his examination of Foucault's critique of reason and the human sciences, Jürgen Habermas makes reference to a passage in a 1969 German translation of Foucault's *Histoire de la folie* in which Schopenhauer's embrace of Asian thought, Nietzsche's fascination with tragedy, Freud's delving into the world of dream and Bataille's flights of archaic inhibition all provide examples of ruptures in cultural identity (see Habermas 240; 412).

Bibliography

Allison, Henry E. *Kant's Transcendental Idealism: An Interpretation and Defense*. New Haven and London: Yale University Press, 1983.

App, Urs. "Notes and Excerpts by Schopenhauer Related to Volumes 1–9 of the *Asiatick Researches.*" *Schopenhauer Jahrbuch* 79: (1998), 11–33.

——. *"Schopenhauers Begegnung mit dem Buddhismus." Schopenhauer Jahrbuch* 79: (1998), 35–56.

Atwell, John E. *Schopenhauer: On the Character of the World: The Metaphysics of Will*. Berkeley: University of California Press, 1995.

——. *Schopenhauer: The Human Character*. Philadelphia: Temple University Press, 1990.

Carnap, Rudolph. *The Logical System of Language*. London: Kegan Paul, 1937.

Chansky, James D. "Schopenahuer and Platonic Ideas: A Groundwork for an Aesthetic Metaphysics." *Schopenhauer: New Essays in Honor of His 200th Birthday*. Ed. Eric von der Luft. Lewiston, N.Y.: Edwin Mellon Press, 1988, 67–81.

Clark, Maudmarie. *Nietzsche on Truth and Philosophy*. Cambridge: Cambridge, University Press, 1990.

Clarke, J. J. *Oriental Enlightenment: The Encounter Between Asian and Western Thought*. New York: Routledge, 1997.

Copleston, Frederich, S. J. *Arthur Schopenhauer: Philosopher of Pessimism*. London: Oxford, 1975.

Dauer, Dorothea. *Schopenhauer as Transmitter of Buddhist Ideas*. Berne: Switzerland: Herbert Lang, 1969.

Desmond, William. "Schopenhauer, Art and the Dark Origin." *Schopenhauer: New Essays in Honor of His 200th Birthday*. Ed. Eric von der Luft. Lewiston, N.Y.: Edwin Mellon Press, 1988, 101–22.

Deussen, Paul. *"Wie Ich zu Schopenhauer kam." Jahrbuch der Schopenhauer-Gesellshaft* 1 (1911): 13–27.

——. *Vedanta, Platon und Kant*. Vienna: Junius, 1917.

Duperron, Anquetil A. H. *"De Kantismo." Oupnek'hat: Secretum Tegendum*. Vol. 1 of 2, Paris: Agentorati, 1801, 711–24.

Gadamer, Hans-Georg. *Philosophical Hermeneutics*. Trans. David E. Lindge. Berkeley: University of California Press, 1977.

——. *Truth and Method*. Trans. Joel Weinsheimer and Donald G. Marshall. New York: Continuum, 1994.

Gardiner, Patrick. *Schopenhauer*. Bristol: Theommes Press, 1963.

Gestering, J. I. *German Pessimism and Indian Philosophy: A Hermeneutic Reading*. Delhi: Ajanta, 1986.

Glasenapp, Helmuth von. "*Schopenhauer und Indien.*" *Ausgewählte Kleine Schriften*. Eds. Heinz Bechert and Volker Moehler. Wiesbaden: Franz Steiner Verlag, 1980.

Gupta, Bina. *The Disinterested Witness: A Fragment of Advaita Vedānta Phenomenology*. Evanston: Northwestern University Press, 1998.

Habermass, Jürgen. *The Philosophical Discourse of Modernity*. Trans. Frederick G. Lawrence. Cambridge: M.I.T. Press, 1996.

Halbfass, Wilhelm. *India and Europe: An Essay in Understanding*. Albany: SUNY Press, 1988.

Halbfass, Wilhelm Ed. *Philology and Confrontation: Paul Hacker on Traditional and Modern Vedanta*. Albany: SUNY Press, 1995.

Hamlyn, D. W. *Schopenhauer*. London: Oxford University Press, 1980.

Hecker, Max, P. *Schopenhauer und die indische Philosophie*. Cologne: Hübscher und Teufel, 1897.

Hegel, G. W. F. *The Phenomenology of Spirit*. Trans. A. V. Miller. Oxford: Oxford University Press, 1977.

Henrich, Dieter. "On the Unity of Subjectivity." Trans. Guenter Zoeller. *The Unity of Reason: Essays on Kant's Philosophy*. Ed. Richard L. Velkley. Cambridge: Harvard University Press, 1994, 17–54.

Holdrege, Barbara A. *Veda and Torah: Transcending the Textuality of Scripture*. Albany: SUNY Press, 1996.

Hübscher, Arthur. *Denker gegen den Strom: Schopenhauer: Gestern-Heute-Morgen*. Bonn: Bouvier Verlag, 1973.

Janaway, Cristopher. *Self and World in Schopenhauer's Philosophy*. Oxford: Clarendon Press, 1989.

Jones, W. T. *Kant and the Nineteenth Century*, vol. 4 of 5 of *A History of Western Philosophy*. San Diego: Harcourt Brace Jovanovich, 1975.

Kant, Immanuel. *The Critique of Pure Reason*. Trans. Norman Kemp Smith. New York: St. Martins Press, 1965.

Kolenda, Konstantin. "Schopenhauer's Ethics: A View from Nowhere." *Schopenhauer: New Essays in Honor of His 200th Birthday*. Ed. Eric von der Luft. Lewiston: Edwin Mellon Press, 1988, 247–56.

Krishna, Daya. "Comparative Philosophy: What It Is and What It Ought to Be." *Interpreting Across Boundaries: New Essays in Comparative Philosophy*. Eds. Gerald James Larson and Eliot Deutsch. Princeton: Princeton University Press, 1988, 71–83.

Larson, Gerald James. "The Age-Old Distinction Between the Same and the Other." *Interpreting Across Boundaries: New Essays in Comparative Philosophy*. Eds. Gerald James Larson and Eliot Deutsch. Princeton: Princeton University Press, 1988, 3–19.

Lucács, Georg. "The Bourgeois Irrationalism of Schopenhauer's Metaphysics." *Schopenhauer: His Philosophical Achievement*. Ed. Michael Fox. Sussex: Harvester Press, 1980, 183–96.

Magee, Bryon. *The Philosophy of Schopenhauer*. Oxford: Clarendon Press, 1983.

Malter, Rudolph. "*Abstraktion, Begriffsanalyse und Urteilskraft in Schopenhauers Erkenntnislehre.*" *Schopenhauer: New Essays in Honor of His 200th Birthday*. Ed. Eric von der Luft. Lewiston: Edwin Mellon Press, 1988, 257–72.

——. *Der eine Gedanke: Hinführung zur Philosophie Arthur Schopenhauers*. Darmstadt: Wissenschaftliche Buchgesellschaft, 1988.

Mandelbaum, Maurice. "The Physiological Orientation of Schopenhauer's Epistemology." *Schopenhauer: His Philosophical Achievement*. Ed. Michael Fox. Sussex: Harvester Press, 1980, 50–67.

Merkel, Rudolf F. "*Schopenhauers Indien-Lehrer.*" *Jahrbuch der Schopenhauer-Gesellschaft* 32 (1948): 158–81.

Mockrauer, Friedrich. "*Schopenhauer und Indien.*" *Jahrbuch der Schopenhauer Gesellschaft* 15 (1928): 3–26.

Mohanty, Jitendra Nath. "Between Indology and Indian Philosophy." *Beyond Orientalism: The Work of Wilhelm Halbfass and its Impact on Indian and Cross-Cultural Studies*. Eds. Eli Franco and Karin Preisendanz. Amsterdam: Pozman Studies, 1997, 163–70.

——. "On Interpreting Indian Philosophy: Some Problems and Concerns." *Essays on Indian Philosophy: Traditional and Modern*. Ed. Purushottama Bilimoria. Delhi: Oxford, 1993, 207–19.

——. *Reason and Tradition in Indian Thought: An Essay on the Nature of Indian Philosophical Thinking*. Oxford: Clarendon Press, 1992.

Müller, Max. "*Damals und Jetzt.*" *Deutsche Rundschau* XLI (1884): 414–19.

Naegelsbach, Hans. *Das Wessen der Vorstellung bei Schopenhauer*. Heidelberg: Carl Winters Universitätsbuchhandlung, 1927.

Nietzsche, Friedrich. *Beyond Good and Evil*. Trans. Walter Kaufmann. New York: Random House, 1989.

——. *The Birth of Tragedy and The Case of Wagner*. Trans. Walter Kaufman. New York: Random House, 1967.

——. *The Gay Science*. Trans. Walter Kaufman. New York: Random House, 1974.

——. *Sämtliche Werke*. Vol. 8 of 15, Eds. Georgio Colli and Mazzino Montinari. Munich: Walter de Gruyter, 1980.

——. *Thus Spoke Zarathustra*. Trans. Walter Kaufman. New Zealand: Penguin, 1978.
——. *Twilight of the Idols / The Anti-Christ*. Trans. R. J. Hollingdale. New Zealand, Penguin, 1990.
O'Leary, Joseph S. "Heidegger and Indian Philosophy." *Beyond Orientalism: The Work of Wilhelm Halbfass and its Impact on Indian and Cross-Cultural Studies*. Eds. Eli Franco and Karin Preisendanz. Amsterdam: Pozman Studies, 1997, 171–204.
Potter, Karl H. "Metaphor as Key to Understanding the Thought of Other Speech Communities." *Interpreting Across Boundaries: New Essays in Comparative Philosophy*. Eds. Gerald James Larson and Eliot Deutsch. Princeton: Princeton University Press, 1988, 19–35.
Quine, Willard Van Orman. *Word and Object*. Cambridge: M.I.T. Press, 1960.
Radhakrishnan, Sarvapali. *Indian Philosophy*, vol. 1 of 2. Delhi: Oxford University Press, 1929.
Radhakrishnan, Sarvapali, Ed. *The Principle Upaniṣads*. Atlantic Highlands: Humanities Press, 1993.
Radhakrishnan, Sarvapali and Charles A. Moore, Eds. *A Sourcebook in Indian Philosophy*. Princeton: Princeton University Press, 1957.
Ricoeur, Paul. *Hermeneutics and the Human Sciences*. Ed. and Trans. John B. Thompson. Cambridge: Cambridge University Press, 1981.
Rorty, Richard. "Review of G. J. Larson and E. Deutsch (eds.), *Interpreting Across Boundaries: New Essays in Comparative Philosophy*." *Philosophy East and West*, 39 (1989): 332–7.
Safransky. Rüdiger. *Schopenhauer and the Wild Years of Philosophy*. Trans. Ewald Osers. Cambridge: Harvard University Press, 1990.
Said, Edward. *Orientalism*. New York: Random House, 1979.
Śaṅkara. *A Thousand Teachings: The Upadeśasāhasrī of Śaṅkara*. Trans. Sengaku Mayeda. Albany: SUNY Press, 1992.
Schmidt, Alfred. "*Schopenhauer und der Materialismus*." *Drei Studien über Materialismus*. Frankfurt am Main: Ullstein, 1979, 21–79.
——. *Die Warheit im Gewände der Lüge: Schopenhauers Religionsphilosophie*. Munich: Piper, 1986.
Schopenhauer, Arthur. *On the Basis of Morality*. Trans. E. F. J. Payne. Providence: Beghahn Books, 1995.
——. *On the Fourfold Root of the Principle of Sufficient Reason*. Trans. E. F. J. Payne. La Salle: Open Court, 1974.
——. *On the Freedom of the Will*. Trans. Konstantin Kolenda. Oxford: Basil Blackwell, 1985.
——. *Gesammelte Briefe*. Ed. Arthur Hübscher. Bonn: Bouvier Verlag, 1987.

——. *Der handschriftliche Nachlass*. Vol. 5 of 5. Ed. Arthur Hübscher. Darmstadt: Wissenschaftliche Buchgesellschaft, 1986.

——. *Manuscript Remains*. Vols. 1 and 2 of 4. Trans. E. F. J. Payne. Ed. Arthur Hübscher . Oxford: Berg, 1988.

——. *On the Will in Nature*. Trans. E. F. J. Payne. New York: Berg, 1992.

——. *Parerga und Paralipomena*. I & II. Vols. 4 and 5 of 5 of *Werke in Fünf Bünden*. Ed. Ludger Lütkehaus. Zürich: Haffmann Verlag, 1988.

——. *The World as Will and Representation*. Vols. 1 and 2. Trans. E. F. J. Payne. New York: Dover Publications, 1966.

Sedler, J. W. *India in the Mind of Germany: Schelling, Schopenhauer and their Times*. Washington, DC: University Press of America, 1982.

Volkelt, Johannes. *Arthur Schopenhauer: Seine Persönlichkeit, seine Lehre, sein Glaube*. Stuttgart: Fromann, 1910.

Young, Julian. *Willing and Unwilling: A Study in the Philosophy of Arthur Schopenhauer*. Dordrecht: Martinus Nijhoff, 1987.